NICK NEEDHAM

2000 YEARS OF CHRIST'S POWER

VOLUME

2

THE MIDDLE AGES

CHRISTIAN
FOCUS

Copyright © Dr N. R. Needham 2016

hardback ISBN 978-1-78191-779-4
epub ISBN 978-1-78191-916-3
mobi ISBN 978-1-78191-917-0

First published in 1998
Revised editions published in 2002 and 2011
Newly revised edition published in 2016
reprinted in 2017
by
Christian Focus Publications Ltd,
Geanies House, Fearn, Ross-shire,
IV20 1TW, Scotland, U.K.
www.christianfocus.com
and
Grace Publications Trust
7 Arlington Way
London, EC1R 1XA, England
www.gracepublications.co.uk

Cover design by Paul Lewis

Printed and bound by Bell & Bain, Glasgow

Dedication

To the Scottish Baptist College, where I took my diploma in pastoral studies in 1991-92, during Dr Ivor Oakley's tenure as Principal, and where I taught the first-year systematic theology students from 1991 to the end of 1993. I don't think the College was particularly medieval; but by the time that you, the reader, have finished this book, I hope that "medieval" will no longer be a term of abuse!

Illustrations and Maps

Contents

Acknowledgements

I would like to pay my debt of thanks to the following:
The Samuel Bill Theological College in Abak, Nigeria, whose students inspired this work; John Appleby of Grace Publications, who seized on the idea when I mentioned to him that I was thinking of writing something like this, and who helped produced the maps for this volume; Phil Arthur and Tim Grass who read through the first draft of this book (independently) and made numerous helpful if occasionally pugnacious comments, especially when it looked as if I was becoming a medieval Papist myself; the St Edward Brotherhood of Brookwood, near Woking, to whose library I owe much of the material about the Eastern Church, and to whose hospitality I owe many a feeling of nutritional satiety – with special thanks to Father Alexis, who read through an early draft of the Eastern chapters and made many helpful suggestions; Nick Houghton and Keith Ives, who helped me track down an otherwise elusive work by John of Damascus, quoted at the end of chapter 1; the Evangelical Library in London, who supplied the portrait of John Huss; the Mount Saint Bernard Abbey, Coalville, Leicester, and Mellifont Abbey, Collon, Ireland, who between them supplied the portrait of Bernard of Clairvaux; Alan Howe, who helped me locate the pictures of Boniface, Anselm of Canterbury, and Hildebrand on the internet, and St John's Abbey, Collegeville, for kind permission to reproduce these images from their "Abbey Refectory"; Alan and Olive Foster, who supplied the photograph of John Wyclif's portrait from St Mary's Anglican church in Lutterworth, and the rector, Mervyn Coussins, who gave kind permission to reproduce it; Father Richard Conrad, who helped me track down a suitable picture of Thomas Aquinas, and SCALA Instituto Fotografico Editoriale of Florence for permission to reproduce it.

A very special note of thanks to the Eastern Orthodox monks of Holy Transfiguration Monastery (Brookline, Boston, Massachusetts 02146-5997, USA), who supplied the eight icons of the great Eastern medieval figures, and kindly gave permission for us to reproduce them.

Preface

For Evangelicals who find the Catholic Middle Ages hard to understand

In my experience, most Evangelicals who have any knowledge of Church history tend to think and speak as if it began on October 31st 1517. This was the memorable day when Martin Luther nailed up his 95 Theses, thus unwittingly sparking off the Protestant Reformation. (Why can't we do what Continental Protestants do and celebrate this as Reformation Day? It's the obvious alternative to Hallowe'en.) But as for what went before Luther's protest – Evangelicals often know nothing about it, and dismiss it all as a period of total darkness.[1] Of course, this means dismissing the overwhelming bulk of the Christian story: writing off the first 1,500 years in favour of the last 500.

If you have read the first volume in this series, it should have become clear by now that I do not share this attitude. Among the precious promises of God's Word are these, spoken by the Saviour Himself: "I will build My Church, and the gates of Hades shall not prevail against it" (Matt. 16:18). Christ's spiritual kingdom is indestructible and perpetual; He has always had, and will always have, an uninterrupted succession of believing people on earth, as His Church continually renews its life from each generation to the next – or rather, as Christ Himself continually renews His Church by His Word and Spirit in every age. Note also Psalm 45:6, Psalm 72:5 & 17, Isaiah 9:7, Daniel 7:13-14, and Matthew 28:20. The higher our view of the 16th century Reformation (and mine *is* high), the more we need to remember these promises of the indestructible, perpetual nature of the Messiah's kingdom, when we contemplate what went before the Reformation. We must especially remember them when we explore the mysterious world of the Middle Ages. The sharp words of the 17th century Anglican theologian, Mark Frank (1613-64), deserve a hearing:

---

1. Total darkness, but with a few flickering lights here and there – notably Augustine of Hippo, and those late medieval figures who are seen as "forerunners" of the Reformation, such as John Wyclif and John Huss.

9

Indeed in itself it is most ridiculous to think the custom, and practice, and order, and interpretation of all times and Churches should be false, and those of yesterday only true, unless we can think the Spirit of Truth has been fifteen or sixteen hundred years asleep, and never waked till now of late; or can imagine that Christ should found a Church, and promise to be with it to the end of the world, and then leave it presently to Antichrist to be guided by him for above fifteen hundred years together.

If you come to this volume with a completely negative attitude to the Middle Ages, seeing them as nothing more than "The Dark Ages" when the knowledge of the living Christ was lost, my suggestion is that you inscribe Mark Frank's words into your mind with a pen of golden fire (along with the promises of Scripture about Christ's never-failing, ever-enduring kingdom, of course).

Yes, there was life in the medieval Church, a great deal of life. What if this life was corrupted by various diseases? Disease attacks life, not death. After all (and this is worth pondering very deeply), the Reformation itself was nurtured in the bosom of medieval Rome. Protestantism sprang not from the dissenting movements – the Waldensians, the Lollards, the Hussites – but from the parent body, Mother Church, whose pious sons wanted to reform her, but were cast out for their pains. As an heir of the Reformation and a Church historian, I often find myself telling people that the great spiritual and theological movement set rolling by Luther and Zwingli was in fact **the best elements of Western medieval Christianity trying to correct the worst elements.** If the history of the New Testament Church in any sense reflects that of Old Testament Israel, the German and the Swiss Reformers were like Josiah and Hilkiah discovering the Book of the Law in the Temple, and calling God's people to Scriptural renewal (2 Kings 22-23). That does not mean there was no spiritual life in Israel before Josiah and Hilkiah came along. God always had His true people and His prophets, even in periods of darkest apostasy, and even when His children were themselves tainted with that apostasy (see, for instance, what Scripture says about Joash in 2 Kings 12:2-3, and Amaziah in 2 Kings 14:3-4).

Having taken all this on board, you may still have serious problems with some of the things the great medieval figures believed and practised. But then, they often quarrelled with each other – over the Trinity, predestination, the Virgin Mary, the sacraments, the papacy, Church-state relations, and many other topics. Regarding the views of those early Church fathers he disagreed with, one of the greatest men of the Middle Ages, patriarch Photius of Constantinople (820-95), uttered words which I have always felt are a model of humility and charity: "We must not accept as doctrine those areas in which they strayed, but we embrace the men themselves." I hope we can say the same about many of our medieval forefathers. I reject certain doctrines believed by (for instance) Anselm of Canterbury and Bernard of Clairvaux, but I embrace the men themselves, and I only wish I had their burning and shining heart of love for the triune God. Human life and history, and Church life and history, are more subtle and complex than a simple "goodies-versus-baddies" approach will allow.

I end this brief introduction with three quotations from three great Reformed thinkers. First we will consider a general statement about the Middle Ages from Philip Schaff (1819-93), one of our most brilliant Church historians from 19th century Germany (where he was born) and America (where he worked). Next we listen to William Cunningham (1805-61), Scotland's greatest Reformed theologian of the 19th century, and not a man to be suspected of medieval or papist leanings. In fact the passage I quote comes in the midst of a fairly scathing criticism by Cunningham of the veneration paid to saints and images by the medieval Church, which Cunningham regarded as idolatry. Lastly we hear the voice of Charles Haddon Spurgeon, the famous English Reformed Baptist preacher, whose praise is in all the churches. Spurgeon extended a generous "catholicity" to those in those own day who, although within the Church of Rome, trusted ultimately in Christ for salvation. One of the blessings of Church history is the satisfaction of discovering that others have already said, and said far better, what one has been spluttering and mumbling about. So let Schaff, Cunningham, and Spurgeon have the last word.

Philip Schaff: The glory of the Middle Ages

It is this precisely which renders the Middle Ages so grand and venerable, that religion in this period appears the all-moving, all-ruling force, the centre around which all moral struggles and triumphs, all thought, poetry and action, are found to revolve. All sciences, and philosophy itself, the science of the sciences, were handmaids to theology, which based itself on the principle of Augustine, *Fides praecedit intellectum* [faith comes before understanding] ... According to the reigning idea, the State stood related to the Church like the moon to the sun, from which it borrows all its light. All forms of life, all national manners, were suffused with magic interest from the unseen world. The holy sacraments ran like threads of gold through the whole texture of life, in all its relations, from infancy to old age. The different arts vied with each other, in the service of the Church. The most magnificent and beautiful buildings of the period are the cathedrals: those giant stone flowers, with their countless turrets, storming the heavens and bearing the soul on high, and their mysterious devotional gloom, visited never by the light of the natural day, but only by mystic irradiations poured through stained glass ... Poetry sang her deepest and most tender strains to the Lord and His Bride; and the greatest poet of the Middle Ages, Dante, has left behind him in his *Divine Comedy* an image simply of the religious spirit and theological wisdom of the age, as occupied with eternity itself and all its dread realities. Truly a great time, and for one who is prepared to understand it, fraught with the richest spiritual interest.

From Schaff's

The Principle of Protestantism

William Cunningham: The godly Catholics of the Middle Ages

We believe that there have always been, and still are, in the Church of Rome, men who, in heart and in the sight of God, were not idolaters, i.e., who were really and in the main worshipping the one only, living, and true God in sincerity and in truth, and resting on the one foundation which has been laid in Zion. It is not easy for men to determine how far their fellow-men, subjected it may be to great disadvantages as to the means of knowing God's will, and involved in great ignorance and darkness, may yet have had a real saving knowledge of God and divine things introduced into their minds and made instrumental by the Holy Spirit in renovating and sanctifying them ... Even during the darkness of the Middle Ages, when the influence of Popery [Cunningham's word for the errors of the medieval Catholic system] in diffusing its corruptions of God's worship and truth was greatest, and when the access to opportunities of gaining sounder knowledge was least, we meet with men who gave unequivocal evidence of having been born again through the belief of the truth. And we doubt not that the Church of Rome has always contained some such men – men who were better than their professed principles – men who had not fully yielded to the natural tendency and the full practical influence of the errors which they professed to hold – men whose character was formed, and whose conduct was regulated, much more by the truth which they embraced than by the errors which they conjoined with it – men who were so deeply impressed with a sense of the glory of God and the all-sufficiency of Christ, as that the errors they held upon the honour due to saints and images exerted but a feeble influence upon the general current of their thoughts and feelings.

From Cunningham's
Historical Theology

C.H.Spurgeon: Roman Catholics who trust in the blood of Christ

In Brussels, I heard a good sermon in a Romish church. The place was crowded with people, many of them standing, though they might have had a seat for a halfpenny or a farthing; and I stood, too; and the good priest – for I believe he is a good man – preached the Lord Jesus with all his might. He spoke of the love of Christ, so that I, a very poor hand at the French language, could fully understand him, and my heart kept beating within me as he told of the beauties of Christ, and the preciousness of His blood, and of His power to save the chief of sinners. He did not say, 'justification by faith,' but he did say, 'efficacy of the blood,' which comes to very much the same thing. He did not tell us we were saved by grace, and not by our works; but he did say that all the works of men were less than nothing when brought into competition with the blood of Christ, and that the blood of Jesus alone could save. True, there were objectionable sentences, as naturally there must be in a discourse delivered under such circumstances; but I could have gone to the preacher, and have said to him, 'Brother, you have spoken the truth;' and if I had been handling his text, I must have treated it in the same way that he did, if I could have done it as well. I was pleased to find my own opinion verified, in his case, that there are, even in the apostate church, some who cleave unto the Lord, – some sparks of Heavenly fire that flicker amidst the rubbish of old superstition, some lights that are not blown out, even by the strong wind of Popery, but still cast a feeble gleam across the waters sufficient to guide the soul to the rock Christ Jesus.

From Spurgeon's
Autobiography vol.2 ch.59

1
Islam and the Church

1. The dawn of the Middle Ages

When the armies of Islam came marching out of the Arabian desert, a new world was born. In the first 600 years after Jesus's death and resurrection, Christianity had set up its victorious banners across Europe, North Africa, and the Middle East, creating "Christendom". (Christendom means "the Christian domain" – a group of nations and territories which, despite political and cultural differences, were united by the fact that Christianity was the public faith in each of them.)[1] However, in the 7th century, Christendom suddenly found its most ancient lands being conquered, and its civilisation supplanted, by the fresh, dynamic, and militant religion of Muhammad. Some historians have argued that this marked the true beginning of the Middle Ages.

Of course, we must not think there was any clean or sudden break between the early Church period and the period we call the Middle Ages. People did not wake up one morning and think, "The Middle Ages begin today." These divisions of time are something historians have invented for their own convenience, to make the study of history easier. Even so, the Christian world

---

1. Christendom is pronounced "Kriss-un-dum". People often use the word today to refer to the idea of a society publicly committed to the Christian faith. From the reign of Roman Emperor Theodosius the Great in the 4th century up to the French Revolution in the 18th, it also meant the political union of Church and state, whichever of the two was the dominant partner. See Volume One, Chapter 7, section 2 for Theodosius.

in the 7th century did experience a number of serious changes, which brought an end to one great chapter in its life-story and opened another. The key changes were:

(i) The rise of Islam. This altered for ever the way that Christians viewed the world; they could never again look out upon the earth without seeing millions of Muslims. The Islamic faith, from its origin to the present day, has always posed the greatest political and military threat, and the most awe-inspiring missionary challenge, to the followers of Jesus Christ.

(ii) The end of the Monophysite controversy.[2] As long as the largely Monophysite populations of Syria and Egypt were citizens of the Byzantine Empire, their doctrinal quarrel with the orthodox Chalcedonians[3] was bound to produce political conflict within the Empire, and to divide the Byzantine Church. So when the forces of Islam conquered Monophysite Syria and Egypt, the controversy between Monophysites and Chalcedonians lost its ability to create theological and political division within Byzantium. (It lost its power to affect the West too; we remember how at least one pope, Martin I, was martyred for opposing a Byzantine Emperor's attempt at compromise with the Monophysites.[4]) The mainstream Eastern Church, centred on Constantinople, was now free to pursue other lines of development, troubled no longer by the internal dispute which had torn it apart for 200 years.

(iii) The birth of the Frankish empire. The 7th century witnessed the rise of Frankish power in the West, reaching its climax with the advent of Charlemagne and the founding of the Holy Roman Empire in the year 800 (see Chapter 2). East and West were now

---

2. For the Monophysite controversy, see Volume One, Chapter 12.

3. A Chalcedonian is someone who accepts the Creed of Chalcedon, drawn up by the Council of Chalcedon in 451. The Creed taught that Christ is one person with two distinct natures, human and divine. See Volume One, Chapter 10, section 4.

4. For Pope Martin's martyrdom, see Volume One, Chapter 12, section 4.

divided by both politics and religion: the Byzantine Emperor and the patriarch of Constantinople faced the Holy Roman Emperor and the pope of Rome. Henceforward the Christian world was in effect two worlds, divided by culture, government, and religious issues. Here were the fateful seeds which finally bore fruit in the great East–West schism of 1054.[5]

These deep historical changes, then, were landmarks which ushered Christianity out of the early Church period into a new era – the Middle Ages (the ages "in the middle" between the patristic age and the age of the Protestant Reformation in the 16th century[6]).

2. Muhammad and the rise of Islam

In more recent decades, some Western scholars have questioned the traditional account of Muhammad's life, or even his very existence. One serious problem is that no biography of Muhammad was written until roughly 150 years after Muhammad's death. The writer was the scholar Ibn Ishaq. Unfortunately even Ibn Ishaq's biography has been lost, and we know it only from quotations in still later writings. However, many non-Islamic sources close to Muhammad's lifetime testify to his historical reality.[7] The following account will reflect the basic outlines of the traditional story.

Muhammad was born in the city of Mecca, an important religious and trading centre near the south-western coast of central Arabia, in 570 or 571. He belonged to the powerful Quraish tribe. His father, however, died before Muhammad's birth, and his mother died when he was only six, so the young Muhammad's uncle, Abu Talib, brought him up; Abu Talib belonged to a poor branch of the family, and Muhammad worked for him as a lowly shepherd. But the hardships of childhood gave way to prosperity

---

5. For the East–West schism, see Chapter 3, section 8.

6. For the Reformation, see Volume Three.

7. See Robert Hoyland, *Seeing Islam As Others Saw It* (Darwin Press: Princeton 1997) for a collection of these testimonies.

in adulthood: Muhammad became a very successful merchant, working for a wealthy widow named Khadijah. Their relationship blossomed and deepened, and despite the fact that Khadijah was 40 years old and Muhammad only 25, they married in the year 595. The marriage produced two boys and four girls; the youngest of the girls, Fatima, became Muhammad's favourite in later years, and married Muhammad's cousin, Ali, who was to be Islam's fourth *caliph* ("leader" – literally, *caliph* means "successor").

Muhammad's commercial journeys from Mecca through Arabia to Syria brought him into contact with Jews and Christians, with whom he discussed religion. Although the prevailing form of Arabian religion was tribal Paganism, there was an economically powerful Jewish minority, and quite a large scattering of Monophysites, plus a smaller number of Nestorians[8] and orthodox Chalcedonian hermits. There were also in Arabia at that time various native groups who, under Jewish and Christian influence, had become dissatisfied with the Pagan idolatry of their homeland; they began to worship the Creator-God alone, but without embracing either Judaism or Christianity. Muhammad became one of these worshippers of the one God. When he was not away on a trading journey, he adopted a habit of meditating alone in a cave on Mount Hira, near Mecca. Muhammad, it seemed, was simply a quiet, sincere, thoughtful man: prosperous, kind to the poor, happily married, with a deeply religious nature, dissatisfied with Paganism and seeking the truth about the one God, the Creator of all.

Then in 610 came the central experience of Muhammad's life, which was to divert the entire river of human history into a fresh and revolutionary channel; for in that year, Muhammad received what he believed to be the first of many personal revelations from God, launching him into his amazing career as the prophet of Allah ("Allah" is simply Arabic for "God"). According to Muhammad, the angel Gabriel appeared to him while he was meditating in the Mount Hira cave, and gave him the following message:

---

8. For the Nestorians, see Volume One, Chapter 10, sections 3 and 5.

Read, in the name of your Lord, who has created all things;
who has created man of congealed blood.
Read, by your most beneficent Lord,
who taught the use of the pen;
who teaches man that which he does not know.
(Qur'an, sura 96)[9]

Muhammad was at first terrified. He did not know whether it was really the angel Gabriel or some demonic deception which had appeared to him. He rushed back home and told his wife what had happened. Khadijah believed in the divine origin of Muhammad's experience, on the basis that God would not allow such a good man as Muhammad to be deceived. So Khadijah became, at the same time, the person who persuaded Muhammad to accept his revelation-experiences as coming from God, and also her husband's first convert. Slowly, quietly at first, Muhammad became the centre of a new religious movement in Mecca, as he began criticising Paganism and idolatry, and calling on people to worship Allah alone. The number of his converts grew; the most important of these earliest Muslims were Muhammad's young cousin Ali, his friend Abu Bakr (who would become Islam's first caliph), his one-time deadly enemy Omar (who would become Islam's second caliph), and his son-in-law Othman (the third caliph).

The new faith, *Islam* (which means "submission"), had its roots in Muhammad's overpowering conviction of the unity or oneness of God. Muhammad interpreted Allah's oneness to mean that He, the Creator and Lord of the universe, was a single individual person, separated by an infinite distance from His creation by His unique possession of divine attributes – there could be no other gods. The divine attribute Muhammad emphasised most was power: Allah alone had power, and therefore He alone was the cause of all things, both good and evil. Idolatry,

---

9. A slightly updated version of the George Sale translation from 1734. This was the first translation of the Qur'an into English, and its style probably echoes the King James Version of the Bible better than any other English translation of the Qur'an.

or violating Allah's oneness by acknowledging any other god, was
the supreme sin. Muhammad's concept of God's oneness (that
God is one single person) ruled out any belief in the Christian
doctrine of the Trinity, which Muhammad felt was no better than
a Pagan idolatry of many gods.[10] He regarded Jesus as his own
forerunner, sinless and virgin-born, a miracle-worker, the greatest of God's prophets apart from Muhammad himself, but not
the divine or eternal Son of God who became flesh. Muhammad
also refused to accept that Jesus had been crucified; God would
not allow His prophets to be treated so shamefully.[11]

Muhammad summed up the new religion in five main duties
(the "five pillars" of Islam):

(a) *Shahadah*, or the confession of faith – "There is no god
but Allah, and Muhammad is His prophet".

(b) *Salah*, or prayer five times a day, said facing towards
Mecca.

(c) *Zakah*, or giving charitable gifts of money as a welfare
contribution to the poor.

(d) *Sawm*, or fasting in the holy month of Ramadan.

(e) *Hajj*, or the pilgrimage to Mecca, which a Muslim must
try to make at least once.

Another sacred duty emphasised in Islam, although it is not one
of the five pillars, is *jihad*, often translated "holy war". The basic
meaning, however, is "struggle". Muslims understand *jihad* as
referring both to the personal struggle for obedience to Allah's
will, and to the struggle to spread Islam in the world – by preaching, writing, diplomacy, warfare.

---

10. Christians have questioned whether Muhammad really understood the
doctrine of the Trinity.

11. This is the traditional view, accepted by most Muslims. Some scholars,
however, have argued that the Qur'an is ambiguous on whether Jesus died, and
that what became the majority view was a later tradition.

The source of divine revelation for the Islamic faith was the Qur'an, a series of 114 messages (or *suras*) dictated to Muhammad (as he claimed) by the angel Gabriel. After Muhammad's death, Islam's third caliph, **Othman** (644-56), collected these suras into a single authoritative edition.[12] The Qur'an is so gloriously majestic and beautiful in its original Arabic that Muhammad pointed to it as the one sure proof that he was inspired by God; the only "miracle" he ever performed was the writing of the Qur'an.[13] Unfortunately, this beauty does not come across in English translation. Indeed, Muslims do not regard translations of the Qur'an as God's Word; they refer to them as "interpretations" of the Qur'an. Also crucial for Islam was the *hadith* – traditions about what Muhammad had said and done; these were important, because Muslims accept Muhammad as the perfect example of how a man should live, and try to model their lives on him.[14] The hadith collectively form the *sunna* or "Path". The Qur'an and the hadith, together with the *ijma* (the consensus of the Muslim community – or, according to some, of Islamic legal scholars), make up the threefold authority which Muslims must follow.

Muhammad's religious movement encountered increasing levels of opposition and persecution in Mecca from the majority of the city's inhabitants, especially the chiefs of the Quraish, the most important tribe. Muhammad's condemnation of idolatry threatened the economic power which the Quraish leaders derived from Pagan ceremonies and pilgrimages connected with the *ka'ba*, an ancient Arab shrine in Mecca. Pagans ridiculed

---

12. In the process, Othman rounded up and destroyed all versions of the Qur'an that had variant readings from his "correct" version. This is a controversial area of Qur'anic scholarship, particularly in Muslim-Christian debates.

13. Or perhaps the "supreme" rather than the only miracle. The traditional *hadith* literature of early Islam does ascribe some miracles to Muhammad, notably predictive prophecies.

14. The collection of the hadith was a laborious process involving the rejection of most alleged traditions of Muhammad's life and sayings. The hard core that survived this purging process was considered reliable. However, this is an area that divided Sunni from Shia Muslims; each has its own collections of hadith. See section 4 for the Sunni-Shia divide.

Muhammad, accused him of being demon-possessed, and beat up, tortured, and killed his followers. Muhammad was protected by his uncle Abu Talib, but when Abu Talib died, Muhammad and his pioneer Muslims were forced to flee from Mecca to the more northerly city of Yathrib, or Medina (as it was later re-named). This happened in the year 622, the year of the *hejira* ("emigration"). The Islamic calendar starts from this event.[15]

The hejira marked the turning point in Muhammad's fortunes. His preaching met with almost total success in Medina. In fact, he became the political and religious leader of the city. Medina was thus the first independent Muslim community; it attracted more and more converts from the surrounding areas, even from Mecca. After several bloody battles between the Muslim forces of Medina and the Pagan Meccans, in 630 Muhammad was able to return to Mecca with an army of 10,000 warriors, a triumphant military conqueror. He won over most of the Pagan population by sparing their lives with a general amnesty, destroyed the images of Mecca's Pagan gods, and made the ancient Meccan shrine, the ka'ba, into the most holy place of Islamic worship.

Before the rise of Islam, Arabia had enjoyed no political unity. It was mostly a patchwork of independent nomadic tribes. By the time of Muhammad's death in 632, he had unified the region both politically and spiritually under his own leadership. This came about partly by the fire of spiritual enthusiasm which Muhammad and his closest followers radiated, winning many sincere converts to Islam, especially in Arabia. However, it also came about partly by military conquest. From the outset, Islam was a faith which spread its territory by the sword. Inspired by an exalted religious ardour, the Arabic Muslim armies under Muhammad's successors, the caliphs, embarked on a military campaign to extend their domain outside Arabia. Within a hundred years, they had created a huge Islamic Empire, stretching from India to Spain. The world had rarely known armies like

---

15.   So the year 622 in the Christian calendar is the year 1 in the Muslim calendar. Islam's calendar is also based on lunar years which are slightly shorter than solar years.

this before: brave, tough, completely sober (Islam did not allow Muslims to drink alcohol), and burning with a zeal for their faith which made them unafraid of death. They swept out of Arabia like a desert storm, swallowed up half the Byzantine Empire and the whole of the Persian Empire, descended on India in the far East, and were soon pouring through North Africa into Spain and France in the West.

To see why the Christian world could offer so little resistance to the Muslim invaders, we have to step back and look at the disunited state of the Byzantine Empire at this period.

3. The Byzantine Empire in the 7th century

As we saw at the end of Volume One, the Byzantine Empire in the 7th century was badly split along geographical lines by the doctrinal conflict between the Chalcedonians and the Monophysites. The Chalcedonians, who accepted the Creed drawn up at the ecumenical Council of Chalcedon in 451, were strongest in Greece, the Balkans, and Asia Minor; the Monophysites, who rejected the Creed of Chalcedon, controlled Syria and Egypt. The doctrinal differences between Chalcedonians and Monophysites had also, by now, become strongly linked with regional and ethnic differences. The mainly Coptic population of Egypt was racially Semitic rather than Greek, and spoke Coptic in preference to Greek. Their hatred of the Byzantine Chalcedonian Emperors encouraged them to feel a sense of Coptic nationalism against rule from Constantinople. There was a similar Monophysite nationalism in Syria. The Syrian Monophysites were also racially Semitic rather than Greek, and developed the use of their own Syriac language in theology and worship.

The Persian wars of 606-29 revealed just how alienated the Syrians and Egyptians were from the Byzantine government. The Sassanid Empire of Persia went on the offensive against Byzantium and invaded Syria, capturing Antioch. By 618 they had conquered Palestine and Egypt too. The Monophysite populations of Syria and Egypt welcomed the Pagan Persians as liberators from the oppressive rule of Byzantium. The Byzantine Emperor Heraclius (610-41) seemed to be in a hopeless situation.

But astonishingly, he raised and trained a new army, and in a series of brilliant campaigns in 622-28 Heraclius not only restored Syria and Egypt to the Byzantine Empire, but carried the war into the centre of Persia, crushed the Persian army at Nineveh, and effectively destroyed Persia as a world power. It was a stunning success for Byzantium. However, Heraclius's forces had to return home; they were too stretched to remain in the Persian heartlands. So the final fruit of Heraclius's destruction of Persian power was that the Persian Empire, and the rich territories east of the Euphrates River, had little military strength left to offer a sustained resistance to the Muslim armies when they arrived.

4. The Islamic conquests

After Muhammad's death in 632, many Arabian tribes rebelled against his successor **Abu Bakr**, who ruled as caliph from 632 to 634 (Muslims refer to the period of a particular caliph's rule as his *caliphate*). Abu Bakr spent much of his brief caliphate subduing the rebellion, and then turned his attention outwards to Syria and Persia. Under the next caliph **Omar** (634-44), the Muslim armies came streaming out of Arabia, and the Islamic conquest of the Byzantine Empire began. In 635, the Muslims besieged and captured Damascus. In 637 they took Jerusalem. In 638, Antioch, Caesarea, and 17 other cities along the Syrian coast fell to Muslim forces. By 639 they had conquered the whole of Syria. In 640 Muslim troops invaded Egypt; Alexandria fell in 641. The Monophysite populations of Syria and Egypt welcomed the Muslims as liberators from Byzantium, as they had welcomed the Persians 20 years earlier.

It seems certain that the Islamic armies would not have been able to conquer Syria and Egypt so easily, unless Syrians and Egyptians had already felt deeply alienated from Byzantine rule. So in a very real sense, the triumph of the Islamic armies was due to the internal theological quarrels of the Eastern Christians. Three of the five great patriarchates – Antioch, Jerusalem, and Alexandria – were now under Muslim control. Meanwhile, another Muslim army had invaded and conquered Persia in 639 – another quick victory for the Muslims, made easier by

Heraclius's shattering of Persian power in 622-28. Further Eastern conquests brought Afghanistan and northern India under Muslim control by the early 8th century.

In the Middle East, the Muslims turned their attention to destroying what was left of the Byzantine Empire, whose frontiers they had rolled back into Asia Minor. Muslim fleets captured or laid waste many of the Mediterranean islands, such as Cyprus (648). By 651, the southern part of Asia Minor was under Muslim control. So too was most of Armenia. The Muslims inflicted a crushing naval defeat on the Byzantines in 655 at the battle of Phoenix (the southern coast of Asia Minor). Finally, under their fifth caliph *Muawiyah* (661-80), the Muslim forces on land and sea gambled all their strength in a supreme effort to capture Constantinople itself. The siege lasted five cruel years (673-78).

However, for the first time, the Muslims met with total failure and defeat. A recently invented Byzantine secret weapon called "Greek fire" ravaged their armies and ships (it was a chemical mixture which burned furiously when it came in contact with water). The defenders of Constantinople hurled Greek fire at the besieging Muslim army and navy, with horrifically destructive effect; Greek fire became the "nuclear bomb" of medieval warfare – devastating, irresistible, and terrifying. Then a storm off the coast of Pamphylia smashed the Muslim fleet. Finally, the great Byzantine Emperor Constantine IV (668-85) wiped out the Muslim army at the battle of Syllaeum in 678. In 679, Constantine IV and caliph Muawiyah ceased hostilities and officially recognised each other's territory.[16]

In the West, Muslim armies swept on from Egypt into North-West Africa. Here they encountered strong resistance from the Berber people. It took the Muslims 50 years of savage fighting to subdue the Berbers, who then embraced the new faith themselves and became strict and zealous Muslims. In 711, an Islamic Berber army crossed over from Africa into Visigothic Spain, and

---

16. Constantine then turned his attention to the Third Ecumenical Council of Constantinople, as we saw in Volume One, Chapter 12, section 5.

by 718 had conquered almost the whole of it – the northern coastlands alone remained under Visigothic Christian control. The Muslims then pushed on into France. At Tours, in north-west France, they were met by a Frankish Catholic army. Here in 732, the Muslim general Abd-er Rahman fought one of the decisive battles of world history against the Frankish general Charles Martel (Martel is French for "hammer").[17] The battle of Tours (or Poitiers – the fighting took place between the two cities) was a decisive victory for Charles Martel and the Franks; it permanently halted the Western progress of the Islamic Empire. The Franks forced the Muslims back into Spain, and there they stayed for the next 700 years. After centuries of struggle between Christians and Muslims in the Iberian peninsula, the great Spanish Catholic king, Ferdinand of Castile and Aragon, finally expelled the last Muslims of Spain back into North Africa in 1492. This Christian-Muslim conflict in Spain, with the eventual triumph of the Christians, is known as the *Reconquista* (the "Reconquest").

The unity of the Islamic Empire was at first impressive, but it did not last. Religious dissension arose after the murder of Othman, the third caliph, in 656. Muslims divided into two parties. One argued that the leadership of the Empire must be hereditary within the family of Muhammad, through Ali and his relatives (Ali was Muhammad's cousin and had married Muhammad's daughter Fatima, so that his children were Muhammad's grandchildren). This group was known as the *Shiat Ali*, "the party of Ali" – or the *Shias*, as they came to be called. Shias held that a living leader (an *imam*), chosen by God from among Muhammad's family, was essential to the right guidance of the Islamic community. By contrast, the other party believed that the nation's elders should freely elect each new caliph (or that the caliph should himself appoint his own successor), and that the caliph did not need to belong to Muhammad's family; this party was called the *Sunnis*. They held that the sunna (the authentic hadith concerning Muhammad, together with the

---

17. For more about Charles Martel, see Chapter 2, section 1.

Qur'an and ijma) was more important than a living leader for the guidance of the faithful. The champion of the Sunnis was Muawiyah, governor of Syria and friend of the murdered caliph Othman; he and others claimed that Ali had arranged Othman's assassination, and they demanded justice.

The Shias and Sunnis plunged the Islamic Empire into its first taste of civil war. Ali emerged from this conflict as the fourth caliph, the last to be accepted (in theory) by all Muslims – the last of the "rightly guided caliphs" (the first four). But Ali was still opposed by Muawiyah, who had built up a formidable army in Syria which owed its loyalty to Muawiyah personally. After Ali's assassination in 661, Muslims then accepted Muawiyah as Islam's fifth caliph (661-80). Muawiyah managed to keep the sons of Ali under control during his caliphate. However, when he died, the Shias refused to recognise Muawiyah's son Yazid (680-83) as the new caliph; for Ali's party, Yazid was an illegitimate tyrant, imposed on the Muslim community by his father. So the Shias under Ali's son *Husein* (626-80) planned a military uprising; Yazid's forces, however, defeated them in battle in 680 at Karbala (on the southern Euphrates, near Babylon). Husein's plans for an uprising had been discovered and quashed by Yazid, so that the Shia "army" at Karbala consisted of little more than Husein's extended family and a few close supporters. His death was ever afterwards considered a martyrdom by Shia Muslims, and Husein himself seems to have gone to Karbala in the spirit of a martyr. The events of Karbala introduced a new theology and spirituality of suffering and martyrdom in Shia Islam that were not really present in Sunni Islam.

The Sunni victors at Karbala had massacred Ali's family, but the Shia party survived the disaster. These fierce internal conflicts created a permanent religious division in the Islamic world between Sunni and Shia Muslims. Shias were always in a small minority (between 10-15%), but their influence was concentrated in one region, Persia (present-day Iran), which became the great Shia stronghold.

The secession of Muslim Spain from the rest of the Islamic Empire in 756 weakened the Empire's political unity. In the 9th century, Shia Persia became effectively independent from the caliphs who ruled in Baghdad. So did Morocco, Tunisia, and Libya in North-West Africa. In the 10th century, Egypt also seceded and became an independent Muslim kingdom. This political and territorial break-up of Islam paved the way for the Western Catholic conquest of the Middle East by the Crusaders in the 11th century (see Chapter 5).

Just as the Christian faith had done, Islam developed its own rich theological traditions and differing schools of thought. Two of its greatest thinkers, the Persian *Avicenna* (980-1037) and the Spanish *Averroes* (1126-98), had a massive influence on Western Catholic theology, through their Arabic translations of the Greek philosopher Aristotle and commentaries on his writings, which Christian scholars then translated into Latin.[18]

Also fascinating to Christian mystics were their Islamic equivalents, the Muslim mystics, or *Sufis* as they were called. *Sufi* (pronounced "soo-fee") comes from the word for the woollen garment worn by early Muslim mystics. It seems likely that Christian mystics and Sufis had quite a wide influence on one another, as well as both drinking at the common fountain of Neoplatonism.[19] The Sufis sang of their love for God "the Beloved" in highly emotional, imaginative poetry that still enchants the world today. The first Sufi of major historic significance was the woman *Rabia of Basra* (717-801), whose surviving poems celebrate an intense personal love-relationship with God. The most globally famous of the Sufi poet-mystics, however, were the Persians *Jalal al-Din Rumi* (1207-73) and *Nur-addin Abd al-Rahman Jami* (1414-92). Rumi in particular won the admiration of the Muslim world, and even Jews and Christians, by his gentle character and beautiful spiritual poems; when he died, it is said that a Christian was heard lamenting, "To us, he was like Moses, David, and Jesus!" The man who stood out as the supreme spiritual giant of medieval Islam was another Persian,

---

18. For the way that Islam channelled Aristotle to the West, see Chapter 7, section 2.

19. For Neoplatonism, see Volume One, Chapter 6, section 2.

Abu Hamid Muhammad al-Ghazali (1058-1111). Al-Ghazali was a sort of Muslim counterpart to Augustine of Hippo, blending a highly intellectual Islamic theology with a warm Sufi mysticism of the heart.[20]

5. Life for the Church under Islamic rule

As we have seen, a "caliph" governed the Islamic Empire; Muslims regarded him as the political successor to Muhammad. The caliphs resided first in Damascus, then from 750 in Baghdad (which is in modern Iraq); they divided their huge territories into provinces called "emirates", ruled on the caliph's behalf by an "emir".

The attitude of the Islamic rulers towards their non-Muslim subjects was twofold. In Arabia itself, the general policy was to regard to all Arabs as bound in perpetuity to Islam, and to use force to uphold this Islamic unity. However, the policy towards non-Arabs was different. When, for example, the Muslims conquered Persia, they made no attempt to force Persians to abandon their ancestral Zoroastrian faith and accept Islam. In fact, the Persian aristocracy continued to practise Zoroastrianism for many years under Islamic rule. Jews and Christians enjoyed a specially favoured status in Islam. Muhammad had recognised both groups as worshippers of Allah, the one true God – those who had received His previous revelations ("people of the book"), although Muhammad thought they had corrupted those revelations. So Muslim rulers certainly did not attempt to force Jews or Christians to convert to Islam. They were allowed to continue worshipping God in their own way. The Monophysite Churches of Syria and Egypt, and the Nestorian Church in Persia, therefore, survived the Muslim conquest. In Damascus, the capital of the Islamic Empire until 750, Christians and Muslims shared the Church of Saint John for worship.

However, there were serious disadvantages for Christians under Muslim rule. Christians in the Islamic Empire became segregated communities of second-class citizens. Their Muslim

---

20. For Augustine, see Volume One, Chapter 9, section 3.

masters required them to organise as a *melet* (nation) under a bishop who was politically responsible for them. A non-Muslim community within an Islamic state were said to be in a condition of *dhimmitude*. This comes from *dhimmi*, an Arabic word meaning "protected". Muslims applied the term *dhimmi* to native non-Muslim populations who surrendered by a treaty (*dhimma*) to Muslim rule. All Christians in *dhimmitude* had to pay a heavy poll tax (a tax not based on property or income – the same amount per person). Christians had to wear distinctive clothing. They were forbidden to own or use swords or horses. No public processions carrying crosses or icons were allowed. Christians were not permitted to ring bells or beat drums to announce services of worship. Marriage between Christians and Muslims was forbidden. Most damaging of all, Islamic law prohibited Christians from evangelising Muslims; conversion from Islam to Christianity was punished by death.

Given these conditions, it is not surprising that the Churches under Islam declined steadily in numbers. The majority of professing Christians converted to Islam to secure the benefits of full citizenship. Despite the official policy of tolerance, Muslims often violently persecuted Christians in local areas. The caliph al-Hakim decreed a systematic persecution of the Church in the period 1015-20, until his fellow Muslims assassinated him for claiming deity.

What is perhaps surprising is the extent to which Christians were able to flourish under Muslim rule. The caliphs employed many Christians (and Jews) as civil servants, much as the German Arian conquerors of the Western Roman Empire had employed Catholics.[21] This was especially true in Persia, where Muslim rulers employed Nestorian Christian scholars to translate the great works of Greek philosophy into Arabic, thus channelling the wisdom of ancient Greece into the new world of Islam. When the caliphs moved the Empire's capital from Damascus in Syria to Baghdad in Persia in 750, the first great principal of Baghdad University was a Nestorian Christian, **Husein ibn Ishaq** (died

---

21. See Volume One, Chapter 11, section 1.

877).[22] Ibn Ishaq translated various writings of Greek philosophers such as Aristotle and Euclid into Arabic.

However, the most distinguished Nestorian thinker and writer under Muslim rule was **Timothy I** (728-823). Timothy was elected *catholicos* (leader) of the Nestorian Church in 780, and was probably the greatest man ever to occupy the office. Highly educated in Greek philosophy and the early church fathers, he translated Aristotle into Arabic and wrote the classic work of Christian apologetics, *Dialogue with al-Mahdi*, which was directed towards Muslims. Al-Mahdi was the caliph from 775 to 785; Timothy enjoyed close and friendly relations with him and his successor Harun-al-Rashid (786-809). Timothy administered the affairs of the Nestorian Church under Islam in a remarkably constructive way, and energetically promoted missionary work among Turks, Tartars, and the tribes of the Caspian Sea.

Timothy was great, but the most outstanding Christian figure who lived and worked under Islamic rule was **John of Damascus** (675-749), often called the last of the Greek church fathers. John was the prime minister of the caliph Abd-ul-Malek in Damascus in the earlier part of his life. Later he retired to the Saint Sabbas monastery near Jerusalem, where he wrote his theological masterpiece, *The Fountain of Knowledge*. The *Fountain* was divided into three parts. Part one dealt with questions of philosophy, and part two with heresies; part three was entitled *Exact Exposition of the Orthodox Faith*, and is one of the most profound and influential presentations of Eastern Chalcedonian theology ever written. John was a firm adherent of the Creed of Chalcedon, and opposed both Nestorianism and Monophysitism; he based his teaching largely on the Cappadocian fathers, and accepted the developments in Christology which Leontius of Byzantium and Maximus the Confessor had pioneered.[23]

---

22. Not to be confused with the Muslim Ibn Ishaq who wrote Muhammad's first biography.

23. For the Cappadocian fathers, see Volume One, Chapter 8, section 3. For Leontius of Byzantium, see Volume One, Chapter 12, section 2. For Maximus the Confessor, see Volume One, Chapter 12, section 4.

John of Damascus (675-749)

The Orthodox Faith was translated into Latin in the 12th century and had quite an impact on the growth of Western systematic theology. John also wrote a thoughtful and powerful defence of icons in the iconoclastic controversy,[24] and a number of the most beautiful and popular of all Greek hymns. Tradition tells us that he was the author of one of the most widely read books in the

---

24. For the iconoclastic controversy, see Chapter 3, section 3.

history of the Byzantine Empire, the religious novel *Barlaam and Josaphet*. The life and writings of John of Damascus, then, show how a great Christian theologian could live and flourish under Islam.

The most tolerant and fruitful Christian-Muslim relationships were those of Muslim Spain (or the "emirate of Cordova", as it was called in the Islamic Empire). In 756, Spain seceded from the Empire and became an independent Muslim state. The Berber Muslims in Spain (they were called "Moors") practised a remarkable degree of religious tolerance towards Christians and Jews; many Christian communities survived unmolested under Spanish Muslim rule for centuries. Islamic Spain had its fair share of Christian martyrs, but generally speaking the Muslim rulers left the Spanish Church alone as long as it made no attempts to criticise Islam or convert Muslims.

In fact, it was in Islamic Spain that Western European culture and civilisation reached their highest development in the early Middle Ages, with a strong contribution from the significant Spanish Christian minority. Its most glorious period was the reign of the great emir Abd al-Rahman III (912-61). Arab culture gained such a powerful hold over the Spanish Church that the Christian scholars of Spain had to translate the Bible and liturgy into Arabic; the Spanish-Arabic liturgy was known as the "Mozarabic liturgy" (see the end of the Chapter for a quotation). Through Muslim Spain the riches of Eastern civilisation, which combined both Greek and Islamic elements, flowed into Western Europe, which was highly uncivilised by contrast. Western Christian scholars often visited the famous Spanish Muslim universities to learn philosophy, mathematics, astronomy, and medicine.

6. Christian responses to Islam

Islam's religious policy of forbidding Muslim conversion to Christianity made missionary work virtually impossible. Christian nations had only two practical ways of combatting the spread of Islam: they could fight it by the sword and by the pen. Fighting

Islamic armies with Christian armies was a far more effective way
of checking the growth of the Islamic Empire than writing books
against Islam. Since Islam's method of expanding its political
authority was by military conquest, the Christian nations felt they
had little option but to resist by defensive warfare.

Still, there were some notable attempts in the Middle Ages by
Christians to evangelise Muslims. The two great trail-blazers of
Christian mission in the Islamic world were the founder of the
Franciscan order, Francis of Assisi (1182-1226), whom we will
consider in Chapter 8, and **Raymond Lull** (1232-1316). Lull
was born into a wealthy Catholic family in Palma on the island
of Majorca, off the east coast of Spain; Catholics had only just
conquered Majorca from Islamic rule. Lull's early life was spent
as private tutor to the sons of the Spanish Catholic king, James
of Aragon. One of James's sons became king of Majorca, and
employed Lull as a royal counsellor, although Lull's chief interest
at this point seems to have been chasing women and writing
pornographic poems about his experiences (or what he wished
to experience). He was, however, shocked into an awareness of
his folly when he discovered that one of his admired ladies had
cancer of the breast. Lull renounced the world, became a hermit
for five years, and then attached himself to the Franciscan order.

Living on Majorca put Lull in close contact with the Muslims
of southern Spain, and he conceived it as his special mission in
life to bring the Gospel to Muslims. He learned Arabic from
a Spanish Muslim slave whose freedom he purchased, and with
financial backing from the king of Aragon he established a special
Franciscan convent at Miramir on Majorca. Here other monks
could learn Arabic and prepare for missionary work among
Muslims. Lull himself went on three missionary journeys to
Tunisia and Algeria in North-West Africa, where his preaching
aroused such fierce Muslim opposition that he narrowly escaped
with his life. One tradition says that on his third journey he
was actually martyred in Tunis (others say he died peacefully
in Majorca). Lull wrote treatises on Christianity in Arabic, and
his influence helped persuade pope Clement V (1305-14) to
decree in 1311 that teachers of Arabic and other Eastern tongues

should be appointed in several universities, so that Christians could learn the languages of Islam and thus be better equipped to understand, refute, and evangelise Muslims. Lull is often seen as the great pioneer Christian missionary to Muslims; he was also a great scholastic theologian,[25] and one of the first Western theologians to write in a language other than Latin (Lull wrote various treatises in Catalan, a form of which was spoken in Majorca).

The Church in the Middle Ages produced a stream of Christian literature aimed at exposing the falsehood of Muhammad's religion and defending the truths of Christianity against Muslim attack. We could compare this literature with the apologies for Christianity against Paganism in the early Roman Empire.[26] Among the greatest Christian apologists against Islam were John of Damascus in the East, and Thomas Aquinas (1225-74)[27] and Raymond Lull in the West.

The Christian apologists of the Middle Ages concentrated their criticisms of Islam on two major points: (i) the claims of Muhammad; (ii) the doctrine of God.

(i) The Christian apologists portrayed Muhammad as a deliberate deceiver, who fabricated his new religion out of Jewish myths and Christian heresies. Often they identified Muhammad with the false prophet of the book of Revelation. They criticised his moral character, especially what they regarded as his excessive indulgence in sexual desire (after the death of his first wife Khadijah, Muhammad took at least 14 wives and several concubines too). Because no new doctrinal or moral revelations were to be expected after Christ and the apostles, they denied that Muhammad was a true prophet. They rejected Muslim attempts to find the coming of Muhammad prophesied

---

25. For scholastic theology, see Chapter 7. For further medieval Catholic efforts at evangelising Muslims, see Chapter 8, section 5.

26. For the early Church apologists, see Volume One, Chapter 3, section 3.

27. For Thomas Aquinas see Chapter 7, section 3.

in the New Testament as a distortion of genuine New Testament teaching (Muslims argued that Christ's predictions of the coming of "another Counsellor" in John 14-16 referred to Muhammad rather than to the Holy Spirit). The apologists also defended the reliability of the New Testament text against Muslim claims that Christians had corrupted it.

(ii) The conflict between the Christian and Muslim doctrines of God centred on the Trinity, the incarnation, divine sovereignty, and the question of pure versus idolatrous worship.

The Trinity. Christian apologists explained and defended the Trinity, seeking to show how it in no way violated the oneness of God. Muslims accused Christians of having three gods; the apologists responded that Father, Son, and Holy Spirit fully and equally possessed one single divine essence, nature, and being: one God in three persons.

The incarnation. Clearly the status of Christ was central to the Christian-Muslim debate. The Christian apologists strove to show that Christ was God incarnate, not (as in the Muslim view) a mere prophet. They often tried to turn the Qu'ran itself against Muslims, pointing out the high claims it sometimes makes for Christ, teaching His unique virgin birth (sura 3:45-47) and calling Him the "Word of God" (sura 4:171).

Divine sovereignty. Christian apologists attacked as blasphemous the Muslim view of God's sovereignty – that God is the ultimate cause of all things, evil as well as good. They argued that God is the cause of all good, but not of evil. Evil is caused by the misuse of free-will by created beings. God creates and sustains the will that does evil, permits it to do evil, and exploits its evil for good, but He does not *cause* it to do evil.[28]

---

28. This Islamic view of divine sovereignty, criticised by the Christian apologists, was the prevailing concept among Islam's professional theologians in

Worship. Muslims accused Christians of idolatry because they worshipped the Virgin Mary (Muslims persistently misunderstood the Trinity to mean the Father, the Mother, and the Son). They also attacked Christians for venerating icons of Christ and the saints. The Christian apologists were on weaker ground here. They could easily refute the false understanding of the Trinity as including Mary. However, it was more difficult for them to prove to Muslims that the religious veneration given to Mary was not worship in the strict sense of the term. (Most Protestants would no doubt be inclined to the Muslim side of the argument here.)[29] They defended the use of icons as teaching aids for those who could not read. The apologists also turned the accusation of idolatry back on the Muslims; they pointed out that at the "grass roots" level, ordinary Muslims placed all sorts of created powers between God and human beings, such as the *jinn* – spirits created from fire that lived on earth and had to be appeased and warded off by magic.

At a theological level, the first Christian apologists against Islam laid down the basic arguments which Christians have

---

the Middle Ages, and seems to be the doctrine taught by the Qur'an. However, not all Muslim thinkers accepted it. Certainly many present-day Muslims would hold the view which I have here ascribed to the Christian apologists!

29.   For the kind of religious veneration Christians were now giving to the Virgin Mary, see the quotation from the *Akathist Hymn to the Most Holy Theotokos* at the end of Chapter 3. Christians had always held Mary in the highest esteem from earliest times, seeing her as the new Eve (not sinless but life-bearing) and Mother of God (that is, not mother of the divine nature, but mother of God incarnate, the Lord Jesus Christ). The belief in Mary's perpetual virginity was also held by all early church theologians except Tertullian. However, the *religious cult* of Mary, both in theology (*e.g.* the belief in her resurrection from the dead and bodily ascension into heaven) and in piety (*e.g.* offering hymns and prayers to her as the most powerful heavenly intercessor), began to grow and develop later – roughly the 5th century onwards. The process was gradual, went to far greater extremes in the West than in the East, and is still continuing in the Roman Catholic Church of today. For the more sober and moderate regard for the Virgin Mary which the early Church fathers expressed, see the quotation from Irenaeus at the end of Volume One, Chapter 4, and also Volume One, Chapter 10, section 3, on Nestorius.

traditionally followed ever since. The only serious difference among conservative Christians today is that many would prefer to think of Muhammad as deceived rather than a deceiver, at least in the earlier part of his career. However, the "Liberal" wing of Christian theology, initiated by Schleiermacher in the late 18th century, has pursued a much more open-minded approach to Islam, seeing it and all other faiths as varying expressions of humanity's common religious experience.

At a more popular level, the Muslim-Christian wars, and the loss of so much ancient Christian territory (especially the Holy Land) to Islam, created a deep emotional fear and hatred of Muslims in Christian lands. This was especially the case in the West. Eastern Christians were in constant contact with Muslims, and came to respect their culture and civilisation; but most Westerners, who had comparatively little contact with Muslims, developed an almost mindless hostility towards them. The West came to see Islam as "the enemy". This would produce bitter fruit in later centuries through the Crusades.

Important people:

The Church

John of Damascus (675-749)
Timothy I (born 728; *catholicos* of the Nestorian Church 780-823)
Husein ibn Ishaq (died 877)
Raymond Lull (1232-1316)

Muslims

Muhammad (570-632)
Caliph Abu Bakr (632-34)
Caliph Omar (634-44)
Caliph Othman (644-56)
Caliph Ali (656-61)
Caliph Muawiyah (661-80)
Husein (626-80)
Rabia (717-801)

Avicenna (980-1037)
Al-Ghazali (1058-1111)
Averroes (1126-98)
Rumi (1207-73)
Jami (1414-92)

The difference that Christ has made to the world

The worship of demons has come to an end; the divine blood has sanctified creation; the altars and temples of idols have fallen; the knowledge of God has taken root in people's minds; the Trinity, three persons in one essence, the uncreated deity, the one true God, now receives humankind's service; people cultivate moral lives; the hope of resurrection has arisen through the resurrection of Christ; the demons tremble at human beings who used to be under their control. And the marvel, indeed, is that all this has come about with success through Christ's cross and suffering and death. Throughout the whole earth, evangelists have preached the Gospel of the knowledge of God; no wars or weapons or armies have put the enemy to flight, but only a handful of naked, poor, uneducated, persecuted, and tormented men, who took their lives in their hands and preached Him who was crucified in the flesh and died. Thus they became triumphant over the wise and powerful, for the all-powerful power of the cross went with them. Death itself, which was once humankind's chief terror, has lost its sting; indeed, although death was once the object of hate and revulsion, people now prefer it to life (Phil. 1:21).

These are the triumphs of Christ's presence; these are the signs of His power. For it was not just one nation that He saved, as when through Moses He divided the sea and liberated Israel from Egypt and the servitude of Pharaoh. No, Christ rescued the whole human race from the corruption of death and the harsh dominion of sin. He did not lead people to goodness by force, He did not swallow them up in the earth or burn them with fire, He did not order the stoning of sinners; no, with gentleness and long-suffering He persuaded people to choose goodness, and to compete with one another and find delight in the struggle to achieve it. In former times, when the Law persecuted sinners, they clung all the closer to their sin, and looked upon sin as their God. But now, for the sake of godliness and goodness, people freely embrace persecutions and crucifixions and death.

Hail, O Christ, the Word and Wisdom and Power of God, You who are God all-powerful! What can we helpless ones give You in return for all these good gifts? For they all come from You, and You demand nothing from us except our salvation, You who Yourself are the giver of salvation, and yet are grateful to those who receive it through Your unspeakable goodness. Thanks be to You who gave us life through Your indescribable humility, and granted us the grace of a truly blessed life, restoring it to us when we had gone astray.

John of Damascus
On the Orthodox Faith, **Book 4, chapter 4**

A dialogue between a Christian and a Muslim

Muslim: In your opinion, what causes evil?

Christian: As I understand it, the cause of evil is un-mistakably the devil and us human beings.

Muslim: How is this so?

Christian: By the use of free-will.

Muslim: Do you actually have free-will, then? Can you act as you desire?

Christian: Yes, free-will has been bestowed on me, but only in two areas.

Muslim: What are they?

Christian: If I do what is right, I have no need to be afraid of the Law. The very opposite – God favours me and embraces me into His mercy. Yet it was through this same free-will that the devil enticed the first man away from God; for God allowed Adam to have free-will, and by that free-will Adam sinned. Thereby Adam fell from the position that God had originally assigned to him. But now let me ask you a question: give me some examples of those things which you would call good and evil.

Muslim: The sun, moon, and stars are good things. This is one example.

Christian: Yes, but that is not what I had in mind. I was referring to human good and human evil. For example, prayer and praise are good, but adultery and theft are evil. Now, if you say that both of these types of good and evil come from God, you make Him unrighteous, contrary to the truth of His nature. If you say that God Himself caused the adulterer to commit adultery, the thief to steal, and the murderer to commit murder, then they would deserve favour for having carried out God's will. But you would then be contradicting your lawgiver and perverting your own scriptures! For they decree that the adulterer and thief be flogged, and the murderer be put to death, when really they should be favoured for fulfilling God's will.

Muslim: In your opinion, who forms the foetus in the womb?

(The Muslim obviously confronts you with this dilemma in order to prove that God Himself is the cause of evil. For if you respond that it is God who forms the foetus in the womb, the Muslim will retort, "So then, God cooperates with fornicators and adulterers!" The Christian should give the following response:)

Christian: Once the seven days of creation were completed, scripture says nothing about God making or creating anything thereafter. If you think I am incorrect, then show me something that God created after that original week (the Muslim will be unable to do this). Everything we can see around us came into existence during those first seven days. This was when God also created the race of humanity, giving the command to reproduce: "Be fruitful and multiply and fill the earth" [Genesis 1:28].

Since Adam was endowed with life and living seed, he sowed seed in his wife. So it was that human beings were begotten, as scripture testifies, "Adam begot Seth, Seth begot Enosh, Enosh begot Cainan, Cainan begot Mahalaleel, Mahalaleel begot Enoch" [Genesis 5:3-18]. Notice, it does not say that God *created* Seth or Enosh or any of these. Adam was the only human being to be created by God. After Adam's creation, human beings begot other humans. And that is how it remains to this day, while the world continues by the grace of God. Once creation had been established, every herb and plant produced others, by organic reproduction, just as God had ordained: "Let the earth bring forth grass and herbs" [Genesis 1:11]. By God's decree, every sprouting tree, herb, and shrub possesses reproductive powers. Because every herb and plant contains a living seed, it germinates when it falls into the soil, whether it sows itself or is sown by another. Then it germinates, not because it has been newly created, but in obedience to God's primal decree.

Likewise, I too, by my free-will, can sow seed either in my wife, or in some other woman, as my desire leads me. That seed will then germinate in obedience to God's primal decree. This is not

because God works in a creative way each day.
God made heaven and earth in the first week –
the whole of created reality in six days; and then
on the seventh day He rested from all His works,
as my scriptures testify.

From John of Damascus's
Dialogue between a Muslim and a Christian

Be born in us today

We praise You, Lord Jesus Christ,
God and Saviour,
Wondrously powerful together with the Father;
We praise You, we call upon You, we pray to You:
Help us with Your pardon, in mercy grant us Your grace.
Arouse in our hearts desires worthy of being fulfilled;
Prompt words that are worthy of being heard;
Grant that our actions may be worthy of Your blessing.
We beg You to renew Your birth in human nature;
Enter into us with Your unseen deity,
As You entered Mary in a special way,
And as You now enter spiritually into Your Church.
Be conceived by our faith;
May our minds, free from corruption, bring You forth,
So that our souls, strengthened by the power of the Most High,
May offer You a home.
Be born in us, not physically, but by manifesting Yourself in us;
Be for us truly Immanuel, God with us.
Be pleased to stay with us and fight for us;
For only in You can we win the victory.

From the *Mozarabic Liturgy* (the Spanish Arabic liturgy)

The lover and the Beloved

They asked the lover, "What is your origin?"
He replied, "Love."
"To whom do you belong?"
"I belong to love."

"Who gave you birth?"
"Love."
"Where were you born?"
"In love."
"Who brought you up?"
"Love."
"How do you live?"
"By love."
"What is your name?"
"Love."
"Where have you journeyed from?"
"From love."
"Where are you going?"
"To love."
"Where do you dwell?"
"In love."
"Have you anything but love?"
"Yes, I have faults and sins against my Beloved."
"Is there pardon in the Beloved?"
"Yes, in my Beloved there is both mercy and justice. Therefore
    I am fixed between fear and hope ..."

The lover met his Beloved and saw that He was very noble and powerful and worthy of all honour. The lover cried out, "How strange it is, that so few people love and honour You as You deserve!" The Beloved replied: "Humankind has grieved Me greatly. I created humanity to know Me, love Me, and honour Me. Yet of every thousand, only a hundred fear and love Me. And of these hundred, ninety fear Me in case I condemn them to hell, and ten love Me from a desire to receive glory. There is hardly one who loves Me for My goodness and nobility." When the lover heard this, he wept bitterly for the dishonour which humankind had done to his Beloved. Then he said: "O Beloved, how much You have given to the human race, and how greatly You have honoured them! Why then has humanity forgotten You?"

Raymond Lull
The Lover and the Beloved, **sections 95 and 212**

The spirituality of the Qur'an[30]

He is God, besides whom there is no God, who knows what is future, and what is present: He is the most Merciful. He is God, besides whom there is no God: the King, the Holy, the Giver of peace, the Faithful, the Guardian, the Powerful, the Strong, the Most High. Far exalted be God above the idols which they associate with Him! He is God, the Creator, the Maker, the Former. He has the most excellent names. Whatever is in heaven and in earth praises Him: and He is the Mighty, the Wise.

Sura 59:22-24

Say, O God, who possesses the kingdom: You give the kingdom to whom You will, and You take away the kingdom from whom You will; You exalt whom You will, and You humble whom You will; in Your hand is good, for You are almighty. You make the night to succeed the day; You bring forth the living out of the dead, and You bring forth the dead out of the living; and You provide food for whom You will without measure.

Sura 3:26-27

Do you not perceive that God knows whatever is in heaven and in earth? There is no private discourse among three persons, but He is the fourth of them; nor among five, but He is the sixth of them; neither among a smaller number than this, nor a larger, but He is with them, wherever they are: and He will declare to them what they have done, on the day of resurrection. For God knows all things.

Sura 58:7

To God belongs the East and the West: therefore wherever you turn yourselves to pray, there is the face of God. For God is omnipresent and omniscient.

Sura 2:115

Whatever is in heaven and on earth is God's; and whether you manifest what is in your minds, or conceal it, God will call you to

---

30. All quotations from the George Sale translation, slightly updated.

account for it, and will forgive whom He pleases, and will punish whom He pleases. For God is almighty.

Sura 2:284

Truly those who hope not to meet Us at the last day, and delight in this present life, and rest securely in the same, and who are negligent of Our signs: their dwelling shall be hellfire, for that which they have deserved. But as to those who believe, and work righteousness, their Lord will direct them because of their faith; they shall have rivers flowing through gardens of pleasure. Their prayer therein shall be, Praise be to You, O God! and their salutation therein shall be Peace! and the end of their prayer shall be, Praise be to God, the Lord of all creatures!

Sura 10:9-10

Fight for the religion of God against those who fight against you; but do not transgress by attacking them first, for God does not love the transgressors. And kill them wherever you find them, and turn them wherever they have dispossessed you; for temptation to idolatry is more grievous than slaughter. Yet do not fight against them in the holy temple, until they attack you therein; but if they attack you, slay them there. This shall be the reward of infidels. But if they desist, God is gracious and merciful. Fight therefore against them, until there is no temptation to idolatry and the religion is God's; but if they desist, then let there be no hostility, except against the ungodly.

Sura 2:190-93

The Qur'an's testimony to the Bible and Christ
We have surely sent down the Law, containing direction and light: thereby did the prophets, who professed the true religion, judge the Jews; and the teachers and priests also judged by the book of God, which had been committed to their custody; and they were witnesses thereof... We also caused Jesus the son of Mary to follow the footsteps of the prophets, confirming the Law which was sent down before him; and we gave him the Gospel, containing direction and light, confirming also the Law which

was given before it, and a direction and admonition to those who fear God: that those who have received the Gospel might judge according to what God has revealed therein. Whoever does not judge according to what God has revealed, they are transgressors.

Sura 5:44, 46-47

O Mary, truly God sends you good tidings, that you shall bear the Word proceeding from Himself. His name shall be Christ Jesus, the son of Mary, honourable in this world and in the world to come, and one of those who approach near to the presence of God; and he shall speak to men in the cradle, and when he is grown up; and he shall be one of the righteous. She answered, Lord, how shall I have a son, since a man has not touched me? The angel said, Thus God creates that which He pleases: when He decrees a thing, He only says to it, Be, and it is.

Sura 3:45-47

O you who have received the scriptures, exceed not the just bounds in your religion, neither say of God any other than the truth. Truly Christ Jesus the son of Mary is the apostle of God, and His Word, which He conveyed into Mary, and a spirit proceeding from Him. Believe therefore in God, and His apostles, and say not, "Three". Forbear this; it will be better for you. God is but one God. Far be it from Him that He should have a son!

Sura 4:171

The spirituality of Islamic mysticism: A poem by the early female Sufi, Rabia of Basra

My Delight,
My Desire,
My Refuge,
My Friend,
My Sustenance for the journey,
My journey's End:
You are my breath,
My confidence,

My companion,
My longing,
My plentiful riches.
O my Life, O my Love,
Without You, I never would have trekked
Over these ceaseless landscapes.
You have bestowed such abundant grace on me,
Done so many good things for me,
Imparted so many gifts to me!
Everywhere I search for Your love:
And then, in an instant, I overflow with it.
O Master of my Heart,
Luminous Eye of Longing in my breast,
While life lasts
I will never be free of You.
Be content with me, my Love,
And I am content.

Rabia of Basra

The spirituality of Islamic mysticism: Three poems by the Persian Sufi, Jalal al-Din Rumi

1. Beyond Heaven
Rise up, lovers!
Let's journey to heaven.
We've seen enough of this world;
The other world awaits us!

But no.
These two gardens are both beautiful,
Both lovely;
But we must travel beyond them both,
And seek the Gardener.

2. Comparisons
My friend, which is sweeter?
Sugar – or He Who creates sugar?

My friend, which is fairer?
The moon – or He Who makes the moon?

Forget sugar; never mind moons.
He has something else in His mind;
He fashions something new.
There are marvels in the sea besides its pearls;
But there are no marvels like the Monarch
Who makes both the sea and the pearls!
Besides the water, there is another Water
Which gushes from a glorious water-wheel;
This Water is flawless, ever-flowing,
And gives life to the heart!

Without knowledge, no-one can build a bath.
Consider, then, that Knowledge
Which creates intellect and awareness!
Without knowledge, you can't extract oil from fat.
Think, then, of that Knowledge
Which fashions sight from the fat of the eye!

Men wait up all night,
Without food, without slumber,
To feast on the dawn-splendour He creates:
How it stuns their souls!
And how glad a dawn for me, when He
Whose light eclipses every despairing moon
Makes His mighty hands
Into a belt around my waist!

3. Sweeter in adversity

The Beloved is sweeter
In this cold and rain:
The Beauty in the heart,
And Love in the brain.

Sweet Beauty in our hearts!
Who compares with You?

Graceful, tender, fair,
Fresh and shining-new.

Let's hide in His shelter
Now the cold winds have come;
For none born of woman
Can offer such a home.

Let's kiss His lips
In the falling snow;
Snow and sugar
Restore the heart's glow.

Jalal al-Din Rumi

2
Charlemagne and the Holy Roman Empire

1. France, the Carolingians, and the papacy

When the Franks settled in France in the 5th century, their kings – such as Clovis, the first to embrace Christianity – belonged to the Merovingian dynasty (named after Clovis's grandfather Merovech).[1] However, the 6th century saw a progressive loss of power by the Merovingian monarchs. The problem was the strength of the Frankish nobility, who were soon acting like little independent sovereigns in their huge private domains. By 630, the Merovingian kings had practically no authority outside their own royal land; and even there, they lost power to the mayors of the royal palace, who became all-powerful prime ministers to a monarch who was only a figurehead. The office of mayor became hereditary in the *Carolingian* family,[2] beginning with Pepin of Laudon (died 639).

Pepin and his Carolingian successors launched a campaign to restore the prestige and authority of the Merovingian monarchy, but only because it increased their own power as mayors of the palace. Part of their strategy for expanding royal authority was the Christianising of the still Pagan tribes in the Netherlands and Germany, such as the Frisians, Hessians, and Saxons.

---

1. For Clovis, see Volume One, Chapter 11, section 1.

2. Pronounced "Carro-lin-jee-un". From *Carolus*, the Latin for Charles – the family was named after its greatest member, Charlemagne (Charles the Great), for whom see section 2.

The Carolingians reasoned that Christian tribes would be less troublesome and rebellious than Pagan ones. If they embraced the Catholic faith, the Germans would come under the authority of a great spiritual organisation which had no local or tribal loyalties; and the Carolingians could then control the Germans through the Church – by putting the right men in positions of power as bishops. In pursuit of this policy, the Carolingian mayors, especially **Charles Martel** (690-741), gave strong support to a new wave of English missionaries to Germany. (This is the Charles Martel who crushed the Muslims at the battle of Tours or Poitiers in 732: see Chapter 1, section 3.)

Two outstanding figures led the English missionaries. The first was **Willibrord** (658-740), from the northern Angle kingdom of Northumbria. Brought up from childhood in the monastery at Ripon, Willibrord spent 12 years as a student in Ireland; then in about 690, he journeyed to the Netherlands at the head of 12 Irish missionaries, according to the traditional Irish practice of sending out mission teams in groups of 13.[3] Willibrord and his companions worked for 50 years in the Netherlands among the southern Frisian tribes; their preaching largely brought about the conversion of the Frisians to Christianity.

The second great English missionary was Winfrid (680-754), born near Crediton in the Anglo-Saxon kingdom of Wessex (south-west England). History knows Winfrid better by his Latin name **Boniface** – "doer of good". Like Willibrord, Boniface spent his childhood in a monastery, at Exeter. As an adult missionary, he at first worked (715 onwards) alongside Willibrord among the Frisians, and then in 718 began a new work among the Hessians and Thuringians of central Germany.[4] He established many monastic communities, including the famous abbey of Fulda in the central German state of Franconia; for 300 years after his death, Boniface's monasteries (especially Fulda) were the life-giving centres of religion and culture in Germany. In all

---

3. For Irish missionary practice, see Volume One, Chapter 11, section 3.

4. See the end of the Chapter for a contemporary account of Boniface's evangelistic labours.

his missionary labours, Boniface received strong support from the papacy, and he in turn upheld papal authority wherever he preached. In 723 Pope Gregory II (715-31) ordained Boniface as a special "missionary bishop" without a church, and in 732 Pope Gregory III (731-41) raised him to the rank of "missionary archbishop". Pope *Zacharias* (741-52) eventually appointed Boniface Archbishop of Mainz (western-central Germany) in 743, with a huge diocese stretching from Cologne in the north to Strasbourg in the south.

Boniface (680-754)

Boniface ended his long and fruitful life as a martyr, killed by
Frisian Pagans in 754. The Church awarded him the honorary title
of "apostle of the Germans"; his decades of missionary enterprise
brought large parts of Germany out of Paganism into the brighter
world of Christendom. As we have seen, both the papacy and
Charles Martel in France gave powerful backing to the missionary
work of Willibrord and Boniface. This religious alliance between
the Carolingians and the papacy grew stronger after Charles
Martel's death in 741 and the accession of his sons Carloman
and *Pepin* (died 768) to power. Martel had placed Carloman and
Pepin in a monastery in their youth, where monks had raised
them to have a genuine concern for the welfare of the Church.
Now that they shared the throne of France, they invited Boniface
to help them reform the Frankish Church. Since Boniface acted
as the pope's representative, these reforms strengthened the bond
between France and the papacy – a bond which was soon to have
serious and lasting consequences.

Carloman became a monk after Boniface's reforms were
completed, leaving his brother Pepin as sole ruler of the Franks.
But in theory, Pepin was still only the mayor of the palace, the
chief servant of Childeric III, last of the feeble Merovingian
kings. The fires of ambition danced in Pepin's heart; he felt that
he, the real ruler of France, should wear its royal crown. So Pepin
obtained the support of Pope Zacharias, and in 751 deposed
Childeric, who retired into a monastery. Then Boniface, again
acting in the pope's name, crowned Pepin king of the Franks –
the first of the great Carolingian royal dynasty. This was the first
time a pope had claimed that his apostolic authority involved the
right to sanction the dethroning of one king and his replacement
by another. It meant that the new royal family in France owed its
legal authority to the papacy.

Political motives inspired the action of Pope Zacharias in
crowning Pepin: Zacharias wanted military allies against the
Lombards in Italy.[5] A new Lombard king, Aistulf, had come
to power in 751, and pursued an aggressive policy of enlarging

---

5. For the Lombards, see Volume One, Chapter 11, section 1.

his territories. He expelled the Byzantine governor of the north Italian city of Ravenna, the Western capital of the Byzantine Empire, and swept all Byzantine forces out of northern Italy. Then his armies threatened Rome itself. Zacharias's successor as pope, Stephen II (752-57), fled into France and threw himself on the mercy of Pepin. To make the Frankish-papal alliance even stronger, Stephen himself personally crowned Pepin king of France in a second coronation ceremony in 754. In return, Pepin invaded Italy with a Frankish army and forced Aistulf to agree not to attack Rome. However, two years later in 756, Aistulf broke the agreement and put Rome under siege. Once again Pope Stephen appealed to Pepin; once again Pepin invaded Italy, and this time he inflicted a crushing military defeat on the Lombards, occupying their lands. Pepin gave all the Lombard cities he had captured to Stephen. This action, known as "the donation of Pepin", created an H-shaped set of papal territories across western-central and north-eastern Italy – the "papal states". Pepin even gave Ravenna to Stephen, rather than restore it to Byzantium. The Byzantine Emperor Constantine V (741-75) protested, but Pepin replied that he felt under no obligation to Byzantium; as far as he was concerned, he had done everything for the glory of God, the apostle Peter, and the pope.

Pepin's action bore three enduring fruits:

(i)   It finally snapped the links between the papacy and the Byzantine Empire. The Eastern and Western branches of the Church had already been drifting apart; that drift now became more like a speeding torrent. The "one holy Catholic and apostolic Church" was beginning to break up into two Churches: the Greek-speaking Eastern Church, centred on Constantinople, and the Latin-speaking Western Church, centred on Rome and the papacy. However, East and West were still in theory united as one Church, and it was not until 1054 that they officially separated (see Chapter 3, section 8).

(ii) It sealed the military, political, and religious bond between the Franks and the papacy. The Frankish monarchy replaced the Byzantine Empire as the centre of Rome's diplomatic and spiritual world.

(iii) It gave the papacy a huge independent state in central and northern Italy. The popes from now on would be secular rulers as much as spiritual leaders. In fact, they often became so absorbed in their secular business that they lost all interest in theology and pastoral work.

It was also around this time (the middle of the 8th century) that a document called the *Donation of Constantine* appeared. This claimed to be a letter from the first Christian Emperor, Constantine the Great (312-37), to Pope Sylvester I (314-35). A story had grown up that Sylvester had miraculously cured Constantine of leprosy; in gratitude, Constantine had supposedly written this letter to Sylvester, in which he acknowledged that the pope was superior to the Emperor, and granted the papacy the right to govern the city of Rome and all imperial territory in Italy and the West. The document was a forgery, exposed by the great Italian scholar Lorenzo Valla in 1440; but for 700 years the popes used the Donation of Constantine to back up their lofty claims.[6]

2. Charlemagne and the Carolingian Renaissance

When Pepin died in 768, his two sons Charles and Carloman succeeded him as joint rulers of France. Carloman died in 771, leaving Charles as sole ruler. He reigned for the next 43 years (771-814) and created the first great Western empire since the fall of Rome in 410. He is called "Charles the Great" or **Charlemagne** (from the Latin *magnus*, "great").[7]

Charlemagne is one of the truly colossal figures of European history. He has been called the "Moses of the Middle Ages", because he led the Germanic peoples out of the wilderness of

---

6. For Lorenzo Valla, see Volume Three, Chapter 1, section 2.

7. Charlemagne is pronounced "Sharl-a-main".

barbarism and gave them a new code of civil and ecclesiastical laws. Medieval Churchmen often compared Charlemagne with Constantine the Great, because the illustrious Frankish king recreated the Western Roman Empire on a Christian basis. His biographer Einhard tells us that Charlemagne was a physical giant of a man, with enough strength and energy for a dozen ordinary mortals; sober and simple in his private life, he was a just and generous ruler, an affectionate father, unswervingly loyal to his friends, and highly popular with his subjects. He had a keen probing mind, a sincere devotion to the Christian faith and the Catholic Church, and a burning sense of personal mission from God to unite the Western nations under a Christian empire. The only real fault in Charlemagne's character was his imperfect standard of sexual conduct: he married and divorced several wives at will, and after the death of his fifth wife he took a number of concubines.

We can look at Charlemagne's reign under the following headings.

Military campaigns

Charlemagne spent most of his long reign fighting wars. A brave warrior and an outstanding general, his armies only ever suffered defeat in battle once. His first great campaign was against the Lombards in Italy. Pope Adrian I (772-95) appealed to Charlemagne to rescue him from the Lombards, who under their last king, Desiderius, were again threatening papal territory. Charlemagne invaded Italy, conquered the Lombard kingdom, deposed Desiderius, and made himself king of Lombardy, thus adding northern Italy to his empire. He fought the Muslims in Spain and brought the Spanish borderlands as far as Barcelona under his control. He also carried out many campaigns on the German frontier, annexing Bavaria, and breaking the power of the Pagan Avars in the Danube valley (modern Hungary).

Charlemagne's longest war was against the Pagan Saxons, which required 18 savage campaigns and occupied over 30 years of his reign. He eventually crushed Saxon resistance through a policy of forcibly resettling large groups of Saxons in other

parts of the Carolingian kingdom, and compelling them to
choose between accepting Christian baptism and being put to
death. This forced conversion of the Saxons aroused protests
from some leading Christians, *e.g.* Charlemagne's chief religious
advisor, **Alcuin of York** (730-804). Alcuin said: "Faith is a free act
of the will, not a forced act. We must appeal to the conscience, not
compel it by violence. You can force people to be baptised, but you
cannot force them to believe." These protests finally succeeded;
Charlemagne abolished the death penalty for Paganism in 797.

The Emperor of the Romans

Many of Charlemagne's Church advisors saw the wide extent of
his kingdom as a re-creation of the Roman Empire in the West.
This led to Charlemagne being recognised as "Emperor of the
Romans" in the year 800. According to tradition, the man behind
this move was Pope **Leo III** (795-816).[8] On Christmas day 800,
while Charlemagne was kneeling at the altar in Saint Peter's
Church, Rome, receiving communion, surrounded by the Frankish
nobility and Roman clergy, Pope Leo suddenly produced a crown
and placed it on Charlemagne's head. Leo's men then shouted out,
"To Charles Augustus, crowned by God, great and peace-making
Emperor of the Romans, long life and victory!" So was born the
Holy Roman Empire. Leo's crowning of Charlemagne signified
that he was not simply king of the Franks; he was the heir of
the old Roman Emperors, the one in whom the Roman Empire
had been reborn, the supreme ruler of the Western world. The
Byzantine Emperors, of course, bitterly resented this unilateral
claim, since they saw themselves as the true heirs of Rome. The
coronation of Charlemagne thus caused East and West to drift
apart still further. At the same time, Leo's act announced that
the new Roman Emperor owed his position to the papacy: Leo
was determined to make the Emperor dependent for his imperial
crown on God's agent, the pope.

Charlemagne was pleased with his new status, but unhappy
at the way Leo had given it to him. He tried to kill the idea

---

8. There are alternative interpretations; I follow the traditional one.

that he owed his authority to the pope by having his son Louis crown himself in Aachen (otherwise called Aix-la-Chapelle), Charlemagne's capital city, presently in north-west Germany. But it was in vain. Leo's act had convinced the people of the Middle Ages that the crown of the Holy Roman Emperor was the gift of the pope.

Culture

Charlemagne's empire saw a mighty flourishing of Christian culture. This is called the *Carolingian Renaissance.*[9] Charlemagne gathered together in his court the most distinguished scholars of Western Europe. Most of these were monks – monasteries had become the focal points of knowledge and culture in the West. Among these scholars were **Paul the Deacon** (720-800), **Paulinus of Aquileia** (730-802), and **Theodulph of Orleans** (750-821). Paul the Deacon, a Lombard, wrote a collection of sermons for the festivals and saints' days of the Church, which preachers in the Western Church used for the next thousand years; he also wrote a *Roman History* and *History of the Lombards*, which are important historical sources. Paulinus of Aquileia, another Lombard, was an outstanding bishop of Aquileia (north-eastern Italy), and a writer of hymns, poems, letters, and a number of theological writings against the Adoptianist heresy.[10] Theodulph of Orleans, a Gothic Spaniard, was another great bishop (Orleans is in northern-central France), theological writer against Adoptianism and in favour of the *filioque* clause,[11] and hymnwriter – the popular hymn "All glory, laud and honour to Thee, Redeemer, King" is by Theodulph.

However, the greatest of Charlemagne's scholars was the English monk, Alcuin of York. Alcuin was the most influential intellect behind the Carolingian Renaissance. Born near the

---

9. "Renaissance" is French for rebirth. The Carolingian Renaissance must not be confused with the great European Renaissance of the 15th century – see Volume Three, Chapter 1.

10. For Adoptianism, see this section under *Religious policy*.

11. For the *filioque* clause, see this section under *Emperor and pope*.

northern English city of York, he became head of its cathedral school, before entering Charlemagne's service in 782. For the next 22 years Alcuin was the grand schoolmaster of the Frankish empire. The most cultured man in Western Europe, he was (among other things) a Bible commentator, textual scholar, liturgical reviser, defender of orthodoxy against the Adoptianists, reformer of monasteries, builder of libraries, and learned astronomer. Alcuin's main contributions to the Carolingian Renaissance were as follows:

Language. Alcuin reformed spelling and developed a new style of handwriting called "Carolingian miniscule", on which our modern printed letters are based. Carolingian scholars revived the Latin language, refined it, and taught it to all educated people. It became the international language of Western civilisation; whatever their native tongue, all educated Westerners could speak Latin.

Literature. In the days before printing was invented, monks had to copy books by hand. Charlemagne's army of monk-scholars made numerous copies of ancient writings; most of our surviving texts from ancient Greece and Rome have come down to us from Carolingian copies. Alcuin oversaw the establishment of monastic libraries throughout Charlemagne's empire where these books were copied and stored. In this way the Carolingian Renaissance helped to preserve and transmit to the present the knowledge and culture of the past.

The Bible. Alcuin revised the text of the Latin Bible and established a standard edition of Jerome's Vulgate.[12]

Education. Charlemagne took a strong personal interest in the spreading of education, advised chiefly by Alcuin. He ordered bishops and abbots to set up schools for training

---

12. For Jerome and the Vulgate, see Volume One, Chapter 9, section 2.

priests and monks. He decreed that every parish[13] should have a school to educate all the male children of the neighbourhood. He founded his own royal academy in Aachen, presided over by Alcuin, which encouraged the study of logic, philosophy, and literature.

Religious policy

Charlemagne saw himself as the spiritual as well as political leader of the Holy Roman Empire, modelling himself on the good Biblical kings of Judah, such as David and Josiah. He interpreted all public disasters as judgments of God on his empire for its sins, and ordered public fasts; for all victories in battle, he ordered public thanksgiving to God. His imperial decrees were more often concerned with religion than with politics. They dealt with the recruitment and education of priests, Church discipline, the religious instruction of the laity, and even theological issues. Charlemagne presided over Church councils and actively participated in them. He assumed authority over the bishops within his empire, nominating men of his choice to vacant bishoprics. He tended to treat the bishops as a department of the Carolingian civil service; many bishops were appointed to secular government positions. He took a strong interest in the monasteries, personally appointing many abbots. He tried to reform the moral lives of the clergy by making them subject to a code called "the rule of Chrodegang" (Chrodegang – died 766 – was the worthy bishop of Metz in north-eastern France). Priests were also now set apart from the rest of Western society in their ordinary everyday dress, the "cassock" (a long black gown worn at all times). It was also at this time that the "alb" (a white linen vestment worn at holy communion) became common.

Charlemagne's religious legislation also affected society at large. For example, he passed strong new laws on the observance of Sunday. Laypeople were forbidden to do any work on Sunday,

---

13.   A parish was a small unit of territory where the life of the inhabitants was organised around their local church, to which they paid tithes. The word comes from the Greek *paroikia*, "district".

except for burying the dead, and transporting food and necessary military supplies. Furthermore, Charlemagne made the payment of tithes universal and compulsory. Ever since the reign of King Pepin, people had paid tithes to their parish church in many places on a voluntary basis. Charlemagne extended the practice throughout his empire and gave it the force of law. Tithes were levied on land, not on persons, and were not paid in cash but in "kind" – corn, wine, hay, livestock. The penalty for refusing to pay tithes to one's parish church was excommunication.

The only great internal quarrel over doctrine in Charlemagne's kingdom was the Adoptianist controversy. Two Spanish bishops, Elipandus of Toledo (718-802) and Felix of Urgel (died 818), put forward the view that although Christ, in His divine nature, was the eternal Son of God, yet in His human nature He was an adopted son of God, just as believers are. Elipandus of Toledo lived in the Muslim kingdom of Cordova, but Felix of Urgel lived in Catalonia, north-eastern Spain. Catalonia had been part of Charlemagne's kingdom since 778; Adoptianism therefore spread and caused great controversy within the Frankish empire. It was strongly opposed by Alcuin, Paulinus of Aquileia, and Theodulph of Orleans; they argued that it was the Nestorian heresy to say that there were two sons in Christ, a divine Son and an adopted human son.[14] Adoptianism was condemned at the council of Frankfurt in 794.

At the root of the controversy lay the question whether "sonship" belonged to "nature" or to "person". The Adoptianists said it belonged to nature; and since Christ has two natures (divine and human), He must have two sonships, an eternal divine sonship and an adopted human sonship. By contrast, Alcuin, Paulinus and Theodulph pointed out that Christ's *divine* sonship belongs to His person, not His nature – it is as a *person* that He is Son of the Father. Father and Son share one and the same nature, the nature of God; what makes them differ from each other is their distinct personhood, revealed in their divine Fatherhood and Sonship. Therefore Christ, the divine Son, cannot have

---

14. For Nestorianism, see Volume One, Chapter 10, sections 3 and 5.

an additional human sonship unless He has a separate human personality, which is the Nestorian heresy.

Emperor and pope

Charlemagne's exalted view of kingship brought him into serious conflict with the papacy. He looked upon himself as *et rex et sacerdos*, "both king and priest". This did not mean that Charlemagne thought he was a priest in the sense of a clergyman, with the right to celebrate the sacraments; but it did mean that he considered himself invested with power directly from Christ to regulate Church affairs within his empire. We can grasp Charlemagne's concept of his own position from two letters that were addressed to him, the first by Alcuin, the second by another Carolingian Churchman, Cathwulf:

> Our Lord Jesus Christ has exalted you as the ruler of the Christian people, excelling the pope and the Emperor of Constantinople in power, in wisdom more illustrious, in the dignity of your leadership more magnificent. The whole safety of the churches of Christ depends on you alone.
>
> Always remember, O my king, in a spirit of reverence and love for God your King, that you stand in God's place. You are established as guardian and ruler of all His members, and you must give an account for them on the day of judgment. The bishop is on a secondary level; he only stands in Christ's place. Therefore take thought within yourself how you can vigorously extend the power of God's law over God's people.

This second quotation from Cathwulf shows that the thinkers of the Carolingian Renaissance saw the king as "vicar of God", standing in God's place ("vicar" means one who stands in the place of another). Cathwulf's point about kings and bishops is that a king is *God's* vicar – standing in the place of the whole Trinity in its divine nature; but the bishop is only *Christ's* vicar – standing in the place of Jesus in His office as Mediator. Other Carolingian writers did not hesitate to describe kings as the vicars of both Christ *and* God. Therefore the king was higher than any bishop; and that included the supreme bishop, the pope. Historians often refer to this vision of the rights and duties of monarchs as the ideal of "sacred kingship". It was not Charlemagne's invention; the Council of Chalcedon in 451 had referred to the Byzantine Emperor Marcian as "priest and king", and Byzantium's rulers saw themselves in these lofty terms.[15] Byzantium, however, had no equivalent of the papacy. The rival claims of Roman pope and Holy Roman Emperor brought a theological and political conflict to Western Christendom which the East never experienced.

Throughout his reign, Charlemagne acted consistently on the theory of sacred kingship, regarding himself as the pope's superior even in doctrinal matters. We can see this particularly clearly in two events:

(i) In 790, without consulting Pope Adrian I, Charlemagne issued the Western Church's response to the "iconoclastic controversy" then raging within Eastern Christianity. This was a dispute over the use of images or "icons" of Christ, Mary, and the saints in worship (see Chapter 3, section 2, for a detailed account). Charlemagne's response came in the so-called *Caroline books* ("books of Charles"), written with the help of his religious advisors, especially Alcuin. The Caroline books took a middle path between the Eastern advocates and enemies of icons. On the one hand, Charlemagne and Alcuin rejected the practice of bowing or kneeling before icons, kissing them, and burning candles or incense in front of them. They also rejected the stories of miracles worked by icons, as human imaginations or demonic deceptions. On the other hand, they accepted that Christians rightly used icons to adorn churches and set forth stories of Christ and the saints. And they accepted that religious honour should be paid to the sign of the cross and to relics of the saints. The council of Frankfurt, which spoke for the churches of France and Germany, officially sanctioned these views in 794. East and West were thus at odds with each other over this important issue of worship. However, the West's opposition to icon-veneration

---

15. For Marcian and the Council of Chalcedon, see Volume One, Chapter 10, section 4.

did not last; by the 10th century, the Western Church had swung over to the Eastern position.

(ii) Despite the veto of Pope Leo III, Charlemagne supported the insertion of the *filioque* clause into the Nicene Creed. The Creed, as originally set forth by the Council of Constantinople in 381, said that the Holy Spirit "proceeds from the Father". From the 6th century onwards, Westerners had begun adding the words "and from the Son" (which in Latin is *filioque* – pronounced "feely-oh-kweh"). This seems to have started in Spain; the Spanish council of Toledo added *filioque* to the Creed in 589. Other parts of the Western Church eventually followed their example. The crowning moment came with the Carolingian Renaissance, whose theologians (*e.g.* Alcuin and Theodulph of Orleans) decisively committed the Church and Empire of Charlemagne to the *filioque* clause.[16] This caused great controversy between East and West. The East protested that the Western Church had no authority to alter one of the ecumenical Creeds, and that in any case this particular alteration was false – the Holy Spirit does not proceed from the Son, but from the Father alone. Pope Leo III agreed with the Carolingian position theologically, but opposed the insertion of the *filioque* clause into

---

16.   In the 640s Maximus the Confessor, one of the greatest Eastern theologians, found the Church in Rome to be in harmony with the East in its views of the Spirit's procession from the Father alone. When Roman theologians in Maximus's time said that the Spirit proceeded "from the Son", they were referring only to the Spirit's procession from the incarnate Christ in salvation, not His procession from the divine Son in eternity. Maximus wrote: "Bringing forward the testimony of the Roman fathers and of Cyril of Alexandria, the Romans do not affirm that the Son is the Cause of the Spirit, for they know that the Father is the Cause of the Son and of the Spirit – of the Son by begetting, and of the Spirit by procession. The Romans merely set forth that the Spirit is *sent* through the Son." This may in fact be all that the Spanish Catholics meant at the Council of Toledo in 589. It was the Carolingian Renaissance which collectively committed the West to the *filioque* clause in the sense rejected by the East, that the Spirit proceeds eternally from Father and Son as from a single source. For a fuller account of the theology of the *filioque* clause, see Chapter 3, section 4. For Maximus, see Volume One, Chapter 12, section 4.

the Nicene Creed. Charlemagne, however, ignored Leo's pro-
tests, and gave his sanction to the *filioque* clause at the council of
Aachen in 809. So again Charlemagne put Western and Eastern
Christianity at odds with each other.

The relationship between Charlemagne and the papacy was
therefore uneasy. The creation of the Holy Roman Empire on
Christmas day 800 paved the way for the fierce conflicts between
popes and Emperors in the later Middle Ages. The papacy stood
for the great spiritual principle of the freedom and independence
of the Church from state control. However, to secure that independence, the popes wanted to place the state under the control
of the Church. Pope Leo III's crowning of Charlemagne could be
used to justify the claim that the papacy had given the Emperor
his crown – and it could also take it away again, if the Emperor
did not obey the will of the pope.

On the other hand, Charlemagne and his successors saw themselves as "sacred kings", the divinely chosen rulers of a Christian
empire, responsible to God for its spiritual as well as secular welfare. Therefore they regarded it as their right and duty to regulate
the affairs of the Church. The pope was, to them, nothing more
than their chief spiritual advisor. As Charlemagne himself put it:

> The king's mission is to fortify, consolidate, spread, and main-
> tain the faith effectively; the pope's mission is to lend support
> the king in this task, by praying for him like Moses with out-
> stretched arms.

So long as Church and state were united, and seen as two
aspects of a single Christian society, the possibility of religious
and political conflict between pope and Emperor was all too real.
Supporters of the pope in this conflict were called "papalists";
supporters of the Emperor were called "imperialists".[17]

---

17. Also known in Italy, rather more exotically, as *Guelfs* (papalists) and
Ghibellines (imperialists). *Guelf* comes from "Welf", after duke Welf of
Bavaria (1070-1101). Welf and his descendants opposed the claims to the
German throne of Emperor Henry IV (1056-1106) and his descendants (the
Hohenstaufen dynasty). Because the Hohenstaufen were anti-papal, the Guelfs

3. Developments in Western worship

One of the gravest problems affecting the life of the Western Church, after the collapse of the Roman Empire in the West in the 5th century, was a widespread decline in the level of education among the clergy. The culture, knowledge, and literacy of any society's clergy tend to reflect the general standards in society at large; and these standards had fallen seriously in Western Europe in the aftermath of the great Germanic invasions of the 400s, with the disruption and devastation they inflicted on the fabric of Western civilisation (see Volume One, Chapter 11). The Carolingian Renaissance did something to improve this state of affairs, but the overall picture remained bleak.

The most obvious evidence of this loss of education in Church life was that most clergy now limited themselves to carrying out liturgical and sacramental functions – celebrating holy communion, hearing confessions, baptising infants, burying the dead. They no longer preached sermons. Western Catholics thus became accustomed to a form of worship in which many things were done but hardly anything was explained. Or at least, it would be more accurate to say that most Western medieval clergy did not preach their *own* sermons; but this did not in fact necessarily mean they preached nothing at all. For this was the period in which *homilies* achieved great prominence in the Church's worship. A homily was a sermon written by someone else and read out to the congregation by the priest.[18] The practice had already sprung up by the 5th century, but it was in the 8th and 9th centuries that it became a normal and widespread factor in preaching. The homilies of the Venerable Bede[19] and of Paul

---

decided to champion the cause of the papacy, on the basis that "my enemy's enemy is my friend". The imperialists were called *Ghibellines* after the important Hohenstaufen town of Waiblingen in Swabia. For Henry IV and his conflict with the papacy, see Chapter 4, sections 5 and 6.

18.   Some might argue that reading out a sermon written by someone else is not "preaching". I am using the word in the broadest sense to mean "delivering sermons".

19.   For the Venerable Bede, see Volume One, Chapter 11, section 3.

the Deacon (see previous section under the heading *Culture*) were especially popular. Collections of homilies were based on the Church lectionary, the fixed system of Bible readings for each Sunday in the year, which had developed since the 3rd century.

It was during the Carolingian Renaissance that the Western liturgy itself was finally standardised. Up until now, Western churches had followed two different liturgies, the Roman and the Gallican (French). Charlemagne desired all churches in his empire to worship according to the same liturgy; and so great was his attachment to all things Roman that he ordered Alcuin to prepare a new scholarly edition of the Roman liturgy for use throughout the Holy Roman Empire. Alcuin added some prayers from the Gallican to the Roman liturgy, but his liturgical reform meant that Western Christendom now followed one standard form of worship derived largely from the Roman church.

The centre of Western worship was the eucharist or holy communion. Of course, ever since the apostolic fathers, holy communion had been at the heart of all Christian worship;[20] but the new Western name for communion, "mass", was accompanied by some important changes in practice too ("mass" probably comes from the closing words of the Western Latin liturgy, *ite, missa est* – "Go, the congregation is dismissed").[21] The most outstanding difference between the eucharist in the early Church and in the Western medieval Church was the role played by the laity. In the age of the early Church fathers, all Christians had taken part in communion every Sunday; but from the 5th century onwards, lay communion had become less and less frequent in the West, so that only clergy and monks took part on a regular basis. By the 6th century, the Western Church required laypeople to receive communion only three times a year, at Christmas, Easter, and Pentecost. Even this was soon cut down to once a year at Easter. Yet parish priests continued to celebrate communion every Sunday, in accordance with early Church tradition; the priest, however, now ate the bread

20. See Volume One, Chapter 3, section 2, under *Church worship*.
21. See Volume One, Chapter 11, section 2, under *Theology*.

and drank the wine by himself, while the laity simply watched. The only place in the West which resisted this development, and where lay communion continued to be frequent until the later Middle Ages, was Rome itself. (Weekly lay communion continued to be the normal practice in the East.)

The reasons behind this huge shift in the way the eucharist was celebrated in the West were twofold:

(i) First, the tremendous feelings of reverence, dread and fear which had become attached to holy communion deterred ordinary laypeople – especially the new Germanic converts – from taking part. They felt unworthy and afraid to approach the awesome mystery of Christ's sacrifice, as it was once again made present and effective in the eucharist for the remission of the sins of the living and the dead. These feelings of awe towards holy communion were deepened still further by the increasing strength of belief that the bread and wine were miraculously and entirely converted into Christ's very flesh and blood (see next section under *Radbertus, Ratramnus, and the communion controversy*).

(ii) Second, the clergy themselves, especially the best educated and most spiritually-minded, discouraged the majority of laypeople from taking part frequently in communion. Strangely, it was not actually the Church's intention to inhibit lay communion; indeed, priests exhorted their congregations to take part more often. However, they also insisted that in order to take part, people had to be serious, committed Christians who lived in obedience to God's commands. The most devout of the clergy were only too aware that many of the Germanic peoples had embraced Christianity in a very loose and shallow way, simply following the religious loyalties of their leader. By stressing that only true Christians with a genuine repentance and love for God could take part meaningfully in communion, the clergy often set the moral and spiritual standard so high that it deterred even the most sincere believers from taking part.

Another important development in Western worship which took place in the 8th century was the distinction between "high mass" and "low mass". High mass was a simplification of the traditional communion liturgy; it is sometimes called "sung mass" because it included singing (in contrast to low mass). All the clergy and laity of a congregation participated in the liturgical part of high mass, and most parish churches celebrated it every Sunday. In low mass, only the priest performed; there was no singing, and the priest spoke the liturgy in a very quiet voice (hence low mass is also called "said mass"). The laity did not take part in any way; they merely watched and carried out their own private devotions. The parish priest celebrated low mass every day. Spiritually-minded laypeople would attend low mass on weekdays, praying and meditating in silence while the priest ate and drank the bread and wine on his own.

4. The Holy Roman Empire after Charlemagne

There were a number of important people, movements and events in the Holy Roman Empire in the period after Charlemagne's death in 814.

Benedict of Aniane and the revival of the monasteries

If Benedict of Nursia[22] was the "father of Western monasticism", another Benedict – *Benedict of Aniane* (750-821) – was its first great reformer. A native of southern France, Benedict began life as an outstanding soldier in Charlemagne's service, but after nearly losing his life in a drowning accident he became a monk in about 775 in a Benedictine monastery at Dijon (eastern-central France). This was a bad experience for Benedict; he thought his fellow monks were more interested in comfort than spiritual struggle. So in 779, he founded his own monastery at Aniane in southern France, where he enforced such a strict rule that all the other monks fled from the monastery! Then he obtained a copy of Benedict of Nursia's original rule (to which, over the centuries, all sorts of additions had been made). Here he found what seemed to

---

22. See Volume One, Chapter 11, section 1 for Benedict of Nursia.

him a perfect balance between prayer, manual labour, and mental work, and Benedict henceforth championed it vigorously against all corrupted versions.

When Charlemagne's son **Louis the Pious** (814-40) became Holy Roman Emperor in 814, he made Benedict his advisor on Church affairs, commissioning him to found a monastery at Inde near Aachen, granting it freedom from all secular control. This was to be an ideal monastery on which all other Frankish monasteries were to be based. Louis also gave Benedict authority over all other monastic communities in France. At a council in Aachen in 817, Benedict and the heads of major Frankish abbeys drew up a standard version of the Benedictine rule which was to be binding on all Frankish monasteries. Benedict's death in 821, and the disintegration of the Empire, meant that this reform had a short life. However, it was a forerunner of the more successful and enduring Cluniac reform a hundred years later (see Chapter 4, section 3).

Gottschalk and the predestination controversy

The central and tragic figure in this controversy was **Gottschalk of Orbais** (805-69), the son of a Saxon nobleman. His parents placed him in the abbey of Fulda when he was a child. He later tried to obtain release from his monastic vows, but the abbot of Fulda, **Rabanus Maurus** (776-856), forced Gottschalk to remain a monk. Rabanus was the man who made Fulda into the greatest centre of religious and secular education in Germany; he wrote a huge number of commentaries, theological and educational treatises, and hymns and poems. Although Rabanus would not release Gottschalk from his vows, he did allow his reluctant monk to move from Fulda to the monastery of Orbais in north-eastern France. In France Gottschalk received ordination to the priesthood. An ardent disciple of Augustine of Hippo and Fulgentius of Ruspe,[23] he began teaching their doctrines of sin, grace and predestination with passionate enthusiasm in Orbais, winning many followers and earning the nickname "Fulgentius". He also

---

23. For Augustine and Fulgentius, see Volume One, Chapter 9, section 3.

wrote religious poetry which scholars have praised as the finest the 9th century has to offer.

Gottschalk's zeal for Augustinianism, which seems at times to have been reckless and imprudent, brought him into conflict with Rabanus, who wrote against him; Gottschalk responded by accusing Rabanus of Semi-Pelagianism. Gottschalk defended his views at the council of Mainz in 848, where he went several degrees beyond Augustine's theology by arguing that (i) Christ died only for the elect (the doctrine of "limited atonement"), and that (ii) the precise number of the non-elect is specified by an eternal decree of God, a predestination to death, which runs parallel to the decree of election to life (the doctrine of "reprobation"). Augustine had never explicitly taught these two ideas. The council condemned Gottschalk and delivered him over to the haughty and intolerant Archbishop **Hincmar of Rheims** (806-82), in whose diocese Orbais was situated. Hincmar, who combined a Semi-Pelagian tendency in theology with a personal tendency to behave like a thug, deposed Gottschalk from the priesthood, had him flogged within an inch of his life, ordered his books to be burnt, and imprisoned him in the monastery of Hautvilliers, near Rheims. Gottschalk spent the rest of his life there, continuing to dispute with Hincmar to the bitter end.

Hincmar's brutal treatment of Gottschalk outraged many Churchmen. Great Catholic scholars leapt to the defence of Gottschalk and his theology – notably archbishop **Remigius of Lyons** (died 875), **Florus of Lyons** (died 860), **Prudentius of Troyes** (died 861), and the monk Ratramnus of Corbie (see next heading on the communion controversy). The church of Lyons produced some of the greatest medieval works in defence of Augustinian theology: the *Reply to the Three Letters* (of Hincmar and Rabanus), *On the Universal Ruin of All Humanity through Adam and the Special Redemption of the Elect through Christ*, and *On Steadfastly Holding the Truth of Scripture and Faithfully Following the Authority of the Holy Orthodox Fathers*. These have all been attributed to archbishop Remigius, although some modern scholars think Florus was the real author. The councils of Valence (855) and Langres (859) also sanctioned a strong

Augustinianism. However, the councils of Quiercy (853) and Savonnieres (859) upheld the more Semi-Pelagian theology of Rabanus and Hincmar. The two parties reached a compromise at the council of Toucy in 860, over which the West Frankish king, **Charles the Bald** (843-77), presided. Hincmar, the most powerful bishop in France, took the leading part in the council, and the compromise agreement favoured his views (*e.g.* it said that God wills the salvation of all human beings, and that Christ died for all).

Despite the council of Toucy, the issues raised by Gottschalk were never really resolved. Approval for Hincmar's Semi-Pelagian views only ever came from local Frankish councils, never from an ecumenical Council, and a full-blooded Augustinianism continued to flourish within Western Christendom.

Radbertus, Ratramnus, and the communion controversy

When the two Frankish monks **Paschasius Radbertus** (785-860) and **Ratramnus of Corbie** (died 868) clashed with each other over the doctrine of the eucharist (holy communion), it was the first serious theological controversy on this issue to disturb the Church. The dispute concerned the relationship between the bread and wine of the Lord's Supper and the flesh and blood of Christ's human body. In the early Church period, as far back as we can go, Christians had always believed that the eucharistic bread and wine could and should, in some sense or other, be called the body and blood of Christ. Still, little or no attempt was made to construct a theological explanation of this belief; it was regarded as a holy and joyful mystery, which human reason should humbly adore rather than seek to explain. Ignatius of Antioch, for example, writing in about AD 110, condemned Docetic heretics because "they do not confess the eucharist to be the flesh of our Saviour Jesus Christ which suffered for our sins and which the Father by His goodness raised up again" (*Letter to the Smyrnaeans*, chapter 7).[24]

---

24. For Ignatius of Antioch, see Volume One, Chapter 3, section 1, and for Docetism, section 2, under *Church teaching*.

In the 4th century, many began to speak of the bread and wine being "converted" into Christ's flesh and blood; but at the same time, they still called the bread and wine "symbols", "figures" and "signs". Often the same theologian would employ both ways of speaking – that the bread and wine were "converted", and were "symbols". This is not such a contradiction as it may seem; in the thought of the ancient world, a symbol made the thing it *symbolised* to be *present* in some way – "presented" it. So it was quite possible for a Christian thinker to hold that the eucharistic bread and wine were symbols of Christ's body and blood *and* that Christ's body and blood were truly present in, or with, or by means of, the bread and wine. Different theologians would emphasise one side of the equation more than the other. For example, Ambrose of Milan[25] tended to stress the conversion of the bread and wine, while Augustine of Hippo emphasised more that they were signs and symbols.

These two lines of thought came in conflict with each other in the 9th century. Paschasius Radbertus was a monk of Corbie monastery in north-eastern France; he was the head of the monastery's school, and in 844 his fellow monks elected him their abbot (he retired in 853). Radbertus was a distinguished scholar who wrote theological treatises, biographies of saints, and commentaries on Psalm 44, Lamentations, and Matthew. His most important work was his *Concerning the Body and Blood of the Lord*, written in 831 and revised in 844. In this book, Radbertus argued that the bread and wine of communion were changed completely into the flesh and blood of Christ, so that the bread and wine no longer existed – they only *seemed* to be bread and wine, but in reality they were now entirely the flesh and blood of the Saviour. When communion was celebrated, the very sacrifice of Christ's flesh and blood on the cross of Calvary became miraculously present and effective for the washing away of sins. However, Radbertus also maintained that the believer ate Christ's flesh and blood in a spiritual sense, and that unbelievers who took part in communion did not receive the Lord's body and blood.

---

25. For Ambrose of Milan, see Volume One, Chapter 7, section 2.

Hincmar of Rheims supported Radbertus, but a number of leading Western theologians strongly opposed him, particularly Ratramnus of Corbie and Rabanus Maurus. Ratramnus and Rabanus were on different sides in the predestination controversy, Ratramnus defending Gottschalk and Rabanus opposing him; but they were united in rejecting Radbertus and his doctrine of communion. Ratramnus was one of Radbertus's monks at Corbie, but he wrote against his abbot at the request of King Charles the Bald, who often asked for Ratramnus's judgment on Church matters. Ratramnus's book, entitled *Concerning Christ's Body and Blood*, argued that the bread and wine of communion remained bread and wine in their own physical nature. At the same time, they became the flesh and blood of Christ – but for the believer alone, and in a mysterious and spiritual sense, rather than a crudely physical way. In, with and through the bread and wine, the Holy Spirit worked secretly to feed and strengthen the souls of Christians with the risen life of Christ.

Neither Radbertus's nor Ratramnus's doctrine triumphed in this controversy; the Western Church tolerated both as valid views. However, Radbertus's view became the increasingly popular one, as we shall see in Chapter 4, section 7.

John Scotus Erigena

One of the greatest thinkers of the Carolingian Renaissance was an Irishman named *John Scotus Erigena* (810-77). Educated in a monastic school in Ireland, Erigena went to France in about 843, where King Charles the Bald appointed him head of the royal academy in Paris. He took part both in the predestination controversy and in the communion controversy. In the predestination controversy, he sided with Hincmar against Gottschalk; but in the communion controversy, he sided with Ratramnus against Hincmar and Radbertus (inventing the phrase that in communion the believer eats Christ's flesh "mentally not dentally").[26] However, Erigena's real achievement was

---

26. Although he took Hincmar's side against Gottschalk in the predestination controversy, Erigena despised Hincmar as a person. When

his translation of the works of Pseudo-Dionysius the Areopagite from Greek into Latin, together with a commentary on Pseudo-Dionysius by Maximus the Confessor.[27] These translations had a profound influence on later Western theologians, *e.g.* Thomas Aquinas.[28]

Erigena's great original work was his *Division of Nature*, published in about 862. This presented a strongly Neoplatonic understanding of Christianity.[29] Erigena took reason as his supreme guide, and said that wherever theology seemed to contradict reason, theological teachings had to be understood in an allegorical sense.[30] He interpreted creation as an emanation from God's essence, arguing that God is the only thing that really exists; he had difficulty separating this doctrine from "pantheism" (the view that everything that exists is God). Just as everything has come from God, Erigena taught that everything would return to God – which made it hard for Erigena to avoid saying that all sinners would finally be saved.

Erigena wrote the *Division of Nature* in a highly poetic style, with a bold freedom from any real respect for Church tradition, and many found it refreshing and attractive. Orthodox Churchmen, however, considered it heretical, and the Frankish council of Sens condemned it. However, the book continued to inspire unorthodox thinkers and groups for centuries, until in 1225 Pope Honorius III (1216-27) ordered all copies of the *Division of Nature* to be burnt. This succeeded in putting a stop to its influence. Only a very few copies have survived for modern scholars to study.

Hincmar died, Erigena wrote a scornful epitaph for his tombstone: "The bones of Hincmar (greedy thief!) here lie: The one good thing he did in life was die."

27.   For Pseudo-Dionysius, see Volume One, Chapter 12, section 3, and for Maximus the Confessor, section 4.

28.   For Thomas Aquinas, see Chapter 7, section 3.

29.   For Neoplatonism, see Volume One, Chapter 6, section 2.

30.   For allegorical interpretation, see Volume One, Chapter 5, section 1, and Origen's theology.

Agobard of Lyons

Another illustrious figure of the Carolingian Renaissance was *Agobard of Lyons* (779-840). Born in Muslim Spain, he emigrated to Lyons in France in 799, was ordained priest in 804, and in 816 became archbishop of Lyons. In a colourful and eventful career, Agobard involved himself in the highest levels of imperial politics; he supported Lothair, son of Emperor Louis the Pious, in a civil war between father and son – the triumphant Louis deposed him from his archbishopric for two years (835-37) as a punishment. Agobard attacked the growing practice of "lay investiture" in the Western Church, by which kings appointed bishops (see Chapter 4, section 2). He was the author of a huge number of books; Agobard's collected works fill 22 volumes. He wrote extensively against Paganism, Judaism, and heresy (especially Adoptianism), and composed many religious poems. Scholars once thought Agobard was the author of *Concerning Images*, an attack on image-worship which anticipated many of the concerns of the Protestant Reformation, rejecting the practice of invoking the saints, and exalting Christ as the only Mediator between God and humankind, the sole object of religious trust.[31] However, modern scholars now doubt whether Agobard wrote this – the real author was probably bishop *Claudius of Turin* (died 827), another distinguished Carolingian scholar.

Agobard's writings give us the fullest picture we possess of Western popular culture at the time of the Carolingian Renaissance. In particular, they reveal how widespread Pagan beliefs and customs were in the "Christian" West. Agobard himself fought tirelessly against this legacy of Paganism as a preacher, teacher, and author. The most notable of his anti-Pagan writings was his *Concerning Hail and Thunder*, in which he criticised the popular belief that evil spirits, rather than God's providence, controlled the wind and rain, and that magic spells could induce these spirits to bestow good weather. In many ways Agobard took an unusually scientific and rational attitude towards nature

---

31. For the Reformation, see Volume Three.

and the world; he has been praised as possessing the clearest intellect of the 9th century.

5. The collapse of the Empire

Charlemagne's son, Louis the Pious (814-40), continued to govern the Holy Roman Empire according to his father's ideals, but without his father's abilities. At the end of his reign, Louis disastrously divided the Empire up between his three sons, Louis the German (843-76), Charles the Bald (843-77), and Lothair (843-55). Louis received the area east of the Rhine river, the "East Frankish kingdom", which became the separate region of Germany; Charles received the "West Frankish kingdom" (France);[32] Lothair received the title of Emperor and a strip of land stretching from the mouth of the Rhine to Lombardy. Further disintegration followed. After Lothair's death in 855, his territory was again divided and became little more than a chaos of small states. The title of Emperor passed to the German kings. However, when the last Carolingian king of Germany, Louis the Child, died in 911, real power had fallen into the hands of the great German tribal chiefs ("dukes") of Saxony, Thuringia, Franconia, Lorraine, Swabia, and Bavaria. France had disintegrated in a similar way by the death of its last Carolingian king in 987.

The popes used the disintegration of the Holy Roman Empire to reassert their own supreme authority over Church affairs: papalism striking back against imperialism. Yet they found that the disappearance of their greatest rival, a powerful Holy Roman Emperor, also meant the loss of their greatest ally. Without an effective Emperor to protect them, the popes fell increasingly under the control of the Roman nobility, and simply became political pawns in the conflicts of different aristocratic factions. By the time of Pope Sergius III (904-11), the papacy had become hopelessly corrupt, incapable of offering any independent moral, spiritual or theological leadership to the Western Church.

---

32. From that point onwards, historians usually refer to the Franks of the West Frankish kingdom as the "French" rather than the "Franks".

Meanwhile the Western Christian world came under fresh military threat from three sources:

(i)   Muslims went on the offensive from North Africa, using sea power to attack Sicily, Sardinia, and the Italian coast. The Spanish Muslim kingdom of Cordova also reached its greatest height of power and influence in the 10th century.

(ii) In 899, a new wave of migrating Asian tribes, the Pagan Magyars, brought war and devastation into Germany, northern Italy, and southern France. The Magyars settled in Eastern Europe and eventually became the nation of Hungary.

(iii) Above all, the Pagan Norsemen – "men of the north", also called Normans and Vikings ("pirates") – began their vast expansion from Scandinavia in 840. The Norsemen worshipped the ancient gods of Germany (Wotan, Thor, Tiwaz, *etc.* – see Volume One, Chapter 11, section 1). A great seafaring people, their ships and warriors brought bloodshed and destruction to Britain, Ireland, France, northern Germany, the Netherlands, Spain, and northern Italy. The 9th and 10th centuries were the "Dark Ages" of political anarchy and constant warfare in Christian Europe. To many Western Christians, it seemed that the end of the world was at hand; it was seriously expected to happen in the year 1000.

So Charlemagne's empire fell to pieces politically after his death. However, the Carolingian Renaissance, which Charlemagne nurtured, had given to Western Europe a unity of Christian culture so strong that it survived the political chaos, and formed the basis for the more stable European society that emerged in the 11th century.

Important people:

The Church

Willibrord (658-740)
Pope Zacharias (741-52)
Boniface (680-754)
Paul the Deacon (720-800)
Paulinus of Aquileia (730-802)
Alcuin of York (730-804)
Pope Leo III (795-816)
Theodulph of Orleans (750-821)
Claudius of Turin (died 827)
Agobard of Lyons (779-840)
Rabanus Maurus (776-856)
Paschasius Radbertus (785-860)
Florus of Lyons (died 860)
Prudentius of Troyes (died 861)
Ratramnus of Corbie (died 868)
Gottschalk of Orbais (805-69)
Remigius of Lyons (died 875)
John Scotus Erigena (810-77)
Hincmar of Rheims (806-82)

Political and military

Charles Martel (690-741)
King Pepin of France (751-68)
Holy Roman Emperor Charlemagne (771-814)
Holy Roman Emperor Louis the Pious (814-40)
King Charles the Bald of France (843-77)

Boniface and the conversion of the Hessians and Thuringians

Now the grace of the Holy Spirit and the laying on of hands confirmed a large number of the Hessians, who at that time had accepted the Catholic faith. But others, who were as yet spiritually weak, refused to embrace the pure teachings of the Church in their fullness. Some of the Hessians continued secretly, and others openly, to offer sacrifices to trees and springs, and to inspect the bowels of sacrificed animals; some practised divination, sorcery, and incantations; some turned their attention to auguries, omens, and other sacrificial rituals; but others, whose minds were more open to reason, forsook all these blasphemous Pagan practices, and committed none of these sins.

Acting on the counsel and advice of these better people, Boniface tried to cut down, at a place called Gaesmere, a certain oak tree of astonishing size, known to Pagans in ancient times as the "Oak of Jupiter". A great crowd of Pagans stood by, watching Boniface, and bitterly cursing in their hearts this enemy of their gods. Taking his courage in his hands, Boniface cut the first notch in the tree. But as soon as he had made this little cut, a powerful blast of wind from above suddenly shook the huge bulk of the oak, and it came crashing to the ground, shattering its topmost branches into fragments. As if God had deliberately willed it (for the brothers present did nothing to cause it), the oak tree burst apart into four pieces, and each piece had a trunk of equal length. When they saw this amazing sight, the Pagans, who had been standing there cursing, stopped their blaspheming, and began to believe and bless the Lord. The holy bishop Boniface instantly conferred with the brothers, built a Christian prayer-house from the timber of the oak, and dedicated it to Saint Peter the apostle.

After achieving with God's help all the things we have already mentioned, Boniface then set out on a journey to Thuringia. Arriving there, he spoke to the elders and chiefs of the people, calling upon them to abandon their blind ignorance, and to return to the Christian faith which they had once embraced. For after the period of rule by their kings ended, control of the Thuringian government had been seized by Theobald and Heden. Under their disastrous rule, which was based more on tyranny and murder than on the loyalty of the people, many Thuringian nobles had been put to death or seized and carried off into captivity, while the rest of the people, engulfed by all kinds of misfortune, had bowed to the domination of the Saxons. So when the power of the Thuringian kings, who had protected piety, was destroyed, the people's devotion to Christianity and true religion also died out; false brothers entered in and corrupted the minds of the people, introducing dangerous heretical factions under the pretence of piety. The chief heretical leaders were Torchtwine, Zeretheve, Eaubercht, and Hunraed – men who lived in fornication and adultery, whom God has already judged (as the apostle says). These individuals aroused a violent conflict against Boniface the man of God; but when they had been exposed and shown to be in opposition to the truth, they received a just punishment for their crimes.

The light of faith illuminated the minds of the Thuringians, the people were freed from the chains of error, and the devil's disciples and crafty seducers of the people (whom we have already mentioned) were driven away. Boniface then gathered in a rich harvest of souls, assisted by a few helpers. At first he suffered from extreme poverty, lacking even the necessities of life; but though he was in difficult circumstances and deep distress, he kept on preaching the Word of God. Gradually, the number of believers grew, the preachers became more numerous, church buildings were restored, and the Word of God was proclaimed all around ...

By this means, the news of Boniface's preaching reached distant lands, so that in a short space of time his fame had spread throughout the greater part of Europe. From England, an extremely large number of holy men came to his aid – readers, writers, and educated men schooled in the other arts. Many of these put themselves under Boniface's leadership and guidance, and by their help the Germans in many places were called out of the errors and blasphemous worship of their Pagan gods. Working in widely dispersed groups among the people of Hessia and Thuringia, the English missionaries preached God's Word in the rural areas and the villages. The number of Hessians and Thuringians who accepted the sacraments of the faith was immense, and many thousands of them were baptised.

From Willibald's
Life of Saint Boniface

Charlemagne: A contemporary portrait

Charlemagne was large and strong, and of a commanding stature, though not well-proportioned, for he seems to have been seven feet tall. The top of his head was round, his eyes very large and lively, his nose rather long, his hair fair, his face happy and pleasant. Whether he stood or sat, he had a great presence and dignity ... He was temperate in eating and drinking, especially in drinking, for he utterly hated drunkenness in anybody, particularly in himself and his companions ... While he was eating his meals, he listened to music, or had books read out to him, books about history and the deeds of men in bygone ages. He gained much delight from the works of Saint Augustine, especially his book *The City of God* ... His speech was quick and flowing, and he expressed himself with the greatest clarity. He did not confine himself to his native language, but took care to learn foreign ones; he acquired such a mastery of Latin that he used to say his prayers in that language as well as his own. He understood Greek but could not speak it very well... He admired culture ardently, and had a great reverence for those who taught it, conferring high honours upon them ...

Charlemagne held the Christian faith as most sacred, having been raised as a Christian from childhood, and he worshipped in the Church with the greatest piety ... He was deeply devoted to the poor, providing for their needs with gifts of charity (which the Greeks call "alms-giving"). He looked after the poor not only in his own country and kingdom, but also those living in poverty in other lands – in Africa, Egypt, Syria, at Carthage, Alexandria, and Jerusalem, to whom he would send money in compassion for their needs. His chief reason for seeking the friendship of foreign kings was that he might be able to be a support and a comfort to the Christians living under their rule ... He endured without a murmur the displeasure of the Byzantine Emperors, who were highly indignant at his assumption of the title "Emperor", and he conquered their dark anger by his great generosity, in which he excelled them beyond any doubt, often sending them ambassadors and greeting them as brothers in his letters to them.

Einhard's
Life of Charlemagne, **chapter 19**

Alcuin: The character of a true bishop

"A bishop must be without blame, as a steward of God" (Titus 1:7). The apostle looks among the stewards for one who is found faithful, not one who eats and drinks with the drunkards, who may do violence to the servants and handmaids of the Lord. No, let the steward wisely await the unknown day of the Lord's coming, and as he waits, give to his fellow servants the food of Catholic doctrine. Let the bishop and the presbyter know that the people are not his servants, but servants together with him. Therefore let him not dictate to them as if they were common slaves, but treat them as sons and teach them with all love.

"Not headstrong". That is, not puffed up with himself, full of pleasure at being a bishop. Let him instead devote himself to good works and seek what contributes to the well-being of the majority.

"Not quick-tempered". A quick-tempered man is like a leaf hanging on a branch that is moved by the slightest breeze. Nothing is more disgraceful than a quick-tempered teacher. A person who is sometimes angry is not quick-tempered, but we truly call a man quick-tempered who is often conquered by this passion.

"Not addicted to wine". It is enough to say, according to the apostle, that there is the abuse of wine, and that wherever you find gluttony and drunkenness, there lust reigns. How surprising that Paul condemned drunkenness in bishops and presbyters, when in the old Law there was a command that priests who entered the temple to serve God must drink no wine at all (Lev. 10:9). The Nazirites too had to abstain from all wine and strong drink, and let their hair grow long (Num. 6:2-5).

"Not violent". We could take this in a simple sense to mean that the bishop must edify his hearer's mind, to stop him stretching forth his hand to murder or to rush into violence. But a more subtle and better interpretation is that the bishop must do nothing to violate the minds of those who understand and see, but must be calm in speech, pure in character. He must not, by contrary behaviour, destroy a soul whom he could have taught by temperance in life and words.

"Not greedy for money". He who seeks such things has set his mind more on things present than things to come. A bishop who desires to imitate the apostle should be content simply with food and clothing. "Let those who serve the altar live from the altar" (1 Cor. 9:13). He says, "Let them live," not, "Let them become rich."

Up to now, the apostle's words have been depicting what a bishop or presbyter ought *not* to be. But now he explains what he ought to be.

"But hospitable, one who loves what is good". Above all else, a bishop must be hospitable. Everyone wants to hear these words from the Gospel spoken to him: "I was a stranger and you took Me in" (Matt. 25:35). How much more should a bishop desire to hear these words! His house ought to be a common guest-house, where pilgrims are kindly received, and their feet washed as a humble duty.

"Chaste, just, holy". If the apostle tells laymen to abstain from sex with their wives on account of prayer (1 Cor. 7:5), what shall we think about a bishop who is to offer up spotless sacrifices of holy prayers every day, for his own sins and the sins of his people?

Alcuin
Commentary on Titus 1:7-8

Radbertus: The reality of Christ's flesh and blood in the eucharist

Christ's body and blood are truly created by the consecration of the sacrament. No-one doubts this who believes the divine words spoken by the Truth: "For My flesh is really food, and My blood is really drink" (John 6:55). When His disciples did not understand this, He clearly identified what He meant by flesh and blood: "He that eats My flesh and drinks My blood abides in Me, and I abide in him" (John 6:56). Therefore, if it is truly food, it is true flesh; if it is truly drink, it is true blood. Otherwise how can His words be true: "The bread which I shall give for the life of the world is My flesh" (John 6:51)? Surely this refers to true flesh. And "the bread which descended from heaven" (John 6:51) surely refers to true bread [the bread of the eucharist]. But because it is not right to devour Christ with our teeth, He chose in the sacrament that this bread and wine be created as His true flesh and blood by the Holy Spirit's power through consecration, by daily creating it to be mystically sacrificed for the life of the world. Just as His true flesh was created by the Spirit from the Virgin without sexual union, so from the substance of bread and wine the Spirit mystically consecrates the same body and blood of Christ. It is plainly of this flesh and blood that He says, "Truly, truly I say to you, unless you eat the flesh of the Son of Man and drink His blood, you have no life in you" (John 6:53) ...

As it is the real flesh of Christ which was crucified and buried, in reality it is the sacrament of His flesh which is divinely consecrated by the Holy Spirit on the altar, by the agency of the priest speaking Christ's word. The Lord Himself proclaims, "This is My body" (Luke 22:19). Do not be surprised by this, O man, and do not ask about what is natural here. If you truly believe that the Holy Spirit's power created His flesh from the Virgin Mary in her womb without human seed, so that the Word might become flesh, truly believe also that what Christ's word brings about in the sacrament by the Holy Spirit is the same body from the Virgin. If you ask, "How exactly does He do this?" – who can explain it, or express it in words? Be assured that the method lies in Christ's efficacy, the knowledge of it lies in faith, the cause of it lies in power, but the effect of it lies in God's will, because God's power over nature effectively works beyond the reach of our reason.

Paschasius Radbertus
Concerning the Body and Blood of the Lord,
Book 4, chapters 1 and 3

Ratramnus: The mystery of Christ's presence by the Spirit

Some of the faithful say that in the sacrament of Christ's body and blood, which the Church daily celebrates, nothing takes place under a symbol or a hidden sign, but is performed with an open manifestation of the reality itself. However, others testify that these elements are contained in a symbolic mystery, and that one thing appears to our bodily senses but another thing to the eyes of faith. This is a serious difference of opinion. The apostle writes to believers that they should all hold the same views and speak the same things, and that no division should appear among them (1 Cor. 1:10); yet believers are divided by a great division when they utter different views about the sacrament of Christ's body and blood ...

"It is the Spirit who gives us life; the flesh profits nothing" (John 6:63). In the sense in which unbelievers understood Him, Christ says that the flesh profits nothing. His flesh bestows life in a different way, when it is received through the sacrament by those who have faith. Christ makes this clear by saying, "It is the Spirit who gives us life." So in the sacrament, His body and blood have an effect which is spiritual in nature. The Spirit gives life, and without the Spirit's effect the sacraments feed the body but cannot feed the soul, which profits nothing. Here arises the question which many express when they say that these things do not happen symbolically but in reality. Those who say this are clearly out of harmony with the writings of the holy fathers. Saint Augustine, the great teacher of the Church, writes in book three of his work *On Christian Doctrine* as follows: "'Unless you eat the flesh of the Son of Man,' says the Saviour, 'and drink His blood, you shall not have life in you.' Christ seems to be commanding a shameful crime [the crime of cannibalism]. Therefore it is a symbol, requiring that we should have a share in the Lord's suffering, and that we should faithfully remember that His flesh was crucified and wounded for us." We see that Augustine says that the sacraments of Christ's body and blood are celebrated in a symbolic sense by believers. For he says that to take Christ's flesh and blood in a fleshly sense involves crime, not religion ...

The Saviour and also Saint Paul teach us that the bread and wine placed on the altar are placed there as a symbol or memorial of the Lord's death, so that what was done in the past may be called back to memory in the present. This is the purpose of the sacrament: through being made mindful of His suffering, we are made sharers in that divine gift by which we have been liberated

from death. When we have arrived at the point where we actually
see Christ [in heaven], we recognise that we will have no need of
such helps, by which we are reminded what His limitless goodness endured for us. For when we see Him face to face, we will
not be moved by any outward memorials of earthly things; but by
contemplating reality itself, we will see how we should give thanks
to the Author of our salvation. Let no-one think, then, that we
are denying that believers receive the Lord's body and blood in
the mystery of the sacrament. Faith receives what it believes in.
However, the eye does not see it, for it is spiritual food, spiritually
feeding the soul, and bestowing a life of eternal blessedness. So
the Saviour Himself says when He commends this mystery, "It is
the Spirit who gives us life; the flesh profits nothing."

Ratramnus

Concerning Christ's Body and Blood,

chapters 2, 31-34, 100-101

In defence of Gottschalk: Salvation by divine grace

With one meaning, one mouth, and one spirit, the most blessed
fathers of the Church declare and approve the unshakable truth
of God's foreknowledge and predestination, in the case both of the
elect to glory, and of the reprobate to punishment (although not to
sin). The fathers boldly state that God's decree here demonstrates
for us an unchangeable order, not of arrangements in time, nor of
things which begin at a particular time, but of the everlasting purposes of God. They affirm that none of the elect can perish – and
that none of the reprobate can be saved, owing to their hard and
impenitent hearts. The truth of holy Scripture and the authority
of the holy orthodox fathers declare this with perfect harmony,
and they require us to believe and accept it without any doubting.
Therefore, even if you condemn the shallowness of the unfortunate
monk Gottschalk, and disapprove his rashness, and blame his loud-
mouthed insolence, you must not for that reason deny divine truth.

According to the Catholic faith, almighty God – even before
the foundation of the world, and before He created anything
– from the very beginning predestined certain souls to His
kingdom, by His own free love, according to the sure, righteous,

unchangeable motives of His own eternal purpose. None of these souls will perish, for His mercy protects them. Others He predestined by His righteous judgment to death, because of their blameworthy ungodliness, which He foresaw. None of these souls can be saved – not because God's power fiercely prevents them, but because of the ungovernable and ceaseless evil of their own wickedness. Nothing remains for us but to renounce anything we may have tasted contrary to God's revelation to us, and faithfully to embrace the truth which is becoming clearer to us. As the apostle says, "For we can do nothing against the truth, but for the truth" (2 Cor. 13:8) ...

Just as the very same man can be healthy, and fall from health into illness by intemperate habits, and then can be made well again by health-giving medicine, so the free choice of the human mind was once sound, but became feeble when the first man sinned. What was sound has been corrupted, what was alive is now dead. Before sin entered, our free choice was truly sound, ruined by no sinful weakness; but through sin itself, it has been so weakened that we may truthfully cry out to God, "O Lord, be merciful to me; heal my soul, for I have sinned against You" (Ps. 41:4). When the good physician heals the soul, a joyful and favoured people exclaims, "O Lord our God, I cried to You, and You have healed me" (Ps. 30:2) ... By deserting Him who is Life and the Fountain of life, humanity became alienated from the life of God, and died, "for the soul that sins shall die" (Ezek. 18:4). Human nature does not have within itself any vital feeling which endeavours after true life, unless it is raised up and made alive by Him who says, "This my son was dead and he is alive again; he was lost and he is found" (Luke 15:24), and is enlivened by the Spirit of whom the apostle says, "The letter kills but the Spirit gives life" (2 Cor. 3:6). So souls are dead and are daily brought to life, of whom the Lord speaks in the Gospel, "The hour is approaching, and now is, when the dead will hear the voice of the Son of God, and those who hear Him will live" (John 5:25).

Reply to the Three Letters
chapters 10 and 21
(traditionally ascribed to Remigius of Lyons)

Gottschalk: A Hymn to God the Life-Giver

You are Three, You are One;
You are all-powerful;
You are good, You are gentle, You are all-merciful;
O graciously grant that my eyes may flow with rivers of tears!
You once changed stone into pools of water,
And cliffs into many-headed fountains;
Therefore You can soften my iron heart.
Yes, You can change my heart of steel into a heart of flesh,
The soul of a beast into the soul of a man,
The old time-worn heart into a new one ...
Freely You created me by Your goodness;
Freely create me afresh, I pray, and restore me to life!
Freely You bestow Your gifts, which is why we say they are "by
    grace".
O Holy Spirit, You bring instant life to those You breathe into;
Together with the Father and His Son, You thunder forth,
    govern and give light;
You increase and You quicken the faith
Which You grant to whomever You choose.
Even more, You make clean those polluted by leprosy,
You make the ungodly righteous;
Together with the Father and the Son, You recreate Your elect
    souls,
And when they are recreated, You also glorify them.

Flying saucers and aliens in 9th century France?

We have seen and heard many people crazy and insane enough
to believe and assert that a certain region called Magonia exists,
from which ships come and sail through the clouds. They say that
these air-ships carry to Magonia the fruits of the earth, which
have fallen because of hail and been ruined by storms, after the
pilots of the air-ships have paid the value of the wheat and other
fruits to the magicians who had caused the storm. Several of these
crazy individuals, who believed that these absurd things could
happen, gathered a crowd and displayed before them four people

in chains – three men and one woman, whom they said had fallen out of these air-ships. They had been keeping these four as prisoners for several days before showing them to the crowd, intending to stone them to death in our presence! However, after I had a long argument with them, truth finally prevailed, so that those who had exhibited the four to the people were put to shame for their folly, like a thief who has been caught, as the prophet says (Jer. 2:26).

From Agobard of Lyons
Concerning Hail and Thunder

Appendix: The Gallican and Roman liturgies

Until Charlemagne's liturgical reforms, the Western Church had used the Gallican (French) liturgy more widely than the Roman in its worship. Readers may be interested to see how these two early medieval liturgies were structured. I present here a simplified outline of each.

* * *

The Gallican liturgy

The Gallican liturgy would have gone something like this:

Part One: The service of the Word

1. Greeting by priest ("The Lord be with you"), response by people ("And with your spirit")

2. *Kyrie eleison* ("Lord, have mercy" – chanted)

3. Hymn – *Benedictus* (Luke 1:68-79) or *Gloria in Excelsis* ("Glory to God in the highest")

4. Collect (set prayer for the day)

5. Reading from Old Testament

6. Reading from New Testament (Acts-Revelation)

7. Hymn – *Benedictus es* ("Blessed are You, O Lord" – the Prayer of Azariah, from the Septuagint version of

Daniel) or *Benedicite* ("Bless the Lord" – the Song of the Three Children, from the Septuagint version of Daniel)

8. Bringing in of the Gospel book, while *Gloria tibi, Domine* ("Glory to You, O Lord") is sung

9. Reading from Gospel

10. Chants – *trisagion* ("Holy God, holy and mighty, holy and immortal, have mercy on us") or *kyrie eleison*

11. Sermon

12. Litany (responsive liturgical prayers), led by deacon

13. Dismissal of all but baptised believers

Part Two: The eucharist

1. Offertory (preparation of bread and wine, wine mixed with water, while a psalm is sung)

2. Litany of the faithful

3. Reading of "diptychs" (official list of the names of those for whom prayer is offered), and prayer for those named in the diptychs

4. Kiss of peace and prayer for peace

5. Dialogue between priest and people

> Priest: The Lord be with you.
>
> People: And with your spirit.
>
> Priest: Lift up your hearts.
>
> People: We lift them to the Lord.
>
> Priest: Let us give thanks to the Lord.
>
> People: It is fitting and right to do so.

6. Prayer of consecration of the bread and wine

7. Singing of the *Sanctus* (Isa. 6:3)

8. Breaking of bread (into nine pieces in the shape of a cross), a piece of bread mixed into the wine

9. The Lord's prayer

10. Act of communion (while Ps. 34 is sung)

11. Prayer of thanksgiving

12. Deacon dismisses the people

* * *

The Roman liturgy

The early medieval Roman liturgy was at first much simpler than the Gallican. After the reforms of Gregory the Great (pope from 590 to 604), it would have gone something like this:

Part One: The service of the Word

1. *Kyrie eleison* ("Lord, have mercy". This was chanted three times. Gregory the Great changed the middle chant to *Christe eleison*, "Christ have mercy")

2. Greeting by priest ("The Lord be with you"), response by people ("And with your spirit")

3. Collect (set prayer for the day)

4. Antiphonal chant

5. Reading from New Testament (Acts-Revelation)

6. Singing of psalm

7. Reading from Gospel

8. Sermon

9. Dismissal of all but baptised believers

Part Two: The eucharist

1. Offertory (preparation of bread and wine, wine mixed with water, while a psalm is sung)

2. Dialogue between priest and people

    Priest: The Lord be with you.

    People: And with your spirit.

    Priest: Lift up your hearts.

    People: We lift them to the Lord.

    Priest: Let us give thanks to the Lord.

    People: It is fitting and right to do so.

3. Prayer of consecration of the bread and wine

4. Singing of the *Sanctus* (Isa. 6:3)

5. Reading of "diptychs" (official list of the names of those for whom prayer is offered), and prayer for those named in the diptychs

6. The Lord's prayer

7. Kiss of peace

8. Breaking of bread, a piece of bread mixed into the wine

9. Act of communion (first the priest, while the *Agnus dei* – "O Lamb of God who takes away the sin of the world, have mercy upon us" – is sung, then the people, while a psalm is sung)

10. Prayer of thanksgiving

11. Deacon dismisses the people

3

The Byzantine Empire: from Leo the Isaurian to the East–West Schism

1. Political and military history 717-1054

The Byzantine Empire, it is worth reminding ourselves, was the Eastern Roman Empire centred on Constantinople, which unlike its Western counterpart had not fallen beneath the weight of the Germanic invasions of the 4th and 5th centuries. The Byzantines called themselves "Romans", not "Byzantines" (a more recent term invented by Western historians). As far as the Emperors and people of Byzantium were concerned, they were simply the ancient Roman Empire in all its glory, still full of life and strength, now sanctified by its adoption of the Christian faith. Charlemagne and the Western Emperors might speak of themselves as the "Holy Roman Empire", but that title more truly belonged, the Byzantines felt, to themselves.

The history of the Byzantine Empire in this period is a highly colourful story of constant wars, on three main fronts: with Muslim Arabs and Turks in the Middle East, with Pagan tribes in the Balkans and the North, and (tragically) with Western Christians. The Empire's territories were constantly shrinking and expanding again. Yet in the midst of this endless conflict, Byzantium was the cradle of glorious achievements in art, literature, theology, and spiritual life.

We pick up the story in 717. This was the year when **Leo the Isaurian** (717-41), founder of the Isaurian dynasty, became

Emperor. (Leo's title comes from Isauria, a mountainous region in southern Asia Minor, where he was once thought to have been born; most historians now agree that he was actually born in Germanica on the borders of Mesopotamia.) Leo employed his power as Emperor to try to reform the Eastern Church by abolishing the use of images or "icons" in worship, which he regarded as idolatrous. This started the great *iconoclastic controversy* which was to tear the East apart for the next 120 years (see section 3).

Leo was also an excellent soldier. At the beginning of his reign, he had to deal with fresh aggression against Byzantium by the Islamic Empire of the Arabs. Once more they invaded Asia Minor and besieged Constantinople in 717-18, but once more the Byzantines devastated them with "Greek fire" and threw back the Muslim onslaught. Both Leo and his son **Constantine V** (741-75) fought successful wars against the Islamic Empire, and brought Asia Minor back under Byzantine control. Constantine V also vanquished the Pagan tribe of the Bulgars, in the area of Eastern Europe known as the Balkans, north of Greece. The Bulgar wars lasted from 756 to 775, and were great victories for the Byzantine armies. However, Constantine V lost Byzantium's Western capital in Ravenna, Italy, to the Franks. This warfare of Byzantines with Franks in Italy shows the degree to which relations had broken down between Christian East and West.

After the death of Constantine V, the Byzantine Empire suffered a series of almost fatal blows on the battlefield. The empress **Irene** (775-802) was a military and political disaster. The Muslim Arabs crushed her armies in Asia Minor in 781, and then the Pagan Bulgars defeated Byzantine forces in the Balkans in 792. A palace revolution eventually deposed Irene in 802, but the next three Emperors were not much better. The Bulgars, under their great warrior-leader Krum, brought the Byzantine Empire to its knees. Byzantium's salvation came only with the death of Krum in 814; under his less militant son Omortag, the Bulgars made peace. The Arabs also went on the offensive again, seizing Crete and Sicily from the Byzantines.

However, salvation was at hand for Byzantium with the new Amorian dynasty of Emperors (820-67), who raised the Empire up from its humiliation to new heights of glory. They waged successful campaigns against the Arabs, fought off an invading army of Pagan Russians who attacked Constantinople in 860, and brought about the conversion of the Bulgars to the Orthodox faith (see section 4). Then came **Basil I** (867-86), who founded the even more illustrious Macedonian dynasty. Under the Macedonian Emperors, the Byzantine Empire experienced its golden age of strength, culture, and prosperity. A series of powerful soldier-Emperors inflicted shattering defeats on the Arabs in Syria and Armenia. The Byzantine navy recaptured the islands of Crete and Cyprus, cleared the Mediterranean of Muslim pirates, and strengthened the Byzantine position in southern Italy. In Syria, Byzantine troops took back the patriarchal city of Antioch. Emperor **Basil II** (976-1025) brought Bulgaria, the nation founded by the Bulgars, into the Byzantine Empire in a 30-year war, lasting from 988 to 1018. Basil also annexed the ancient Christian kingdom of Armenia. Most important of all for the future of Eastern Christianity, the Eastern Church oversaw the conversion of the Russians.[1] There was a mighty flourishing of art, literature, and commerce throughout the Empire, and the Emperors carried out many just social reforms. During the long reign of Basil II, the Byzantine Empire became the greatest power in the entire Christian and Muslim world.

2. Eastern worship

Since most of the readers of this book will probably be Protestants, this is a good place to say something about the pattern of worship that developed in the Eastern Byzantine Church. This form of worship has changed very little, and still characterises Eastern Orthodoxy today.[2] It is in many ways quite different from Western worship, both Protestant *and* Roman Catholic.

Eastern Orthodox church buildings have no pews, no pulpit, and no organ (or any other musical instrument). There are no

---

1. For the conversion of Russia, see Chapter 6.

2. The Eastern Church is referred to as "Eastern Orthodoxy" after the great East–West schism of 1054. See section 8 of this Chapter.

religious statues, but covering the walls is an abundance of flat two-dimensional images of Christ, Biblical characters, and Orthodox saints. These pictures are known as "icons" (see under next heading, *The iconoclastic controversy*). The icons often have olive-oil lamps burning beneath them. The idea behind the icons is that the worship of the congregation on earth is a joining and sharing in the worship of the glorified Church in heaven; the icons are a window into that heavenly worship, revealing the presence of the saints and angels. It is in company with them, and with the help of their prayers, that believers on earth approach and worship the Trinity.

An Orthodox church interior is divided in half by a step (or set of steps), and then an icon-screen known as the *iconostasis* ("icon-stand"), which is covered in icons. The icon-screen separates the communion table from the rest of the church. Historians are not sure when this separation first arose; there is some evidence to suggest that it dates back to the early 5th century. At first the icon-screen was a simple plain screen. In the 9th century, after the iconoclastic controversy, the screen began to be adorned with some icons; the almost total covering of the screen with icons (as in Orthodox churches today) was a later development – perhaps as late as the 14th or 15th century.

The icon-screen has three doors, signifying the Trinity; the middle door is a set of double doors called the "holy doors". On the left of the holy doors is an icon of the Virgin Mary, on their right an icon of Christ. These central doors then lead through to a room which Westerners would call a sanctuary, but Orthodoxy calls the whole room the "altar". The altar is always at the east end of the church and represents heaven. Normally, clergy alone are allowed to enter the altar. It contains a draped square block from which the priest celebrates the eucharist; this draped block is what Roman Catholics would call the altar, but Orthodox call it the "holy table" – or sometimes the "throne of God". Atop the holy table are a crucifix, two candles, and a copy of the Gospels. Behind the holy table lies a seat for the bishop, and benches for lesser clergy. The holy table is always positioned over relics of Orthodox saints, and Orthodox churches often house other relics.

Those leading Orthodox worship give the Bible readings, sermon, and prayers from the steps before the icon-screen. Portable lecterns (*analogia*) are positioned wherever necessary for the Bibles and liturgical books to rest on; some icons will also be on analogia. An Orthodox congregation will stand throughout most of the service, including holy communion when they receive the bread and wine.[3] An Orthodox priest serves communion from a special spoon, so that people receive the bread and wine at the same time, the bread soaked in the wine. This method of serving communion seems to have had its origins in Syria, perhaps as early as the late 4th century; however, the practice of drinking from the cup lasted in some parts of Byzantium until the 9th or 10th century. The bread is ordinary leavened bread, baked in flat round cakes about four centimetres thick, stamped with a cross and the Greek letters IC XC NI KA ("Jesus Christ conquers"). The communion wine is mixed with hot water. In some parts of the Orthodox world today, *e.g.* Greece, it is still the custom (dating from earliest patristic times) for the worshippers themselves to supply the communion bread and wine. The East never went down the later Western path of withholding the wine from the laity. At the end of a communion service, those parts of the bread which were not consecrated for eucharistic use are handed out to all worshippers, including non-Orthodox; this bread is called the *antidoron* ("instead of the gift"). The same custom prevailed until recently in French-speaking Catholic churches.

In an Orthodox service, Eastern worshippers, unlike their Protestant and Roman Catholic counterparts, do not all do the same thing, or watch or listen to the same thing, at the same time. (The idea that the entire congregation must all be doing the same thing at the same time is largely Western in origin.) Each

---

3. As we saw in Volume One, Chapter 3, section 2, under *Church worship*, pews were quite a late development, appearing in the Western Church only from the 14th century. They have never appeared in any Eastern church until very recently. The seats attached to the sides of the walls in Eastern churches are for those who are weak through illness or old age – from which we perhaps get the expression, "The weak go to the wall."

Eastern worshipper is free – within limits – to participate in the worship in his own way. Various worshippers will therefore go from one part of the church to another, in order to call upon Christ or different saints at different icons; they will make the sign of the cross, or bow, or kneel down, at different parts of the service, according to their own feelings of devotion. At some points in the service, the priest will "cense" the icons and congregation, *i.e.* he will spread incense about from a special container (a censer). The theology behind censing *icons* is that incense is being offered to God for His presence and work in the saints; the *worshippers* are censed because human beings themselves are the true icon (image) of God. Some parts of an Orthodox service are sung – by the people, or a choir, or a reader alone (it varies from one Orthodox region to another); in almost all Orthodox churches, no musical instruments accompany the singing.[4] Much traditional Orthodox singing follows the pattern of "antiphony", which employs two singers (or "chanters", as they are called) or two choirs. In Orthodox antiphonal singing, one chanter will sing the first part of a hymn or prayer, and then the second will complete it.

Because Eastern Orthodoxy has been so conservative in its attitude to worship, it is possible for non-Orthodox to see in most Orthodox churches today the same basic pattern of worship that was practised in the Byzantine Empire a thousand years ago.

Byzantine worship in our period (717-1054) was enriched by some of the most eminent hymnwriters ever to have written in Greek. The theologian John of Damascus (675-749), whom we have already met in Chapter 1, section 3, penned some of the Eastern Church's greatest hymns, especially the Canon for Easter Day ("the golden canon"), which Eastern Orthodox sing on the midnight before Easter. John's brother, **Cosmas the Melodist** (died

---

4. In the 19th century, a few Greek Orthodox congregations in Western Europe introduced organs. In the 20th century, some Greek Orthodox congregations in America also installed organs. This is exceptional not normal in Eastern Orthodoxy, and traditional Orthodox have strongly condemned it as a betrayal of the ancient apostolic practice.

760),[5] is often regarded as the supreme Eastern hymnwriter; the Eastern Church commemorates his life and death in the rhyme,

> Where perfect sweetness dwells has Cosmas gone;
> But his sweet songs to cheer the Church live on.

Cosmas was, like his brother, a monk in the Saint Sabbas monastery near Jerusalem. He and John used to read each other's hymns and suggest improvements. *Andrew of Crete* (660-740), a native of Damascus who became archbishop of Gortina in Crete in 692, wrote the long Great Canon which Eastern Orthodox still sing today on the Thursday of mid-Lent week; it goes through the main Old Testament events and the life of Christ. *Germanus of Constantinople* (634-733), patriarch of Constantinople from 715, wrote various hymns, but is better known for having clashed with Emperor Leo the Isaurian over Leo's iconoclastic policy (see next section) – Leo deposed Germanus in 730. *Theophanes the Branded* (died 820) was another hymnwriter who suffered for his opposition to iconoclasm; the iconoclast Emperor, Leo the Armenian (813-20), had him branded with a red-hot iron (hence "Theophanes the Branded") and banished. Theophanes has earned a noble place among the East's great composers of hymns, surpassed in beauty only by John of Damascus and Cosmas the Melodist. Theodore of Studium (759-826), yet another martyr to iconoclastic fury, also wrote some important hymns for Lent and saints' days (see section 5 for Theodore). These hymnwriters, along with Romanos the Melodist whom we met in Volume One, Chapter 12, section 6, are the kings of Eastern hymnody.

3. The iconoclastic controversy

In the 8th and 9th centuries, the great iconoclastic controversy of 726-843 almost tore the Eastern Church apart. The dispute was over *icons* – pictures of Christ, the Virgin Mary, and the saints and angels in heaven. Eastern icons were almost always *pictures*

---

5. Cosmas is also known as "Cosmas of Jerusalem" and "Cosmas of Maiuma" (in later life, much against his will, he became bishop of Maiuma, near Gaza in Palestine).

(two-dimensional images: drawings, paintings, mosaics, wood, or stone carvings in low relief), not *statues* (fully three-dimensional images); to this day, Orthodoxy opposes statues of Christ, Mary, saints, and angels. By the 8th century, the use of religious icons had become widespread in Eastern Christendom. People would bow down in their presence, burn lamps and candles in front of them, kiss them, and pray before them. The idea behind such actions was that the icon revealed the presence of Christ – even an icon of a saint did this, because it was Christ *in* the saint who made him or her into a saint – and the bowing, kissing, and lamp-lighting were physical acts intended to express the heart's love and honour towards Christ (much as a subject would bow before his king, or a child kiss its mother).

Emperor **Leo the Isaurian** (717-41) declared war on this cult of icons. A passionate man with huge staring eyes, looking like some fierce combination of cat and wolf, Leo believed he had a personal mission from God to cleanse the Empire from the sin of image-worship, which would otherwise bring down divine wrath on Byzantium. The opposition of Muslims to all religious icons may have influenced Leo: perhaps Islam was God's judgment on icon-worshipping Byzantium. Furthermore, Leo had the most exalted views of his own authority in religious matters; "I am both Emperor and priest," he proclaimed. Other Emperors thought this of themselves, but Leo acted on the belief with all-consuming energy, harnessing all the power of the Byzantine state to try to destroy icons and those who venerated them. His loyal army backed him, but the monks and popular opinion opposed him bitterly. It was one of the most striking examples in all history of a mighty government trying, and failing, to force religious change on an unwilling people. Leo and those who wanted to get rid of icons were called *iconoclasts* (icon-breakers); the supporters of icons were known as *iconodules* (icon-venerators) or *iconophiles* (icon-lovers).[6]

---

6. Less reverently, iconoclasts have been called "smashers", and iconodules "kissers".

Leo opened the war against icons in 726. On the palace gate in Constantinople stood a gigantic golden icon of Christ, the most prominent image in the city; a squad of Leo's soldiers pulled it down. The act aroused the most passionate feelings. A mob of enraged women seized the officer in charge and beat him to death with mops and kitchen tools. Leo ordered the execution of the rioters. Popular demonstrations against Leo broke out. In Italy, whole communities threw off their allegiance to Byzantium, most famously in Venice (thus creating the independent republic of Venice, which would later play a vital part in the downfall of the Byzantine Empire). Pope Gregory II (715-31) gave his full support to the Italian rebels. Indeed, throughout the iconoclastic controversy, the popes backed the iconodules, for two reasons: (i) the papacy accepted the iconodule position as theologically correct, although the actual veneration of icons in the Western Church had not developed so fully as it had in the East; (ii) the popes also objected to the way that the iconoclast Emperors were subjecting the Eastern Church to the authority of the state, as if the Emperor were the supreme judge of doctrinal and spiritual matters. The iconoclastic controversy therefore opened up yet again the painful wounds of East–West division.

Still, the hostility of Pope Gregory did not deter Leo the Isaurian in the slightest. In 730 he deposed Constantinople's stubbornly iconodule patriarch, the hymnwriter Germanus I (715-30), replacing him with an iconoclast, Anastasius (730-54). Then Leo issued his famous edict against icons. It decreed the destruction of all icons and the punishment of all who continued to harbour them. The chief victims of Leo's edict were the monasteries which housed vast numbers of icons; many Byzantine monks fled to the West, with the most precious of the icons hidden beneath their robes.

Leo's son, Constantine V (741-75), continued the campaign against icons. Constantine, in fact, was animated by an iconoclastic zeal and a hatred of monks that bordered on mania. He forcibly evicted thousands of monks from their monasteries, and then converted the monasteries into barracks for his troops; the monks themselves he banished, mutilated or executed.

Constantine's most celebrated martyr was the leading iconodule **Stephen of Saint Auxentius** (died 767), abbot of a monastery in Bithynia (Asia Minor). Constantine tried everything to silence Stephen and destroy his far-reaching influence: first he exiled him to a small island, then he imprisoned him in Constantinople itself. But the prison was overflowing with persecuted iconodules, and Stephen led them in worship, forming a sort of church-in-prison. Finally Constantine's patience snapped and he condemned Stephen to death. Imperial soldiers marched him through the streets of Constantinople, beating and cursing him, and calling on the crowds to stone "this enemy of the Emperor". The crowd responded; a zealous iconoclast split Stephen's head open with a wooden club. Iconodules venerated him as "Stephen the New Martyr" (after Stephen the deacon, Acts 7). Constantine also called an ecumenical Church Council in Constantinople in 754 which, packed with 338 iconoclast bishops, condemned icons. The Church as a whole, however, did not recognise the "ecumenical" status of this Council, because Constantine did not invite delegates from the iconodule patriarchs of Antioch, Alexandria, or Jerusalem, or the Roman papacy.

The persecution of iconodules died down in the short reign of Constantine's son, Leo IV (775-80). This was due to the influence of his amazingly beautiful wife, the Empress **Irene**, whose thirst for power was matched only by her enthusiasm for icons. After Leo's death, Irene ruled the Empire in the name of her young son Constantine VI (780-97), and reversed the iconoclastic policy of the first three Isaurian Emperors. She called another ecumenical Council at Nicaea in 787 which pronounced in favour of icons. This is called the Second Council of Nicaea, to distinguish it from the one that met in 325. Two ambassadors of Pope Hadrian I took part in the Council, which meant that its decrees were binding on the Western as well as the Eastern Church. This was the seventh of the ecumenical Councils of the Church which both Easterners and Westerners recognised, before the great East–West schism of 1054; it was the last ecumenical Council acknowledged by the East (the West had other Councils which it considered ecumenical after

1054). See the end of the chapter for the text of the Second Council of Nicaea's decree.

The Second Council of Nicaea did not settle the controversy immediately. Irene's iconodule policies alienated the army, which was loyal to the memory of the great iconoclastic Emperor Constantine V. A revolution replaced Irene in 802 with a succession of six more iconoclastic Emperors. Despite the fact that most of these Emperors brutally persecuted iconodules, the monks remained firm supporters of icons, and popular opinion stayed on their side. The controversy was finally brought to an end by *Theodora*, another Empress ruling on behalf of a young son (Michael III). After coming to power in 842, Theodora summoned a Council in 843 which re-affirmed the iconodule position of the Second Council of Nicaea. The Eastern Orthodox Church celebrates this final victory of the iconodule position on the first Sunday of Lent, in a festival known as "the Triumph of Orthodoxy".[7] From now on, the use of religious icons was to be an essential part of Eastern Orthodox spirituality. Orthodoxy sees icons as the place where heaven and earth unite, sacred meeting-places with the spiritual world, manifestations of Christ's presence.

The iconoclastic controversy was partly a clash between Church and state. Religious motives may have inspired Leo the Isaurian, but many of the Emperors who came after him pursued an iconoclastic policy for political reasons. To them, it was just a way of imposing their will on the Eastern Church, and subjecting it to the authority of the state. This is shown by the way that iconoclastic Emperors replaced religious icons with self-glorifying pictures of themselves. However, we should not ignore the very deep spiritual and theological issues which were also involved in the controversy. The chief ones were the following. (I have put the iconoclast arguments first, and then in more detail the iconodule response. I have arranged it this way round, simply because it was the iconodules who finally triumphed, and their position became the accepted view throughout the Eastern

---

7. In Eastern Orthodoxy, Lent is the six weeks before Easter week.

Church and within Eastern Orthodoxy to the present day. It is as well for everyone concerned – both friend and foe – to know what the Orthodox theology of icons actually is.)

(i) Do icons violate the 2nd Commandment which forbids the making of images? Iconoclasts took their stand on this command, and rejected all manmade religious icons. The only proper visual images of Christ, they argued, were the bread and wine of the eucharist, the sign of the cross, and the Chi-Rho sign. (The *cross* must not be confused with the *crucifix*. A cross is empty. A crucifix has the figure of Christ hanging on it. Iconoclasts rejected the crucifix, but accepted the cross.) In response, the iconodules – whose greatest theologians were John of Damascus and Theodore of Studium[8] – held that the 2nd Commandment forbids the making of Pagan icons, images of false gods, not icons of Christ who is the Truth. They admitted that in Old Testament times, icons of the true God were impossible, owing to His invisible spiritual nature; but His taking flesh in Jesus Christ, they argued, had changed all this (see next point). Further, they did not regard icons as "graven images"; icons were not statues "in the round", but paintings or mosaics "in the flat".

Finally, they pointed out that God positively sanctioned many icons in the Old Testament system of worship: the golden cherubim over the ark of the covenant (Exod. 25:18-22), the cherubim woven into the tabernacle curtain (Exod. 26:31-32), the pomegranates woven into the high priest's robe (Exod. 28:33-34), the olive-wood cherubim in the inner sanctuary of the temple (1 Kings 6:23-28), the carved figures of cherubim, palm trees and open flowers on the temple walls and doors (1 Kings 6:29-35), the 12 bronze oxen carrying the bronze sea, and the bronze carts with carved oxen, lions and cherubim, in the temple court (1 Kings 7:23-51), and the brazen serpent which was a symbol of the crucified Christ (Num. 21:8-9, John 3:14-15). They also argued that the ark of the covenant was itself a symbol of Christ, the true dwelling place of God, and that the Israelites performed acts of reverence to the ark by bowing down before it (Josh. 7:6).

---

8. For Theodore, see section 5.

Iconodules of course maintained that they did not actually worship the icon itself; it would indeed be idolatry to worship a picture. They worshipped, not the physical substance of the icon, but the adorable person represented by the icon. In the words of **Leontius of Neapolis** (died 650):

> When I worship the icon of God, I am not worshipping the nature of the wood and the colours (God forbid!); but, holding to the non-living portrait of Christ, I intend *through* it to hold and worship Christ Himself.

However, iconodules did give special *honour* to the icon for the sake of the beloved person it portrayed. The Second Council of Nicaea distinguished between the absolute worship that believers should give to Christ (which they called *latreia*), and the limited, secondary veneration they should give to icons (which they called *proskunesis*). This was similar to the distinction between the love a man might have for his wife, and the secondary affection he might feel for a picture of his wife.

(ii) Does the fact that the Son of God became a man enable us to portray Him as a man? Iconoclasts said that only Christ Himself is the image of God; a picture cannot reproduce that image. All that a picture of Christ can depict is His human nature, not His divine nature; it therefore depicts only half of Christ, robbing Him of His deity. Iconodules argued that those who rejected pictures of Christ were not taking seriously the fact that He became a true man. Before the incarnation, no picture of God was possible, because no-one had seen Him. In Jesus Christ, however, God has become man; and it is the mark of a real flesh-and-blood man that he can be seen and depicted. So if Christ cannot be depicted, He cannot have been a real man. In other words, iconodules accused iconoclasts of undermining Christ's true humanity. In response to the iconoclast argument that a picture could not portray Christ's divine nature, iconodules said that no picture could ever portray the *nature* of God, which is invisible; but a picture of Christ is a portrait of a divine *person*, the eternal Son of God, *in the human form* which He took upon Himself in the incarnation. Since the human form which the icon depicted was *God's* human form, the picture did not deny the divine nature of Christ.

(iii) What was the practice of the early Church? This was in some ways the strongest argument of the iconoclasts. Up until the 4th century, the fathers of the Church did not set forth any theology of Christian icons, and sometimes condemned pictures of Christ; the positive veneration of icons they regarded as Pagan. When church buildings became common in the course of the 4th century, however, the practice of adorning them with icons of Christ was equally common, as we saw in Volume One, Chapter 7, section 3, under the heading *Church worship*. One interesting difference between East and West was that the East tended to depict Christ as a man; the West tended to depict Him in symbolic form, often as a lamb (the East rejected this on the grounds that it could degenerate into Pagan animal-worship: the incarnation required that the Saviour be depicted as a human being). To get around the fact that they could not find much support for icons in the writings of the early Church fathers, iconodules appealed to an "unwritten tradition" within the Church in favour of icons. They pointed out that the great Church historian of the 4th century, Eusebius of Caesarea, bore witness to this unwritten tradition in his *History of the Church*, even though Eusebius himself was personally opposed to icons.[9]

(iv) What was best for uneducated people who could not read? Iconoclasts said that icons would lead such people astray into idolatry: they would worship the icon as if it were a divine object. Iconodules, by contrast, argued that icons were like books for those who could not read: they portrayed the people and stories of the Bible and early Church history, so that the illiterate could see and learn about them. "What the written word is to those who can read," said John of Damascus, "the icon is to the illiterate.

---

9. "The features of the apostles Paul and Peter, and indeed of Christ Himself, have been preserved in coloured portraits which I have examined." Eusebius's *History of the Church*, book 7, paragraph 18. For Eusebius see Volume One, Chapter 7, section 1.

What speech is to the ear, the icon is to the eye." Iconodules also asked if there was any real difference between portraying Biblical people and stories with words, and portraying them with pictures. If one was allowed, why not the other? Words and icons were just different ways of picturing the same thing; one could "paint a picture" in people's minds by using words, or one could paint an icon on wood to the same effect.

Although the most important aspects of the iconoclastic controversy centred on icons of Christ, it also involved icons of the Virgin Mary, the saints, and the angels. The question was not whether believers should ask Mary and the saints and angels in heaven to pray for them; both iconodules and iconoclasts accepted this practice of "invocation" ("calling upon" the inhabitants of heaven to intercede for believers on earth). It was purely a question whether believers should use icons of Mary, saints, and angels as aids to their invocations – ways of focusing their minds on the heavenly inhabitant whose prayers they were seeking. Iconodules said yes: iconoclasts said no.

The iconoclastic controversy was an essentially Eastern affair. There was no Western equivalent. Western Christendom accepted that Christ, Mary, saints, and angels could be portrayed in icons, but did not attach the same theological or spiritual significance to icons as the East came to do after the triumph of the iconodules. Relics were far more important than icons in the West. At the time of the iconoclastic controversy, many Westerners actually rejected the practice of bowing or kneeling before icons, kissing them, and lighting lamps and candles in front of them. Because the Second Council of Nicaea in 787 had condemned those who did not honour icons in this way, many Western theologians rejected the Council, despite its approval by the papacy. (For Western attitudes at the time, see the previous Chapter, section 2.)

It was not long, however, before Westerners adopted and sanctioned Eastern customs, and went even further, by venerating not only two-dimensional pictures but also three-dimensional statues of Christ, Mary, saints, and angels. This turned the tables completely, and led the East to accuse the West of gross idolatry through venerating graven images! In the thought of the Eastern Church, statues cannot represent spiritual realities, because a statue belongs to this present world too much – it is too solid and material and "in the world", and therefore liable to lead people astray into worshipping the statue itself. People are less likely to worship a flat two-dimensional icon of Christ or a saint (the East argues), because it is more obviously a mere image of a higher spiritual reality. Eastern iconography (the painting of icons) underlined this point by deliberately refusing to depict Christ and the saints in a realistic manner. Iconographers painted them in a special stylised form, violating normal artistic laws of perspective, in order to express the truth that the person depicted was not just an earthly creature, but a heavenly being, transfigured by God's glory.

4. Photius the Great and the filioque controversy

The iconoclastic controversy was hardly over, when one of the grandest, most influential and most controversial figures in Byzantine history became patriarch of Constantinople. This was Photius (820-95), known to the Eastern Church as **Saint Photius the Great**. He was born into a wealthy iconodule family, which the iconoclastic Emperors and their patriarchs excommunicated and persecuted. Photius himself grew up under the last of the iconoclasts, Emperor **Theophilus** (829-42), whose soldiers beat, tortured, imprisoned, and exiled iconodule bishops and monks. Both Photius's parents died young, apparently as a result of persecution during Theophilus's cruel reign – Photius described them as martyrs.

However, there was a more positive side to the brutal Theophilus; he acted as imperial patron to a notable revival of culture which quickened the intellectual and literary life of the Empire, a revival which continued under his successors, the great iconodule empress Theodora (842-56) and her son Michael III (842-67). Central to this cultural awakening was the University of Constantinople. Founded by Constantine the Great, the University was reorganised by Theophilus, who appointed the great iconoclast philosopher, **Leo the Mathematician** (born 790, died some time after 869), as its chief teacher. Leo's fame as a scholar was so far-flung that the ruler of the Islamic Empire, Caliph Mamun, offered Theophilus huge sums of money and an everlasting peace treaty, if Theophilus would only send Leo to Baghdad! Theophilus refused; he wanted the brilliant Leo in Constantinople. Under Leo's guidance, the study of science, and of the ancient Pagan poets and philosophers of Greece, blossomed richly at the University.

Leo's two most outstanding students were Cyril of Thessalonica (for Cyril, see section 7) and Photius himself. Not just as a student, but throughout Photius's whole life, an unquenchable thirst for knowledge possessed him; he read every book on every subject that came his way, and made himself the most learned man in the Byzantine Empire – indeed, some have called Photius "the wisest man of the Middle Ages". His vast knowledge included all matters of theology. Photius's mind was a star of flaming brightness; his personality, however, remains shrouded in baffling mystery. He was obviously a man of almost superhuman energy and purpose, and his contemporaries say he had a "sweet expression of face" and "noble and attractive manners"; but his real feelings and motives are so difficult to grasp that different historians have come to opposite conclusions about his virtue and integrity – usually depending on whether they agree with Photius's theology! Still, it is clear that over the men of his own times Photius exercised a strange facination. Under the influence of his personal presence and his persuasive words, the hardest hearts of Photius's most determined enemies would often melt like ice into water.

Photius's career was at first totally secular; he was by turns a civil servant, a diplomat, and a lecturer in Constantinople University. However, when in 858 dark political factors brought about the fall of Constantinople's patriarch *Ignatius* (appointed 843), the young Emperor Michael III (known as "Michael the Drunkard", for all-too-obvious reasons) chose Photius as his new patriarch. Photius was horrified; all he wanted was to live a quiet life of study. But the Emperor and his court would not take no for an answer. Reluctantly, Photius submitted. Because

Photius was a layman, Michael had to get him set apart to the five "orders" in the Church – monk, reader, sub-deacon, deacon, priest – at the rate of one a day, in order to enable Photius to accept ordination as patriarch on day six. Today many reckon Photius the greatest patriarch Constantinople has ever enjoyed, without equal as a penetrating theologian and a practical Church leader. At the time, however, the deposed patriarch Ignatius still had loyal supporters. Ignatius was a steadfast iconodule, who had suffered terribly under Emperor Theophilus for his devotion to icons; the extreme wing of the now triumphant iconodules, who wanted to show no mercy to former iconoclasts, looked on Ignatius as their champion, and rejected the more moderate Photius as an illegal usurper.

In 861 the papacy became caught up in the quarrel between Ignatius and Photius. At the invitation of Emperor Michael, Pope *Nicholas I* (858-67) sent two Western bishops, Rodoald of Porto and Zacharias of Anagni, to Constantinople to help settle some minor points left over from the iconoclastic controversy. However, Nicholas really wanted Rodoald and Zacharias to do two things: (a) to negotiate with Byzantium about papal authority over the churches of southern Italy (then under Byzantine control) and the Balkans, and (b) to investigate the deposition of Ignatius. As far as (b) was concerned, Nicholas's aim was to assert the sovereignty of Rome over Constantinople, by establishing his right as pope to judge which of the two claimants, Ignatius or Photius, should be patriarch. (Nicholas was one of the most extreme advocates of the papacy's exalted claims who had thus far occupied the papal throne.) However, once Rodoald and Zacharias had arrived in Constantinople, Photius and his supporters persuaded them, perhaps with bribes, to give their approval to a synod which condemned Ignatius and upheld Photius's claims.

Pope Nicholas exploded with fury. He had been denied the chance to act as arbiter between Ignatius and Photius, and had received no concessions over southern Italy or the Balkans. So in 862, Nicholas disowned what Rodoald and Zacharias had done (he also deposed both men from their bishoprics), and recognised Ignatius as the rightful patriarch of Constantinople. In 863, he solemnly excommunicated Photius. The Byzantine Emperor Michael III responded to Pope Nicholas's awesome decrees in the most cutting way possible: he simply ignored them and continued to accept Photius as his patriarch.

Rome and Constantinople were clearly shaping up for a massive conflict over Photius. This came closer to open war through the passionate rivalry between Western and Eastern missionaries in Bulgaria.[10] Each group of missionaries was competing for the religious loyalties of the Bulgarian nation, especially its leader, Boris. In 865 Boris accepted baptism from Eastern clergy, but when Constantinople would not give him an independent Bulgarian Church, he began looking to the West. These events inflamed bad feeling between the two rival groups of missionaries, who began attacking each other on every issue on which East and West differed – and the quarrel came to focus its deadly heat on the *filioque* clause. This was the insertion into the Nicene Creed which some Western Catholics in Spain began to make in the 6th century; the insertion made the Creed teach that the Holy Spirit "proceeds from the Father *and from the Son*". (The Latin for "and from the Son" is *filioque*.) The first Holy Roman Emperor, Charlemagne, gave his sanction to the *filioque* clause at the council of Aachen in 809.[11]

Photius responded to Western attacks on the East's rejection of the *filioque* clause by writing in 867 an encyclical (circular) letter to the other Eastern patriarchs, in which he denounced the *filioque* as heretical. The letter also condemned the Western Church for all the practices in which it varied from the East, *e.g.* the Western insistence on clerical celibacy. Finally, Photius summoned a Church council in Constantinople which excommunicated Pope Nicholas. So the ultimate breakdown of relationships had occurred; Rome and Constantinople were now officially out of communion with each other. It looked as if Western and Eastern Christianity, the two wings of the one holy

---

10. See section 7 for a fuller account of missionary work in Bulgaria.

11. See Chapter 2, section 2, under the heading *Emperor and pope.*

apostolic Church of Christ, had broken apart into two separate and hostile Churches. The event is known (in the West) as the "Photian schism".

At this point, however, the chances and changes of Byzantine politics suddenly toppled Photius from the patriarchate. The Emperor, Michael, had by now become quite incapable of governing; he spent most of the time either getting drunk or recovering from his drinking bouts. His right-hand man, Basil the Macedonian, who was the real power behind the throne, murdered the besotted Michael in his bed in 867, and took his place as Emperor **Basil I** (867-86), founder of the mighty Macedonian dynasty. To strengthen his grip on power, Basil deposed Photius, who was too closely linked with the previous regime; besides, Photius had insulted the new Emperor by refusing to admit him to holy communion, stained as Basil was with Michael's blood. Basil imprisoned Photius in a monastery, and reinstated Ignatius as patriarch, thus winning the allegiance of Ignatius's party. Then Basil assembled another Church council in Constantinople in 869, known as the *anti-Photian council*; it reversed all the decisions taken in the council of 867 which had excommunicated Pope Nicholas. So the downfall of Photius restored peace and fellowship between Rome and Constantinople.

The theological dispute over the *filioque* clause, however, was by no means dead. Photius's encyclical letter of 867 had made it a central and burning issue in the frictions between East and West. Photius also wrote a highly influential book on the subject, his *Treatise on the Mystagogia of the Holy Spirit*, which scholars regard as Photius's theological masterpiece (*mystagogia* means "interpretation of a mystery"). In the *Treatise*, Photius stated clearly all the Eastern objections to the *filioque* clause. He accused the West of destroying the unity of the Trinity by its teaching that the Spirit proceeds from the Son as well as from the Father. In Eastern thought, the Father is the unique source or fountain of the divine nature; the Son and the Spirit are God because they possess all the fullness of God the *Father's* essence and attributes (all except His actual Fatherhood) – the Son by eternal generation, the Spirit by eternal procession. So when

Eastern believers heard Western theologians saying that the Spirit proceeds from the Son as well as from the Father, the East felt that Westerners were making the Son into another source of the divine nature. But if there were two sources of God's nature, the unity of God was destroyed; Father and Son became two separate Gods.

The gulf between East and West here was a basically different approach to the doctrine of the Trinity. Following the Cappadocian fathers, the East tended to begin with the *persons* of the Trinity, and saw their unity as lying in *the person of God the Father*. For Eastern theologians, the Father guarantees that the three persons are only one God, because the Father alone is the "fountain of deity", the one source of the Son and the Spirit, causing them each to possess the fullness of His divine essence. Therefore the Holy Spirit proceeds only from the Father. (The East never tired of pointing out to the West that the Bible explicitly says the Spirit "proceeds from the Father" in John 15:26, but nowhere says He proceeds from the Son too.) Of course, Eastern thinkers admitted that in the experience of salvation, the Spirit came to believers from the Father *through* the Son; but that, they said, was only because the Father had first of all *given* the Spirit to the Son as head of the Church.

By contrast, the West began, not with the persons, but with the *nature* of God. Following Augustine of Hippo, Western theologians tended to think of God's nature or essence before the three persons of the Trinity, and to see the oneness of the Trinity as lying in the *one common nature* shared by Father, Son, and Spirit. Because Western thinkers started with God's nature, they viewed the divine persons as little more than inner relationships within the divine nature. Therefore the one divine nature, as it existed in both Father and Son, was the source of the Holy Spirit. The main reason why the West was so insistent on bringing Father and Son together as the common origin of the Spirit was Western zeal for the equality of the Son with the Father; Western thinkers argued that it would undermine the full deity of Christ if He were not equal with the Father as source of the Spirit. (The East responded that, on this argument, it would undermine the full deity of the Spirit if He were not equal with the Father as the source of the Son!)

The East, of course, also objected to the *filioque* clause on the grounds that the West had no right to insert it into the Nicene Creed. The Creed was the ecumenical property of East and West alike; how could the West alter it without the East's consent? This was a powerful objection. However, the arguments over the *filioque* went much deeper, revealing serious differences between East and West in their whole approach to the fundamental Christian doctrine of the Trinity. The Eastern approach emphasised the persons of the Trinity and tended to speak of "three persons in one essence"; the Western approach emphasised the divine essence and tended to speak of "one essence in three persons".

Photius's deposition did not bring his career to an end. Ignatius proved unequal to the weighty and complex burdens of the patriarchate, and Emperor Basil's thoughts began to turn back to Photius. In 873 he released Photius from imprisonment, making him tutor to his sons. Photius's intellectual brilliance and personal charm conquered the Emperor's heart, and even won over Photius's arch-enemy Ignatius, to whom Photius ministered in Ignatius's final illness. When Ignatius died in 877, Basil I instantly appointed Photius patriarch again. In 879, Photius summoned another Church council which met in the heavenly splendour of Hagia Sophia, and undid all the decisions of the anti-Photian council of 869. From 879 to 886, Photius ruled in both Church and state in the Byzantine Empire, after the death of Basil's favourite son Constantine hurled the Emperor's mind to the brink of insanity (Basil felt he was being judged by God for having murdered Michael the Drunkard 10 years before). While Basil brooded in his mental darkness, Photius reigned. Never had a patriarch of Constantinople climbed to such exalted heights of power.

However, when Basil I died in 886, and his son Leo the Philosopher (whom Photius had taught) became Emperor, Leo deposed Photius, accusing him of having plotted to make himself Emperor after Basil's death. Actually Leo wanted to install his brother Stephen as patriarch. Leo exiled the fallen Photius to a monastery in Armenia, where he died nine years later. His death seemed to wipe away all the stains of past controversies. Leo immediately had Photius's body brought to Constantinople and entombed in Hagia Sophia; there, the Emperor and his court publicly honoured Photius's name, together with that of Ignatius who had once been Photius's greatest foe – the final reconciliation: "Ignatius and Photius, the Orthodox patriarchs, in everlasting memory."

Photius left behind him a great number of important writings, especially his *Treatise on the Holy Spirit.* Also influential was his *Nomocanon,* a collection of ecclesiastical and imperial laws, regarded as authoritative throughout the Eastern Orthodox world. Sermons, Bible commentaries, poems, letters, and theological writings by Photius all survive to show us the depth and brilliance of his learning, if not the hidden springs of his mysterious personality (although his letters are quite charming and glow with apparent Christian sincerity). However, Photius's greatest legacy was the uncompromising way he had championed the cause of the Eastern Church against the papacy, and stiffened Eastern determination to resist Western encroachments, especially over the *filioque* clause. The quarrel between Photius and Pope Nicholas did not cause the separation between Eastern and Western Christianity; the causes of separation were already there, in the divergent theology and practice of East and West. But the Photian schism of 863-67 provided obvious and painful proof that the two great branches of the Church were drifting far apart in a way that involved even the fundamental Christian doctrine of the Trinity.

5. Byzantine monasteries and Simeon the New Theologian

Monasteries were an essential feature of life in the Byzantine Empire. Many of Byzantium's leading theologians and spiritual writers were monks, and the higher ranks of the clergy (from bishop upwards) normally came from the monasteries. In the West from about the 11th century, monks belonged to different monastic "orders" (Augustinian, Cluniac, Carthusian, Cistercian, Dominican, *etc.*). By contrast, the East had no such orders; all monks were simply monks, living according to the guidelines drawn up by Basil of Caesarea in the 4th century. For this reason Westerners sometimes say that Eastern monks belong to the "Basilian" order, but this is not correct – Basil's guidelines do not constitute a distinct "order".

Theodore of Studium (759-826)

There were two great monastic centres in the Byzantine Empire. The first was the *Studium* in Constantinople itself, which housed 1,000 monks. Founded in 463, it had its own pattern for monastic life, the *Typicon* or "Studite rule", which other monasteries often adopted, *e.g.* the Monastery of the Caves in Russia (see Chapter 6, section 1). Studium's most famous archimandrite (leader) was Theodore, called **Theodore of Studium** (759-826) to distinguish him from several other Theodores. He was a native of Constantinople, of noble birth, who joined the monastery of Saccudion in Bithynia, Asia Minor, in 787, and was elected its abbot in 794. To escape Muslim aggression, the monks migrated to the Studium in Constantinople in 797, where Theodore launched a successful campaign of monastic reform. His adaptation of Basil's monastic rules, the *Typicon*, placed a deeper stress on community life and on education in the Scriptures and the early Church fathers, and became widely used throughout the East. Theodore was also one of the most resolute champions of icons in the iconoclastic controversy, for which he suffered persecution under the iconoclast Emperors. Emperor Leo the Armenian (813-20) threw Theodore and all his monks in prison; Theodore himself died in exile, while his brother Joseph (also a monk of Studium and fervent iconodule) was tortured to death by Emperor Theophilus (829-42). Theodore was also important in developing Byzantine hymn-writing. His many letters are one of our richest sources of knowledge of Byzantine people, customs, and events of his times.

The other great centre of Byzantine monasticism was *Mount Athos* in northern Greece, often called "the holy mountain".[12] According to tradition, the Virgin Mary had once stopped here on a journey from Palestine to Cyprus, and every Pagan shrine and statue had instantly fallen to the ground. Athos was henceforth specially consecrated to Mary; no other woman was allowed to set foot on the peninsula (women are still barred today). Multitudes of hermits had lived in the wooded hills and chestnut groves of Mount Athos since the 4th century; but it

---

12. The "ath" in Athos is pronounced like the "math" in mathematics.

was in 963 that Athos's first great cenobitic monastery, the Great
Lavra, was founded by *Athanasius of Trebizond* (920-1003),
who modelled his community on the Studium. Other monasteries sprang up, and by the 11th century Athos had become
almost an independent monastic republic, with 40,000 monks
in residence. There were 20 main or "ruling" monasteries. Many
Eastern leaders came from among the Athonite monks; one
monastery alone gave the East 26 patriarchs and 144 bishops.
Today, Mount Athos is the most important centre of Eastern
Orthodox monasticism, although the number of monks living
there has declined sharply in the 20th century; in 1965 there
were only 1,491 monks in residence.

The monastic movement within the Eastern Church gave
rise to a special type of monk – the "elder" (in Greek, *geron*; in
Russian, *starets*). The elder was a monk who gained a reputation
for spiritual wisdom and discernment, and whom other people,
both monks and non-monks, therefore sought out as a spiritual
guide (or "director"). His particular gift was to see what God's
will was for each individual who consulted him. An elder was not
officially ordained to this role; it was a role that he simply found
himself fulfilling by virtue of his gifts and reputation. Easterners
often see Antony, the Egyptian desert father of the 4th century,
as the first elder.[13]

One of the most famous and interesting Eastern monks of
this period was *Nilus of Calabria* (died 1005). Nilus was Greek
by race, but born at Rossano in Calabria (south-western Italy) –
southern Italy at that time was part of the Byzantine Empire and
was called "Greater Greece". After his wife died, Nilus committed
himself to the life of a hermit in about 940, taking Antony of
Egypt as his example. He then founded several monastic communities, became abbot of the monastery in his native Rossano,
and won a vast reputation for sanctity, boldly rebuking popes
and Holy Roman Emperors for their sins. In the 990s, Muslim

---

13. The West also had monastic elders, especially in the Celtic Church, but
it was a tradition that had largely died out by the time of the East–West split
in 1054. An elder did not in fact have to be a monk, but usually was.

invaders ravaged Calabria, forcing Nilus and his 60 monks to flee. Their most obvious escape-route was eastward into the safety of Byzantine Greece; but Nilus knew how admired he was in the East and feared he would become proud if he settled there. So he took his monks north, into the Latin-speaking part of Italy where the papacy reigned, and sought refuge in the celebrated monastery of Monte Cassino, founded by the great Benedict of Nursia.[14] Monte Cassino welcomed Nilus warmly; the abbot invited him and his monks to worship in the monastic church at times when the Western monks were not using it. So despite the deep and growing gulf between Eastern and Western Christendom, divine worship sounded forth in Monte Cassino alternately in both Greek and Latin. Nilus himself even learned Latin so that he could worship together with the Western monks.

Eventually, Nilus left Monte Cassino, received the blessing of Pope Gregory V (996-99) in Rome, and founded the monastery of Grottaferrata just outside the papal city, where he died in 1005. It is strange to think that within a mere 50 years, the happy blending of Greek East and Latin West which shone forth in Nilus's life would no longer be theologically valid, owing to the bitter and enduring East–West Schism of 1054 (see section 8).

Far greater than Nilus in historic influence was the monk **Simeon the New Theologian** (949-1022), often called the greatest of the Byzantine mystics. Simeon was born to a wealthy family in the village of Galatia in Paphlagonia (along the southern coast of the Black Sea). His early career as a civil servant in the court of Emperor Nicephorus II Phocas (963-69) clashed with his deep yearning for the monastic life; but his spiritual director, a monk of Constantinople's great Studium monastery, advised the young Simeon to remain a civil servant for a time, until his life in Christ had grown and he could make a mature decision to become a monk. The director's name was also Simeon – he is known as Simeon the Reverent, to distinguish him from his more famous disciple. The relationship between the two men was deep, intimate and lifelong, and was to plunge Simeon the

---

14. For Benedict of Nursia, see Volume One, Chapter 11, section 1.

New Theologian into stormy waters of persecution after his master's death. Young Simeon eventually joined the Studium, but his spiritual intensity (especially his love of praying by himself) alarmed many of the other monks, who began criticising and mocking him. To spare him, Simeon the Reverent had his pupil transferred to Constantinople's Saint Mamas monastery, where he was soon elected abbot in 980. He produced a steady stream of written sermons, hymns, and treatises on the ascetic life.

Simeon the New Theologian (949-1022)

After the death of Simeon the Reverent, Simeon the New Theologian regarded his old master as a saint who was now in heaven, and honoured him with passionate devotion. This provoked much hostility, especially from Stephen, a former metropolitan of Nicomedia, now an official of the Constantinople patriarchate. Stephen seems to have conceived some sort of personal hatred for Simeon; he attacked him unceasingly, accusing him of fostering an extravagant and unauthorised cult of his dead master, and criticising his spiritual writings as the work of a shallow, uneducated man. Stephen raised up a host of enemies for Simeon; it was in some ways a conflict between those (like Stephen) who emphasised the official organised Church and its authority, and those (like Simeon) who placed an even higher value on individual conscience and the inner life of the Spirit. Opinions about Simeon eventually became so divided in Constantinople, that Patriarch Sergius II (999-1019) asked Simeon to leave the city in 1009, for the sake of the Church's peace. Simeon submitted meekly and settled just outside Constantinople near the Church of Saint Marina. There, a rich friend helped him found a new monastery, where he enjoyed the peace that had escaped him in the turbulent Byzantine capital.

Simeon was certainly an unusual and striking person. Whenever he led his monks in worship, his face (they said) shone like an angel. He often made prophecies about individuals (which apparently came true), and had a ministry of healing-through-prayer. A highly valued spiritual grace in the mysticism of the Eastern Church is "the gift of tears" – a burning anguish of repentance in the heart which issues forth in weeping profusely over one's sins. Simeon possessed this gift in abundance; people often noticed that he was bathed in tears when he was sitting alone. Simeon's faith was also unusual. Unlike other Byzantine mystics, he spoke freely and openly about his personal experience of God. He was a fierce critic of a merely "nominal" Christianity. Baptism and church attendance, Simeon insisted, were spiritually worthless unless they bore fruit in a changed life.

> "Is Christ's name not on people's lips everywhere," Simeon said, "in cities, villages, monasteries, and on mountains? But if you search carefully to see if people actually obey Christ's commands, you will hardly find one among thousands and tens of thousands who is a real Christian in word and in deed."

Through his preaching, writing, and counselling, Simeon spent his life trying to turn people away from a religion that was all ritual and ceremony, to an inward spirituality of the heart. He exalted the inner voice of conscience as the meeting place between God and the soul, and insisted that a true knowledge of God could not come through doctrine alone, but through committed spiritual practice, especially prayer, in which the believer came to know God personally in feeling and experience. The practice of prayer, Simeon held, would bring to the believer the glorious vision of God as light – the uncreated divine radiance that shone from Christ on the mount of transfiguration (Matt. 17:1-9). Here was a theme taken up by the "hesychast" movement and Gregory Palamas – but their story belongs to Chapter 9, section 3. Simeon also taught a doctrine of "Christian perfection", which seemed to suggest that a believer on earth could become free of all actual sin (or at least all "disturbing passions"), leading to a special indwelling of the Holy Spirit.

Controversial in his lifetime, after Simeon's death the Eastern Church gave its verdict in his favour and against Stephen of Nicomedia, and Simeon became one of the East's most revered and beloved saints. His writings earned him his majestic title of "the New Theologian"; prior to this, Easterners had given the title "Theologian" only to the apostle John and Gregory of Nazianzus, because they were seen as matchless in their teaching about the nature of God and the Trinity.[15] The East could express its respect for Simeon in no higher way than by ranking him on this most exalted plane with John and Gregory.

6. Dissenting movements: Manichees, Paulicians, and Bogomils

Not everyone in the Byzantine Empire accepted Orthodoxy as his religion. There were groups of dissenters. The main dissenting movements were the Manichees, Paulicians, and Bogomils,

---

15. See Volume One, Chapter 8, section 3 for Gregory of Nazianzus. In Eastern Orthodox thought, the word *theology* normally refers to the doctrine of God. To refer to the doctrines of creation and redemption, *i.e.* what God has done outside of Himself, Orthodoxy uses the word *economy* (from the Greek word for "administration" or "dispensation").

who were all in varying degrees the spiritual descendants of the Gnostics.[16] We have already examined the beliefs of the Manichees in Volume One, Chapter 6, section 2; they were the Gnostic sect to which Augustine of Hippo had belonged before his conversion.[17] They were still active in parts of the Byzantine Empire.

The Paulicians were a distinct Gnostic group who originated in Armenia in the 7th century and spread to southern Asia Minor. Their founder, **Constantine**, taught that an evil and inferior god had created the physical world. All matter was therefore evil, and Constantine rejected the use of all material things (the water of baptism, the bread and wine of holy communion, icons) in worship. The evil creator-god was the god of the Old Testament, and also of some parts of the New Testament; Constantine accepted only the Gospels and Paul's letters as having come from the true God of heaven. This reverence for the apostle Paul is probably why Constantine and his followers were called "Paulicians"; Constantine even changed his name to Silvanus to make the point that he was a disciple of Paul (see 2 Cor. 1:19, 1 Thess. 1:1, 2 Thess. 1:1). According to Constantine, Jesus was an angel sent by the true God to reveal the way of salvation by which souls could escape from the evil of matter.

The Byzantine state persecuted the Paulicians, although the oppression was less severe under the iconoclastic Emperors, whose opposition to icons had something in common with Paulician beliefs. It was rumoured that one iconoclast Emperor, Constantine V (741-75), was a secret Paulician himself. However, after the final triumph of the iconodules in 843, the Emperors persecuted the Paulicians without mercy. As a result, the Paulicians formed themselves into armed bands, and fought fiercely and brilliantly in self-defence. Indeed, they often allied themselves with the Muslim Arabs against Byzantium. Paulicians could still be found in Armenia as recently as the 19th century.

The Bogomils arose in Bulgaria in the 10th century. Our main source of information about them is a detailed apologetic treatise

---

16. See Volume One, Chapter 4, section 1.

17. See Volume One, Chapter 8, section 3.

which a Bulgarian Orthodox priest called **Cosmas** (not to be confused with Cosmas the Melodist) wrote against them in about 970. According to Cosmas, they were named after their founder, a priest called **Bogomil**, which means "dear to God" – so we could translate "Bogomils" as "the friends of God". Bogomil probably derived his religious ideas from Paulicians whom the Byzantine authorities had forcibly resettled in Bulgaria, but Bogomilism was a more complex Gnostic system than Paulicianism. Bogomil taught that the Supreme God had two angel-sons, Satanael the elder, and Christ the younger. Satanael rebelled against the Supreme God and seduced many lesser angels to follow him. He then persuaded these fallen angels to inhabit bodies of flesh which he had created as part of an evil world of matter – so that human souls are really angels who have fallen away from heaven. (Later Bogomils altered this original teaching and made Satanael into an uncreated and eternal power of evil, who invaded heaven, kidnapped large numbers of angels, and imprisoned them in human bodies.) Cosmas sums up for us the Bogomils' extreme hostility to the physical creation:

> They say that everything exists by the will of the devil. The sky, the sun, the stars, the air, the human race, church buildings, crosses: everything that comes from God, they ascribe to the devil. In short, they consider all that moves on the earth, animal, vegetable and mineral, to be the devil's work.

This attitude led Bogomils, like all Gnostics, to deny the inspiration of the Old Testament, with its doctrine of the divine creation of matter, to reject marriage and meat-eating, and to banish everything physical from their worship (water baptism, holy communion, icons). To set humankind free from the tyranny of Satanael and his monstrous world of matter, Bogomil taught that the Supreme God sent his younger son, Christ, to the earth as Jesus of Nazareth. Satanael killed Jesus, but he was resurrected in a spirit-body and returned to heaven. Likewise, after death, God would give eternal spirit-bodies to all the followers of Jesus.

Bogomils flourished in Bulgaria in the 10th century; by 1150, there were Bogomil missionaries working in Western Europe, where they enjoyed close relationships with the Cathars and Albigensians.[18] However, they died out in their native Bulgaria after 1393, when the Muslim Turks conquered the land.

Orthodox theologians like Cosmas wrote many apologetic works against the Manichees, Paulicians, and Bogomils, often referring to all three groups simply as "Manichees". Interestingly, even their Orthodox opponents admitted that these Gnostics lived blameless moral lives. "In their outward life," Cosmas tells us, speaking of the Bogomils, "the heretics are clothed in the appearance of being sheep. They are gentle, humble, peaceful, and pale from all their insincere fasts. They do not speak an idle word, nor laugh abrasively, nor indulge in smutty jokes. When people see their great humility, they imagine they are Orthodox and able to show them the way of salvation." The good character of many Manichees, Paulicians, and Bogomils has led some Protestants to wonder whether these despised Gnostics were in reality true evangelical Christians, Reformers before the Reformation, whose beliefs were misrepresented by their foes. But there is no evidence of such misrepresentation. History shows that an outwardly pure life is, by itself, no sure sign of a true Christian.

7. Byzantine missionary activity

Under the Byzantine Empire in this period, there was a huge expansion westwards and northwards of the Eastern Church into Moravia, Bulgaria, Serbia, Romania, and Russia.

Moravia. The Moravians, Bulgars, and Serbs were all peoples of the Slavic race. The Slavs had come from central Russia and spread through the plains of Eastern and Central Europe in the 5th and 6th centuries. They worshipped various Pagan gods, *e.g.* Perun, the god of thunder, Dazbag, the god of the sun, and Jarovit, the god of springtime. The Moravians were the first Slavs to show interest in Christianity. (Moravia occupied roughly the same

---

18. See Chapter 8, section 3.

territory as the eastern part of the modern Czech Republic.) In 860 the Moravian prince Ratislav asked the Byzantine Emperor Michael III to send missionaries to instruct his people in the Christian faith. The patriarch of Constantinople, who at that time was Photius the Great (see section 4), sent two Greek brothers, **Cyril of Thessalonica** (died 869) and **Methodius** (died 885). Cyril was a personal friend of Photius; they had been fellow students at Constantinople University under Leo the Mathematician, and then they had both given lectures there.

Cyril of Thessalonica (died 869) and Methodius (died 885)

Cyril was no stranger to missionary work. Before the Moravian mission, he had worked among Arabs from 855 to 856, and among the Khazars (north-east of the Black Sea) from 860 to 861. However, it was Cyril and Methodius's mission to the Slavic Moravians that proved to be of lasting historic significance. The two brothers created for the first time a written alphabet for the Slavic language ("Slavonic"); the alphabet used today in south-eastern Europe and in Russia is based on this, and is called "Cyrillic", after Cyril. It was an important factor in the spread of Byzantine Christianity and culture among the Slavic peoples. Cyril and Methodius's missionary work among the Moravians was successful at first. Tensions, however, developed between the Byzantine brothers and their missionaries on the one side, and Western Frankish bishops on the other, who wanted the Moravians to be under the spiritual authority of Rome, not Byzantium. Another source of controversy was the use of Slavonic as the language of worship; the West preferred all worship to be in Latin, regardless of the native tongue of the people. After the deaths of Cyril and Methodius, the Franks expelled their converts from Moravia, and Moravian Christianity eventually developed along Western Roman lines.

Bulgaria. The Eastern Christians who had been driven out of Moravia went south into Bulgaria to continue their work in a more friendly setting. The Bulgarian leader or "tsar", **Boris** (852- 88), had accepted baptism into the Eastern faith in 865, but then turned to the West when Constantinople would not grant him an autonomous Church of Bulgaria (see section 4 for the way this sparked East–West controversy over the *filioque* clause). However, in 870, the Byzantine Emperor Basil I and Patriarch Ignatius of Constantinople won Boris back to the Eastern fold, by recognising the right of the Bulgarians to an independent national Church. Eastern Christianity spread rapidly through the work of the Moravian missionaries. There was a setback when Tsar Vladimir, son of Boris, renounced Christianity and tried to take Bulgaria back into Paganism. But the attempt was short-lived; his father Boris came out of the monastery to which he had retired, led an army against Vladimir, crushed him in battle, had him blinded and imprisoned, settled his other son Simeon on the throne as a Christian – and then retired to his monastery again! Under **Simeon** (893-927), the greatest of the Bulgarian tsars, a great Slavonic Christian literature was born, and a new Slavonic culture based on Byzantine civilisation. However, because the Bulgarian Church used its own Slavonic tongue, it was able to develop its own native form of the Eastern faith. In 927 Constantinople promoted the archbishop of Bulgaria to the rank of patriarch.

The experience of Bulgaria illustrates one of the chief differences between Eastern and Western Christianity. When the West evangelised a people, it brought them into complete submission and conformity to the authority of Rome (*e.g.* through the use of Latin as the language of worship). The East, by contrast, allowed the peoples it evangelised a much greater freedom from Constantinople. The new nationally-based Eastern Churches often became *autocephalous* (Greek for "self-governing") – they were given their own spiritual leader, sometimes a patriarch, sometimes an archbishop or metropolitan, who was not answerable to the leader of any other autocephalous Church.

Serbia. The missionaries of Cyril and Methodius also evangelised the Slavic people of Serbia in the 9th century. As in Moravia and Bulgaria, there was a struggle in Serbia for the nation's religious loyalty between East and West, but the East won. The victorious supporters of the Eastern faith introduced worship in the Slavonic tongue, and created a new Slavonic Serbian culture after the pattern of Byzantium.

Romania. The Romanian people lived in the kingdoms of Moldavia and Wallachia, between Bulgaria and Russia. Unlike the Moravians, Bulgarians, and Serbians, the Romanians were not originally part of the Slavic race; they were mainly Western and Latin in origin. Roman legions had settled in the region in the 2nd century, intermarrying with the native Dacians; and from this Roman-Dacian union, the Romanian nation was born. However,

Slavic tribes who settled in the area in huge numbers in the 6th century brought Romania into the Slavic world. Christianity had already existed among the Romanians since the 2nd century, but Byzantine and Bulgarian missionaries succeeded in winning them over into the Byzantine form of doctrine and piety. The Romanians adopted the Slavonic language for worship, but it was a peculiar form of Slavonic, mingled with their ancestral Latin.

Greece. Many of the Pagan Slavs had settled in Greece; the Eastern Church successfully evangelised them. The greatest of the Greek missionaries to the Slavs was ***Nikon the Penitent*** (930-1000), who worked among the Slavic colonists of the Mani peninsula. Nikon, the son of a landowner in Armenia Minor, ran away from home as a youth to join the monastery of Chryse Pente. He spent the years 961-8 evangelising the Muslims of Crete, and then settled in Sparta, southern Greece, in the 970s, where he founded a monastery and preached among the Pagan Slavs. Nikon's passion for evangelism was combined with a profoundly gloomy outlook on life, which he described as "smoke and children's games".

Russia. For the conversion of Russia to the Eastern Byzantine form of Christianity, see Chapter 6.

8. The Great East–West Schism

The Eastern and Western wings of the one universal Church had been drifting apart ever since the fall of the Roman Empire in the West in 410. East and West spoke different languages (Greek in the East, Latin in the West – someone once made the witty comment that "East and West did not understand each other, because they did not understand each other"). They lived in different cultural and political worlds (East – the ancient Christian Byzantine Empire; West – the new Germanic and Norse kingdoms, comparatively uncivilised, and only just converted from Arianism and Paganism). Over the centuries, a great many differences, disagreements and misunderstandings had grown up between Eastern and Western Christendom. These included the following:

(i) The rivalry between Rome and Constantinople. During the Middle Ages, Rome's claims became ever more exalted. The popes began by claiming a place of special honour among bishops; they ended by claiming absolute authority over the entire Church. The East denied the papacy's claims, rejected the idea that the Church has a visible earthly head, and held that the five ancient patriarchates of Rome, Constantinople, Antioch, Jerusalem, and Alexandria should together offer leadership to Christians.

(ii) Differences in religious practice. These varied in their seriousness. The West did not allow priests to marry; the East allowed them to marry prior to ordination, and almost all Eastern priests were in fact married men (although bishops had to be celibate). The West used unleavened bread in communion; the East used leavened bread. In baptism, the East continued the early Church practice of immersing people three times in the name of the Trinity; the West had come to tolerate a variety of practices – threefold immersion, single immersion, and affusion, although affusion increasingly became the Western norm.[19]

(iii) Theological differences. These were increasingly serious. The East, for example, did not teach the Western doctrine of purgatory, which was becoming ever more central in Western spirituality. The West held that some aspects of sin's penalty could be removed on earth by penance or by an indulgence. If a believer died without paying all the punishment he owed, he had to pay off his outstanding debt by sufferings in the fire of purgatory. However, the pope (according to the Western theory, when fully developed) had the power to release souls from purgatory, because

---

19. In the West, baptism by "affusion" (pouring) began to replace baptism by immersion during the Carolingian Renaissance (see Chapter 2). However, leading Western theologians continued to argue that immersion was better than affusion; this was the view of Peter Lombard, Bonaventura, Thomas Aquinas, and Duns Scotus (for these theologians, see Chapter 7, section 3). The West considered threefold immersion, single immersion, and affusion as all being valid modes of baptism. The East held that threefold immersion was the only valid form of baptism.

God had given the papacy control over the "treasury of merits" of the saints. The pope could transfer these merits to souls in purgatory by means of an indulgence, thus paying off their temporal punishment for them and releasing them. By contrast, the East denied the existence of purgatory, rejected the idea that the righteous were punished after death, and did not believe either in the "treasury of merits" or in indulgences. However, Easterners did accept that true believers, whose Christian lives had fallen seriously short of God's standards, would not be immediately admitted into heaven; they would have to wait in a condition of shadow and sorrow until God had mercy on them. Still, no punishment, no torment, and no purifying fire were involved. All the Church on earth could do was pray humbly and lovingly for these souls, especially at holy communion; but neither the pope nor anyone else on earth had any spiritual power over them – this was the prerogative of Christ alone.[20]

The language barrier contributed to the theological divide. Greek was ideally suited to expressing Christian truth with the concepts, concerns, and precision of *philosophy*. Byzantine theologians therefore tended to approach (for example) the doctrine of the Church and salvation in basically *ontological* terms, as a transforming spiritual union between the natures of God and humanity in the person of Christ the God-Man ("ontological" comes from the Greek word for "being"). By contrast, Latin had an inbuilt atmosphere of "law", inherited from the deep-rooted traditions of the Western Roman Empire. Western theologians therefore tended to see the Church and salvation more in *legal* terms – the Church as an administrative organisation, salvation as the remission of penalty.

Furthermore, in Western thinking, dominated as it was by Augustine's theology, the doctrine of original sin was central. For Western theologians, all human beings were born with the guilt and corruption of Adam's sin resting upon them. Salvation

---

20.   For penance, see Chapter 7, section 3, footnote 15; for indulgences, see Chapter 5, section 5; for the treasury of merits, see Chapter 7, section 3, under the teaching of *Thomas Aquinas*.

was therefore understood as being fundamentally a deliverance from the debt of guilt and the stain of depravity. Death was the consequence of sin; the atoning work of Christ dealt with sin and thereby conquered death. Such views were not unknown in the East, but Easterners generally tended to approach the whole question of salvation from a different standpoint. In Eastern thought, the fundamental problem was perceived as *death* rather than sin. Easterners agreed that the human race had fallen in Adam, but they saw mortality and death, rather than original sin, as the inheritance which Adam transmitted to his offspring. Eastern theology looked upon death as an all-pervading cosmic force, which alienated both the soul and the body of human beings from their true destiny. "Original sin", for Easterners, usually meant the grip that death had on human nature through Adam's sin; they rejected any idea of Adam's guilt being imputed to his descendants. Salvation, accordingly, meant liberation from the objective power of death. Sin was the consequence of death; the atoning work of Christ conquered death and thereby dealt with sin. Given these differing outlooks, it is not surprising that Western piety came to be centred increasingly on the cross of Christ, whereas Eastern piety tended to focus more on His resurrection.

However, the most crucial doctrinal difference between East and West was over the doctrine of the Trinity and the *filioque* clause in the Nicene Creed. As we have seen, the East held that in the inner life of the Trinity, the Holy Spirit proceeds from the Father alone, whereas the West maintained that the Spirit proceeds from Father and Son as a single source. The East also objected profoundly to the way that the West had inserted the *filioque* clause into the Nicene Creed, thus altering the first and greatest of the Church's ecumenical Creeds. The papacy itself had resisted this insertion of the *filioque* into the Creed for centuries, even though it was committed to the doctrine of the *filioque*, but in the early 11th century (no-one is surely exactly when) Rome finally officially inserted the clause into the Creed. As we observed earlier, the East–West divide over the *filioque* clause revealed fundamentally different ways of understanding the

Trinity. The East began with the person of God the Father, and saw Him as the personal source of the divine essence, and thus the personal bond of unity in the Trinity; the West, by contrast, began with the divine essence itself, and saw it as the source of the three divine persons and their common bond of unity.

Political and military events sparked off the final breach between East and West. The Byzantine Emperor, Constantine IX (1042-55), had made an alliance with the Holy Roman Emperor, Henry III (1039-56), and Pope Leo IX (1049-54) against the Normans, who were threatening both Byzantine and papal land in southern Italy. As a result of this alliance, Constantine IX demanded that the patriarch of Constantinople, **Michael Cerularius** (1043-58), acknowledge the superior authority of Rome over Constantinople. Cerularius refused; he was as determined as Photius had been to uphold the ecclesiastical freedom and independence of Constantinople. As the quarrel worsened, in 1052 Cerularius closed down the Latin-speaking churches of Constantinople. Then in 1053 he and Leo of Ochrida, the scholarly metropolitan of Bulgaria, addressed a letter to the pope and all Western Catholics in which they detailed the errors of Western religious practice – the use of unleavened bread in communion, fasting on Saturdays, eating the meat of strangled animals (Acts 15:29), and not singing the Alleluia during the season of Lent. Pope Leo IX replied through Cardinal Humbert of Silva Candida,[21] sending Cerularius a letter setting out all the exalted claims of the papacy in the most uncompromising terms.

The victory of the Normans over Leo IX's army at the battle of Civitate (south-eastern Italy), in which Leo was taken prisoner, brought a temporary halt to the East–West quarrel. The Norman threat to Byzantine land in Italy was now greater than ever, compelling Cerularius to make peaceful overtures to Leo. Pope Leo sent ambassadors to Constantinople, led by Cardinal Humbert. However, the meeting between Cerularius and Humbert was an utter disaster: not so much a fruitful exchange of views, more like the proverbial head-on collision

---

21. For more about Humbert, see Chapter 4, sections 4 and 5.

between the irresistible force and the immovable object. The patriarch and the cardinal were two of the most high-spirited, stubborn, aggressive men who have ever lived in the history of humanity, each completely lacking in any of the graces required for diplomacy.

When news reached Constantinople that Pope Leo had died, Cerularius refused any longer to acknowledge Humbert's right to negotiate. Eventually Humbert lost all patience with Cerularius. Together with the other papal delegates, on July 16th 1054 Humbert marched into Hagia Sophia, and laid on the holy table a document excommunicating Cerularius and all who dared to follow him in his blasphemous criticisms of the most holy faith of the Roman Church. In language of thunder, the document anathematised the Easterners along with all Arians, Manichees, a list of other heretics, and even "the devil and his angels", and ended with a resounding "Amen, amen, amen!" Cerularius responded by anathematising Humbert and the other papal ambassadors.[22]

The West received Humbert's action with approval. Its effect was to break Eastern and Western Christianity apart into two separate Churches (referred to, from this point onwards, as the Western *Catholic* Church and the Eastern *Orthodox* Church[23]). Since both sides believed that there could only be one true Church, this East–West split meant that neither side regarded the other as true Christians any longer. The Holy Spirit dwelt only in the true Church; therefore, in Eastern eyes, the West had cut itself off from all grace and salvation by excommunicating the

---

22. Interestingly, Cerularius did not excommunicate the pope or Westerners in general. It was the West that excommunicated the East. "Anathematising", we recollect, means "banning from the Church"; it comes from the Greek word *anathema*, "given over".

23. The use of "Catholic" to describe the Western Church, and "Orthodox" to describe the Eastern Church, after 1054, is simply a customary way of speaking that has developed over the years. In reality, of course, the Eastern Church still claimed to be Catholic (in the sense of "universal" – the universal Church), and the Western Church still claimed to be Orthodox (in the sense of "believing correctly").

Easterners, and in Western eyes the East had been cut off from grace by Humbert acting in the pope's name.[24]

It took some time for the consequences of 1054 to become clear in the practical relations between all Easterners and Westerners at the local level. It was the Crusades, and the outrages committed by the Western Crusaders against Eastern Christians, which made the great schism into a burning grass-roots reality. (For the Crusades see Chapter 5.) The excommunications and anathemas between Rome and Constantinople were officially lifted by Pope Paul VI and Patriarch Athenagoras in 1965 – both Paul and Athenagoras were committed to the ecumenical movement. But the two Churches have still (as yet) not reunited.

Important people:

The Church

Leontius of Neapolis (died 650)

Germanus of Constantinople (born 634; patriarch 715-30; died 733)

Andrew of Crete (660-740)

Cosmas the Melodist (died 760)

Stephen of Saint Auxentius (died 767)

Theophanes the Branded (died 820)

Theodore of Studium (759-826)

Pope Nicholas I (858-67)

Cyril of Thessalonica (died 869)

Ignatius of Constantinople (843-58, 869-77)

Methodius (died 885)

Leo the Mathematician (born 790, died some time after 869)

Photius the Great (born 820; patriarch of
    Constantinople 858-69, 877-86; died 895)

---

24.   Theologically, neither the Eastern Orthodox nor the Western Catholics would have admitted that the other side was a "Church" at all, after the schism. They held that there could be only one Church, the one Body of Christ. By separating from the one Church, Westerners (according to the East) and Easterners (according to the West) had ceased to be part of the Church at all; they were now simply a deviant religious organisation which wrongly claimed the name of "Church".

Cosmas (active 970s)

Nikon the Penitent (930-1000)

Nilus of Calabria (died 1005)

Athanasius of Trebizond (920-1003)

Simeon the New Theologian (949-1022)

Michael Cerularius (patriarch of Constantinople, 1043-58; died 1059)

Political and military

Emperor Leo the Isaurian (717-41)

Emperor Constantine V (741-75)

Empress Irene (780-802)

Emperor Theophilus (829-42)

Empress Theodora (842-56)

Emperor Basil I (867-86)

Tsar Boris of Bulgaria (852-88)

Tsar Simeon of Bulgaria (893-927)

Emperor Basil II (976-1025)

Others

Constantine (founder of the Paulicians: mid-7th century)

Bogomil (active 927-50)

In defence of icons

"You cannot see My form," Scripture says (Exod. 33:20, Deut. 4:12). What wisdom the Lawgiver displays! How can anyone depict the Invisible? How can anyone picture the Inconceivable? How can anyone draw what is without limits, beyond measure, infinite? How can anyone give a form to the Formless? How can anyone paint Him who has no body? How can anyone depict a Mystery? But clearly, when you look at God becoming man, you can then depict Him clothed in human form. When the Invisible One becomes visible to our flesh, you may then draw His likeness. In His divine nature the Logos is without body and form, beyond measure and boundless, existing in the form of God; but when He empties Himself and takes the form of a servant, and is found in a body of flesh in substance and stature, you may then draw His image and show it to anyone who is willing to look at it. Yes, depict His wonderful stooping down, His birth from the Virgin, His baptism in the Jordan, His transfiguration on Mount Tabor, His sufferings which have liberated us from our sinful passions, His death, and His miracles which are the sign of His divine nature, since He worked them in the flesh through divine power. Make icons of His saving cross, His tomb, His resurrection, His ascension into heaven. Use every sort of drawing, word, colour ...

In previous times God who is without form or body could never be depicted. But now, when God is seen in the flesh conversing with human beings, I make an image of the Creator whom I see. I do not worship physical matter; I worship the Creator of matter who became matter for my sake, who willed to make His dwelling-place in matter, who worked out my salvation through matter. I will never cease honouring the matter which brought about my salvation! I honour matter – but not as if it were God ... Through matter my salvation has come to me. Was not the thrice-happy and thrice-blessed wood of the cross made of matter? The holy and exalted hill of Calvary – was it not matter? The life-bearing cave, the holy and life-giving tomb, that fountain of our resurrection – was it not matter? The ink in the holy pages of the Gospel Scriptures – is it not matter? The life-giving holy table of the Lord, from which we receive the bread of life – is it not made of matter? Gold and silver are matter, and from them we make crosses, patens[25] and chalices. And over and above all this, the body and blood of our Lord are matter! ... Do not despise matter; it is not despicable. God has not made anything despicable. To think such a thing is Manichaeism. The only thing that is despicable is what does not have its source in God – our own invention, our own wilful choice to disobey God's law – that is, sin.

John of Damascus
***Concerning the Divine Images*, Book I, chapters 8 and 16**

---

25.   A paten is a plate which covers the top of a communion cup, or on which communion bread is served.

The decree of the Second Council of Nicaea (held in 787) on icons

To make our confession of faith short, we keep all the Church traditions handed down to us without changing them, whether they are handed down in writing or speech. One of these traditions is the making of pictures which represent things described in the Gospel history. This tradition is useful in many ways, but especially because it depicts the incarnation of the Logos of God as something real and not merely imaginary ...

We, therefore, following the royal pathway and divinely in-spired authority of our holy fathers and the traditions of the Catholic Church (for the Holy Spirit dwells in her, as we all know), define with all certainty and accuracy as follows: just as the form of the precious life-giving cross should be set forth in paintings and mosaics and other suitable materials in the sacred churches of God, and on vestments and on hanging cloths and in pictures, both in houses and by the wayside, so also should the venerable and holy icons be set forth in the same way – that is, the form of our Lord God and Saviour Jesus Christ, of our pure lady the Theotokos [Mary], of the honourable angels, and of all saints and all godly people. For as often as we see these in artistic representations, they lift up our minds to the memory of those who are depicted, so that our desires are kindled towards them. We ought to give proper greeting and honourable rever-ence (*proskunesis*) to the icons. We must not, indeed, give icons the true worship (*latreia*) of faith which belongs to the divine nature alone. But we may offer incense and lights before icons, as also before the form of the precious life-giving cross, according to the ancient and godly custom. For the honour we pay to the icon passes on to what the icon represents; he who reveres the icon reveres the person represented by the icon.

The Eastern Liturgy: From Andrew of Crete's Great Canon for Lent

My God is my help and protector, and I will declare His glory. He is my father's God, and I will exalt His majesty; for He has made His glory triumphant. Be merciful to me, O God, be merciful to me!

Where shall I begin as I mourn the deeds of my poverty-stricken life? O Christ, what first-fruits shall I offer in my weeping now? But as You are gracious, grant me the forgiveness of my sins. Be merciful to me, O God, be merciful to me!

Come, poverty-stricken soul, together with your flesh, confess to the Creator of all. From now on, abandon the folly of your past life and bring tears of repentance to God. Be merciful to me, O God, be merciful to me!

I have rivalled the first-created man, Adam, in transgression; I knew that I was deprived of God, of His eternal kingdom and His delight, because of my sins. Be merciful to me, O God, be merciful to me!

Alas for my poverty-stricken soul! You are like the first Eve! You saw evil, and were desperately wounded; you touched the tree, and recklessly tasted the food of folly. Be merciful to me, O God, be merciful to me!

Instead of a fleshly Eve, I have an Eve in my mind, in thoughts of sensual passion, which seem so sweet but always turn to bitterness when swallowed. Be merciful to me, O God, be merciful to me!

Adam was righteously exiled from Eden for not keeping one single command of Yours, O Saviour. What then will I suffer, when I constantly thrust away Your words of life? Be merciful to me, O God, be merciful to me!

By my own deliberate choice I have walked in the footsteps of the murderer Cain, giving life to my sinful flesh and murdering my soul and its conscience, warring against it by evil deeds. Be merciful to me, O God, be merciful to me!

O Jesus, I have not been like Abel in righteousness; I have never brought You suitable gifts, godly deeds, pure offerings, or an unblemished life. Be merciful to me, O God, be merciful to me!

O my poverty-stricken soul, we are like Cain; to the Creator of all, we have together offered defiled deeds, a polluted sacrifice, a worthless life. For this we are condemned. Be merciful to me, O God, be merciful to me!

As the potter shapes the clay, You fashioned me, forming me with flesh and bones, breath and life. Now, O my Creator, Redeemer and Judge, accept me as I come repentant. Be merciful to me, O God, be merciful to me!

O Saviour, I openly confess to You the sins I have committed, the wounds of my soul and body, inflicted on me by murderous and criminal thoughts within. Be merciful to me, O God, be merciful to me!

Even though I have sinned, O Saviour, I know that You are the Lover of humankind. Your chastening is merciful, Your compassion is zealous. You see the tears, and run like the father to meet the prodigal son. Be merciful to me, O God, be merciful to me!

Andrew of Crete
part of the First Ode of his Great Canon for Lent

The Eastern Liturgy: Christmas joy

Christ is born! Tell forth His fame!
Christ from heaven! His love proclaim!
Christ on earth! Exalt His name!
Sing to the Lord, O world, with exultation!
Break forth with glad thanksgiving, every nation!
    For He has triumphed gloriously!

Man in God's own likeness made,
Man by Satan's lies betrayed,
Man by sting of death dismayed,
Banished from hope of life and of salvation,
By Christ today is made a new creation:
    For He has triumphed gloriously!

God the Maker, when His foe
Dragged us down to death and woe,
Bowed the heavens and came below,
And in the Virgin's womb His palace making

Became true man, our human nature taking:
    For He has triumphed gloriously!

    Christ the Wisdom, Word and Might,
    God and Son and Light of light,
    Concealed in Mary from the sight
Of worldly monarch and demonic spirit,
Was born on earth, that we might heaven inherit:
    And He has triumphed gloriously!

Cosmas the Melodist
Canon for Christmas Day

The Eastern Liturgy: The Day of Judgment

The Lord draws near, the righteous royal Assessor,
The just to save, to punish the transgressor:
    We weep, we mourn, we pray,
    Considering that Day
When all the secrets of all hearts must be
Made clear in blaze of bright eternity!

O'er Sinai's Mount, with darkest clouds assembling,
Moses saw God's eternal glory, trembling:
    Yet he could only see
    God's feebler majesty.
And I – I must behold His fullest face:
O spare me, Lord! Embrace me in Your grace!

David of old beheld in speechless terror
The session of the Judge, the doom of error:
    And what have I to plead
    For mercy in my need?
Nothing but this: O Saviour, make me true
Before that Day – convert my soul to You!

Here, fires of deep damnation roar and glitter,
The worm is deathless, and the cup is bitter;
    There, morn that has no morrow,

Pure joy that has no sorrow,
And those so favoured, they defy the abyss,
Raised up to God's right hand and unknown bliss!

My soul with many an act of sin is wounded,
With mortal weakness is my flesh surrounded;
   My life is nearly o'er –
   The Judge stands at the door!
Poor sinner, what will be your destiny
When Christ summons your soul its end to see?

Theodore the Studite

Canon for Apocreos, Ode Nine

The Spirit of the Father

[Photius tackles the Western argument that the Son's equality with the Father demands that the Spirit must proceed from the Son as well as from the Father]: You should consider this – if the Father and the Son both cause the Spirit to proceed from Them, why do the Father and the Spirit not both beget the Son for the same reasons? ...

[Photius tackles the Western argument that the phrase "Spirit of the Son" (Gal. 4:6) proves that the Spirit proceeds eternally from the Son]: John the Baptist, in whom godliness was constantly visible and shining, first gathered the believers out of the multitude, and then initiated them into the primary mysteries of grace, teaching holy doctrine. For he saw that the more-than-human Man, the Fountain of life and immortality, the Master and Creator of all, did not fall short of any righteousness. He saw the Master being baptised in the world-cleansing waters of the Jordan. Seeing the heavens opened, John testified with wonder and amazement; he saw the all-Holy Spirit descending in the form of a dove. And so the faithful prophet of the Word cried out, "I saw the Spirit descending as a dove and abiding on Him" (John 1:32). The Spirit, descending from the Father, abides on the Son and in the Son (if you will accept this latter phrase) ... The prophet Isaiah, expounding almost equal truths, says of Christ's person, "The Spirit of the Lord is upon Me, because He has anointed Me"

(Isa. 61:1). Now, having already heard that the famous Gregory and Zacharias[26] said, "The Spirit abides in the Son," (for perhaps your lack of shame has melted into fear), why do you not in this respect instantly think of Paul's statement, "the Spirit of the Son"? … Is this not the correct meaning of the statement "the Spirit of the Son"? I am convinced that the reason why Scripture says the Spirit is "of the Son" is perfectly certain – and Scripture does not say it for the reasons *you* say it in your contentious misdeed [of altering the Nicene Creed]. Scripture says "Spirit of the Son" because the Spirit is "in the Son". Which statement gives the meaning closest to the apostolic statement: "The Spirit *abides in* the Son," or "The Spirit *proceeds from* the Son"? …

[Photius now tackles the Western argument that the phrase "Spirit of Christ" (Rom. 8:9) proves that the Spirit belongs to Christ as much as to the Father, and therefore proceeds eternally from the Son]: Scripture says "the Spirit of Christ" because the Spirit anoints Christ. For the Truth says, "The Spirit of the Lord is upon Me, because He has anointed Me" (Isa. 61:1). The Spirit anointed Christ – but in what way? Did the Spirit anoint the Logos in His humanity, according to the flesh and blood He took when He became man? Or did the Spirit anoint Christ in His eternally existing deity? If you say the latter, I reckon you have said something utterly rash and insolent. The Spirit did not anoint the Son as God. He anointed Christ as Man. Accordingly, since the Spirit anoints Christ, He is called "the Spirit of Christ". But you say that this Scriptural title, "the Spirit of Christ", means that the Spirit proceeds from Christ. If so, it would mean that the Spirit proceeds from Christ, not according to His deity, but according to His humanity. And therefore, the Spirit does not proceed before time began, but started to proceed at the time when the Son took humanity upon Himself!

Photius

Treatise on the Mystagogia of the Holy Spirit, **Chapters 9, 84 and 91**

---

26.   Gregory is Pope Gregory the Great (590-604), for whom see Volume 1, Chapter 11, sections 2 and 3. Zacharias is Pope Zacharias (741-52), for whom see Chapter 2, section 1.

The glory of Jesus

Desiring to save the world, O Dayspring of the East, You came to the dark West of our nature, and humbled Yourself even unto death. Therefore Your name is exalted above every name, and from all created beings of heaven and earth You hear "Alleluia!"

O Christ, father of the age to come, make Your holy angels a rampart for us, and cleanse us from every stain, as You cleansed the ten lepers; heal us, as You healed the covetous soul of Zacchaeus the tax-collector, that we may cry to You with contrition and say –

O Jesus, never-failing Treasure,
O Jesus, everlasting Wealth,
O Jesus, true and essential Food,
O Jesus, inexhaustible Drink,
O Jesus, Clothing of the poor,
O Jesus, Defender of widows,
O Jesus, Protector of orphans,
O Jesus, Champion of those in troubles,
O Jesus, Companion of pilgrims,
O Jesus, Pilot of voyagers,
O Jesus, Peaceful Haven of the storm-tossed,
O Jesus, raise me from my fallenness;
O Jesus, Son of God, have mercy on me!

In my unworthiness I offer You a contrite hymn; like the Canaanite woman I cry to You, "O Jesus, have mercy on me!" For I do not have a daughter possessed, but my flesh is violently possessed by passions and disturbed with anger. Grant me healing as I cry aloud to you, "Alleluia!"

Paul once persecuted You, O brilliant Beacon-Light shining on those in the darkness of ignorance; but then, illuminated by Your light and perceiving the power of Your divinely wise voice, the fury of his soul was quenched. In the same way, give light to the darkened eyes of my soul as I cry such things as these –

O Jesus, my supremely powerful King,
O Jesus, my all-powerful God,
O Jesus, my immortal Lord,
O Jesus, my most glorious Creator,

O Jesus, my supremely good Guide,
O Jesus, my most loving Shepherd,
O Jesus, my Master so rich in mercy,
O Jesus, my Saviour, Friend of Humankind:
O Jesus, enlighten my passion-darkened senses,
O Jesus, heal my sin-wounded body,
O Jesus, cleanse my mind of empty thoughts,
O Jesus, guard my heart from sinful desires;
O Jesus, Son of God, have mercy on me!

Grant me Your grace, Jesus, You who forgive all debts, and receive my repentant soul, as You received Peter who denied You. Call my downcast soul to Yourself, as You long ago called Paul who persecuted You. Hear me as I cry to You, "Alleluia!"

While singing the glory of Your incarnation, we all praise You, and together with Thomas we believe that You are our Lord and our God, You who sit with the Father, and will come again to judge the living and the dead. O grant that on that day I may stand at Your right hand, I who now cry out to You –

O Jesus, King of peace, bestow Your peace on me.
O Jesus, sweet-scented Flower, make me fragrant.
O Jesus, longed-for Warmth, warm me.
O Jesus, eternal Temple, shelter me.
O Jesus, majestic Garment, clothe me.
O Jesus, Pearl of great price, make me rich.
O Jesus, precious Gem, enlighten me.
O Jesus, Sun of righteousness, shine on me.
O Jesus, holy Light, make me radiant.
O Jesus, deliver me from weakness of soul and body.
O Jesus, rescue me from the hands of the Enemy.
O Jesus, save me from the eternal torments of hell.
O Jesus, Son of God, have mercy on me!

From the *Akathist Hymn to Our Sweetest Lord Jesus Christ,*
Letters sigma, tau, upsilon, phi, chi, and psi (authorship uncertain;
written between the 9th and 11th centuries)

Eastern devotion to the Blessed Virgin: The mystery of Mary

When the angel learned the secret command,
He hastened and stood before Joseph's dwelling
And spoke to the Maiden who knew not wedlock:
"The One who has bowed the heavens by His descent
Is held and contained, without change, completely in you.
Seeing Him receive the form of a Servant in your womb,
I stand in awe and cry out to you:
     Rejoice, O Bride unwedded!"

An angel, the chief of angels, was sent from heaven
To cry, "Rejoice!" to the Mother of God.
And beholding You, O Lord, taking bodily form,
He stood in awe, and with his angelic voice
He cried aloud to Mary such things as these:
"Rejoice, you through whom joy shall shine forth;
Rejoice, you through whom the curse shall be cancelled.
Rejoice, O restoration of fallen Adam;
Rejoice, O redemption of the sorrows of Eve.
Rejoice, O height hard for human thought to ascend;
Rejoice, O depth difficult for the eyes of angels to explore.
Rejoice, for you are the Throne of the King;
Rejoice, for you bear Him who bears all.
Rejoice, O star that makes the Sun appear;
Rejoice, O womb of the divine incarnation.
Rejoice, you through whom creation is renewed;
Rejoice, you through whom the Creator becomes a babe.
     Rejoice, O Bride unwedded!"

Beholding herself in chastity,
The holy maid spoke boldly to Gabriel:
"Your strange words seem hard for my soul to receive.
How can you speak of a seedless conception?"
Crying aloud, Alleluia!

Seeking to know knowledge unknown,
The Virgin cried to him who ministered to her:
"How can a Son be born from a chaste womb?
O tell me!" Then he spoke to her in awe, crying aloud:
"Rejoice, you who are initiated into God's ineffable plan;
Rejoice, you who have faith in what demands silence.
Rejoice, O prelude to the miracles of Messiah;
Rejoice, O pinnacle of His teachings.
Rejoice, O heavenly ladder, by which God came down;
Rejoice, O bridge, leading earth's people to heaven.
Rejoice, O far-famed marvel of the angels;
Rejoice, O much-wept wounding of the demons.
Rejoice, you who ineffably give birth to the Light;
Rejoice, you who reveal the mystery to none.
Rejoice, you who soar beyond the knowledge of the wise;
Rejoice, you who enlighten the minds of the faithful.
    Rejoice, O Bride unwedded!"

The Power of the Highest then overshadowed
Her who knew not wedlock, that she might conceive,
Manifesting her fruitful womb as a sweet meadow
To all who wish to reap salvation,
While chanting, Alleluia!

Carrying God in her womb, the Virgin hastened
To Elizabeth, whose unborn babe immediately perceived
Her greeting and rejoiced, leaping as though with songs,
And cried out to the Theotokos:
"Rejoice, vine that bears the unfading Bloom;
Rejoice, land that yields the untainted Fruit.
Rejoice, you who tend the man-befriending Farmer;
Rejoice, you from whom blossoms forth the Sower of our
    Life.
Rejoice, O field bearing a wealth of compassions;
Rejoice, O table loaded with an abundance of mercies.
Rejoice, for you revive the garden of delight;
Rejoice, for you prepare a Refuge for souls.

Rejoice, O acceptable incense of intercession;
Rejoice, oblation for the whole world.
Rejoice, O favour of God to mortals;
Rejoice, O access of mortals to God.
    Rejoice, O Bride unwedded!"

Experiencing a storm of doubting thoughts within,
The chaste Joseph was troubled;
For he suspected an unchaste union,
As he beheld you unwed, O blameless one.
But when he learned of your conception through the Holy
    Spirit,
He cried, Alleluia!

The Creator showed a new creation to us His creatures
When He sprang forth from the seedless womb;
And the womb which had never been defiled
He preserved undefiled, so that we who behold this marvel
May praise Mary as we cry out:
"Rejoice, flower of perfect purity;
Rejoice, crown of chastity.
Rejoice, you who shine forth the image of the Resurrection;
Rejoice, you who show forth the Life of the angels.
Rejoice, tree of good Fruit which nourishes the faithful;
Rejoice, wood of leafy branches, where many are sheltered.
Rejoice, you who bear the Guide of those going astray;
Rejoice, you who give birth to the Redeemer of captives.
Rejoice, you who supplicate the Righteous Judge;
Rejoice, you through whom many transgressors receive
    forgiveness.
Rejoice, robe of confidence for the naked;
Rejoice, tenderness that vanquishes all desire.
    Rejoice, O Bride unwedded!"

Seeing a strange Child-birth,
Let us estrange ourselves from the world
By lifting our minds to heaven.

For this is why the Most High God
Was manifest on earth as a lowly Man,
That He might lift to the heights those who cry to Him,
Alleluia!

Completely present with those below
Was the Word which cannot be contained,
Yet in no way was He absent from those above.
For this was a divine condescension,
Not a mere change of place;
And His birth was from a Virgin chosen by God
Who heard such words as these:
"Rejoice, enclosure of the uncontained God;
Rejoice, gateway of the solemn Mystery.
Rejoice, doubtful rumour of the faithless;
Rejoice, undoubted boast of the faithful.
Rejoice, all-holy chariot of Him who rides on the Cherubim;
Rejoice, sweetest dwelling-place of Him who sits on the
   Seraphim.
Rejoice, you who make differing things agree;
Rejoice, you who unite Motherhood and Virginity.
Rejoice, you through whom transgression is annulled;
Rejoice, you through whom paradise is opened.
Rejoice, O key of the Kingdom of Messiah;
Rejoice, O hope of blessings everlasting.
   Rejoice, O Bride unwedded!"

From the *Akathist Hymn to the most holy Theotokos*
(authorship uncertain; its roots are probably in the 6th century)

The Saviour came so that the Spirit might come

The Logos did not shun the universe, but chose to go down into
the most pure womb of the ever-Virgin Mary, to be born, and to
be nourished with milk. He willed to grow, to become a mature
man, to thirst, to hunger, to be crushed with labours, and to pour
out sweat. He submitted Himself to the envy which the Jews felt
on account of His miracles, which revealed and proved His divine
nature. He was voluntarily impaled with thieves on the cross, as

if He were an evildoer, died a shameful death by His own will, was buried, rose again, and ascended into heaven – all so that He could send down upon believers the Holy Spirit who proceeds from the Father. And indeed, Christ did send the Spirit! For this was the entire goal and purpose of Christ's incarnation: that the Holy Spirit might enter into the souls of those who believe in Christ – those who confess Him as the God-Man, a single Christ in two natures, divine and human, without division and without confusion. God's purpose in Christ's taking human nature was that this Holy Spirit might become "the soul of the souls" of believers, if I may express it that way. This is the reason why we are called Christians ("anointed ones"), and we are reshaped, recreated, renewed, and sanctified (to a degree) by this Holy Spirit, in our mind, in our conscience, and in all our senses. Those who have received the Spirit in this way should no longer have any corrupt life in themselves, which could set their souls on fire with an inclination and longing for fleshly pleasures and worldly lusts...

And so it is absolutely necessary for everyone to engage in all possible efforts to receive from above, from Christ our God, this joy and this glory – that is, the grace of the Holy Spirit, in order to have the power to sin no more. For what someone does by free-will, he can also destroy by free-will; but free-will cannot destroy what comes from our very nature. If we have now become corrupt and mortal in our very nature, free-will alone cannot make us incorruptible or immortal. From the time of Adam's banishment from paradise, when we became corruptible and mortal through sin, right up until the present day, not a single human being has ever been free from corruption or death. So if we are ever to regain the original state in which God created us, to become free from corruption, no human free-will whatsoever can raise us up to this state. Only the power of God can do this, received by human beings through union with the divine nature.

Simeon the New Theologian
The First-Created Man, Homily 38

4
The Cluniac Revival, Hildebrand, and the Investiture Controversy

1. The conversion of the Norsemen and Central Europe

The war and devastation which the Pagan Norsemen of Scandinavia brought upon Western Europe in the 9th and 10th centuries almost destroyed Christian civilisation. The Norse warriors showed no respect for religion – burning churches and monasteries, slaughtering priests and monks, raping nuns. To their victims, it seemed impossible that these savage killers could ever embrace the Christian faith. But the impossible happened.

It began in England. The Norsemen of Denmark (the Danes) conquered and colonised much of the north-eastern half of the country, and then pushed south to try to take over the rest of England. England at that time was divided into a number of separate Anglo-Saxon kingdoms, which fell one by one to the Danish invaders. However, the English people of the southern kingdom of Wessex fought back under their outstanding young Christian king, *Alfred the Great* (born 849; reigned 871-99). Alfred finally crushed the Danish army decisively in 878 at the battle of Edington (in Wiltshire, south-western England), and forced the Danes to accept a peaceful division of the land. One of Alfred's terms of peace was that the Danish king, Guthrum (died 890), and his court, should be baptised; Alfred hoped this would discourage the Pagan Danes from persecuting the Christian English in the Danish half of the island. So the Danes in England submitted to the Christian faith, and under Alfred's grandson, king Athelstan (925-39), they became part of a politically and spiritually united Christian England.

From his own lifetime to the present day, many people have admired King Alfred for the noble quality of his mind and spirit; he is the only English king who has ever received the title "the Great". His mighty contribution to the development of English Christian culture also earned him the title of the "Charlemagne of England".[1] In fact, far more than Charlemagne, Alfred came to symbolise the ideal of Christian kingship among the English-speaking peoples; for although Alfred ruled over a much smaller domain than Charlemagne, and made no impact on the culture of mainland Europe, the English king's virtuous moral character was unblemished by the sexual impurity that spoiled that of the first Holy Roman Emperor.

Alfred saw it as his God-given destiny to create a flourishing Christian civilisation in his kingdom of Wessex. Acting as a "sacred king", he consecrated his royal power to the supreme mission of organising Church affairs, raising moral and academic standards among the clergy, and promoting the religious knowledge of the English people. He gave away half his income to the building and maintenance of churches and schools. He personally translated into English a number of the great Latin works of theology, spirituality, and philosophy – Augustine of Hippo's *Soliloquies*, Boethius's *Consolation of Philosophy*, Gregory the Great's *Pastoral Care*, as well as the first 50 Psalms.[2] In carrying out this task, Alfred relied on the advice of an international team of scholars whom he gathered from Britain, Ireland, and France; his favourite and constant companion was a learned Welsh priest-monk, Asser, who wrote a biography of Alfred and taught the king to read Latin so that he could translate Augustine, Boethius, and Gregory into English.

---

1. For Charlemagne, see Chapter 2, section 2.

2. For Augustine, see Volume One, Chapter 9, section 3; for Boethius, see Volume One, Chapter 11, section 1; for Gregory the Great, see Volume One, Chapter 11, section 2.

In his private life Alfred was a devout, humble, prayerful Christian. He knew the liturgy and many of the Psalms by heart, and swore an oath to divide his time equally between the political affairs of his kingdom and the spiritual affairs of his faith. A mysterious lifelong illness, which often left him in agony for lengthy periods, softened his naturally warlike spirit into something more generous and gentle. Soon after Alfred's death, an Anglo-Saxon historian described him like this:

> Alfred, immovable pillar of the people of Wessex, a man filled with justice, energetic in the conduct of war, prudent in speech, and – above all else – learned in holy writings; for he translated innumerable books from Latin into the English tongue, with such variety and ability, that not just scholars but anyone who wished could understand what they meant. O Christ the Redeemer, save his soul!

King Alfred was the real founder of the English nation. The Anglo-Saxon kingdoms of England had never come together politically before the Norse invasions; Alfred united half the island around his own kingdom of Wessex, paving the way for the complete unification of England under his grandson Athelstan. Alfred also founded the English navy, created a new and stronger English army, built fortified towns and cities which could withstand Danish attacks, and initiated the official recording of English history through the *Anglo-Saxon Chronicles*. So Alfred's Wessex became the spiritual heart of that new Christian England which was eventually to have such a profound influence on the world from the days of John Wyclif onward.[3]

In France, too, the Norsemen (or "Normans" as the French called them) accepted Christianity. After the Normans had conquered the northern French coast, the French king, Charles the Simple (898-923), made a peace treaty in 911 with the Norman leader, Rollo. The treaty made Rollo's land into the French duchy of "Normandy" ("land of the Normans"), owing allegiance in theory to France's king. Part of the treaty involved Rollo and the

---

3. For John Wyclif, see Chapter 10, section 4.

Normans embracing the Christian faith. In the mid-11th century, a band of French Norman warriors brought southern Italy under their control, snatching it from the Byzantine Empire, and then conquered Sicily too, seizing it from the Muslims. These events transformed the Normans into the militant champions of the Western Catholic Church against Islam and Eastern Orthodoxy. In 1066 they invaded and conquered England, and Duke William of Normandy became King William I of England ("William the Conqueror", 1066-87).[4]

The conversion of the Norse kingdoms of Denmark, Sweden, Norway, Iceland, and Finland followed. Western European missionaries had been at work in Denmark, Sweden, and Norway since the early 800s. However, it was the revival of Germany as a great Christian power in the 10th century which made the Norse kings take Christianity seriously (see section 2).

Denmark. In 972, King Harald Bluetooth (died 986) of Denmark and his entire army accepted Christian baptism. There was a Pagan reaction under king Sweyn (986-1014), but Sweyn's son Canute (1019-35) was a strong Christian, and Denmark became a fully Christian kingdom in Canute's reign. Canute was king of England as well as Denmark, and made good use of English monks and priests in evangelising and Christianising his Danish kingdom.

Norway. King Olaf Tryggvason (995-1000) made Christianity into Norway's national faith. Tryggvason was a typical Norse

---

4. The Norman Conquest of England brought the English Church into much closer relations with Rome and the papacy. When William invaded England, he had the blessing of Pope Alexander II (1061-73). This was because the English archbishop of Canterbury, Stigand (died 1072), had shown favour to a rival of Alexander II for the papal throne (this rival set himself up as "Pope Honorius II" between 1061 and 1064). On top of this, William of Normandy was a close ally of the reforming party which then controlled the papacy (see sections 4 and 5). This reform party thought that the English Church fell disgracefully short of their reforming ideals, especially in the matter of the celibacy of the clergy. Before William conquered England, most English priests were lawfully married men; after the Norman Conquest, William and his Norman bishops gradually enforced celibacy on all English clergymen.

warrior, who spent his five years as king of Norway using rough Norse methods to persuade his aristocracy to accept the new faith – be baptised or die! There was a Pagan reaction after Tryggvason's death, but King Olaf Haraldsson (1015-28) effectively made Norway a Christian kingdom.

Sweden. Sweden became officially Christian under King Olaf Skotkonung (994-1024). Christianity prospered, however, only in the south-west of Sweden; elsewhere, most people continued to practise Paganism. It was only in the reign of King Sverker (1130-55) that the Christian faith really put down roots throughout the land. Sverker was determined to Christianise his country; the spearhead of his Christianising campaign were monks from the recently founded Cistercian order in France, whom Sverker summoned to his aid.[5] The success of the campaign was shown when the city of Uppsala, previously the stronghold of Paganism, yielded to Christianity and became the new centre of the Swedish Church; Sweden's first archbishop, Stephen (a Cistercian monk), was consecrated in Uppsala in 1164.

Iceland. From the 870s the Norsemen settled this northern island just below the Arctic Circle, where they developed one of the most cultured and democratic societies in the Western world. Iceland received the Christian faith through missionaries sent by King Olaf Tryggvason of Norway. The response of the Icelanders to the preaching of the Norwegian evangelists was to divide into a Christian and a Pagan party; a religious civil war seemed to be on the horizon. However, the democratic traditions of Icelandic culture prevailed, and the nation agreed to submit the great religious question to one of their wisest men. After a long period of meditation, the sage finally reported back that the new faith in Christ was better than the old Paganism. This decision was accepted by all, and the Icelandic parliament made Christianity the national religion in the year 1000.

---

5. For the Cistercians, see Chapter 5, section 3, under the heading *Bernard of Clairvaux and the Second Crusade.*

We may ask why, in democratic Iceland, the two religions could not live together peacefully, and why the Icelanders felt they must all embrace either the one faith or the other. The answer is that no-one in the Middle Ages could imagine a society with two or more religions. People saw religion as the "glue" that held society together. Therefore each society – even a democratic one – could have only one faith. Democracy did not guarantee religious toleration; it only ensured that a society would make a democratic decision about which faith the whole society would practise.

Finland. The beginnings of the Church in Finland are obscure. Sweden and Russia played a part in introducing Christianity, both in its Western Catholic and Eastern Orthodox forms. Missionaries were at work in the 1100s, and in 1220 an English missionary called Thomas, bishop of Rantemakia, officially organised a Finnish Catholic Church. At the same time that the Swedish monarchy established its sovereignty over Finland, Western Catholicism triumphed over Eastern Orthodoxy as the official Finnish faith in 1249 (although there is even today a large Orthodox minority in Finland).

At the same time that the Norsemen were embracing Christianity, other tribal peoples in Central Europe were also abandoning Paganism for the Christian faith in its Western form. Chief among these were the Magyars, the Bohemians, the Poles, and the Croats.

The Magyars. These were an Asiatic people who migrated into central Europe under their warrior-leader Arpad (896-907). In a series of campaigns between 899 and 955, they brought far greater bloodshed and destruction into Germany and surrounding areas than the Norsemen ever did. Decisively crushed, however, by the German Emperor Otto the Great (see next section) at the battle of Augsburg in 955, the Magyars settled down to create the kingdom of Hungary. Their leader Geza (972-97) accepted Christian baptism, established a strong monarchy, and used royal power to advance the Church and the Christian faith throughout his dominion, a process completed by his successor, King Stephen I (997-1038).

The Bohemians (or Czechs) were a Slavic people, strongly influenced by Western Christianity from the 850s onwards. The Christian faith first became a powerful force among them under King Wenceslas,[6] but he was murdered by his Pagan brother Boleslav in 929. Boleslav's son, however, King Boleslav II (967-99), was a committed Christian who successfully promoted the interests of the Church throughout Bohemia.

The Poles were another Slavic people who from the 7th century had occupied north-eastern Europe, between Germany and Russia. In 966, the Polish ruler, Duke Miezko I (960-92), was baptised into the Christian faith by Western missionaries; the main Christian influence on him seems to have been his Bohemian wife, Dobrawa, the sister of King Boleslav II of Bohemia. Miezko entered into close diplomatic relations with the German Emperor Otto III (983-1002), and placed Poland under the special protection of the pope.

The Croats were also Slavs, neighbours of the Serbs.[7] United by race and language, the two groups became divided by religion: the Serbs embraced Eastern Christianity, while the Croats turned West towards the papacy. The decisive moment for the Croats came in the reign of King Demetrius Zvonomir (1074-89), who liberated his people from the Byzantine Empire; Pope Gregory VII (Hildebrand – see section 5) crowned Demetrius king of Croatia in 1076.

2. The German Empire

After the collapse of the Holy Roman Empire and the Norse invasions, the revival of a strong Christian society in Western Europe sprang from a partnership between the monasteries, which had

---

6.   This is the "good king Wenceslas" of the traditional Christmas carol.

7.   For the Serbs, see Chapter 3, section 7.

preserved the culture of the Carolingian Renaissance, and the Western monarchies. The most important of these monarchies was in Germany. By 900, Charlemagne's Empire in Germany had almost broken up into six tribal states – Saxony, Thuringia, Franconia, Lorraine, Swabia, and Bavaria. However, the invading Magyar peoples from Asia forced a fresh unity on Germany. To protect themselves, the Germans banded together under a new king, Henry I (919-36), who inflicted on the Magyars their first great defeat at the battle of Riade (in Thuringia) in 933. Henry's son, **Otto the Great** (936-73), revived the Carolingian ideal of the Holy Roman Empire, fighting successful wars against Magyars, Norsemen, and Slavs, and making Germany into a great national power. Like Charlemagne, Otto also invaded Italy to rescue the lands of the papacy from Lombard aggression. As a reward, Pope John XII (955-64) crowned Otto as Holy Roman Emperor in Rome in 962.

One of Otto's most effective instruments in rebuilding the Holy Roman Empire was the German Church. Otto saw himself as the spiritual as well as political head of the Empire – the "sacred kingship" ideal of Charlemagne – and he made great use of bishops in his government, setting them in positions of power as secular lords (counts, dukes, princes). There were two reasons why Otto did this. First, bishops had received a good education in the monasteries, unlike most laypeople, so they could act as intelligent servants of royal policy, reading written instructions and sending back written reports. Second, bishops were celibate – they had no children (or no legitimate children). When a bishop died, he had no son to inherit the land over which Otto had set him; Otto could therefore appoint a man of his own choice as the new count, duke, or prince. This practice went hand-in-hand with Otto choosing who would be bishop (not just choosing a bishop to be a duke, but choosing the man who would be the bishop).

This control of the clergy by the secular authorities was a widespread development all over Western Christendom. It was a consequence of a new social system whose seeds had been sown by the collapse of the Roman Empire in the West in the 5th century. With the disappearance of a strong central government, people had to look to a powerful local lord for protection against violence and injustice. Since the lord's power was based on the amount of land he owned, land became all-important in the new system.

In 8th century France, Charles Martel drew these new social arrangements into the Frankish political structure.[8] Keenly aware of the Spanish Muslim threat to his Frankish kingdom, Martel created a permanent class of armed warriors on horseback ("knights") to keep the fearsome Muslim cavalry in check.[9] Martel gave land to the knights as a royal grant, perhaps as a reward for past services rendered, perhaps on condition that the knights in future would fight for the French monarchy. The greatest of the knights developed into a powerful military and landowning aristocracy. The least powerful of the knights ruled a small area organised around a manor house (a castle-like dwelling); his land was worked by "peasants", farm-labourers who were the lowest and poorest class in medieval society.

Until very recently this social system was called "feudalism" (from the Latin *feudum*, a grant – the grant of land from a superior to an inferior). Complex interpretations of feudalism as an all-embracing system of life were developed. These were based on the idea that medieval society was a series of grades like the steps of a ladder, with the king at the top and the peasant at the bottom, each lower grade bound to the higher by an oath of loyalty. This has now been challenged and rejected by most modern experts in medieval history. Western medieval life, they argue, was too diverse to be understood in this simple way, and there is little evidence that oaths of loyalty between inferior and superior were the universal glue that held medieval society together. Consequently "feudalism" is no longer favoured as a model for understanding Western medieval life. Unfortunately the idea of feudalism is so widespread in older studies (written before the 1980s) that a great gulf has opened up between present-day

8. For Charles Martel, see Chapter 2, section 1.
9. For more about the knights, see Chapter 5, section 2.

studies and all previous approaches. Whether this revolution will be permanent remains to be seen. The present volume, however, will refrain from speaking of feudalism.

Whether or not oaths of loyalty were involved, the new social structure, in which land was so important, made a deep impact on the Church. The local landowner would build the local church on his own land at his own expense; so the church's land and land-based property (*e.g.* the manse) belonged to the clergy only as a gift from the local lord. Naturally enough, the lord saw it as his right to choose who would occupy the local church and its land as priest or bishop. This attitude swept away the ancient tradition of the clergy being elected by the votes of church members, and bishops being elected by clergy and people together. When a king (who was of course a layman) appointed ("invested") the man of his choosing as a bishop (or an abbot), this was called "lay investiture". It took place through a ceremony in which the king bestowed on a bishop or abbot his ring and staff, the symbols of spiritual office. This practice of lay investiture was soon to cause controversy so fierce that it almost tore Western Europe apart.

3. The Cluniac revival

In the partnership between monastery and monarchy which rebuilt Western Europe after the Norse invasions, one monastery in particular led the movement for establishing Christian values in society – the monastery of Cluny in south-eastern France. Founded in 909 by William the Pious, duke of Aquitaine, Cluny was led by a series of great abbots: **Odo** (abbot 927-42), Maieul (943-94), Odilo (994-1049), **Hugh the Great** (1049-1109), and Peter the Venerable (1122-57).[10] Cluny's role in restoring the vigour and purity of the Western monasteries, and in helping to shape a new Christian West, has been described as the "Cluniac revival".

---

10. Other monastic reform movements which sprang up under the influence of the Cluniac revival were the Camaldolese order (founded 1012), the Carthusians (1084), and the Cistercians (1098). For the Cistercians, see Chapter 5, section 3, under the heading *Bernard of Clairvaux and the Second Crusade*.

Abbot Odo was the real inspiration behind the Cluniac revival. He deliberately established "daughter" monasteries from Cluny. In 931, Pope John XI (931-35) gave Cluny the right to control the other monasteries it had founded. This meant that these monasteries did not have abbots of their own; they only had "priors", normally second-in-command to an abbot. The priors of the Cluniac monasteries were personally appointed by Odo, and took a vow of obedience to the abbot of Cluny. So a great network of Cluniac monasteries spread across France and Germany, all under the central direction of Cluny – there were a thousand Cluniac monasteries by the year 1100. This organisation of monasteries was called the *Cluniac order*. The idea of a monastic order was something new in Christian history. Before the Cluniac revival, all monasteries had simply been part of a general monastic movement. Cluny introduced the new concept of a special organisation of monasteries, bound together by particular ideals, with a single leader at the top. (The idea never caught on in the East.)

The main thrust of the Cluniac revival was to reform and purify existing monasteries, and establish new and better ones. Central to this Cluniac vision of reformed monastic life was the Cluniac liturgy. A Cluniac monk devoted almost the whole of his day to services of worship, and Cluniacs constructed and decorated their monastic churches with awesome beauty and magnificence, to make worship as glorious an experience as possible. The Cluniac reformers were also committed to the Benedictine rule, the most widely used code for monastic life in the West.[11] By the 10th century, most Western monasteries had become very ill-disciplined, ignoring the Benedictine rule in practice; by the 11th century, through the impact of the Cluniac revival, strict obedience to the Benedictine rule had become widespread throughout Western Europe. Cluny also produced one of the greatest Christian poets of the Middle Ages, **Bernard of Cluny** (active 1140s), who wrote the poetic masterpiece, *De Contemptu Mundi* ("Concerning Contempt for the World"),

---

11. For the Benedictine rule, see Volume One, Chapter 11, section 1.

from which English hymnwriters have taken several English hymns about heaven.[12]

From its very foundation, Cluny enjoyed freedom from all secular or political control – unusual in this era. In 999, it also received from Pope Gregory V (996-99) freedom from episcopal authority (control by bishops). Cluny was subject only to the pope. However, until the reform of the papacy in the mid-11th century, the papacy was itself corrupt and powerless. That meant that the abbots of Cluny were free to pursue their own policies, without interference from popes or kings. The abbots of Cluny, rather than the popes, were the central figures in the Christian life of Western Europe until Hildebrand became pope in 1073.

Despite Cluny's freedom from political control, there grew up a strong alliance between the Cluniac monks and the secular rulers (duke, prince, king, Emperor). Indeed, the Cluniac revival itself helped to spread Christian ideals to the ruling classes, because part of the Cluniac policy was to take the sons of the aristocracy into Cluniac monasteries to give them a solid Christian education. An especially powerful partnership grew up between Cluny and the *kings* of Western Christendom. The abbots of Cluny believed that the best hope of making Europe into a truly Christian society lay in strong Christian monarchies being established, which could then govern society according to Christian ideals.

What did the kings get out of the Cluniac movement? Four things, chiefly:

(a) Strong support for the ideal of "sacred kingship". The Cluniacs encouraged the view of kingship that Charlemagne had represented: the king was a spiritual figure whose power came directly from Christ; he was equal to the priest; he had a duty to regulate the affairs of the Church. Such an exalted view obviously strengthened the king's position in society, surrounding monarchy with the heavenly sanctions of religion.

---

12. See the end of the Chapter for Bernard's poem.

(b) A supply of well-trained civil servants. Men trained in Cluniac monasteries (especially bishops) often became government officials, carrying out political, economic, and diplomatic functions (see previous section).

(c) An army from the huge lands owned by the monasteries. Those who lived on these lands were obliged to give military service to the king.

(d) Efficient monasteries where Cluniac monks honoured God and prayed for society.

4. The "cleansing of the papacy"

While Otto the Great and his successors were rebuilding the Holy Roman Empire, the papacy was in a state of almost hopeless moral and spiritual degradation. It had become a political pawn in the hands of the Roman aristocracy, who fought over who should "own" the papacy. Things reached crisis point in 1044. There was a violent rebellion in Rome against Pope Benedict IX (1032-45), a scandalously immoral man. Another pope, Sylvester III, briefly ascended the papal throne in 1045, but Benedict's political allies then managed to put Benedict back in power. Benedict, however, tired of being pope, sold the papacy to a third candidate, Gregory VI – but Benedict later changed his mind and reclaimed the papacy. So when the Holy Roman Emperor, *Henry III* (1039-56), arrived in Rome in 1046 so that the pope could officially crown him Emperor, he found three rival popes!

Henry III was the most striking product of the Cluniac revival. He was the perfect Cluniac king: holy and pure in his personal life, just and wise as a ruler, and a dedicated Christian reformer of Church and society. Henry called a synod at Sutri, a small town just north of Rome; the synod deposed all three popes. Henry himself then placed a good German bishop on the papal throne – Pope Clement II (1046-47). This act of Henry is known as "the cleansing of the papacy". Acting as a "sacred king", the Holy Roman Emperor lifted the papacy out of its pit of spiritual corruption and put it in the hands of a party of committed reformers. The most important of these reformers were:

Humbert of Moyenmoutier (died 1061), a scholar who in 1050 became bishop of Silva Candida, one of Rome's suburban churches. Usually known as "Cardinal Humbert" (see next section for cardinals), he was a reformer gifted with a bold confidence in the righteousness of his cause which heroically swept aside every obstacle (or, alternatively, he was a troublemaker cursed with a ruthless pig-headed arrogance which crushed everyone who dared to disagree with him – it depends which histories you read). Humbert's place in Church history is assured, as he was the one who excommunicated Patriarch Cerularius of Constantinople in 1054, thus creating the permanent schism between Eastern and Western Christianity (see Chapter 3, section 8).

Peter Damiani (1007-72), a Camaldolese monk and, from 1057, bishop of Ostia on the Italian coast, another of Rome's suburban churches. Damiani was famous for his personal sanctity and outspoken criticisms of immorality among the clergy. His many writings – theologicial treatises, sermons, lives of saints, letters, poems – are a perfect mirror of the age and society in which he lived. He was the man chiefly responsible for making popular the practice of "self-flagellation" (whipping or scourging oneself). This practice already existed in Western Christendom, although not in the East – another example of the growing divergence between Western and Eastern piety. Damiani, however, was the man who shaped flagellation into an orderly system. The flagellant would scourge himself with a leather thong on his bare back while chanting the Psalms; Damiani defended the practice against critics, arguing that it was a voluntary imitation of the sufferings of Jesus. Self-flagellation became very popular in the West, especially among monks, and particularly in the 13th and 14th centuries.

Humbert and Damiani were important, but the man who came to dominate the reform movement which the "cleansing of the papacy" had initiated was a native of Tuscany (north-western Italy), a former chaplain of Pope Gregory VI, called *Hildebrand* (1015-85, pope from 1073). The reform movement takes its name from him: the *Hildebrandine reform*.[13]

---

13. Or the Gregorian reform, after Hildebrand's papal name, Gregory VII.

5. Hildebrand and the investiture controversy

The cleansing of the papacy by Henry III at the synod of Sutri created a series of reforming popes: Clement II (1046-47), Damasus II (1048), **Leo IX** (1049-54), Victor II (1055-57), Stephen IX (1057-58), Nicholas II (1059-61), and Alexander II (1061-73). Of these, Leo IX was the most effective. Leo travelled about Western Europe, promoting reform with unbounded boldness and energy, and introduced committed reformers into the papal court as his chief advisors, including Humbert, Damiani, and Hildebrand himself.

The reformers had two main aims:

(i) The reformation of the papacy itself. The Hildebrandine reformers wanted to make the papal court in Rome into a truly Christian institution which practised the highest moral standards: a spiritual example to the rest of the Church. To achieve this, they wanted to free the papacy from political control by the Roman aristocracy. The more radical of the reformers, like Humbert and Hildebrand, wanted to make the papacy independent even of the Holy Roman Emperor. They were reviving the old Western view of Church-state relations: the Church must be independent of the state so that it can pursue its own spiritual purposes. But along with this, they also elevated the claims of the papacy to more soaring heights than ever before. For the Hildebrandine reformers, the pope was the infallible successor of the apostle Peter, standing in Peter's place (Peter's "vicar"), sanctified by Peter's merits, almost a reincarnation of Peter (when Hildebrand became pope, he said, "I am Peter's vicar; he now lives in my body"), and exercising absolute apostolic authority over all other bishops and churches – and indeed secular governments – throughout the entire world. The papacy as the Protestant Reformers knew it, and as we know it today, came to birth through the Hildebrandine reform movement.

(ii) The purification of the Western Church from "simony" and sexual immorality among the clergy. "Simony" means buying or selling a position of authority in the Church, *e.g.* a bishopric. This was a common abuse; kings often sold bishoprics, and Pope Benedict IX had sold the papacy itself to Pope Gregory VI (see previous section).

Hildebrand (1015-85)

(The Latin words around Hildebrand's head quote his dying words: "I have loved righteousness and hated iniquity".)

As for sexual immorality among the clergy, for the Hildebrandine reformers this did not just mean clergymen living with concubines, or committing adultery and fornication; it also meant clergymen getting married. The reformers insisted on the celibacy of the clergy. This was partly a desire to take the high ascetic ideals of the monastery into the Church at large: a priest, like a monk, should be "married to Christ", free of the worldly distractions of marriage and family, totally devoted to the kingdom of God. It was also partly a desire to stop clergymen having sons who would then inherit their father's priesthood or bishopric like a piece of property, without regard to the spiritual fitness of the son.

The Hildebrandine reform movement made slow and hard-fought progress in the Church. The reformers purified the papal court from abuses, and took over the crucial positions of power. They secured a great victory in 1059 at the Lateran council in Rome. Here, the reformers succeeded in placing the election of the pope exclusively in the hands of the "cardinal" clergy of Rome. These were clergy who belonged to the immediate staff of the pope – seven bishops, 28 priests, and 18 deacons. The cardinal bishops were in charge of Rome's suburban churches; to them the Lateran council now granted the power of choosing a new pope. They were then to present their candidate to the cardinal priests and deacons, who either confirmed or rejected their choice.

This reform liberated the papacy from political control: neither the Roman aristocracy, nor the Holy Roman Emperor, were to have any more say in who became pope. (The Emperor Henry IV did not protest, because he was only nine years old at the time, and the Holy Roman Empire was divided between different factions of nobles.) However, what if an Emperor tried to use force to secure the election of a pope of his own choosing? To guard against this possibility, the reformers made an alliance with the Normans of southern Italy, led by Robert Guiscard. In return for official papal recognition of the land he had conquered, Guiscard promised to use his Norman army to support lawful elections to the papacy.

The Lateran council of 1059 also passed strict new laws about the celibacy of the clergy. This incidentally removed an ancient and painful thorn from the papacy's side by leading to the final triumph of the church of Rome over the church of Milan. The Milanese had for long maintained a spirit of independence against the papacy, rooted in Milan's historic fame as the church of Ambrose, one of the greatest fathers of the West.[14] Up till now, Milan had championed the right of the clergy to marry; by the sweeping use of his authority as a papal ambassador, Peter Damiani forced the Milanese to submit to the new order of absolute celibacy for all clergy.

In 1073, at the age of 50, Hildebrand himself was elected pope, and took the name Gregory VII. He had been the guiding hand behind the reforming popes. Now, by the overwhelming popular choice of the entire people of Rome, it was his own turn to sit on the papal throne. Judged by the impact he made on Church and society, he was perhaps the greatest of all the popes in history. What kind of man was Hildebrand? Physically he was not very impressive: a short man with a rather weak voice. But he had shining, piercing eyes; his friend Peter Damiani called him a "holy Satan". He possessed a dominating force of will, an all-consuming devotion to justice and righteousness, and a burning zeal for the purity and reformation of the Church. At the same time, he was remarkably broad-minded and tolerant of various doctrinal disagreements which he did not think important in the Church's life (see section 7). He had an amazing ability to get his friends and allies to do what *he* wanted them to do. He also had a supreme talent for dividing opinion about himself into violent extremes of adoration and hatred; people either admired Hildebrand intensely as a heaven-sent spiritual hero, or detested him bitterly as an ambitious power-mad schemer.

Hildebrand saw life in military terms as a raging conflict between light and darkness. The chief agents of darkness were the secular rulers – the counts, dukes, princes, and kings. They were nothing but glorified thugs, murderers dressed up in robes and crowns, children of Cain and Satan who oppressed the poor and filled the earth with injustice. To bring about justice, the

---

14. For Ambrose, see Volume One, Chapter 7, section 2.

agents of light – the Church, headed by the papacy – must take control of these evil rulers and force them to serve the cause of God. Only in this way could the righteous establish a truly Christian society. Hildebrand had a deep, heartfelt sympathy for the poor, "Christ's poor ones", and saw himself as their special protector against the oppression of the powerful. His negative view of kingship was a complete break with the Cluniac tradition which saw the Christian king as the brightest hope of creating a society based on Christian beliefs and values. However, in Hildebrand's thinking, it was not the Christian king, but the papacy itself which was God's appointed agent for establishing His kingdom on earth.

It was around this time that Western Christianity began to speak of Christians on earth as "the Church Militant", contrasted with those now in heaven as "the Church Triumphant". ("Militant" means "fighting", "engaged in war".) Previously it had been the custom to think of Christians on earth as "the pilgrim Church" and those in heaven as "the Church at rest". This change from the "pilgrim" to the "warrior" image reflects the new world-conquering aggression and self-confidence which the Hildebrandine reform movement brought to the Church.

Soon after becoming pope, Hildebrand published in 1075 a statement known as the *dictatus papae* ("papal decree") which outlined his view of the papacy. Here are some of its claims:

1. The Roman Church was founded by God alone.

2. Only the Roman pope is rightly called universal.

3. The pope alone can depose and reinstate bishops.

9. The pope is the only one whose feet all princes must kiss.

12. The pope may depose Emperors.

16. No council may be called ecumenical without the pope's authority.

19. The pope may be judged by no-one.

22. The Roman Church has never erred, and (as Scripture testifies) it shall never err, to all eternity.

23. The Roman pope, if properly ordained according to Church law, is sanctified by the merits of Saint Peter.

26. He who is not in conformity with the Roman Church should not be considered a Catholic.

Not all of this was new in what it claimed; other popes, especially since the cleansing of the papacy in 1046, had said similar things. But the whole tone of the *dictatus papae* was new – its grand, sweeping, universal, self-confident assertiveness. And what was definitely new was Hildebrand's fierce, unbending resolve to put it all into practice.

As pope, Hildebrand was determined to destroy the political power that secular rulers exercised over Church affairs. The reformers had freed the papacy itself, but other problems remained. The point at which Hildebrand chose to strike was the practice of "lay investiture". As we saw in section 3, this was the action by which a king would "invest" or appoint a man of his own choosing as a bishop or abbot. The land over which bishops and abbots ruled was important to the Western kings for its economic and military resources. So they felt they had the right to make sure that suitable men were in charge of these lands. Hildebrand saw it differently: the appointment of bishops and abbots by secular rulers was an unholy violation of the Church's independence from state control. Hildebrand particularly objected to the ceremony in which a king bestowed on a bishop or abbot his ring and staff, the symbols of their spiritual office. This implied that bishops and abbots owed their spiritual authority to the king – which is indeed what Western kings believed, holding as they did to the "sacred kingship" ideal.

In 1075, Hildebrand decreed that the Holy Roman Emperor, Henry IV, must cease from the practice of lay investiture. He picked on the Holy Roman Emperor because he was the most important of the Western monarchs, claiming to represent the authority of a reborn Roman Empire; Hildebrand knew that if he could defeat him, he could defeat anyone. The battle between the "papalist" and "imperialist" vision of Western Christendom had begun.

Hildebrand's foe, Emperor *Henry IV* (1065-1105), was one of the most naturally gifted rulers and soldiers ever to wear the crown of the Holy Roman Empire. His moral character, however, was a cause of scandal to his contemporaries; his adulteries alienated the devout, and his tyranny outraged lovers of political freedom. Henry had been involved in a civil war with his own German nobles for many years; it was only in 1075, at the age of 25, that he managed to establish his own power over the whole of Germany. The German Church had strongly supported Henry in the civil war against his nobles. German bishops, inspired by the Cluniac ideal, wanted to see a powerful Christian monarchy created in Germany as the basis for a Christian society, and despite Henry's obvious faults the Church backed him as the best hope of strong, stable government.

So when Hildebrand issued his challenge to Henry, the German bishops at first supported the Emperor. Henry defied Hildebrand's demand to cease from investiture, and appointed a new archbishop of Milan. When Hildebrand protested, Henry called a council at Worms (western-central Germany) in January 1076. Here most of the German bishops joined in condemning Hildebrand and rejecting him as pope. Henry was trying to assert his authority as Emperor over the pope, just as his father Henry III had done in 1046 at the synod of Sutri when he had "cleansed" the papacy. It was Henry III's cleansing of the papacy which had put the Hildebrandine reformers in power; now, Henry IV thought it was time to cleanse the papacy again – by getting rid of Hildebrand! Henry sent an official letter to Hildebrand from the council of Worms which shows what Henry thought of this new pope:

> To Hildebrand, not pope but a false monk. How dare you, who have won your power by deceit, flattery, bribery, and force, stretch forth your hand against the Lord's anointed, despising the command of the true pope, Saint Peter: 'Fear God, honour the king' (1 Pet. 2:17)? You do not fear God, and you dishonour me whom He has appointed. Condemned by the voice of all our bishops, leave the apostolic throne and let someone else sit there, someone who will preach the healthy doctrine of Saint Peter and

not exploit religion as a cloak for violence. I, Henry, king by the
grace of God, with all my bishops, say to you – come down, come
down from the papal throne, and be damned through all ages!

Hildebrand's response to this threatening letter came like a bolt
of lightning. He excommunicated Henry and released all Henry's
subjects from their obligation of loyalty to him. Henry's closest allies, the German bishops, afraid for their own position,
obeyed Hildebrand and refused all further cooperation with the
Emperor. So at one stroke, Henry lost two-thirds of his army
which came from Church lands. Henry's German nobles seized
this chance to rebel again, and at a council in Tribur (just north
of Worms) in October 1076 they suspended Henry from his
imperial office. With no effective army, Henry was powerless.
The nobles also invited Hildebrand to come to another council
to be held in 1077 at Augsburg (southern Germany). It looked
as if they would elect a new Emperor to replace Henry, and that
Hildebrand would preside over the election. The Holy Roman
Emperor, the most exalted king in Western Europe, had been
toppled from his throne simply by the word of the pope.

Henry was desperate. With his family and a few loyal supporters, he journeyed down into Italy. He found Hildebrand at
Canossa in the north, in a castle with Hugh the Great, the abbot
of Cluny. Hildebrand had taken refuge in the castle of Canossa,
protected by his wealthy and powerful friend the countess of
Tuscany, because he feared that Henry would take military action against him. However, the Emperor came without an army.
For three days in January 1077, Henry stood outside the castle
gate with his wife and children, barefoot in the freezing snow,
crying out to Hildebrand that he had repented, pleading for
mercy. Inside the castle, Hugh the Great of Cluny interceded
with Hildebrand on Henry's behalf. Hugh was as opposed to
lay investiture as Hildebrand was, but he was also a gentler,
more moderate person who wanted to see friendly cooperation
between Church and state. As abbot of Cluny, Hugh was also
a highly respected figure in the Church whom Hildebrand could
not afford to ignore.

Henry's action had placed Hildebrand in a difficult position. As a priest, it was his duty to accept Henry's repentance and restore him to Church membership. Yet if Hildebrand did this, Henry would regain all his power in Germany – and then probably use it to destroy Hildebrand. So for three days Hildebrand hesitated, as Henry outside the castle and Hugh inside begged him to show pity. Finally, Hildebrand's priestly conscience gave way. He allowed Henry into the castle. Weeping, the young Emperor promised to obey the pope's demands to cease from the practice of lay investiture. Hildebrand received him back into the Church. From one point of view, it was the ultimate scene of the Church triumphing over the state: the Holy Roman Emperor, the supreme ruler of the Western world, lay prostrate at the feet of the pope, crying for mercy. However, Hildebrand must surely have guessed that the Emperor's tears of repentance were also the ultimate act of kingly hypocrisy and insincerity.

Hildebrand's forgiveness restored Henry's power in Germany, because it gave him back his army from Church lands. When Henry returned to Germany, a new civil war broke out. Henry's foes elected Rudolf of Swabia as Emperor. The German bishops supported Henry against the rebellious nobles. Both Henry and Rudolf looked to Hildebrand for support; for three years Hildebrand wavered between them, as the war raged. At last in March 1080, provoked by a high-handed demand from Henry that Hildebrand must excommunicate Rudolf, the pope came down on Rudolf's side and excommunicated Henry again. This time, however, the German bishops stayed loyal to Henry; they did not recognise Rudolf's claim to the throne, and saw Henry as the only hope for peace and stability in Germany. Henry called a council at Brixen (northern Italy) in June which deposed Hildebrand from the papacy, and appointed archbishop Guibert of Ravenna in his place.

In October Henry won the civil war when Rudolf was killed in battle. The victorious Emperor invaded Italy in 1081, conquered the north, and finally in 1084 captured Rome itself. Hildebrand locked himself away in the Roman castle of Sant' Angelo. Henry placed the archbishop of Ravenna on the papal throne as Pope Clement III; Clement then crowned Henry as Holy Roman Emperor. Robert Guiscard and his Normans rescued Hildebrand from Sant' Angelo, but they wrecked Rome in the process, committing appalling outrages. Hildebrand went with his dubious Norman allies into exile, to Salerno in southern Italy, and died there in 1085. His last words were: "I have loved righteousness and hated iniquity; therefore I die in exile."

6. The end of the investiture conflict

It looked as if Henry IV had won. But the struggle for the independence of the Church did not die with Hildebrand. For some time there continued to be two rival popes, one in Rome chosen by Henry, the other in exile chosen by the reformers loyal to Hildebrand's ideals. However, the great reforming pope, Urban II (1088-99), a fervent disciple of Hildebrand, soon won most of Western Europe to his cause by sheer moral force of character, brilliant diplomacy, and his masterminding of the 1st Crusade (see Chapter 5, section 2). The Emperor's rival pope lost control of Rome in 1096. The papacy was now firmly in the hands of Hildebrand's followers.

The struggle over lay investiture between the Hildebrandine reformers and the secular rulers continued under Pope Urban II and his successor Pope *Paschal II* (1099-1118). Paschal was so committed to the spiritual independence of the Church from state control that in 1110 he offered an astonishing proposal to the new Emperor, Henry V (1106-25). If the Emperor would give up all pretence of investing bishops with their spiritual authority, Paschal would surrender all the Church's secular possessions in the Holy Roman Empire to the Emperor; bishops would live in simple apostolic poverty. This proposal was not to the liking of most German bishops, and Paschal had to withdraw it. However the distinction Paschal had made between the spiritual and secular aspects of investiture provided the key to the final settlement of the controversy in 1122. At Worms in western Germany that year, Pope Calixtus II (1119-24) and Emperor Henry V agreed on two points:

(i) The Emperor would invest a bishop or abbot with his authority over the *land* that went with his office.

(ii) The bishop's spiritual superior (his archbishop) would invest him with his *spiritual* authority over the Church – the Emperor would no longer confer the ring and staff.

This agreement had already taken effect in France in 1106 and in England in 1107; it meant that a new bishop had to be acceptable both to the state and to the Church. The treaty between Henry V and Pope Calixtus in 1122, establishing the same policy for the Holy Roman Empire, was called the "Concordat of Worms". Such a compromise between papalism and imperialism would have disappointed Hildebrand, but it secured for the Church a lot more independence than it had enjoyed before. It also dealt a crushing blow to the "sacred kingship" ideal that bishops owed their spiritual office to the king. The new Western Christian Europe, with the papacy as its acknowledged spiritual head, had taken shape.

7. The controversy over communion

The dispute between Radbertus and Ratramnus in the 9th century over the doctrine of the eucharist broke out afresh in the 11th century.[15] This time, the two main antagonists were *Berengar of Tours* (1000-1088) and *Lanfranc of Canterbury* (1005-89). Berengar was head of the cathedral school in Tours (north-western France), and later archdeacon of Angers (west of Tours). A popular theological teacher, his study of the Bible and the early Church fathers led Berengar between 1040 and 1045 to reject the teaching of Radbertus (that Christ's flesh and blood are so totally present in communion that the bread and wine simply cease to exist). Berengar preferred Ratramnus's view, that the bread and wine physically remain bread and wine, and that Christ's body and blood are truly present in them, but in a spiritual manner, received by faith into the soul, not by the mouth into the body.

---

15. For Radbertus and Ratramnus, see Chapter 2, section 4.

This caused great controversy, because by the mid-11th century Radbertus's view had become the widely accepted one in the West. Berengar's chief opponent was Lanfranc, an Italian who in 1045 was elected prior of the monastery of Le Bec in Normandy, and later in 1070 (as a consequence of the Norman Conquest of England) became archbishop of Canterbury. Lanfranc defended Radbertus's doctrine, and took it still further by maintaining that even unbelievers who take part in the eucharist eat Christ's flesh and drink His blood.

Berengar had few supporters and was put on trial for heresy by a local French council in Tours in 1054, where Pope Leo IX presided. Berengar was saved from condemnation by none other than Hildebrand, who believed that both Berengar's and Lanfranc's views should be allowed in the Church. However, the great majority of Catholic Churchmen did not share Hildebrand's tolerance. In 1059, at a council in Rome under the papacy of Nicholas II, Berengar was again tried and, this time, condemned. Led by the unsubtle and heavy-handed Cardinal Humbert, the council bullied Berengar into signing a very crude doctrinal statement which said that Christ's flesh is physically chewed by the teeth of all those who receive communion. Ashamed of having betrayed his real beliefs, Berengar found his courage after returning to France, renounced the doctrinal statement he had signed in Rome, and taught his own doctrine with renewed vigour. Lanfranc wrote against him in 1063; Berengar replied with *Concerning the Holy Supper, against Lanfranc*, his chief work on the subject. Abandoned by his friends, Berengar was reviled by all; his life was even threatened.

In 1079, Berengar's old protector Hildebrand (who was now pope) summoned him to Rome, apparently hoping to make him secure against his enemies. However, the council that met to settle the issue was so completely hostile to Berengar that it defied Hildebrand, and commanded Berengar to withdraw his heresy or be put to death. Hildebrand could no longer protect him without risking his own reputation. Berengar was not the stuff of which martyrs are made; he once more gave in, and signed a doctrinal statement which taught Lanfranc's view of the eucharist.

Hildebrand then threw the full strength of his papal authority around the humiliated Berengar, threatening to excommunicate anyone who henceforward accused him of heresy or harassed him in any way. Berengar bitterly regretted his lack of courage in signing the doctrinal statement, and spent the last nine years of his life in retirement on an island near Tours.

The triumph of Lanfranc's doctrine of communion over Berengar's shows that by the mid-11th century the Western Church was committed to a belief that the bread and wine of the Lord's Supper ceased to exist after the words of consecration, and were miraculously replaced by the very flesh and blood of Christ. However, it would need the mighty intellect of the 13th century theologian Thomas Aquinas to work out a clear doctrinal expression of this belief, which he did by means of the doctrine of "transubstantiation" – see Chapter 7, section 3, under *Thomas Aquinas*.

8. Civil courts and Church courts: The martyrdom of Thomas Becket

The Hildebrandine concept of the Church's independence from the state included the belief that the clergy should not be subject to the authority of the civil or secular courts. Clergymen who committed crimes, the Hildebrandine reformers felt, should be tried only by Church courts. This view of the Church's independence, when put into practice, could provoke explosive conflict between Church and state, since it struck at the power of Western kings to punish their own subjects for criminal offences.

The most famous conflict took place in England. In the aftermath of the Norman Conquest in 1066 (see section 1), King William the Conqueror, who supported many aspects of the Hildebrandine reform, introduced into English law the twofold system of civil courts and Church courts. William intended the Church courts to deal only with strictly religious cases, such as breaking an oath sworn in God's name. However, the English Church courts extended their power enormously throughout the following century. By the time *Henry II* (1154-89) became king, an English clergyman who committed murder would be tried by a Church court and merely fined for his offence, whereas a civil court would try a lay murderer and, if it found him guilty, sentence him to death. (Church courts could only fine or at most imprison, but imprisonment was rare; it cost the Church too much money to build and maintain prisons, and fining criminal clergy was obviously more profitable.) The only way a civil court could punish a criminal clergyman was if a Church court stripped him of his priesthood. But the Church hardly ever took this step; it seemed to undermine the accepted doctrine that ordination was a sacrament (like baptism) which bestowed a permanent priestly character on an ordained man.

King Henry II was determined to undo this state of affairs, and make the English clergy subject to the civil courts in all criminal cases. However, Henry's high-spirited archbishop of Canterbury, *Thomas Becket* (1118-70), fiercely opposed him, and defended the right of the clergy to be tried by Church courts alone. King Henry actually had many of the English clergy on his side in his struggle with Becket, but he utterly shipwrecked his cause in 1170 when he told some of his knights, in an outburst of rage, that he wished someone would get rid of that trouble-maker Becket for him. Four of the knights took their royal master at his word, went to Canterbury cathedral, and murdered Becket at the altar, smashing his skull open so that his brain spilled out.

Shock-waves of horror and outrage electrified the whole of Catholic Europe. People everywhere hailed Becket as a martyr and a saint, especially when his relics, and prayers addressed to him, produced one of the most abundant crops of miracles (real or alleged) in the Middle Ages. Pope Alexander III (1159-81) forced King Henry to do public penance and give up his campaign against the Church courts; Becket's tomb in Canterbury became one of the most popular sites of pilgrimage for devout Catholics from all over the Western world. The medieval state had lost yet another battle with the medieval Church.

9. The Catholic mystics of the 12th century

A number of important Catholic mystics flourished in the 1100s, in the years following the investiture controversy. The most outstanding were Bernard of Clairvaux, Hugh and Richard of Saint Victor, and Hildegard of Bingen. We will look at Bernard of Clairvaux (1090-1153) in the next Chapter, because of his close involvement with the 2nd Crusade.

Hugh of Saint Victor (1096-1141) is a rather mysterious figure, of whose life we know almost nothing. Probably from Saxony, he joined the abbey of Saint Victor in Paris when he was 18, and became its director of theological studies in 1133, when he was 37. Strongly Augustinian in his theology, Hugh was nicknamed "the second Augustine"; among his many writings, the greatest and most mystical was his *The Moral Ark of Noah* (see the end of the Chapter).

Richard of Saint Victor (1123-73) was a native of Scotland who also joined the abbey of Saint Victor at an early age, becoming its prior in 1162. Among his writings were his *Concerning the Trinity*, *Benjamin the Less* and *Benjamin the Greater*. In *Concerning the Trinity*, Richard argued that the statement "God is love" requires God to be a Trinity; love must be a relationship between persons, and where two persons love each other perfectly, they will desire a third person whom they can both love in common. In *Benjamin the Less* and *Benjamin the Greater*, Richard set out his mystical teaching, in which he emphasised the importance of moral obedience, love, and testing everything against Scripture, in pursuing the supreme experience – the vision of the Trinity "above reason and aside from reason".

Hildegard of Bingen (1098-1179) was the abbess of the Benedictine convent of Disibodenberg from 1136 to 1148, and then abbess of the new Rupertsberg convent (which she founded) from 1150 to 1179, both convents being situated near Bingen in western Germany. She was certainly one of the most striking and influential women in the entire history of the Church. A mystic who described herself as "a feather on the breath of God" and received many visions (recorded in her three works, entitled *Scivias* – "Know the Ways", *The Book of Life's Merits*, and *The Book of Divine Works*), one of the greatest hymnwriters and musicians of the Middle Ages, a playwright, a biographer of saints, a scientific student of nature who wrote detailed books on herbs, trees, and fish, a healer to whom people flocked from all over Europe to be miraculously cured: Hildegard was all these things, and combined with them a reputation for holiness of life that won the warmest admiration of Bernard of Clairvaux. Kings, Emperors, abbots, bishops, and popes asked her advice and begged her for her prayers. Three times she went on preaching tours through Germany and France, denouncing corruption in the Church, warning people of God's coming judgment, summoning them to repentance, and exhorting them to seek salvation in Christ Himself rather than relying on priests and ceremonies. Many of Hildegard's 77 spiritual songs were recorded for the first time in the 1980s and found a whole new audience of modern admirers.

10. The rise of musical instruments in worship

The period which this Chapter covers witnessed the dawn of a revolution in Western worship – the introduction of musical instruments. As we saw in Volume One, the early Church did not use instruments in its worship, regarding them as Jewish or Pagan, but not part of the apostolic tradition of Christian worship.[16] This was the situation that prevailed in both East and West for many centuries; and in the Eastern Church, this ancient pattern of worshipping without instruments has remained unchanged to the present day. In the Western Church, however, signs of change began to appear in the Middle Ages. We first hear of a musical instrument being used in Western worship in the 8th century, for in the year 757 the Frankish king Pepin presented an organ to the church of Saint Corneille in Compiegne, north of Paris.[17] We also, from the 8th century onwards, occasionally find the harp, violin, and cithern depicted in some Western musical

---

16.   For the early Church's attitude, see Volume One, Chapter 3, section 2.

17.   For King Pepin, see Chapter 2, section 1. Some historians think that an organ may first have been introduced into Western worship slightly earlier, in Rome itself, by Pope Vitalian, pope from 657 to 672.

manuscripts. In the period 900-1100, which this Chapter deals with, organs began to become common features of the great Western abbeys and cathedral churches. We know, for instance, that archbishop **Dunstan of Canterbury** (born 909; archbishop 961-88) installed an organ in Malmesbury abbey and several other places in England.

At first, the organ was used simply to give the right note for the monks and choirs (like a tuning-fork). Soon, however, new developments in Western Church singing gave a strong impetus to a more complex use of the organ and other instruments in worship. Up until now, the established style of singing had been Gregorian chant,[18] which was "unison plainsong" – that is, all the singers sang the same words, to the same tune, at the same time. But in our period a new style called "part-singing" (or "polyphony") began to become popular. In part-singing, different singers sang the same words to a slightly variant tune; more complicated forms of part-singing involved singing different words at the same time. To help the singers sing their own parts, abbeys and cathedrals used an organ to accompany the words of one singer or group of singers, adding other instruments (*e.g.* pipes and cornets) to accompany the words of other singers.

This period (900-1100) did not actually lead to a widespread use of instruments in ordinary parish churches and thus in normal Western Catholic worship. Even in the great abbeys and cathedrals, the organ's use was limited to the important Church festivals. Churches did not begin to employ the organ in the celebration of ordinary masses until the 12th century. Some historical sources speak of an "organ controversy" in the 13th century, which resulted in the Catholic Church's declaring against the use of organs. Thomas Aquinas[19] (1225-74), the greatest Western theologian of the 13th century, seems to confirm this, for Aquinas simply repeated the way that the early Church fathers had condemned all musical instruments in Christian worship:

---

18. For Gregorian chant, see Volume One, Chapter 11, section 2, under the heading *Church worship*.

19. For Aquinas, see Chapter 7, section 3.

The Church does not use musical instruments such as the harp or lyre when praising God, in case she should seem to fall back into Judaism. As Aristotle says, 'We must not introduce flutes into teaching, nor any artificial instrument such as the harp, nor anything of the kind, but only such things as make people morally good.' For musical instruments usually move the soul more to pleasure than create inner moral goodness. But in the Old Testament, they used instruments of this kind, both because the people were more coarse and carnal, so that they needed to be aroused by such instruments and with worldly promises, and also because these bodily instruments were symbolic of something.

In fact, it was not until after Aquinas, in the 14th and 15th centuries, that the playing of musical instruments became a widespread, regular and accepted feature of ordinary Western worship. The first great church organist known to history was the Italian Francesco Landino (died 1390), of the Church of Saint Lorenzo in Florence. Even so, it was the age of the Cluniac revival and the investiture controversy that planted the seeds of this revolution in the worship of the Western Church. The adoption of musical instruments in Western worship became one more barrier between East and West, Orthodoxy and Catholicism.

Important people:

The Church

Odo of Cluny (abbot of Cluny 927-42)

Archbishop Dunstan of Canterbury (909-88)

Pope Leo IX (1049-54)

Humbert of Moyenmoutier (died 1061)

Peter Damiani (1007-72)

Hildebrand (born 1015; pope 1073-85,
   took the name "Gregory VII")

Berengar of Tours (1000-1088)

Lanfranc of Canterbury (1005-89)

Hugh the Great (abbot of Cluny 1049-1109)

Pope Paschal II (1099-1118)

Bernard of Cluny (active 1140s)
Hugh of Saint Victor (1096-1141)
Archbishop Thomas Becket of Canterbury (1118-70)
Richard of Saint Victor (1123-73)
Hildegard of Bingen (1098-1179)

Political and military

King Alfred the Great of Wessex (871-99)
Holy Roman Emperor Otto the Great (936-73)
Holy Roman Emperor Henry III (1039-56)
Holy Roman Emperor Henry IV (1065-1105)
King Henry II of England (1154-89)

The laws of King Alfred

The Lord spoke these words to Moses and said: I am the Lord your God. I led you out of the land of the Egyptians and out of their bondage.

1. Do not love other strange gods above Me.

2. Do not speak My name idly, for you shall not be guiltless towards Me if you speak My name idly.

3. Remember to hallow the rest-day. Do your work for six days, and rest on the seventh. For in six days Christ made the heaven and the earth, the seas, and all creatures that are in them, and rested on the seventh day. Therefore the Lord hallowed it.

4. Honour your father and your mother whom the Lord has given you, and you may live long on the earth.

5. Do not murder.

6. Do not commit adultery.

7. Do not steal.

8. Do not speak false witness.

9. Do not covet your neighbour's goods unjustly.

10. Do not make for yourself golden or silver gods ...

[Then follow laws taken from Exod. 20:1-17.]

These are the judgments which the almighty God Himself spoke to Moses, and commanded him to keep. After the only-begotten Son of the Lord our God, that is, our Saviour Christ, came to the earth, He said that He came not to break nor to forbid these commandments, but with all good to increase them; and He taught mercy and humility. Then after His suffering, before His apostles were scattered throughout the earth to teach, and while they were together, they converted many Pagan nations to God. When they were all assembled, they sent messengers to Antioch and Syria, to teach them the law of Christ ... [Then follows Acts 15:23-29.]

I, then – Alfred, king – gathered these together, and commanded many of those to be written down which our forefathers held, those which seemed good to me; and many of those which did not seem good to me, I rejected by the counsel of my witan [the king's supreme council, made up of bishops, nobles and courtiers].

From *The Dooms of Alfred*

Hildebrand on kings and clergymen

Who does not know that kings and princes sprang from men who were ignorant of God, who by pride, robbery, treachery, murders, and in short by almost every crime prompted by the devil, the prince of this world, have striven with blind greed and intolerable arrogance to dominate over their fellow human beings who are their equals? When kings try to force God's priests to bow to their feet, to whom can we better compare these kings than to Satan, the head of all the sons of pride? He tempted the highest priest Himself, the Head of priests, promising Him the kingdoms of the world, and saying, "All these I will give You, if You will fall down and worship me". Who can doubt that Christ's priests must be considered the fathers and masters of kings, of princes, and of all believers? It is surely pitiful madness for a son to try to make his father submit to him, or a pupil to force his teacher to be subject to him, or for a person to seize by his power and bind with sinful bonds someone who he believes can bind and loose him in heaven as well as on earth ...

Which layman (not to mention priests) in his last hour has ever begged the help of an earthly king for the salvation of his soul? Which king or Emperor is able by his royal office to rescue a Christian from the devil's power through holy baptism, to number him among the sons of God, to strengthen him with the divine anointing? Which king can by his words make the Lord's body and blood, the greatest act in our Christian faith? Which king possesses the power to bind and loose in heaven and earth? For all these reasons it is clear that the priestly office far exceeds the kingly in power. Which king can ordain a clergyman in the holy Church, or depose him for any fault? In the ordained offices of the Church, a greater power is needed to depose than to ordain. Bishops can ordain other bishops, but cannot depose them without the authority of the apostolic throne [the papacy]. Who then with even a moderate understanding can hesitate to give priests priority over kings? If priests can discipline kings for their sins, who better than the Roman pope can exercise this discipline?

In brief, any good Christian has a better right than a bad prince has to think himself a king. For a good Christian seeks the glory of God, and rules over himself strictly, whereas a bad prince seeks his own interests rather than God's, and is an enemy to his own soul and a tyrannical oppressor of others. Faithful Christians are the body of Christ, the true King; evil rulers are the body of the devil. Faithful Christians rule over themselves in the hope that they will reign eternally with the Supreme Emperor, but the reign of bad princes ends in their destruction and eternal damnation together with the prince of darkness, the king of all the sons of pride.

Hildebrand
Letter to bishop Hermann of Metz (**1081**)

Hildebrand's decree on lay investiture

We have learned that laypeople perform investiture in many churches, contrary to what the holy fathers have established, and that this causes many disturbances to arise in the Church, on account of which the Christian faith is trodden under foot. Therefore we decree that no clergyman shall be invested as bishop or abbot by the hands of an Emperor, or a king, or any layperson, male or female. If anyone presumes to do this, let him know clearly that such investiture lacks the authority of the apostles, and that he himself shall be excommunicated until he offers suitable satisfaction.

Pope Paschal II's solution to the investiture conflict

From Bishop Paschal, servant of the servants of God, to his beloved son Henry [Emperor Henry V] and his successors for ever. The institutions of God's law, and sacred canon law, both forbid priests to be involved in secular affairs, or to go to a civil court except to save the condemned or on behalf of others who suffer harm. Thus the apostle Paul says, "If you have secular judgments, constitute as judges those who are of low degree in the church." Indeed, in parts of your kingdom, bishops and abbots are so taken up with secular affairs that it forces them to go often to court and to perform military service – and such things are hardly ever carried on without plunder, sacrilege, and arson! Servants of the altar become servants of the royal court, receiving cities, dukedoms, margravates, sums of money, and other things that belong to the king's service. In this way the custom (so intolerable to the Church) has grown up, that elected bishops should not be consecrated unless they have first been invested by the hands of the king. This is the cause of the wickedness of heretical simony and the sometimes vast ambition by which episcopal thrones have been invaded without an election taking place.

Aroused by these evils and many others, which have come about mostly through investitures, our predecessors – the Popes Gregory VII [Hildebrand] and Urban II, of blessed memory – frequently summoned episcopal councils and condemned those lay investitures, decreeing that those who obtained churches through them should be deposed, and the donors [the laypeople performing the investiture] be excommunicated. This is in agreement with the chapter in the apostolic canons which says, "If any bishop employs worldly powers and through them obtains a church, let him be deposed and isolated, along with all who have dealings with him." Following in the footsteps of these canons, we too have confirmed their decree in an episcopal council.

And so, my most beloved son, King Henry, you who are Emperor of the Romans by God's grace through our office, we decree that the royal properties and privileges [now held by the Church] which plainly belonged to your kingdom in the times of Charles, Louis, and your other predecessors, must be given back to you. We forbid, indeed we prohibit under threat of anathema, that any bishop or abbot, present or future, take possession of these royal properties, including the cities, dukedoms, margravates, counties, sums of money, tolls, markets, royal advowsons, rights of the judges of the hundred courts, and the courts which plainly belonged to the king together with what pertained to them, the military posts and camps of the kingdom. From now on, bishops and abbots shall not concern themselves with these royal properties and privileges, unless by the king's favour. Nor shall any of our successors on the apostolic throne be allowed to disturb you or your kingdom in this matter.

Again, we decree that the churches, together with the offerings and hereditary possessions which plainly were not royal property, shall remain free – just as you promised on your coronation day in the sight of the entire Church. For it is suitable that bishops should be free of secular cares and look after their people, and not be absent from their churches any more. As the apostle Paul says, let them keep watch as those who must render an account for the souls of the people (Heb. 13:17).

Decree of Paschal II
February 12, the year 1111

The glory of heaven

The world is very evil,
    The times are waxing late;
Be sober and keep vigil,
    The Judge is at the gate –
The Judge Who comes in mercy,
    The Judge Who comes in might,
To bring an end to evil,
    To vindicate the right.

And now we fight the battle,
    But then shall wear the crown
Of full and everlasting
    And passionless renown!
And now we watch, and struggle,
    And now we live in hope,
And Zion in her anguish
    With Babylon must cope.
But He Whom now we trust in
    Shall then be seen and known;
And they that know and see Him
    Shall have Him for their own!

For you, O dear, sweet Country,
    My eyes their vigil keep;
For love's own sake, beholding
    Your blessed name, they weep.
The story of your glory
    Is unction to the breast,
And medicine pure in sickness,
    And love, and life, and rest.

The Cross is all your splendour,
    The Crucified your praise;
His glory and His blessing
    Your ransomed people raise:
"O Jesus, Gem of Beauty,

True God and Man!" they sing,
    "The ever-fruitful Garden,
        The ever-golden Ring!
The Door, the Pledge, the Husband,
        The Guardian of His Court;
The Day-star of Salvation,
        The Porter and the Port!"

You have no shore, fair Ocean!
        You have no end, bright Day!
Sweet Fountain of refreshment
        To pilgrims far away!
Upon the Rock of Ages
        Your holy towers rise;
Yours is the crown of triumph,
        And yours the golden prize!

Jerusalem the golden,
        With milk and honey blest,
Beneath your contemplation
        Sink heart and voice oppressed.
I know not, O I know not
        What social joys are there,
What radiancy of glory,
        What light beyond compare!

And when my tongue would sing them,
        My spirit fails and faints;
O vainly would it picture
        The assembly of the Saints!
They stand, those halls of Zion,
        All jubilant with song,
And bright with many an angel,
        And all the martyr throng:
The Prince is ever in them;
        The daylight is serene;
The pastures of the Blessed
        Are decked in glorious sheen.

There is the Throne of David,
    And there, from care released,
The song of those who triumph,
    The shout of those who feast;
And those who, with their Leader,
    Have conquered in the fight,
For ever and for ever
    Are clad in robes of white!

Jerusalem, exulting
    On that securest shore,
I hope you, wish you, sing you,
    And love you evermore!
I ask not for my merit;
    I seek not to deny
My merit is destruction –
    A child of wrath am I;
But yet with faith I venture,
    And hope, upon my way;
And for the prize perpetual
    I labour night and day.

The best and dearest Father
    Who made and saved my soul,
Bore with me in defilement
    And cleansed my squalour foul –
When in His strength I struggle,
    For very joy I leap:
When in my sin I stumble,
    I weep – or try to weep;
But grace, sweet grace celestial
    Shall all its love display,
And David's royal Fountain
    Purge every sin away!

Selected verses from Bernard of Cluny's
Concerning Contempt for the World

The love of God heals restless hearts

When I was sitting among the brothers and responding to questions they were asking, and we had raised and set forth many matters, all of us suddenly began to marvel passionately at the unstable and restless nature of the human heart. We began to sigh. They pleaded with me to show them why the human heart was so tossed by whirling thoughts, and by what art of discipline we might remove this evil. I indeed wished to satisfy my brothers, as far as God helped me, and to untie the knot of their questions, by authority and by argument. I knew it would please them best if I wrote down my thoughts to read them out at the table. I planned first to show them the origin of these violent changes in the human heart, and then the path that can lead the mind to keep itself in stable peace. I had no doubt that this was properly the work of God's grace, not human labour; still, I know that God wishes us to cooperate. Besides, it is good for us to know the greatness of our weakness and the method of repairing it, since such knowledge will deepen our gratitude.

God created the first man in such a way that if he had not sinned, he would always have seen in constant contemplation the face of his Creator; by always seeing Him, he would always have loved Him; by always loving Him, he would always have clung close to Him; by clinging to Him Who is eternal, he would have possessed everlasting life. The one true good of Adam was clearly the perfect knowledge of his Creator. But he was banished from the Lord's face; because of his sin, he was struck with the blindness of ignorance, and lost the intimate light of contemplation; forgetting the sweetness of divine things, he inclined his mind to earthly desires. Thus he became a wanderer and a fugitive over the earth. By his disordered lust for earthly things, he became a wanderer; and by his guilty conscience, which feels every man's hand against it, he became a fugitive. Every temptation will conquer the one who has lost God's help.

So the human heart, which divine love had kept secure, and which had kept itself in unity by loving only One, now began to flow out in all directions through earthly desires. For the mind which does not know how to love its true good is never stable and never rests. Here is the source of restlessness, ceaseless labour, disquiet – until we turn and cling again to God. The sick heart trembles and staggers; the cause of its disease is love of the world; its remedy is love of God.

Hugh of Saint Victor
The Moral Ark of Noah, **Prologue**

The Trinity: An illustration

Just as one flame contains three realities in a single fire, so there is one God in three persons. How? The flame is made of a shining brightness, a purple energy, and a glowing heat. It has a shining brightness so that it can give light, a purple energy so that it can be active and alive, and a glowing heat so that it can burn. The shining brightness represents the Father, who reveals His brightness to believers in His fatherly care. The purple energy contained within the brightness (by which the same flame manifests its power) represents the Son, who from the Virgin took a body in which the divine nature demonstrated its miraculous powers. The glowing heat represents the Holy Spirit, who pours Himself glowingly into the minds of believers. But where there is no shining brightness, no purple energy, and no glowing heat, there is no flame to be seen. Likewise, where neither the Father, nor the Son, nor the Holy Spirit is honoured, God receives no worthy worship. And so, just as we see these three realities in the one flame, so we must understand three persons in the unity of the divine nature.

Hildegard of Bingen
Scivias, **Book 2, chapter 2, section 6**

A conversation between Hardness of heart and Mercy

My fourth vision gathered like a cloud of thick smoke. It assumed a human shape, but with no arms or legs; it only had huge dark eyes that stared without blinking. It remained in the darkness, completely still and unmoving. Then it spoke:

Hardness of heart: I have produced nothing; I have not brought anyone into existence. So why should I concern myself about anything? I will just leave things as they are; I will help others only if they are useful to me. God created everything, so let Him look after it all. If I got involved even a little bit in other people's business, I wouldn't do them any good or any harm. I could go round feeling pity for everybody and everything, but that would rob me of all *my* peace. What would become of me? What sort of life would I have if I had to supply an answer to every happy or sad voice? All I know is that I myself exist; and everyone else should think in the same way.

Again I heard a voice coming from the cloud, as follows:

Mercy's reply: What are you saying, you thing of stone? The plants radiate the fragrance of their flowers. Precious jewels reflect their splendour to others. Every created being longs for a loving embrace. The whole natural world serves humankind, offering all its abundance in this service. But you do not even deserve a full human shape. All you are is a merciless stare, an evil cloud of smoke in the darkness! But I, Mercy, am a soothing herb. I live in the dew, in the air, in all that is green. My heart fills to overflowing, and I help others. I was there when the first words sounded forth: "Let there be!" These words gave birth to all creation, which stands today as humankind's servant. But you are banished. With a loving gaze I look at life's demands, and I feel myself to be a part of all. I lift up the broken-hearted and lead them back to wholeness, because I, Mercy, am the balm for all suffering, and my words are true. But you, Hardness of heart, remain what you are: a bitter cloud of smoke.

Hildegard of Bingen
The Book of Life's Merits, chapter 1, sections 16-17

Song to God the Father

O great Father,
Great is our need!
So we pray to You now
By Your Word
Through which You have filled us
With what we lacked.
O may it please You, Father
(For it is proper)
To look upon us now,
In case we fail
And darken Your name within us.
For Your name is our help
In time of need.

Song for the Holy Spirit

The Holy Spirit is Life
And gives life,
Animating all living things.
He is the root of every created being,
And He purifies all things,
Washing away sins,
Anointing wounds.
He is shining Life,
Worthy of praise!
He awakens
And He enlivens
All things.

Song for the Virgin Mary

O sweet branch from the stump of Jesse!
O how marvellous a thing,
That God saw this girl's beauty
Like an eagle that fixes its eye on the sun!

And when the Most High Father
Saw this girl's splendour,
He desired His Logos
To become flesh in her.

For in God's hidden mystery
The Virgin's mind was flooded with light,
And from her there sprang forth
In a miraculous way
A bright Flower.

For when the Most High Father
Saw this girl's splendour,
He desired His Logos
To become flesh in her.

Hildegard of Bingen

5

The Crusades

1. What were the Crusades?

The Crusades were a series of military expeditions to the Middle East by Western Catholics, inspired and blessed by the Catholic Church, with the aim of recapturing the Holy Land (especially Jerusalem) from the Muslims. There were four main Crusades:

First Crusade:	1096-99
Second Crusade:	1147-49
Third Crusade:	1189-92
Fourth Crusade:	1202-4

There had, of course, been a long tradition of warfare between Christians and Muslims before the Crusades. The Byzantine Empire and the Islamic Empire had been fighting each other in and around Asia Minor ever since the Muslim armies first came streaming out of Arabia in the 7th century. However, the wars of the Byzantines against the Muslims were *not* Crusades. This is because they were not wars led by the Church for a religious purpose (as the Crusades were); the Byzantine-Muslim wars were "ordinary" wars, led by the Byzantine state for reasons of national self-defence, or the reconquest of Byzantine territory which the Muslims had seized. The Eastern Church resolutely refused to award the crown of martyrdom to Byzantine soldiers who had fallen in battle against Muslims – a stark contrast to the Western attitude, where the Church saw fighting and dying in a Crusade as a spiritual act that washed away the warrior's sins. So when the First Crusade was preached in 1095, a new and specifically

Western Catholic phenomenon was born, which had profound effects on Western society and the Western Church.

2. The causes of the Crusades

It was the great Byzantine Emperor **Alexius I Comnenus** (1081-1118) who triggered off the Crusades. In 1094, Alexius appealed to Pope **Urban II** (1088-99) for help in fighting the Seljuk Turks. The Turks, the new rulers of the Muslim world in the East, had decisively beaten the Byzantines at the battle of Manzikert in 1071, and conquered the bulk of Asia Minor.[1] Alexius asked for Western troops to increase the strength of his own Byzantine army, so that he could reconquer Asia Minor. What he got instead was the First Crusade.

Before Alexius made his appeal to Urban II for Western troops, Western Europe was already full of people who had gone on pilgrimage to the Holy Land, to visit the scenes of Jesus's life and death, especially His tomb (which was, according to tradition, located in the Church of the Holy Sepulchre in Jerusalem). Any physical object which was associated with Christ or the saints, *e.g.* part of their body or clothing, was highly valued; believers viewed these "relics" as channels through which God would bestow grace and favour on those who venerated them.[2]

Because the Son of God had trodden and sanctified its very soil, the Holy Land gained a unique status in the eyes of Western Christians (not to the same degree for Easterners, who never felt any need to "liberate" Jerusalem from the Muslims).[3] People therefore felt that pilgrimages to the Holy Land were a special way of acquiring God's blessing.

---

1. See Chapter 3, section 1.

2. For relics, see Volume One, Chapter 7, section 3, under the heading *Church worship*.

3. This difference of attitude between East and West may perhaps reflect the greater degree to which Western piety was focused on material "things" and "places". The East of course had its *icons*; but it resolutely refused to imitate the West in having *statues*, on the grounds that statues were too grossly materialistic to be genuine windows into spiritual realities (as we saw in Chapter 3, section 3).

Until the Seljuk Turks took control in 1055, the Muslim rulers of the Holy Land had always treated Christian pilgrims well. The Turks, by contrast, treated them badly. Western pilgrims came back from Palestine and filled Europe with terrible stories of Turkish hostility and persecution. Catholic Europe was outraged. In addition, there was a growing feeling in the West at this time that the forces of Christianity could defeat and expel the Muslims from Christian lands they had conquered. Under King Ferdinand I of Castile (1035-65), the Christian reconquest of Muslim Spain had begun, which Spanish Catholics regarded as a Crusade in their own land. Between 1060 and 1090, the Catholic Normans of southern Italy destroyed Muslim power in Sicily. Perhaps it seemed natural to continue this successful drive against Islam into the East.

Pope Urban II had reasons of his own for supporting the Byzantine appeal for help. As we saw in the last Chapter (section 6), Urban was a disciple of Hildebrand, and was in exile from Rome where the Holy Roman Emperor Henry IV had set up a rival pope, Clement III. Urban thought that the way to defeat Henry and his rival pope, and so secure the victory of the Hildebrandine reform movement, was to make himself the leader of a great popular cause. So from the outset, Pope Urban intended to answer the Byzantine appeal for troops by launching a great religious Crusade to liberate the Holy Land. He correctly calculated that this would unite Catholic Europe behind him. In November 1095, Urban called together a council of clergy and nobles at Clermont in southern France to consider the situation in the East. On the ninth day of this council, he preached one of the most epoch-making sermons in Christian history. Urban called on the kings and nobles of Catholic Europe, especially the French, to stop fighting each other, unite, and rescue the Holy Land from the Turks. The assembled crowds responded with an outburst of wild enthusiasm, crying out, "God wills it! God wills it!" (in Latin, "Deus vult!") This became the motto of the First Crusade.

We must always remember that the Crusades were genuine expressions of popular religious enthusiasm. Hundreds of thousands of Western European men sincerely wanted to free the tomb of Christ from the Muslims, as an act of devotion to their Saviour. The Crusades, in fact, were simply pilgrimages carried out in the form of warfare. The very name the Crusaders took for themselves suggests this religious motive, because the word "crusade" comes from the Latin *crux*, meaning "cross". A Crusading knight would have the sign of the cross sewn into his outer clothing as a token of his allegiance to Christ; the more zealous would brand it into their flesh. "To take the cross" meant to become a Crusader. Urban II encouraged this spirit by using the words of Christ in Mark 8:34 as a Crusade text – "Whoever desires to come after Me, let him deny himself, and take up his cross, and follow Me." Different national groups were soon wearing distinctive crosses; in the Third Crusade, for instance, the English wore white crosses, the French red, and the Flemish green.

The military power behind the Crusades was the nobility (or aristocracy) of Western Europe, a warrior class for whom fighting was a way of life. They fought on horseback and were called "knights"; they were the backbone of Europe's ruling class.[4] The Cluniac revival in the 10th and 11th centuries tried to bring the violence of this warrior class under control by creating a moral and spiritual code to govern their behaviour.[5] This was called the code of "chivalry" (from the French *chevalerie*, "cavalry" – warriors on horses). We can see the code of chivalry best summed up in the *Book of the Christian Life* by Bishop **Bonizo of Sutri** (died 1098), a friend of Hildebrand. The *Book*, published in about 1090, offered a complete set of chivalric values for the Christian knight, including courage, justice, chastity, sobriety, loyalty, and prudence. The code of chivalry often took Charlemagne as the supreme example of a true Christian knight.[6] In practice, it meant that when a young noble reached his maturity, the Church blessed his sword in a special ceremony, and he promised

---

4. For the origin of the knights and their place in the medieval social system, see Chapter 4, section 3.

5. For the Cluniac revival, see Chapter 4, section 3.

6. For Charlemagne, see Chapter 2, section 2.

to use it to defend churches, women, orphans, the poor, and servants of God, and to fight against injustice and the enemies of Christianity. Western Catholics therefore came to see the knight as a kind of spiritual figure, like a priest or a monk.

In these ways, then, the Catholic Church tried to Christianise the knights of Western Europe. The Crusades provided a great outlet for the energies of these Christian warriors: by attacking the Muslims and freeing the Holy Land, they were doing the thing they enjoyed most (fighting), and also fulfilling the spiritual ideals of chivalry by acting as champions of the Christian faith. Abbot **Guibert of Nogent** (1053/65?-1125) in north-eastern France said:

> In our times God has instituted holy wars, so that knights may find a new way of gaining salvation. They do not have to abandon secular affairs completely by choosing the monastic life or any religious profession, as was once the custom, but they can in some degree attain to God's grace by pursuing their own knightly careers, in the freedom and the armour which is their habit.

(Guibert was an interesting figure. He was a disciple of the "father of scholastic theology", Anselm of Canterbury – see Chapter 7, section 3 – and wrote notable treatises on the incarnation, the veneration of Mary, and the eucharist, opposing Berengar of Tours – see Chapter 4, section 7. He also produced a history of the First Crusade, and a remarkable attack on the abuse of relics, in which he condemned such absurdities as the claim of certain monks of Saint-Médard to possess a tooth of Jesus! Guibert's autobiography is a mine of information about the history and customs of his times.)

The spiritual nature of Crusade warfare was underlined by the fact that before every battle, a Crusader had to confess his sins to a priest and take holy communion. The papacy also offered heavenly rewards to the Crusading knights, promising them complete pardon from all the "temporal penalties" of their sins. This pardon was called an "indulgence". In the Second Crusade, Pope Eugenius III (1145-53) actually promised eternal life to all who fought the Turks in the Holy Land. By the time of the Third

Crusade, someone could get an indulgence for all his sins merely by hiring a knight to crusade on his behalf.[7]

The chief inspiration behind the Crusades, then, was religious: they were armed pilgrimages which expressed the ideals of chivalry and offered a pathway to God's grace and even eternal life. Historians of a previous generation, unable to understand religious motives, used to emphasise that the Crusades had other, less spiritual attractions for the Western nobility. For example, a Crusade offered some nobles an opportunity to win land for themselves. The Western custom of inheritance, "primogeniture", meant that the oldest son inherited all his father's property; so there were many younger sons of the nobility who had no land. The Middle East opened up for them a huge field for conquest. The Crusades were also attractive because they offered the noble warrior a chance to prove how good a fighter he was and achieve military glory for himself. These secular motives must have played a part in the Crusades, but we have to recognise that a deeply religious concern lay at the bottom of it all, however misguided the modern student may feel it was.

3. The history of the Crusades

Although we divide up the Crusades into a number of separate expeditions, we must remember that after the First Crusade there was a constant trickle of Catholic soldiers going to the Holy Land to join the Crusaders who were already there, to defend and extend the territory they had already won from the Turks. Fighting was going on all the time. What we call "the Second Crusade", "the Third Crusade", *etc.*, were the times when the West made specific and concentrated attempts at destroying Turkish power.

The First Crusade, 1096-99

Before the official Crusade called for by Pope Urban II took place, there was a tragic episode known as the "peoples' Crusade". A French monk named **Peter the Hermit** (1050-1115), claiming

---

7. For a detailed account of the theology of "temporal penalties" and "indulgences", see Chapter 7, section 3, under the heading *Thomas Aquinas.*

to be guided by visions, went about preaching the Crusade with an almost evangelistic passion. Judged by his popularity, Peter was probably the most successful preacher of the entire Middle Ages. Wherever he preached the Crusade, people wept for their sins, reformed their lives, forgave their enemies, mended their broken or failing marriages, and freely gave money to the Church. Peter gathered an army of some 20,000 ordinary people, mostly peasants (not knights). Inspired by his wondrous visions of victory over the Muslims in the Holy Land, they marched to Palestine through southern Germany, massacring Jews on the way. This was the first serious outbreak of violent anti-Judaism (religious hostility to Jews) in medieval Europe.[8] However, when the peoples' army arrived in Asia Minor, they were themselves massacred by the Turks – it was a case of an unruly mob of poorly armed peasants fighting professional Turkish soldiers. Peter the Hermit escaped the slaughter and was present with the triumphant Crusading army of knights when it captured Jerusalem in 1099.

By contrast with Peter the Hermit's mob of peasants, the knights of the First official Crusade were an impressive assembly of Western Europe's greatest French nobles: Hugh of Vermandois, brother of King Philip I of France; **Godfrey of Bouillon** (1060-1100), a descendant of Charlemagne; Godfrey's brothers Eustace and Baldwin; Raymond of Toulouse, a veteran campaigner against the Muslims in Spain; and several great Norman nobles – Bohemund (a Norman warrior of southern Italy), his nephew Tancred, Robert of Normandy (oldest son of King William the Conqueror of England[9]), and his brother-in-law, Stephen of Blois. Unfortunately the Crusaders appointed no single commander, and the expedition was cursed by constant quarrelling among the various leaders. Some of them were men of integrity, such as Raymond of Toulouse, Tancred (who was

---

8. For more about anti-Judaism, see Chapter 8, section 2.

9. William the Conqueror, who died in 1087, had divided his Norman empire by giving England to his younger son William Rufus (1087-1100), and the French duchy of Normandy to his older son Robert. For William the Conqueror, see Chapter 4, section 1.

praised by his own generation as the perfect model of a chivalrous Christian knight), and especially Godfrey of Bouillon, whom his contemporaries called "a holy monk in armour". However, many of the others were far from being men of pure Christian lives.

The Crusading armies gathered at Constantinople in the winter and spring of 1096-97. It was a huge force – as many as 300,000, according to some high estimates. They arrived at just the right time: the empire of the Seljuk Turks had broken up into warring factions. The disunity of the Turks enabled the Crusaders to defeat the separate Turkish forces one by one. The Crusaders began by recapturing Nicaea from the Turks in 1097. They defeated a Turkish army at Dorylaeum in July. Then followed the siege of Antioch, which was long and bitter; it fell to the Crusaders after eight months in June 1098. Three days later, they were themselves under siege in Antioch from a Turkish army, but managed to inflict a crushing defeat on their Muslim besiegers. It then took the Crusaders another year to reach Jerusalem, by which time their forces had been reduced by battle, famine, and pestilence to a mere 20,000 men. But it was enough: they captured Jerusalem in June 1099 after a siege of six weeks. Once inside the Holy City, the Crusaders spared no-one; they carried out a merciless massacre of its entire Muslim and Jewish population, including women and children.[10]

The military results of the First Crusade were the restoration of western Asia Minor to Byzantine rule, and the setting up of four independent "Crusader states" in Syria and Palestine: the County of Edessa, the Principality of Antioch, the County of Tripolis, and the Kingdom of Jerusalem. These are often called the "Latin" kingdoms because their rulers belonged to the Latin-speaking Catholic Church. The jewel of the Latin kingdoms was Jerusalem. Godfrey of Bouillon was offered the title "king" of

---

10. We should not feel too morally superior to the Crusaders. Ours is the age in which, during the Second World War, Britain carried out "obliteration bombing" of German cities, and America dropped atom bombs on Hiroshima and Nagasaki, thereby massacring in the name of democracy far greater numbers of women and children than the Crusaders ever managed.

Jerusalem, but refused to wear a crown of gold in the city where his Lord had worn a crown of thorns. Instead he took the more lowly title "Defender of the Holy Tomb". Godfrey died a year later in 1100, and was succeeded by his brother, Baldwin, who did take the title "king of Jerusalem" and reigned until 1118, enlarging his kingdom by capturing cities like Caesarea in 1101 and Beirut in 1110.

The creation of these Latin Crusader states did far more than the schism of 1054 to breed real practical division between Eastern Orthodox and Western Catholic Christians. Wherever the Crusaders conquered, they forcibly took over the churches of Easterners and set up their own Western Latin bishops, to whom they expected Eastern believers to submit. Indeed, the sometimes brutal way the Crusaders trod down the native Orthodox peoples of the Middle East became so hateful to the Orthodox, that they were soon fighting alongside the more tolerant Muslims to throw out the oppressive Crusaders!

Bernard of Clairvaux and the Second Crusade, 1147-49

The fall of the Latin kingdom of Edessa to a Turkish army in 1144 gave rise to the Second Crusade. Pope Eugenius III proclaimed it, but the real force behind the Second Crusade was **Bernard of Clairvaux** (1090-1153).[11]

Bernard was one of the brightest spiritual stars of the entire Middle Ages. Born in Fontaines (eastern-central France), he was the third son of Tescelin Sorrel, a Crusading knight who had taken part in the capture of Jerusalem in 1099. Tescelin's six sons were trained to follow in his military footsteps as knights – all, that is, except Bernard. We are told that his mother Alice had a dream about Bernard being destined for higher things. So he was sent to a theological college in Chatillon, where priests instructed students in grammar, logic, rhetoric, and the Scriptures. It seems that Bernard was a very imaginative boy who loved solitude, and often had vivid and sometimes overpowering dreams.

---

11. Clairvaux is pronounced "Clair-voh".

He was particularly affected by a childhood dream in which he saw the Virgin Mary and the Christ-child; the deep impression made by this dream on Bernard's mind and emotions stayed with him throughout his life.

Bernard of Clairvaux (1090-1153)

Bernard had an unusually close relationship as a child with his devout mother Alice. When she died in Bernard's late teens, the bereavement seems to have shaken him to the depths of his being. There followed a period of intense inner conflict, in which he felt himself torn violently between the call of the monastery and the worldly life of a carefree, irresponsible young noble who had the means to indulge his appetites quite liberally. His ultimate decision in the year 1112 at the age of 22 to become a monk took the form of a tumultuous self-surrender to Christ, which Bernard always referred to as his conversion. The monastery he joined was the Cistercian community in Citeaux, near Fontaines (in Latin, Citeaux is *Cistercium* – hence "Cistercian").[12] The Cistercian order of monks was a reformed branch of the Benedictines. Their headquarters was at the Citeaux monastery, founded in 1098; they were distinguished as a monastic order by the extreme plainness and simplicity of their liturgy, vestments, and church interiors (partly because of their commitment to a simple lifestyle – vast amounts of money were not to be spent on fabulous church adornments).

In 1115, Bernard and 12 other monks from Citeaux set up a new Cistercian community in the county of Champagne. The monastery was established in a place called "the valley of Wormwood", a desolate and forbidding wasteland; but Bernard, the abbot of the new community, changed its name to "the valley of Light" – which in French is "Clairvaux". And so the famous monastery of Clairvaux was founded, which soon outshone the mother community in Citeaux, simply because Bernard was in Clairvaux. The man lent his lustre to the monastery. Clairvaux flourished under Bernard's rule, becoming the parent to 68 new Cistercian communities. By the time Bernard died there were 338 in total, scattered over the face of Europe and the Middle East, as far north as Sweden, and as far east as Palestine.

Bernard soon became one of the greatest preachers of the Middle Ages, and probably one of the great preachers of all time. His nickname was "The Honey-flowing Teacher", because his sermons seemed to drip with the love of Christ. Bernard expressed his own ideal of preaching in the following pithy epigram: "Not

---

12. Citeaux is pronounced "see-toh". As with Clairvaux, the "x" is silent.

so much to explain the words as to reach people's hearts." The controlling theme of his preaching was always Love: God's love for man as revealed in Christ, man's responsive love for God and for his neighbour. Martin Luther[13] said of Bernard's written sermons, "In his sermons Bernard is superior to all the teachers, even to Augustine himself, because he preaches Christ so excellently."[14] The other distinguishing feature of Bernard's sermons was their pervading sense of eternal realities. To listen to Bernard was to feel the things of earth grow strangely dim in the light of God's glory and grace. Bernard preached outside as well as inside the abbey at Clairvaux, and people of all sorts found his sermons gripping. It was said that if Bernard was due to preach in a particular locality, mothers hid their sons and wives hid their husbands, in case they were so captivated by Bernard's eloquence that they ran away from home to become monks!

In doctrinal matters, Bernard was a disciple of Augustine of Hippo, setting out the chief features of Augustinian doctrine in his treatise *On Grace and Free-will*. Bernard wrote several books which many have regarded as spiritual masterpieces on the Christian life – *On Loving God*, *Steps of Humility and Pride*, and *Sermons on the Song of Solomon*. His interpretation of the *Song* as an allegory of the spiritual love-union between Christ the Bridegroom, and the faithful soul as His Bride, is largely responsible for Bernard's reputation as a "mystic".

A number of popular hymns are said to have been written by Bernard: "Jesus, Thou joy of loving hearts", "Jesus, the very thought of Thee", "O Jesus, King most wonderful", and "O sacred head, sore wounded". The attribution is doubtful in some cases; but even if Bernard did not actually write any of these hymns, they faithfully reflect his spiritual outlook, with their warm emotional focus on the sweetness and beauty of Jesus in His human nature, His tenderness and sufferings. In fact, Bernard pioneered a revolutionary new trend in Western piety towards a greater emphasis on the human Jesus, and the centrality of

---

13. For Luther, see Volume Three, Chapters 2 and 3.

14. For Augustine, see Volume One, Chapter 9, section 3.

companionship with Jesus the Man of Sorrows in the believer's life. Jesus the suffering Son of Man, hanging on a cross, tended to replace Christ the risen Son of God, enthroned in heaven, as the main focus of Western Catholic spirituality.

Bernard did more than any other man of his time to popularise the adoration of the Virgin Mary, for whom he felt a special veneration – "the violet of humility, the lily of chastity, the rose of purity, and the splendour of heaven", as Bernard called her. If Christ was the Mediator between God the Father and humankind, Mary was the intercessor with Christ. "If you are terrified by the thunders of the Father," said Bernard, "go to Jesus. If you are afraid to go to Jesus, then run to Mary." However, despite Bernard's devotion to Mary, he very strongly opposed the view that Mary was conceived without sin – the doctrine of the immaculate conception (which at that time was not an official Catholic doctrine, but only a theological opinion).[15]

Bernard had a prolonged and famous controversy with Peter Abelard.[16] Abelard was the great intellectual and the great sinner of his day. Thousands flocked to his theology lectures in Paris until the scandal of his love affair with his young pupil Heloise became public. Bernard could not stand the man and spent most of his life trying to curb his influence. He thought Abelard was an arrogant free-thinker: "The only thing Abelard does not know," fulminated Bernard, "are the words, 'I do not know'!" He accused Abelard of joining with Arius in his views of the Trinity, with Nestorius in his views of Christ, and with Pelagius in his views of grace and free-will. The two protagonists had a healthy respect for each other. Abelard respected Bernard's position in the Church, and said he felt like an ant in the presence of a lion; Bernard respected Abelard's intellectual powers, and said he felt like David taking on Goliath. The real difference between them was ultimately one of spirit and attitude. Bernard wanted the mind of the Christian to receive and adore

---

15. See the quotation at the end of the Chapter, and the account of Thomas Aquinas's theology in Chapter 7, section 3.

16. See the account of Peter Abelard's theology in Chapter 7, section 3.

in humility the mysteries of the faith; Abelard wanted the intellectual freedom to argue about everything and discover truth
through unfettered discussion and disputation. In this battle of
giants, Bernard triumphed, and Pope Innocent II condemned
Abelard to perpetual silence and confinement. Abelard died a
year later, under the protection of Peter the Venerable, abbot of
Cluny, who tells us that Abelard passed into eternity meek and
penitent, a true philosopher of Christ. Depending on one's point
of view, Bernard appears in this controversy either as a narrow-
minded persecutor of a more brilliant man, or as the undaunted
champion of orthodoxy against a dangerous speculator.

Bernard's reputation as a preacher, a writer, and a founder of
monasteries was so far-flung that he was in constant demand for
advice. It has been said of Bernard that "in his solitude he governed all the churches of the West." Bernard's counsel was sought
on the appointment of bishops and other high dignitaries in the
Church. His influence scaled new heights in the 1130s when the
cardinals elected two rival popes, Innocent II and Anacletus II.
Bernard supported Innocent and toured Western Europe campaigning on his behalf. Bernard's offensive swung the Catholic
nations decisively behind Innocent, and in 1134 Bernard and
Innocent entered Rome together, where Innocent was enthroned
as the true pope. Bernard took back with him from Italy to
Clairvaux a young man also named Bernard, who became the
older Bernard's favourite disciple. In 1145 this younger Bernard
became Pope Eugenius III. Bernard of Clairvaux's sway reached
its pinnacle, since Eugenius retained all his affection for his old
master and consulted him frequently. Bernard wrote a spiritual
handbook for Eugenius in which he warned him against becoming so involved in a thousand and one tasks and affairs that he
forgot himself and drifted into hardness of heart.[17]

Bernard's dominating position in the life of the Western
Church in the 1100s was quite remarkable. He was never

---

17. The great Protestant Reformer John Calvin had a high opinion of this
handbook; in its pages, he says, "Bernard speaks as though the very truth itself
were speaking" (Calvin's *Institutes*, Book 4, chapter 2, section 11).

anything more than abbot of Clairvaux, yet kings, Emperors, and popes sat at his feet. All attempts to elevate him to a higher office in the Church he resisted fiercely and successfully. One thing that contributed to Bernard's influence was his reputation as a miracle-worker. Spectacular healings and exorcisms occurred when Bernard prayed for people. Bernard himself referred to these marvels in a rather diffident sort of way:

> Signs and wonders have been wrought by holy men and by deceivers. I am not conscious of being either. I know that I do not have those holy merits to which miracles testify. The miracles are not meant to honour me but to admonish others.

The fall of the Latin kingdom of Edessa to a Turkish army in 1144 gave rise to the Second Crusade of 1147-49. Bernard's involvement in the Second Crusade came about because Pope Eugenius III was (as we saw) a former monk of Bernard's, and Eugenius asked him to act as a sort of publicity agent for the Crusade. Bernard agreed and preached passionately all over Western Europe, exhorting people to go to the rescue of the kingdom of Jerusalem. Here is a typical example of Bernard's Crusade preaching:

> The earth trembles and shakes, because the King of heaven has lost His country, the country where once He appeared to men, where He walked among them for more than 30 years, the country made glorious by His miracles and holy by His blood, the country where the flowers of the resurrection first bloomed. And now, because of our sins, the enemy of the cross has begun to lift his blasphemous head there, and to devastate with his sword that blessed land of promise. The great eye of providence surveys these acts in silence; it wishes to see if there is anyone who seeks God, anyone who suffers with Him in His sorrow, anyone who will restore His heritage to Him. I say to you, the Lord is testing you!

Bernard's appeals were successful. The Second Crusade was led by King Louis VII of France (1137-80) and the Holy Roman Emperor, Conrad III (1138-52). However, once the Crusaders arrived in the East, they met with total disaster. The Eastern Byzantine Christians, who had not asked the Crusaders to come, received them badly. Most of the Crusaders perished in Asia Minor through famine, fever, and Turkish attacks. Their one serious military operation, the siege of Damascus, was a failure. Catholic Europe was shaken to the core. Many blamed the collapse of the Crusade on the ill-will and treachery of the Byzantines. Bernard of Clairvaux, however, blamed it on the sins of Western Catholics; God was judging and punishing them for their ungodly lives:

> It seems that our sins have provoked the Lord, and He has forgotten His pity and has come to judge the world before the appointed time. He has not spared His own people; He has not spared even His own name. The Pagans say, 'Where is their God?' We promised victory; behold – desolation!

Bernard's involvement in the Second Crusade contrasts strangely with his moderate and gentle attitude to heretics and Jews within Catholic Europe. He advocated tolerance towards the Jews, and maintained that the only weapons the Church should use against heretics were argument and persuasion. However, these were the days before the founding of the inquisition. Once the inquisition was established, the Church buried Bernard's tolerant opinions in silence.[18]

Bernard was swiftly canonised (officially proclaimed a saint) in 1174, only 21 years after his death. His fame lived on through his writings, although obviously he was held in higher regard among the Cistercians than anywhere else. As a popular saint he was eclipsed by Francis of Assisi in the 1200s.[19] Also, as the doctrine of Mary's immaculate conception became ever more fashionable, Bernard suffered for his staunch denial of it. The more fervent worshippers of Mary declared that in heaven Bernard bore a blemish on his glorified breast to atone for what

---

18. For the inquisition, see Chapter 8, section 3.
19. For Francis of Assisi, see Chapter 8, section 4.

he had said against the Virgin. However, his reputation endured and even survived the storms of the Protestant Reformation in the 16th century. When the Reformers broke with the papacy, they made severe criticisms of many medieval saints and theologians; but they could never bring themselves to speak very harshly of Bernard. Martin Luther, in his commentary on Galatians, extolled Bernard as a shining example of a man who lived by genuine heartfelt faith in Jesus Christ: "Bernard, a man so godly, so holy, so pure, that we should commend and prefer him before all the theologians of the Church."

At about the same time as the Second Crusade, a band of knights from England and Flanders (modern Belgium), who were sailing to the Holy Land, stopped on the way in 1139 to attack the Muslim city of Lisbon, on the western coast of Islamic Spain. They captured it, slaughtered the Muslim population, settled there, and founded the new Catholic nation of Portugal. No-one at the time could foresee it, but in the 15th century the Portugese would create a vast overseas empire based on naval power, opening up America to European colonisation and conquest.

The Third Crusade, 1189-92

After the failure of the Second Crusade, the disunited Muslims of the Middle East began to find their unity again. A brilliant Kurdish general called **Saladin** (1137-93) took control of Egypt, and by 1186 his empire surrounded the kingdom of Jerusalem. He crushed the Latin army at the battle of Hattin in July 1187 and captured Jerusalem. The West had controlled the city from 1099 to 1187. Fortunately Saladin was more merciful than the Crusaders had been when they took Jerusalem, and he allowed its conquered Christian inhabitants to leave peacefully. Saladin was a just and wise ruler whose standards of conduct often put the Crusaders to shame.

The whole West was shocked by the fall of Jerusalem. It is said that Pope Gregory VIII (October-December 1187) died of grief, but not before proclaiming the Third Crusade. The three greatest kings of Catholic Europe led the Crusade: King Philip Augustus of France (1180-1223), the Holy Roman Emperor Frederick Barbarossa (1152-90), and above all, King **Richard I** of England (1189-99), known to history as "Richard the Lionheart". Various disasters almost wrecked the expedition. The Holy Roman Emperor Frederick drowned near Tarsus in 1190; without his leadership, his German army proved hopelessly ineffective. Philip Augustus of France and Richard of England quarrelled constantly. However, the Crusaders captured the great city of Acre near Mount Carmel, north of Jerusalem. Acre, not Jerusalem, was really the most important Latin city in the Middle East, because it was the centre of international trade and commerce.

After the Crusaders had taken Acre, Philip Augustus went back to France. Richard the Lionheart stayed on for another year. He failed to capture Jerusalem, but his amazing exploits in battle won him the admiration even of the Muslims. For years afterwards, Muslim women used to frighten their children into obedience by telling them that if they did not do as they were told, Richard the Lionheart would get them! Richard finally made a treaty with Saladin in 1192, which gave the Crusaders a strip of coastland from Acre to Ascalon (south-west of Jerusalem), with Christian right of access to Jerusalem guaranteed.

More than any other, the Third Crusade inspired the imagination of Western Europe. Men poured out a flood of poetry, story, and song to celebrate the contest between Saladin and Richard the Lionheart, two of the greatest warrior-leaders of any age. To this day, the Third Crusade is the one most people know something about.

The Fourth Crusade, 1202-1204

Pope Innocent III (1198-1216) proclaimed the Fourth Crusade. This time the Crusading soldiers were entirely French. They had at first intended to conquer Egypt from the Muslims, but they were being ferried there in ships provided by the great Italian trading republic of Venice; and Venice insisted, as part of the payment, that the French first of all conquer for them the city of Zara in Dalmatia (modern Croatia) – Zara had recently seceded from the Venetian empire and joined the Catholic kingdom of

Hungary. So the Fourth Crusade began with the Crusaders shedding the blood of their fellow Catholics as they stormed and captured Zara. Innocent III was outraged and excommunicated both the French and the Venetians. He eventually restored the French Crusaders to the Church on their professions of repentance, but he refused to lift the sentence from the Venetians. The Crusade therefore continued as a sort of unholy alliance between the Catholic French and excommunicated Venetians.

At this point Alexius Angelus, the son of the deposed Byzantine Emperor Isaac II (1185-95), diverted the French and Venetian force from its original aim of conquering Egypt. Alexius promised the Crusaders large payment, and the submission of the Orthodox Church to the papacy, if they would help him regain the Byzantine throne. The Venetians welcomed Alexius's proposal; they wanted to secure control of all Eastern trade. On top of this, the head ("doge") of the Venetian republic, Enrico Dandolo, had a personal vendetta against the Byzantines; he had been blinded in a street fight in Constantinople 30 years previously, and was further embittered against Byzantium by the difficulty he found in renewing trade agreements with them after he had become doge. With his personal and political hostility against Byzantium, Dandolo has been seen as the real mastermind behind the Fourth Crusade's attack on Constantinople.

Pope Innocent III forbade the Crusaders to fight the Byzantines, but they ignored Innocent, went to Constantinople, deposed the Byzantine Emperor, and placed Alexius on the throne. When Alexius could not keep his lavish promises of payment, the French and Venetians besieged and captured Constantinople in 1204. Amid scenes of appalling violence, the triumphant Crusaders looted the Byzantine capital's fabulous treasures (it was mostly the Venetians, not the French, who did the looting). A French noble, Baldwin of Flanders, became Emperor of a new Latin kingdom of Constantinople; other French nobles shared out large parts of the Byzantine Empire among themselves. The new Catholic rulers of Byzantium set up a Western Catholic patriarch of Constantinople, and made the Orthodox Church subject to the pope. Even so, except where Western force compelled them, the Orthodox people of Byzantium scorned the papacy and remained loyal to their own Church and their own patriarch.

The Fourth Crusade was one of the darkest episodes in Christian history. For the first time, a Crusading army fought fellow Christians, both Catholics in Zara and Orthodox in Constantinople, simply for material gain. The Byzantine Empire received a mortal wound from which it never really recovered, even though the Byzantines recaptured Constantinople from the Latins in 1261. An enduring legacy of deep hatred for the Western Catholic Church was left among the Eastern Orthodox.

Other Crusades

There were other Crusades, but none to rival the first four. The most important of the others was the so-called Sixth Crusade of 1228-29, led by the Holy Roman Emperor **Frederick II** (1210-50). Frederick was one of the strangest, most cultured and most gifted rulers of the whole Middle Ages, admired by historians as a law-maker. He had a great sympathy for Muslim culture.[20] A determined foe of the papacy, with which he was frequently in military conflict, he had been excommunicated by Pope Gregory IX (1227-41). Frederick's appearance in the Holy Land was more of a state visit than a Crusade. Without fighting, in 1229 he secured from the Sultan al-Kamil of Egypt, by diplomacy alone, possession of Jerusalem, Bethlehem, and Nazareth. Frederick then crowned himself king of Jerusalem. The Holy City was once more in Christian hands, until 1244 when it was again captured by Muslims and permanently lost to the West. By the end of the 13th century, all the Latin territory in the Middle East had fallen to the Muslims; the last to fall was the great Crusading capital of Acre in 1291. Western Christendom and the papacy continued to talk about further Crusades for several hundred

---

20. Frederick was referred to as a "baptised sultan" (a sultan was a Turkish Muslim ruler); he wore a Turkish costume, and had a Turkish bodyguard and several wives. For more about Frederick, see Chapter 8, section 1.

years, but none was ever launched. When Acre fell, the Crusades against Islam were over.

4. The Hospitallers, Templars, and Teutonic Knights

The Crusades gave rise to a number of great religious-military monastic orders. The most important were *the Knights of Saint John of Jerusalem, the Knights of the Temple,* and *the Teutonic Knights.* These orders combined the monastic way of life with the warrior-code of chivalry; their members were both monks and knights at the same time. Their purpose was to transport pilgrims to the Holy Land, give them shelter and protection while they were there, and do battle with the Muslim Turks.

The Knights of Saint John were founded in 1048, before the First Crusade, but it was as a result of the Crusades that they really blossomed and flourished. Pope Paschal II (1099-1118) gave them official papal recognition in 1113. They were often called the *Hospitallers,* because they ran a hospital for sick pilgrims in Jerusalem. The Knights of the Temple were founded in 1118; their name came from their base near the site of the Jerusalem temple, and their monastic rule was written by none other than Bernard of Clairvaux in 1128. They were often called the *Templars.*

The Hospitallers and the Templars fought with outstanding courage and discipline against the Turks. Both became vast and wealthy organisations. After Jerusalem was recaptured by Muslim forces under Saladin in 1187, the Hospitallers and Templars were based in Acre. When Acre fell in 1291, the Hospitallers moved their headquarters first to Rhodes, then to Malta, from where they defended Christian Europe against Muslim attack for the next 300 years. The Templars settled in France. However, in what many consider one of the foulest crimes of the Middle Ages, the French king Philip the Fair (1285-1314) forcibly disbanded the Templars in 1312, and put many of them to death, on false charges of heresy, merely because he wanted to seize their money and property.

The Teutonic Knights were somewhat different from the Hospitallers and Templars. They were an almost exclusively

German order of monk-knights, founded by merchants of the German cities of Lubeck and Bremen in 1190 during the Third Crusade, and given papal recognition in 1191 by Pope Clement III (1187-91). Most of the activities of the Teutonic Knights took place in Germany and Eastern Europe rather than Palestine. They began campaigning against the Pagan Prussians in 1226, in the territory covered by present-day coastal Poland, conquering Prussia completely by 1283. German settlers and Dominican[21] missionaries followed in the footsteps of the victorious Knights, thus bringing Prussia within the Catholic fold (although only the eastern part of Prussia actually remained under the control of the Knights – the west was conquered by Poland).

The Teutonic Knights also vanquished and Christianised Latvia and Estonia. In a strange twist of history, the last great Pagan people of Eastern Europe, the Lithuanians, came to embrace Catholic Christianity through their fierce conflict with the Teutonic Knights. Seeking military assistance to fight off the Knights, the Lithunian king, Jagiello, made an alliance with Queen *Jadwiga* (1382-99) of Catholic Poland; the terms of the alliance were that Jagiello should marry Jadwiga, thus uniting Lithuania and Poland under a single monarchy, and that Jagiello and his people should accept the Christian faith. Jagiello was baptised, married and crowned king of Poland-Lithuania in 1386, taking the name *Vladislav II Jagiello* (1386-1434). In this way Lithuania, the final outpost of Pagan Europe, became officially Christian. And the Teutonic Knights were kept out of Lithuania.

5. The effects of the Crusades

The Crusades had many effects on Europe and the Middle East. These were the most important:

(i) They heightened the prestige and influence of the papacy in the West. The Crusades were inspired by the popes. The papacy appeared as the champion of

---

21. For the Dominicans, see Chapter 8, section 4.

Christianity, uniting Christians against the Muslim menace, and organising the resources of the West in defence of the Holy Land and the Latin Crusader states.

(ii) They encouraged the use of "indulgences" by which the popes could pardon all the "temporal penalties" of sin. Originally, indulgences were granted for some outstanding good deed (*e.g.* going on a Crusade). Soon they were being sold for cash: the payment of money to the Church was regarded as the good deed, in return for which penalties were cancelled. Eventually, indulgences were extended to cover souls already in purgatory. The theory was that if a believer had not paid off in this life the temporal penalties of his sins, he must pay them off by sufferings in purgatory. Buying an indulgence for a dead friend could therefore hasten his passage from purgatory to heaven.[22]

(iii) The Crusades established the idea and practice of using a religious war to destroy the enemies of the Catholic Church. The papacy would soon be using Crusades against heretical or dissenting groups within Western Christendom, such as the Albigensians in France and the Hussites in Bohemia.[23]

(iv) They helped the development of strong monarchies in Western Europe. The power of the Western nobility was weakened by their loss of control over many local communities; towns and cities bought their independence with money paid to the nobility, their landowning overlords, to finance the nobles' Crusading

---

22. For more about the theology of purgatory, see Chapter 7, section 3, under the heading *Thomas Aquinas*.

23. See Chapter 8, section 3 for the Albigensians, and Chapter 10, section 5 for the Hussites.

expeditions. In these and other ways, the Crusades contributed to the growth of stronger national monarchies in the West.

(v)   They inflicted lasting damage on relationships between Eastern Orthodox and Western Catholic Christianity because of the religious oppression to which the Crusaders subjected the Orthodox peoples of the East. The fall of Constantinople to a Crusading army in 1204 hastened the fall of the Byzantine Empire, and Byzantium's weakness paved the way for the Muslim conquest of Eastern Europe.

(vi) They left a lasting legacy of bitterness and hatred between Christians and Muslims. Prior to the Crusades, Byzantine Christians and Muslims had fought each other often enough, but they had a genuine respect for each other. *Nicholas Mysticus*, one of the greatest patriarchs of Constantinople (895-925), said:

Two empires, the Muslim and the Byzantine, surpass all other empires on earth, like two great lights in the heavens. For this reason alone, if for no other, they ought to be partners and brothers. Although we are separated in our ways of life, our customs, and our worship, we ought not to be completely divided.[24]

However, Mysticus's respect for Islamic culture did not yet exist among Western Catholics. The conduct of the Crusaders towards Muslims in the Holy Land was utterly ruthless. They made no attempt at evangelism; the Muslims were simply seen as enemies of Christ to be killed without compassion. The Crusades therefore introduced a new note of cruelty and religious intolerance into Christian-Muslim relationships. To this day, Arabic and

---

24. Mysticus actually had two periods as patriarch, 895-906 and 911-25. The Byzantine Emperor Leo VI (886-912) deposed Mysticus in 906 for opposing his fourth marriage (each of his previous three wives had died). Church law in Eastern Orthodoxy allows a person to marry only three times. After Leo's death, Mysticus regained his position as patriarch.

Turkish Muslims think of Christianity in terms of the Crusades, and see the "Christian West" as the present-day representative of the Crusading knights who slaughtered so many Muslim men, women and children in the Holy Land in the Middle Ages.

Important people:

The Church

Nicholas Mysticus, patriarch of Constantinople (895-906, 911-25)
Bonizo of Sutri (died 1098)
Pope Urban II (1088-99)
Peter the Hermit (1050-1115)
Guibert of Nogent (1053/65?-1125)
Bernard of Clairvaux (1090-1153)

Political and military

Byzantine Emperor Alexius I Comnenus (1081-1118)
Godfrey of Bouillon (1060-1100)
Saladin (1137-93)
King Richard I of England (1189-99)
Holy Roman Emperor Frederick II (1210-50)
Queen Jadwiga of Poland (1382-99)
King Vladislav II Jagiello of Poland-Lithuania (1386-1434)

On to the Holy Land!

O nation of the French, nation from across the mountains, nation beloved and chosen by God! It is clear from your many works that you are a nation set apart from all others by the position of your country, and by your Catholic faith and the honour you give to the holy Church. We address our sermon to you: for you our exhortations are intended ... From Jerusalem and the city of Constantinople has gone forth a horrible tale which has often reached our ears. It is reported that a nation from the kingdom of the Persians, an accursed nation, a nation totally alienated from God [the Seljuk Turks], has violently invaded the lands of the

Eastern Christians, reducing their population by plunder and by fire. They have taken away many captives to their own country, and killed others by cruel tortures. They have destroyed God's churches or taken them over for the practice of their own religion. They destroy the altars after defiling them by their own uncleanness. For they force circumcision on the Christians and spread the blood of circumcision on the altars or pour it into baptismal vessels ...[25]

Therefore let hatred depart from among you, let your quarrels cease, let wars end, let all contentions and controversies slumber! Set out on the road that leads to Christ's holy tomb; seize that land from the wicked nation of Turks, conquer it for yourselves. Scripture says that the land there is flowing with milk and honey, and that God gave it into the power of the children of Israel. Jerusalem is the centre of the world; its land is fruitful above all others, like another paradise of delights. The Redeemer of the human race made that land illustrious by His coming, He made it beautiful by His presence, He sanctified it by His suffering, He redeemed it by His death, He glorified it by His burial. And yet this royal city, this centre of the world, is now held captive by the enemies of Christ! It is subjected to those who do not know God and to their Pagan worship! She seeks and desires her freedom; she does not cease to beg you to come to her aid. From you above all she asks for help, because God has bestowed on the French above all other nations great glory in warfare, as we have already said. So then, undertake this journey for the forgiveness of your sins, with the assurance of imperishable glory in the kingdom of heaven!

Sermon of Pope Urban II
at the council of Clermont, November 1095

---

25. It is interesting that Pope Urban refers to the Eastern Orthodox as true Christians who need to be liberated from Islamic persecution. This is 41 years after the East–West schism of 1054. Ironically, as we have already noted, it was the Crusades themselves which made that schism into a practical reality, through Western ill-treatment of Eastern believers.

The capture of Jerusalem, June 1099

On Wednesday and Thursday we attacked the city, day and night, from all sides. Before we attacked, our bishops and priests preached to us, exhorting us to march in a procession for God's glory around Jerusalem, and to pray, distribute charitable gifts, and fast. Then on Friday 15th July 1099, at dawn, we attacked the city from all sides, but we met with no success, and we were all overwhelmed with astonishment and trembling with fear. Godfrey of Bouillon and his brother, Baldwin, Count of Boulogne, were fighting with great courage in the siege-tower. Then another of our knights named Lethold clambered up onto the city wall. As soon as he was on the top, all the defenders of the city fled along the walls and through the city. Our soldiers, with Lethold at their head, chased after the defenders, killing them and cutting them to pieces right up to the Temple of Solomon. There was such a massacre there, we were wading in blood up to our ankles.

Count Raymond of Toulouse led his troops from the south right close to the wall, together with a siege-tower. But at this point, the Emir [the Muslim ruler] in David's Tower surrendered to Raymond, opening up to him the gate where the pilgrims paid their pilgrimage taxes. Then our pilgrims entered the city, chasing the Muslims all the way to the Temple of Solomon, killing as they went. At the Temple the enemy made a stand, and we fought a fierce battle for the entire day, so that enemy blood was splashed all over the Temple. At last we defeated the Pagans, and our soldiers captured a large number of men and women in the Temple; they either killed them or let them live, as they chose. On the roof of Solomon's temple there was a huge gathering of the Pagans, both men and women. Tancred and Gaston of Bearn had given their banners to these people [as flags of truce, putting them under Tancred and Gaston's protection]. Soon our army was all over the city, grabbing gold and silver, horses and mules, and dwellings packed with treasures of all kinds. Our entire army came to worship at the Church of the Holy Sepulchre, not only rejoicing but weeping with joy.

The next morning our men crept up onto the roof of the Temple and attacked the Muslims, both men and women, cutting

off their heads with our swords. Those who were not killed threw
themselves off the Temple roof. When Tancred saw this, he was
very angry [because people under his protection had been killed]
... Our men gave orders that all the dead Muslims should be cast
out of the city because of the terrible stench; almost the entire
city was overflowing with their corpses. The Muslims who were
still alive dragged the bodies out and piled them in front of the
gates; these piles were as large as houses. No-one ever saw or
heard of such a slaughter of Pagans. Funeral pyres were formed
of their dead bodies like pyramids. God alone knows how many
we killed. Raymond of Toulouse had the emir and the others
with him brought to him at Ascalon, safe and unharmed.

Jerusalem was taken by the Christians on Friday 15th July.
A week later, they elected Godfrey of Bouillon to be ruler of the
city, that he might keep the Pagans in subjection and protect the
Christians.

From *The Deeds of the Franks*
by an unknown writer who took part in the First Crusade

A maiden's love and longing for her Crusading knight

I will sing to bring courage to my heart,
Otherwise I may die or go mad
Because of my so great loss.
For no-one returns from that far-off country
Where my beloved now is,
The man whose name comforts my heart
Whenever I hear it spoken.

O God, when they shout "Onward!"
Please give Your help to that pilgrim
For whom my heart trembles!
For the Muslims are wicked men.

I will endure my loss for a year.
My beloved is on a pilgrimage;
O God, grant that he will return!

In spite of all the pressure my family puts on me,
I will never consent to marry another man.
Anyone who suggests that to me is a fool!

O God, when they shout "Onward!"
Please give Your help to that pilgrim
For whom my heart trembles!
For the Muslims are wicked men.

I live with hope, for he pledged himself to me,
And I accepted his pledge.
And when the sweet wind blows
From that sweet country where my beloved is,
I turn my face towards it gladly,
And then I can almost feel him
Beneath my mantle of fur.

O God, when they shout "Onward!"
Please give Your help to that pilgrim
For whom my heart trembles!
For the Muslims are wicked men.

From a song by Guiot of Dijon
(written about 1190)

A peaceful encounter between a Muslim and a Crusader in Jerusalem

I saw one of the Franks[26] walk up to al-Amir Mu'in al-Din, may Allah's mercy be upon his soul. This happened when he was in the Dome of the Rock [the mosque in Jerusalem]. The Frank said to Mu'in al-Din, "Do you want to see God as a child?" Mu'in al-Din replied, "Yes." So the Frank went ahead of us and showed us a picture of Mary with Christ (peace be upon him!) as a child in her lap. The Frank said, "This is God as a child." But Allah is exalted far above what these unbelievers say about Him.

From the *Book of Instruction* of the Syrian Muslim noble,
Usamah ibn Munqidh

---

26. Muslims called all Crusaders "Franks", *i.e.* French.

Clairvaux in the days of Bernard:
A visitor's impressions

I stayed with Bernard a few days, unworthy though I was. Whichever way I turned my eyes, I marvelled; I thought I saw a new heaven and a new earth, and also the old pathways of our fathers the monks of Egypt, marked with the recent footsteps which the men of our day had left in them. There at Clairvaux the golden age seemed to have returned and revisited the world. At the first glance, as you enter, after going down the hill, you can feel that God is in this place. In the simplicity of its buildings the silent valley speaks of the genuine humility of Christ's poor ones dwelling there. The silence of noon was the silence of midnight, broken only by the chants of the choral services, and the sound of the implements in garden and field. No-one was idle. In the hours not devoted to sleep or prayer, the brothers kept busy with hoe, scythe, and axe, taming the wild land and clearing the forest.

William of Saint Thierry (1075-1148)

Vita Prima, **Book 1, chapter 7**

God's love for humankind revealed
in the incarnation

Thanks be to God, through whom we have such overflowing consolation in this pilgrimage, this exile, this present misery. I have often exhorted you never to forget that we are pilgrims, far away from our native land, heirs who have been thrown out of our inheritance. For those who never experience desolation cannot know consolation. And that is why people who live in the world, absorbed in its affairs, do not seek after mercy, for they do not feel their misery. But listen, you to whom it is said, and not said in vain, "Be still and know how gracious the Lord is." Listen, you whom worldly interests do not hold back; listen, you who really know what exile means. Here is your comfort: help has come down from heaven! "The kindness and love of God for humanity have appeared" (Titus 3:4).

The kindness was always there, for the Lord's mercy is eternal; but it was hidden until "His love for humanity appeared." Before that, it was promised but not felt, so that many did not believe in it. But look! He no longer promises peace, He sends it; He no longer predicts it, He presents it to us. God the Father has sent a sort of sackful of His mercy to earth: a sack that must be torn open through Christ's suffering, so that the price of our redemption may pour out of it. It is only a small sack, but it is full. "Unto us a small child is given," (Isa. 9:6), yet "in Him dwells the fullness of deity" (Col. 2:9). For "when the fullness of time had come" (Gal. 4:4), the fullness of deity also came. He came in flesh to show Himself to people living in the flesh; and His love for humanity appeared, so that human beings might truly know His kindness. What better way was there for Him to commend His kindness to me, than by His taking my flesh – *my* flesh, not the flesh Adam had before he fell?[27] What could so mightily declare His mercy as this act of clothing Himself with our misery? And the smaller He made Himself, the kinder He showed Himself; the smaller He becomes *for* me, the dearer He becomes *to* me.

Bernard of Clairvaux
Sermon on Titus 3:4

The experience of salvation: God's sovereignty, human responsibility

We must therefore be careful, whenever we feel these things happening invisibly within us and with us, not to ascribe them to our own will, which is weak; nor to any necessity on the part of God, for there is none; but solely to that grace of which He is full. It is grace which arouses our free choice, by sowing the seed of the good thought; it is grace which heals our free choice, by changing its disposition; it is grace which strengthens it so as to lead it to action; it is grace which saves it from experiencing a fall. Grace so cooperates with free choice, however, that only in

---

27. Bernard means that Adam's flesh before he sinned was free from the curse and power of death, whereas now, after the fall, our flesh is doomed to die. Christ took *our* flesh, with all its liability to misery and death (although He did not take our moral corruption). Thus Christ shows how much He loves us by submitting to such lowliness.

the first case does grace go a step ahead of it; in the other cases, grace accompanies free choice. What was begun by grace alone is completed by grace and free choice together, in such a way that they contribute to each new work not singly, but jointly – not by turns, but at the same time. It is not as if grace did half the work and free choice the other half; but each does the whole work, according to its own contribution. Grace does the whole work, and so does free choice – with this one qualification: the whole work is done *in* free choice, but the whole work is done *by* grace.

From Bernard of Clairvaux
On Grace and Free-will

Not under law, but under grace

O Lord my God, why do you not pardon my offences and forgive my sins? Then, when You have freed me from the burdens of my self-will, I will be able to live under the light burden of Your love. Then slavish fear will not rule me, nor will a mercenary spirit of self-love move me. Instead Your Spirit will inspire me, the Spirit of freedom who leads Your children (Rom. 8:14). Your Spirit bears witness with my spirit that I too am one of Your children (Rom. 8:16). We both have the same law, O Lord; and as You are, so I can be in the world. These are the people who follow the apostle Paul's advice: "Owe nobody anything, except to love one another" (Rom 13:8). Such people are surely God's people in this world! They are not slaves. They are not hired mercenaries. They are His sons and daughters.

But even children have the law! Of course, someone may point out the text which says, "The law is not made for a right-eous person" (1 Tim. 1:9). But we need to understand that the law decreed by the spirit of slavery is very different from the liberating and joyful law of the Spirit. God's children cannot be under the first of these laws, but they cannot live without the second. Do you want to know why the law is not for a righteous person? "For you did not receive the spirit of slavery again to fear" (Rom. 8:15). However, the righteous do have the law of love, for Paul adds, "you received the Spirit of adoption." Finally, hear the righteous man who confesses that even though he is not under the law, he does still have a law: "To those who are under the law, I became as a man under the law, so that I might win those who are under the law; to those who are without the law, I became as a man without law (though I am not without law towards God, but under law towards Christ), that I might win those who are without the law" (1 Cor. 9:20-21).

So it is not correct to say, "The righteous do not *have* the law." What we must say is, "The law is not *made* for the righteous," in the sense that God does not force it on them against their wills. No, the righteous welcome God's law with open arms, as a gift from God's generosity. So the Lord says to us very suitably, "Take My yoke upon you" (Matt. 11:29). It is as if He were saying, "I am not putting My yoke on the unwilling, but only on those who desire it. However, if you don't want My yoke, you will always have unrest in your souls; you will never find refreshment."

Bernard of Clairvaux
On Loving God, **chapters 13 and 14**

The Virgin Mary: Glorious but not sinless

I am afraid, because some of you want to introduce change into important matters, inventing a new festival [the festival of Mary's immaculate conception] which is unknown to the Church, unapproved by reason, unjustified by ancient tradition. Are we indeed wiser and more godly than our fathers? You will say, "We must glorify the Mother of God as much as we can." That is true. But the way we glorify the Queen of heaven requires discernment. This royal Virgin has no need of a false glorification, since she possesses true crowns of glory and signs of honour. Glorify the purity of her body and the holiness of her life; marvel at the abundance of this Virgin's gifts; venerate her divine Son; exalt her who conceived without experiencing lust and gave birth without experiencing pain. What do we need to add to these dignities?

People say that we must revere Mary's *own* conception which came before the glory of her giving birth to God, because (they say) if Mary herself had not first been conceived without sin, she could not have been the glorious birth-giver of God. But by this reasoning, we would have to demand the same kind of veneration for holy Mary's own father and mother [as sinless – how else could they have given birth to sinless Mary?]. And then we might equally demand the same veneration for Mary's grandparents, and great-grandparents, and so on to infinity! But how could sin not have existed in Mary's conception, which took place according to lustful human passion? Therefore let no-one say that the holy Virgin was conceived by the Holy Spirit and not by human nature. I say decisively that the Holy Spirit descended *upon* Mary, but not that He came *with* her ...

No-one is given the right to be conceived in holiness. Only the Lord Christ was conceived by the Holy Spirit, and He alone is holy from His very conception. Apart from Christ, the words spoken by one of Adam's offspring – "Behold, I was conceived in iniquity" (Ps. 51:5) – must be applied to all Adam's offspring, both out of a feeling of humility and in recognition of the truth. How can we demand that Mary's conception be holy, when it was not the work of the Holy Spirit, and took place according to lustful human passion? The holy Virgin rejects any glory given to her which in fact glorifies sin; for she cannot justify a new doctrine which men have invented in defiance of Church teaching – a new doctrine which is the mother of folly, the sister of unbelief, and the daughter of light-mindedness.

Bernard of Clairvaux

Epistle 174

6
Holy Russia: Orthodoxy among the Slavs

The great East–West schism of 1054 broke the one Catholic Church apart into two rival Churches, the West centred on Rome and the papacy, the East centred on Constantinople. North and west of Constantinople, however, there stretched huge lands larger than Western Europe, inhabited by the Slavic peoples; and here, the Eastern Byzantine type of Christianity flourished outside the political boundaries of the Byzantine Empire. This was especially the case in Russia, where the Eastern faith took the vast and majestic form of the Russian Orthodox Church. Today, this is the largest Orthodox Church in the world.

The story of how Russian Christianity came to birth under the inspiration of Byzantium begins in the 10th century, with the contact between the Byzantine Empire and the Russian city of Kiev.

1. Christianity in Kievan Russia
The most powerful and prosperous city in Russia in the 10th century was Kiev. The rulers of Kiev were a tribal group called the Rus, who eventually gave their name to the whole of the surrounding country ("Russia" – land of the Rus). The Pagan Rus, who may have been related to the Norsemen,[1] were a race of aristocratic warriors, who had extended their dominion from Kiev to the neighbouring Slavic tribes and towns. The Rus

---

1. For the Norsemen, see Chapter 4, section 1.

encouraged trade with the nearby Byzantine Empire, and this opened Kiev to Christian influence. By 945 a church had been established in the city. The Russian Princess Olga, who ruled Kiev from 945 to 964 (while her son Svyatoslav was only a child), was converted to Christianity, receiving baptism into the Eastern faith in Constantinople in 957. Olga's conversion did not, however, lead to the Christianisation of Kiev, and Svyatoslav, who ruled in his own right from 964, did not follow his mother's religious example – he was afraid that his Pagan warriors would laugh at him if he became a Christian.

The whole-hearted acceptance of Christianity by Kievan Russia came through Olga's grandson, Prince **Vladimir** (980-1015). Russian tradition says that Vladimir invited representatives of the four great religions of the world – Judaism, Islam, and Eastern and Western Christianity – to come to Kiev and expound the merits of their respective faiths. Judaism and Islam did not impress him, but he found it difficult to decide between the two wings of the Christian Church. So he sent delegates to Rome and Constantinople. This tipped the balance in favour of the East. When Vladmir's delegates arrived in Constantinople and witnessed Byzantine worship in the Church of Hagia Sophia, it overwhelmed them:

> We did not know whether we were in heaven or on earth, for surely there is no such splendour or beauty anywhere on earth. We cannot describe it to you; all we know is that God dwells there among human beings.

This report reveals an important aspect of Orthodoxy as it took root in Russia: Russians were always to prize their beautiful form of worship more highly than doctrinal orthodoxy or codes of morality. In the Slavonic language, the word for Orthodoxy is *Pravoslavie*, "right glory". (The word "Orthodoxy" in Greek also literally means "right glory".)

The report of the Russian delegates from Constantinople persuaded Vladimir to embrace the Eastern Byzantine form of Christianity – in the year 988, according to tradition. Many of the Rus followed their leader's example and were baptised in the river Dnieper. The new converts hurled the idol of the Rus's chief Pagan god, Perun, down the hilltop above Kiev. Vladimir then set out to make Kiev into a Christian kingdom, modelled on the Byzantine Empire. The patriarch of Constantinople appointed a metropolitan bishop in Kiev to lead the Russian Church (Constantinople was to nominate the metropolitans of Kiev for the next 500 years).

Vladimir married Anna, sister of the great Byzantine Emperor Basil II (976-1025). He invited Byzantine monks to settle in Kiev; the monks brought Byzantine culture and civilisation with them, translating the Byzantine liturgy and other religious writings into Slavonic by means of the Cyrillic alphabet.[2] This gave Russians something that Western Christians did not have, for Western worship and theology were in Latin which most Westerners did not understand. By contrast, through the translation of Byzantine theology and liturgy into Slavonic, the Russians had a religion in their own native language. A distinctive Russian style of church building came into existence too, marked out by an onion-shaped dome. Further, Vladimir took very seriously his social responsibilities as a Christian ruler; he established a highly organised system of social services for the poor and deprived of Kiev – the best welfare system known to us anywhere in medieval Europe. He also set up Christian schools which trained the younger generation of Russians in the new religion.

After Vladimir's death in 1015, conflict broke out between his twelve sons. One of them, Svyatopolk, decided to kill his two younger brothers, Boris and Gleb, as rivals to the throne; but Boris and Gleb, taking literally Christ's command to "turn the other cheek" (Matt. 5:39), refused to offer any resistance to Svyatopolk, and were murdered by his soldiers. Later Russians looked on Boris and Gleb as saints and martyrs who had deliberately chosen to imitate Christ in His voluntary and innocent suffering. This sense of identifying with the suffering Christ became one of the most powerful themes in Russian Christianity.

---

2. See Chapter 3, section 7 for the Cyrillic alphabet.

Svyatopolk's actions brought on a long civil war, from which another of Vladimir's sons, **Yaroslav the Wise** (1019-54), emerged as the ultimate victor, vanquishing all his rivals by 1036. Under Yaroslav's rule, Kiev became the intellectual and artistic capital of all Russia. Christianity prospered too; Yaroslav had the Bible translated into Slavonic, and in the middle of the 11th century a great monastic revival swept through Kiev. The chief figures in this movement were two outstanding monks, **Antony** and **Theodosius** (died 1074). Antony, who had lived in the great Byzantine monastic community of Mount Athos,[3] founded the "Monastery of the Caves" just outside Kiev in about 1051. This became the most important centre of religious life in Kievan Russia for the next 200 years. His successor, Theodosius, reorganised the monastery, introducing the "Studite rule" of the great Byzantine monastery of Studium in Constantinople. Theodosius was one of the greatest and best-loved of Russian saints. Like Boris and Gleb, he emphasised the need to endure suffering humbly for Christ's sake, and not to fight back. Of noble birth, Theodosius renounced his riches, identified with the poor and outcast, and worked with slaves in the fields; his life had an abiding impact on Russian spirituality through the popular biography of him written by his fellow monk **Nestor** (1056-1111). Nestor also wrote an important work called *Annals*, our chief source of information about early Russian Church history.

As we have seen, Russian Christianity followed the Byzantine pattern very closely. This meant that Russia was intimately involved in the final spiritual breach between Byzantium and Rome. In 1054 Cardinal Humbert, acting in the name of the papacy, excommunicated Patriarch Michael Cerularius of Constantinople and all who adhered to his Eastern "errors" (*e.g.* the Eastern view of the Trinity), thus bringing about the great East–West schism.[4] So after 1054, we speak about "Eastern Orthodoxy" rather than simply "the Eastern Church". As part of the Eastern Christian

---

3. See Chapter 3, section 5 for Mount Athos and Studium.

4. See Chapter 3, section 8 for Humbert, Cerularius, and the East–West schism.

world, Russia naturally sided with Constantinople against Rome in the schism; and so after 1054, the Russian Church is known as the Russian *Orthodox* Church, and its faith is from now on called *Russian Orthodoxy*.

The work of Antony and Theodosius, and the founding of the Monastery of the Caves, made monasticism into the single most important channel for the development of Russian Orthodox spirituality and theology. In the 12th century especially, the growth of the monastic movement in Kievan Russia was amazing. Prior to 1100, there were 20 known monasteries in Russia; but in the 1100s, no fewer than 50 new monasteries were founded. Russian monasticism fell into the three types well-known in the Eastern world: (a) eremitic (solitary) monasticism; (b) cenobitic (community) monasticism; (c) skete-type monasticism.[5]

Other great Christian figures in Kievan Russia included:

Hilarion of Kiev, the first native Russian metropolitan of Kiev (from 1051), one of the most learned authors and eloquent preachers of the Kievan period. Hilarion's most famous work was his *Sermon on Law and Grace*, which expounded the distinction between Old and New Testaments, based on the apostle Paul's contrast in Galatians 4:21-31 between Abraham's two sons – Ishmael, son of the slave Hagar (symbolising the Old Testament, the religion of law and compulsion), and Isaac, son of the freewoman Sarah (symbolising the New Testament, the religion of the Spirit and freedom). Hilarion's *Sermon* also stressed the importance of history in God's purposes. Hilarion thought that Russia had a special place in the outworking of God's historical plan – a view which came to be shared by many Russian Orthodox believers. Through its baptism into Christ, Russia had become the spiritual equal of Byzantium, Hilarion felt; and accordingly, he cooperated with Yaroslav the Wise in boldly affirming the Russian Church's equality of dignity with Constantinople.

---

5. For all three types of monasticism, see Volume One, Chapter 7, section 3.

Cyril of Turov (1130-89). Cyril was bishop of Turov (north-west of Kiev), and the outstanding theologian and writer of his times. He became famous in his own lifetime for his sermons, letters and written prayers, which were still popular in Russia 500 years after his death. An accomplished student of the early Church fathers, Cyril's spiritual outlook was, in some ways, closer to Augustine of Hippo[6] than was normal for an Orthodox thinker; Cyril emphasised the overwhelming power and majesty of God, and the utter helplessness of the sinner who can only cry out for God's mercy. His most celebrated masterpiece was his series of eight sermons for the eight Sundays of Easter, beginning with Palm Sunday.

Disaster befell Kievan Russia in the 13th century. A new military power had risen in the far East – the Mongols. The great warrior-leader, **Genghis Khan** (1196-1227), unified the nomadic tribes who lived in the region between the Gobi desert and Lake Baykal (present-day Mongolia), established his headquarters at Karakoram, and embarked on a devastating campaign of world conquest. In the early 1200s the Mongol armies invaded Russia and decisively defeated the Russians at the battle of the river Kalka in 1223. The death of Genghis Khan in 1227 brought a temporary halt to the Mongol advance, but they returned in 1236 led by Genghis's grandson Batu Khan. In 1240 Batu's forces captured Kiev and massacred its inhabitants. The only thing that saved the whole of Europe from being conquered by the Mongols was the sudden death in 1241 of their "great khan" (Emperor), also named Batu. The Mongol tribal leaders had to return to Karakoram to elect a new great khan – Western Europe was saved.

However, southern Russia (modern Ukraine) remained completely under Mongol domination; the Mongol rulers compelled even the princes and cities of northern Russia, too, to pay annual tribute. The Russian Mongol kingdom broke away from the wider Mongol empire as an independent state, and became known as the *Golden Horde* (from the yellow costumes worn by Genghis Khan and his ruling tribe). It had its capital at Sarai,

---

6. For Augustine, see Volume One, Chapter 9, section 3.

near the Caspian Sea. The Mongol rulers of Russia are sometimes called the *Tartars*, from the name of a tribe which provided the Mongols with an advance guard of "shock troops". After the destruction of Kiev by the Mongols, Russian Orthodox believers would often look back on Kievan Russia as the greatest era of Christianity in Russian history – a spiritual ideal which all succeeding generations must strive to imitate.

2. Serbian Orthodoxy

The Russians were the largest Slavic group, but other branches of the Slav family were also central in the story of Eastern Orthodoxy. None were more important than the Serbs, and no Serb was spiritually greater than *Sava* (1175-1236). Sava, indeed, was the outstanding Orthodox leader of his time, honoured by all the Orthodox nations. He is often called "the Enlightener of the Serbs" because of the way he almost single-handedly cemented the Serbian people's loyalty to Orthodoxy against Western Catholic influence. As we saw in Chapter 3, section 7, the Serbs had embraced Eastern Christianity in the 9th century, but the papacy did not give up the struggle to win them over to the Western Church. Sava's life shows us the kind of religious and political conflicts that embittered relationships between Eastern Orthodoxy and Western Catholicism after the great schism of 1054.

Sava was born with the name "Rastko", the third child of King Stephen Numanja (1151-96) of Serbia. King Stephen made Rastko, at the age of 15, a prince over a strip of Serbian territory. But the young Rastko's thoughts were turning even now towards heavenly glories; he had already committed himself to a celibate life, although by all accounts he was a strikingly beautiful boy. When a Russian Orthodox monk from Mount Athos visited the Serbian court in 1193, Rastko's heart burned within him at the descriptions of monastic life on Athos – here was what his soul thirsted for! – so he persuaded the monk to take him back secretly to the holy mountain. An indignant King Stephen sent soldiers after his runaway son; Rastko just managed to keep one step ahead of them. By the time the exhausted troops arrived at the Russian monastery on Athos where Rastko had fled, it was too late. The 18-year-old prince had been swiftly "tonsured" (enrolled as a monk) and taken the new name "Sava", after the famous 6th century Palestinian monk Sabbas the Sanctified.[7] The baffled soldiers had to journey back home empty-handed. Thus began Sava's illustrious spiritual career.

Sava (1175-1236) and Simeon the Myrrh-Gusher (died 1200)

---

7.   For Sabbas, see Volume One, Chapter 12, section 2. "Sava" is another way of spelling "Sabbas".

At that point in the history of Mount Athos, there was no Serbian monastery, so Sava joined a Greek one. In fact, Sava's first great contribution to Serbian Orthodoxy was to establish a monastic community for Serbs on Athos. This came about when his father, King Stephen, now aged 82, resigned from the Serbian throne in 1196 so that he could end his days as a monk, taking the name *Simeon*. Simeon joined Sava on Athos (the ex-king was no longer angry with his son for preferring monastic to court life); after an emotional reunion, father and son set about rebuilding the ruined Greek monastery of Hilander[8] for use by their fellow Serbs. Their influence at the Byzantine court in Constantinople prompted Emperor Alexius III (1195-1203) to issue a decree granting Hilander to the Serbian people in 1199, as an independent, self-governing monastery. From that day onward, Hilander became a vital, thriving centre of Serb religion and culture, attracting multitudes of young Serbian men to Mount Athos and the monastic life. Having founded Hilander, Sava then built a private cell for himself and became a hermit, enriching his solitude by writing many hymns, prayers, treatises, and a biography of his father who died in 1200.

Meanwhile, Serbia had toppled into a bloody civil war between Simeon's second son, King Stephen II (1196-1228), and Simeon's other son Vukan. Stephen controlled the northern and eastern region of Serbia, Vukan the southern and western part. Here the struggle between Catholicism and Orthodoxy reared its head, for Vukan received the backing of pope Innocent III (1198-1216), the most politically powerful figure ever to occupy the episcopal throne of Rome;[9] in return for Innocent's support, Vukan placed the Serbian Church in his domain under papal authority. The war between Stephen and Vukan thus took on the colours of a religious conflict between Orthodox and Catholic. Things began to look distinctly bad for the Orthodox when a Catholic Crusader army overthrew the Byzantine Empire in 1204, capturing Constantinople and setting up a new French

---

8. Or Chilander.
9. For Innocent III, see Chapter 8.

Catholic kingdom.[10] Byzantium itself, the spiritual mother of
Serbian Orthodoxy, lay prostrate beneath the swords of Catholic
conquerors. The new French lords of the East even placed Mount
Athos under the control of a Catholic bishop in 1205.

In the midst of these hammer-blow disasters for Orthodoxy,
King Stephen pleaded with his brother, Sava, to return to devastated Serbia and help him heal the wounds of the nation. Sava
finally agreed and arrived back in Serbia in 1207. He brought
with him the coffin bearing the body of Simeon, the father of
Sava, Stephen and Vukan. When the coffin was opened, Simeon's
body was still fresh ("incorrupt"), despite having been dead for
seven years, and exuded a sweet-smelling oil and myrrh. This, in
the Middle Ages, was the accepted sign that a dead believer was
a true saint, and that his soul was now glorified in heaven; it is
the origin of our phrase "the odour of sanctity".[11] So Serbs hailed
Simeon as a saint ("Simeon the Myrrh-gusher"). The presence
of his body, with its proofs of sanctity, helped to reconcile the
battling brothers Stephen and Vukan; the civil war soon ended,
and Stephen reigned as rightful king, although for years he was
politically dependent on the support of the papacy.

Sava became abbot of the Studenitsa monastery. From there,
he spent all his energies in revitalising the Orthodox faith among
the Serbs, preaching, teaching, founding and reforming monasteries, building churches, and establishing "iconography" schools
(to teach people how to paint icons). Sava's personality adorned
his efforts, for in the eyes of his contemporaries he was one of
those quiet, humble, serene souls whose very manner seemed
to proclaim that knowing Christ was the centre of his life, and
of all true life. Serbs learned to look on Sava – Orthodox Serbs
still do – as the supreme example of a Christian man. His ex-
traordinary reputation was officially recognised in 1219, when
Byzantine Emperor Theodore I Lascaris (1206-22) and Patriarch

---

10. For the fall of Constantinople in 1204, see Chapter 5, section 3, under
The Fourth Crusade, and Chapter 8, section 3.

11. It is still the accepted proof of sanctity in conservative Orthodox and
Roman Catholic circles today.

Manuel I of Constantinople (1215-22)[12] appointed him Serbia's first archbishop, thereby granting the Serbian Orthodox Church a large measure of national independence.[13] Sava then crowned his brother Stephen in 1220 as Orthodox king of the Serbs, thus breaking all political ties between the Serbian monarchy and the papacy. From now on, Serbia was to be an Orthodox nation in every respect – religion, culture, politics. No-one did more to bring this about than Sava.

When Sava died in 1236, he had become such an internationally revered saint that not only Orthodox, but Catholics and even Jews came from far and wide to pay honour to his body. After the Turkish Muslim conquest of Serbia in 1389, Sava's shrine remained such a powerful symbol of both Serbian Christianity and Serbian nationhood that, in 1595, the Muslim authorities dug up Sava's body and burnt it, to try to desecrate and destroy his memory.

3. Mongol rule in Russia and the rise of Moscow

As we saw in section 1, Orthodox Kievan Russia fell to the Mongol armies in 1240. The Mongols were a Pagan people; however, they acknowledged a supreme God, and allowed their conquered subjects to worship Him according to their own religious traditions. The Russian Orthodox Church, therefore, survived the Mongol conquest. Indeed, during the period of Mongol rule under the Golden Horde (1240-1480), it was chiefly Russian Orthodoxy which kept Russian national feeling alive. This was because the Church forbade intermarriage between Russians and Mongols,

---

12.   The Emperors and patriarchs of Constantinople were in exile in Nicaea until Emperor Michael VIII Paleologus (1261-82) reconquered the city from the Catholic French and re-established the Byzantine Empire. See Chapter 9, sections 1 and 4.

13.   A synod of Serbian bishops elevated their archbishop to the rank of patriarch in 1346, at a time when the Serbian nation was at its strongest under the mighty King Stefan Dushan (1336-56). This caused a temporary breach with Constantinople, but in 1375 the patriarch of Constantinople recognised the new Serbian patriarch as fully independent leader of an autocephalous Serbian Orthodox Church.

and also because Russian nationalism and Russian Orthodoxy became fused together in opposition to the non-Christian beliefs of the conquering Mongols. Russian Christians made little effort to evangelise their Mongol masters, who in fact soon abandoned their ancestral Paganism, but only to embrace Islam. However, very few Mongols actually settled in Russia; they were a small upper-class of ruling lords, whose ranks were spread thinly over the land they had conquered.

An important centre of Christian civilisation in Russia which escaped the Mongol conquest was the northern city of Novgorod. By 1150, Novgorod had become one of the most prosperous trading cities in Europe, and had secured a large measure of political and ecclesiastical freedom from the rule of Kiev. When Kiev fell to the Golden Horde in 1240, Novgorod became for a time the guardian of Russia's national freedom and Orthodox faith. It was ruled at this period by Prince **Alexander Nevsky** (born 1219; ruled 1236-51), one of the greatest heroes of the Russian Orthodox faith and of Russian national history. Nevsky was a sort of holy warrior-king. He fought off two attempts by Western Catholic Crusading armies to conquer northern Russia. First, in 1240, he defeated an invading Swedish army at the battle of the river Neva; then in 1242 he crushed an invading army of German Crusaders, the Teutonic Knights, at the battle of the Ice on the frozen Lake Peipus.[14] Nevsky made peace with the Mongols and paid tribute to them, but he refused to have any dealings with Western Catholic powers. This was because the Mongols, although they were not Christians, allowed Russian Orthodox believers to practise their faith; by contrast, Western Catholics forced the Orthodox to submit to the papacy, as they had done in Constantinople.[15] With bold defiance Nevsky declared to ambassadors of the pope:

> Our doctrines are those preached by the apostles. We carefully keep the traditions of the holy fathers of the seven ecumenical

---

14. For the Teutonic Knights, see Chapter 5, section 4.

15. This was the period of Catholic rule in Byzantium – see Chapter 5, section 3 on the Fourth Crusade.

Councils. As for your words, we do not listen to them, and we do not want your doctrine.

Nevsky was instrumental in the rise of Moscow as the new centre of Russian national life. Moscow was south-east of Novgorod, in central Russia, protected by thick forests, with a large population, and outside the sphere of direct Mongol rule. Nevsky established a dominion there for his son Daniel, who ruled Moscow from 1276 to 1303, expanding its power. The growing empire of Moscow was called "Muscovy". Its first great ruler was Ivan I (1325-41), who took the title *grand prince* in 1328. Under Ivan and his successors, Moscow became the centre of anti-Mongol resistance in Russia.

The new status of Moscow as champion of Russia's faith and liberty was symbolised by the fact that the metropolitans of Kiev moved to Moscow. Peter, metropolitan from 1308 to 1326, made Moscow into the new residence of the leader of the Russian Orthodox Church. A strong alliance between Church and state developed in Muscovy. The central figure here was **Sergius of Radonezh** (1314-92), whom Russians regard as their greatest national saint, the Russian equivalent of Sava. In Russian terms, Sergius resembled Theodosius of Kiev: born into a rich family, he gave up his privileged status and lived in voluntary poverty, to identify with the humility and suffering of Christ. Sergius began his religious life as a hermit in the forest of Radonezh, 25 miles north of Moscow. Reputed to receive visions and work miracles, he attracted a growing band of spiritual disciples, and in about 1340 formed them into the "Monastery of the Holy Trinity". This became in the new kingdom of Moscow what the Monastery of the Caves had been in Kiev – the centre of Russian Orthodox spiritual and theological vitality. (See the quotation at the end of the Chapter for the origins of the Monastery of the Holy Trinity.)

Sergius was the main spiritual force behind a mighty new wave of colonist-monks, who spread out into the northern forests of Russia, established monasteries as centres of Orthodox Christianity and civilisation, and evangelised the Pagan natives.

One of the most important of these missionaries was **Stephen of Perm** (1340-96), who evangelised a Finnish tribe of northern Russia known as the Zyrians, giving their language a written form for the first time, and translating the Bible and the Orthodox liturgy into it. The lives of Sergius of Radonezh and Stephen of Perm were preserved for future generations by **Epiphanius the Wise** (active early 1400s).

Sergius of Radonezh (1314-92)

In his epoch-making biographies of Sergius and Stephen, Epiphanius created a totally new literary style for the Russian tongue, called *pletenie sloves* ("weaving of words"), in which verbs were used sparingly in favour of complex patterns of nouns and adjectives.

The Monastery of the Holy Trinity inspired a powerful new tradition of Russian religious art. These monk-artists did not attach their names to the icons they painted, but we know that two of the most distinguished, **Daniel Chorney** (died 1430) and his more celebrated disciple **Andrei Rublev** (1370-1430), were active around the year 1400. Rublev, one of the world's greatest religious artists, painted the most famous Orthodox icon of all, a strangely captivating picture of the three angels who visited Abraham in Genesis 18. The three angels in Rublev's icon are usually reckoned to represent the Trinity. This seems the most likely interpretation, but it is not absolutely certain. The central angel is probably Christ, not God the Father, and the other two figures may simply be angels. What prompts interpreters to identify the central figure as Christ is that He is wearing a blue robe over a red one, and in Orthodox icons of Christ these colours represent His incarnation (blue = humanity, red = deity). It has been said of Andrei Rublev and his icons:

> He takes the colours of his palette not from the traditional canons of colour, but from Russian nature around him, the beauty of which he acutely sensed. His marvellous deep blue is suggested by the blue of the spring sky; his whites recalled the birches so dear to a Russian; his green is close to the colour of unripe rye; his golden ochre summons up the colour of autumn leaves. He translated the colour of Russian nature into the lofty language of art.[16]

Icons were as important in the Orthodoxy of Russia as they were in Byzantium; they hung in vast numbers on the walls of churches, and inside the huts of peasants and the palaces of princes. Russians believed that some icons possessed miraculous powers;

---

16. These are the words of the art critic Viktor Lazarev.

the famous icon of Our Lady of Vladimir (a picture of the Virgin Mary and the Christ-child) was reckoned to have saved Moscow three times from foreign invasion. The 14th century also witnessed a flourishing of hesychastic spirituality in Russia.[17] This stemmed from the great monastic community of Mount Athos in Greece, where a large number of Russian monks had taken up residence. Russian monks also settled in other Greek-speaking parts of the Byzantine Empire, and made many translations into Slavonic of the writings of the Mount Athos monks and other Greek religious works. So the spiritual riches of Byzantium flowed into Moscow.

Sergius of Radonezh was a close friend and advisor to the grand princes of Moscow, and supported their plans for expanding the power of Orthodox Muscovy. When Grand Prince **Dmitri Donskoi** (1359-89) went into battle against the Golden Horde, he first sought and obtained Sergius's blessing. Donskoi inflicted a serious defeat on the Mongol army at the battle of Kulikovo in 1380 – the first time that native Russians had beaten the Golden Horde. Then the Mongol ruler of Samarkand, Tamerlane (1360-1405), tried to recreate the united Mongol empire of Genghis Khan, which led him too into war with the independent kingdom of the Golden Horde. Tamerlane defeated them and destroyed their capital city of Sarai in 1395. However, Tamerlane's subsequent wars with India and Persia, and his death in 1405, saved Russia from being annexed as part of a revived and reunited Mongol empire.[18]

The result of these conflicts was the break-up of the Golden Horde into a number of smaller Mongol Muslim states around the Crimea and the Caspian Sea. This enabled the Russian Orthodox kingdom of Muscovy to become the dominant power in the region. By the time of Grand Prince **Ivan III** (1462-1505), Moscow had enough military and political strength for Ivan to proclaim himself "sole ruler of all Russia". Native Russians had still been paying tribute to the Mongol states for some time after

---

17. See Chapter 9, section 3 for hesychasm.

18. For more about Tamerlane, see Chapter 8, section 5.

the collapse of the Golden Horde, out of fear of military reprisals; but Ivan III threw off the Mongol yoke decisively in 1480, by putting an end to all payment of tribute. Islamic Mongol rule was finally over. Orthodox Russia was free.

The Russian Orthodox Church also became free from the ecclesiastical rule of Constantinople in this period. Up until then, the patriarch of Constantinople had always appointed the leader of the Russian Church, the metropolitan of Kiev. However, at the Council of Florence in 1439, Metropolitan Isidore of Kiev (along with other Orthodox delegates) accepted the submission of Orthodoxy to the papacy, in return for Western military support against the Ottoman Turks. This agreement was known as the *Union of Florence*.[19] Pope Eugenius IV (1431-47) made Isidore a Catholic cardinal and papal legate. Isidore returned to Moscow in 1441, only to find that the Russian Orthodox Church, of which he was the spiritual leader, angrily rejected the Union to which he had committed it. He was thrown in prison, and later allowed to escape back to Italy.

This meant that Russian Orthodoxy no longer had any metropolitan. However, the Russians could not ask the patriarch of Constantinople to give them a new one, because Constantinople had accepted the Union of Florence. After waiting for several years, a council of Russian bishops met in 1448 and decided to take independent action and elect their own metropolitan – Jonas, bishop of Ryazan (south-east of Moscow), metropolitan from 1448 to 1461. After the Byzantine Empire had fallen to the Turks in 1453, and the patriarchs of Constantinople had abandoned the Union of Florence, Moscow and Constantinople re-established communion with each other; but the Russians continued to elect their own metropolitan. From then onwards, the Russian Orthodox Church was *autocephalous* (self-governing) under the metropolitan of Moscow. The papacy appointed its own metropolitan of Kiev in 1458, under the terms of the Union of Florence, and Kiev became the centre of a separate Ukrainian Orthodox Church in communion with Rome. However, in 1470,

---

19. See Chapter 9, section 4 for the Union of Florence.

the Kievan metropolitan abandoned the Union of Florence, rejected the papacy, and placed himself back under the authority of the patriarch of Constantinople.

The 14th and 15th centuries in Russia saw the outbreak of the first great movements of Russian religious dissent. First came the *Strigolniki* ("shaven-heads"), who arose in the great northern cities of Novgorod and Pskov in about 1375. They were originally a movement for religious reform, led by two Orthodox deacons, Nikita and Karp, who protested against low moral standards among the clergy and (especially) the practice of simony in the Church (buying and selling positions of spiritual leadership). The protest movement, however, took on a religious life of its own, and the Strigolniki were soon rejecting the priesthood and sacraments altogether, and denying the doctrine of the resurrection and the practice of praying for the dead. Their greatest opponent was Stephen of Perm, whose writings against the Strigolniki are almost our only source of information about them.

The second half of the 15th century then witnessed another great dissenting movement, the *Judaisers*. Much debate has raged around their origins and beliefs; it seems that they were a strange blend of Judaism and Gnosticism, perhaps influenced by the Bogomils of Bulgaria.[20] The main effect the Judaizers had was to divide Russian Orthodox opinion on how to deal with heresy. Some, led by Nilus of Sora (1433-1508), opposed persecution, holding that argument and persuasion were the best methods to win heretics back to Orthodoxy. Others, led by Joseph of Volokalamsk (1439-1515), maintained that the state should suppress heresy by force. However, the conflict between Nilus and Joseph was much wider in scope than the treatment of heretics, and we must leave that story until Volume Three.

4. Moscow, Russian Orthodoxy and the Byzantine Empire

Orthodox Christianity had first come to Russia through the Byzantine Empire. When Constantinople was captured by the

---

20. For the Bogomils, see Chapter 3, section 6.

Turks in 1453, ending a thousand years of Byzantine civilisation, the torch of Orthodoxy passed from Byzantium to Moscow. A new Russian Orthodox Empire stepped forth to champion the faith of Eastern Christianity. This transfer of spiritual status from Byzantium to Russia was symbolised in a number of ways:

(i)   In 1472, Grand Prince Ivan III of Moscow married Sophia, the niece of Constantine XI, last of the Byzantine Emperors. This established a royal blood-link between the ruling families of Byzantium and Russia.

(ii) Ivan III also took over the Byzantine sign of the double eagle. This had symbolised Byzantine power: Byzantine armies had carried the sign before them into battle. Ivan made it the official emblem of Russian power too, thus proclaiming that Moscow had inherited the empire of the Byzantines.

(iii) Grand Prince Ivan IV (1533-84), known as "Ivan the Terrible", assumed the title *tsar*. This comes from the title of the Roman and Byzantine Emperors, *Caesar*. Ivan III had been addressed in this way too; but Ivan IV actually had himself crowned as successor of the Caesars, using the coronation ceremonies with which Byzantine Emperors had been enthroned.

(iv) Russian Orthodox theologians began to look on Moscow as "the third Rome". The first Rome was Rome itself, which they believed had departed from the true faith under the corrupt papacy. The second Rome was Byzantium or Constantinople, which had also betrayed the true faith by surrendering to the papacy in the Union of Florence, and for its sin had fallen to the Muslims. The third Rome was Moscow – the new spiritual capital of the Orthodox Christian faith. The Russian monk **Philotheus of Pskov**, abbot of the Three Hierarchs Monastery in Pskov (north-eastern Russia) and writer of spiritual letters, was the first to express this exalted view of Moscow. He put it like this in a celebrated letter to Tsar Basil III in 1510:

I want to add a few words on the present Orthodox empire of our ruler. On earth, he is the only Emperor of Christians, leader of the apostolic Church, which no longer stands in Rome or Constantinople, but in the blessed city of Moscow. Moscow alone shines in the whole world, brighter than the sun. All other Christian empires have fallen, and in their place stands alone our ruler's empire, in accordance with the prophetic writings. Two Romes have fallen, but the third stands, and a fourth there will not be.

Having secured their national independence from the Mongols, and their spiritual independence from the Byzantines, the Orthodox people of Russia became imbued with a sense of their special divine mission and destiny. In much the same way that Protestant Britain and America would later regard themselves, Russia became in its own mind "Holy Russia" – God's chosen land, where the Christian empires of Rome and Byzantium lived on, and where the faith of Christ and the apostles was preserved in its purity in the Russian Orthodox Church, at a time when the rest of the Christian world had fallen either into heresy or under Muslim control. As Philotheus said, Moscow shone brighter than the sun as the third Rome, and there would not be a fourth.

Important people:

The Church

Antony (mid-11th century)
Theodosius (died 1074)
Hilarion of Kiev (mid-11th century)
Nestor (1056-1111)
Cyril of Turov (1130-89)
Simeon the Myrrh-gusher (died 1196)
Sava (1175-1236)
Sergius of Radonezh (1314-92)
Stephen of Perm (1340-96)

Daniel Chorney (died 1430)
Andrei Rublev (1370-1430)
Epiphanius the Wise (active early 1400s)
Philotheus of Pskov (active early 1500s)

Political and military

Prince Vladimir (980-1015)
Prince Yaroslav the Wise (1019-54)
Genghis Khan (1196-1227)
Prince Alexander Nevsky (1236-51)
Grand Prince Dmitri Donskoi (1359-89)
Grand Prince Ivan III (1462-1505)

Christ comes to Russia

Blessed be the God of Israel and the God of Christianity, who has visited His people and brought them salvation! He did not hate His creation, which for ages was possessed by Pagan darkness and devil-worship. He gave light to the children of Abraham by giving them the tablets of His Law, and afterwards He delivered all the nations by sending them His Son, His Gospel, and His baptism, and by giving them resurrection unto life eternal ...

When Abraham and Sarah were old, while Abraham was sitting at the door of his tent in the heat of the day, God appeared to him by the oak trees of Mamre. Abraham ran to meet Him, bowing himself humbly to the earth, and then hastened into the tent to Sarah. Likewise, when the end of the age was approaching, God appeared to humanity, came down to the earth, and blessed the womb of the Virgin Mary. And He was received by the spotless Virgin into the very tent of her flesh. And the Virgin said to the angel, "Behold the maidservant of the Lord; may it indeed be to me according to your word." Once the Lord granted Sarah to bear a child, and she gave birth to Isaac, the free son of a free mother. And when our Lord again visited humanity, He appeared unrecognised and hidden from human eyes; and then not the Law, but grace and truth were born – not a servant, but the Son.

And Sarah's child grew up and was weaned; and Abraham held a great feast on the day of Isaac's weaning. And when Christ was on earth, grace did not immediately reveal itself, because Christ lived in seclusion until He was thirty. But when He had grown and was weaned, then grace was revealed by a Man in the river Jordan. Our Lord [God the Father] invited many and held a feast where He offered up the fatted calf of this present age, even His beloved Son Jesus Christ. God summoned multitudes to this feast from heaven and earth, joining angels and human beings together into one Church ...

This blessed faith now spreads across the whole world. Finally it reached the Russian people. Although the lake of the Law had dried up, the fountain of the Gospel became abundant in water, reaching us and overflowing into our land. Now, together with all Christians, we give glory to the holy Trinity, while the Jews remain dumb ...

With a voice of celebration, Rome praises Peter and Paul, through whom they came to believe in Jesus Christ, the Son of God; Asia, Ephesus, and Patmos praise John the Theologian; India praises Thomas; Egypt praises Mark. All lands, cities, and people honour and glorify the teacher who brought them to the Orthodox faith. Therefore let us summon our own strength and humbly praise our teacher and guide, the great prince of our land, Vladimir, the grandson of Igor of olden times, the son of glorious Svyatoslav, who ruled in their own day with courage and bravery, famous in many lands for their triumphs and heroism. And they did not reign in a poor or unknown land, but in Russia, which is known and celebrated by everyone throughout the world ...

Arise from your grave, O revered prince; arise and cast off your sleep! You are not dead; you only sleep until the day of universal resurrection. Arise! You are not dead! It is not right that you should die. For you have put your faith in Christ, who carries the whole world on His shoulders. Cast off your deep sleep, lift up your eyes, and see what honour the Lord has granted you! Still you live upon the earth, remembered through your sons. Arise, behold your son George, your beloved child, whom God brought forth from your loins. Behold him adorning the throne of your land. O rejoice and be of good cheer! Behold your son's godly wife, Irina. Behold your grandchildren, your great-grand-children; see how they live, how God cares for them. Behold how they maintain their devotion in the tradition you handed down to them, taking part in the mysteries of the holy Church, glorifying Christ, venerating His holy name. Behold your city, shining with majesty! Behold your blossoming churches! Behold the Christian faith flourishing! Behold your city adorned and gleaming with holy icons, fragrant with incense, praising God, filling the air with holy songs! And beholding all this, rejoice and be of good cheer, and praise the Lord, the Creator of all.

From Hilarion of Kiev's
Sermon on Law and Grace

The glory of Sunday

In this past Easter week, there was joy in heaven, but terror in the lower regions. Life was renewed and the world set free, hell was destroyed, and there was victory over the grave, the resurrection of the dead, the destruction of Satan's deceitful power, the salva-tion of humankind by Christ's rising from the tomb, the impov-erishing of the Old Covenant, the Sabbath placed in bondage, the enriching of Christ's Church, and the enthroning of Sunday. Yes, last Easter week there was universal change, for heaven opened up the earth, cleansing it from Satanic impurities ... All creation was revived! For people no longer think that the air, the sun, the fire, the springs, and the trees are gods. Fathers no longer sacrifice their own children, sending them to hell. Death is no longer wor-shipped. For the mystery of the cross has brought idolatry to an end, conquering Satan's power. Christ has given Himself to God as a sacrifice for all, thus putting a stop to the blood-sacrifices of goats and calves, and throwing the Old Covenant into the shad-ows. Sunday ceased to be a day devoted to human pleasure, for it was sanctified by the resurrection; Christ rose from the dead on that day, so that Sunday is now supreme ...

Today the sun rises and shines in the height, and joy warms the earth, for today Christ, the true Sun, has risen from the grave, saving all who trust in Him. Today the moon comes down from its high place and bows before the greater lights. As it was prophesied, the Old Covenant and its Sabbath have ceased, instead giving honour with its prophets to Christ's Covenant and Sunday. Today the winter of sin has ended in repentance, and wisdom has melted the ice of unbelief. Today the season of spring appears afresh, giving life to all earthly things; the stormy winds now blow gently, begetting fruits, nourishing seeds, bringing forth the green grass. For "spring" is the beauty of faith in Christ, which through baptism gives rebirth to humanity; the "stormy winds" are evil, sinful thoughts, changed to goodness through repentance, and begetting soul-saving fruits. The soil of our life, receiving God's Word like a seed, and undergoing a joyful labour through the fear of God, brings forth a spirit of salvation.

From Cyril of Turov's
Sermon on the first Sunday after Easter

The reign of Yaroslav the Wise: The benefit of reading books

Yaroslav devoted himself to books, constantly reading them day and night. He gathered many scribes, and translated books from Greek into Slavonic. He wrote and collected many books for the instruction of true believers and their religious education. For as one man ploughs the land, another sows, and others reap and eat an abundance of food, so it was with Prince Yaroslav. His father Vladimir ploughed and broke up the soil when he enlightened Russia through baptism, and Yaroslav sowed the written word into the hearts of the faithful, and we in turn reap the harvest by receiving the teaching of books.

For the benefit of learning from books is great. Books reveal to us and teach us the way of repentance, for we gain wisdom and purity from the written word. Books are like rivers which water the whole world; they are the wellsprings of wisdom. Books have a depth which no-one can measure; they comfort us in sorrow; they are the bridle of self-control. For great is wisdom. As Solomon says in praise of wisdom: "I, Wisdom, dwell with prudence, and search out reason and discretion. The fear of the

Lord is the beginning of wisdom. Counsel belongs to me, and sound wisdom; I am understanding, I have strength. Kings reign by me, and rulers decree justice. By me princes rule, and nobles, all the judges of the earth. I love those who love me, and those who seek me earnestly will find favour" (Prov. 8:12-17). If you seek wisdom attentively in books, your spirit will derive great profit. He who often reads books converses with God or holy men. If you have the words of the prophets, the teachings of the Gospel-writers and the apostles, and the lives of the holy fathers, your soul will gain great profit from these.

Thus Yaroslav was a lover of books. He wrote many and put them for safe-keeping in the Church of Saint Sophia which he built himself. He adorned this church with gold, silver, and ecclesiastical vessels, and its people sing the usual hymns to God at the customary times. Yaroslav also built other churches in the cities and districts, appointing priests and paying them out of his own wealth. He ordered them to teach the people, because that is their God-given duty, and to be often in the churches. Priests and Christian laypeople thus grew in number. Yaroslav rejoiced when he beheld the multitude of his churches and his Christian subjects, but the sight afflicted the devil, since this new Christian nation had overthrown him.

From *The Tale of Bygone Years*
(a contemporary chronicle of Russian history),
the entry for the year 1037

Sava of Serbia's dying prayer

O Lord of my father [Simeon], how great Your power is, how sweet Your love! Your mercies toward me have been beyond measuring; how then can I measure Your mercies toward all creation? Truly, there is nothing dark for Your eyes, there is nothing confusing for Your wisdom, and nothing can compare with the beauty of Your holiness. From my birth, You have guided me with Your right hand, and nourished me with Your wisdom's milk and honey. I have merely been Your instrument in shepherding one of Your nations toward Your heavenly sheepfold. O merciful Lord, bless the people of my father Saint Simeon, and make them great in holiness among the nations. O my God, I worship You, I praise You; for now you have granted my desire to die in a foreign land.[21] Forgive me all my doubts! All the good things I received from You, I have given back to others; and now, last of all, I return my soul itself into Your hands. Be merciful to my sinful soul, O my Lord Christ; take it to the dwelling place of my father Simeon, through the intercession of Your holy mother the Virgin Mary and all Your saints.

Sergius of Radonezh: A hermit becomes an abbot

Who can tell the story of his labours? Who can number the trials he endured, living on his own in the wilderness? At various times the devil, in different disguises, wrestled with the saint, but the demons were never successful when they attacked Saint Sergius. It didn't matter what visions they called up, they could not conquer the firm and courageous spirit of the ascetic. One moment, Satan himself laid traps for him; next, wild beasts invaded his sanctuary – for there were a lot of wild beasts living in this wilderness. Some of them stayed at a distance; others came near the saint, surrounded him, even sniffed him.

One particular beast, a bear, would often come to the holy man. Realising that the animal didn't mean him any harm, but came simply to get food, the saint brought a small slice of bread and put it on a log or stump; and the bear learned to come for the meal that Sergius prepared for him, ate it, and went away again. If Sergius had no bread, and the bear didn't find his usual slice, the animal would wait around for a long time, staring about him on all sides – he looked like a moneylender waiting to be paid a debt! Sergius at this point didn't have a well-stored larder in the wilderness; he only had bread, and water from a spring, and not even much of these two things. So he often didn't have any bread, and then both he and the bear would go hungry. Sometimes, though the saint only had a single slice of bread, he actually gave it to the bear, because he didn't want the beast to be disappointed when he came for his food.

---

21. Sava died in Bulgaria.

Sergius worked hard at studying the holy Scriptures in order to get a knowledge of everything good; in his private contemplations, he trained his mind to long for the eternal joy of heaven. The most marvellous thing was that no-one knew the extent of his ascetic and godly life, lived in solitude. Only God, Who sees everything hidden, observed it. Whether Sergius lived two years or more in the wilderness by himself, we do not know; only God knows. And the Lord, seeing his quite remarkable faith and patience, had compassion on him; desiring to give him relief from his lonely labours, He put it into the hearts of certain God-fearing monks to visit Sergius. The saint asked them, "Do you think you can endure the hardships of this place – hunger, thirst, being deprived of all kinds of things?" They responded, "Yes, reverend father, we are willing, with God's help and your prayers." Holy Sergius, seeing their faith and zeal, was amazed and said: "My brothers, I wanted to live alone in this wilderness and even to die here. But if God wants to gather many brothers here and to establish a monastery in this place, then God's will be done. I welcome you with joy. Let each of you build a cell for himself. And let it be known to you, if you come to live in this wilderness, that the beginning of righteousness is to fear the Lord."

To increase his own fear of the Lord, Sergius spent night and day studying the Word of God. He was a young man, physically strong and healthy, and could do the work of two men or more. What the devil did now was to direct all his energies to wounding Sergius with the darts of lust. The saint, aware that these were attacks of the enemy, disciplined his body and trained his soul, gaining the mastery through fasting; and so he was protected by the grace of God. He hadn't yet been raised to the priestly office, but lived in company with his brother monks, going to church with them every day for the various religious services – nocturns, matins, the hours, and vespers. To celebrate communion with them, a priest who was an abbot used to come from one of the villages. At first, Sergius himself didn't want to become either a priest or an abbot, because of his deep humility. He was always saying that the origin and root of all evil lay in the pride of authority and the ambitious desire to be an abbot ...

But within a year, the abbot who had received Saint Sergius into the monastic life had fallen sick and, after a short illness, passed out of this life. Then God put it into the hearts of the brothers to go to blessed Sergius, and say to him, "Father, we can't continue without an abbot. We want you to be our abbot, the guide of our souls and bodies" ... Groaning inwardly, Sergius said, "Fathers and brothers, I will say no more against it. I will submit to God's will. He sees into our hearts and souls. We will go into the town to see our bishop" ... Our blessed father Sergius begged the bishop to give them an abbot, a guide for their souls. The venerable bishop Athanasius replied: "You yourself, my son and my brother, will be the father and abbot of your brother monks. For God called you to this in your mother's womb." Blessed Sergius refused, insisting that he was unworthy. But Athanasius said to him, "My beloved, you have acquired every good quality – except obedience." Blessed Sergius bowed right down, and replied, "May God's will be done. Praise be to the Lord for ever and ever." And they all responded, "Amen."

From *The Life, Acts, and Miracles of Sergius of Radonezh*
by Epiphanius the Wise

7

The Universities and the rise of Scholasticism

1. The universities

The 12th and 13th centuries saw a great flowering of knowledge, especially theology and philosophy, in Western Christendom. It reached its high point in the 13th century, which many consider to be the "golden age" of Western Catholic civilisation in the Middle Ages. At the heart of this flowering of knowledge was the university.

The institution of the university came to the West from the Muslim world. The most important Muslim university was al-Azhar University in Cairo, Egypt. Al-Azhar was founded in 970; it still exists today, one of the world's oldest centres of learning. These Islamic universities had a strong influence on the development of European education, *e.g.* in the use of Arabic rather than Roman numbers.[1] However, the greatest impact Islamic universities had on the West was simply the way they acted as channels for the Muslim world's medical, scientific, mathematical and philosophical knowledge to flow into Western academic institutions. (At that time, the Islamic world far surpassed the West in intellectual achievement.)

Western universities began to appear in the 12th century. They developed out of schools which were attached to cathedral

---

1. Arabic numbers are the basis of the numbers we use today – 1, 2, 3, 4, 5, and so on. For Roman numbers, see the section *Roman numbers* in *A Chapter on Time* in Volume One.

churches and abbeys. Many of these schools were originally founded to train boys for the Church, *e.g.* to sing in choirs – the earliest known choir school seems to have been the one attached to York cathedral, established in the 7th century. However, such schools also often provided a free general education to boys living in the neighbourhood. The first universities were those of Bologna (northern Italy) and Paris (northern France). There had been a law school in Bologna since 890; this formed the basis of what became Bologna University, given official recognition by the Holy Roman Emperor, Frederick Barbarossa (1152-90), in 1155. In Paris, there was a famous school attached to Notre Dame Cathedral, which by 1150-70 had taken on the features of a university.

The other Western universities were modelled on Bologna and Paris. In Bologna, the university was a "corporation" (a sort of trade union) of students; the students controlled the policies of the university, and hired and fired the teachers. In Paris, the university was a corporation of teachers; they controlled policy and set the fees for the students. The name "university" arose out of these methods of organisation. A university organised on the Bologna model was called in Latin a *universitas scholarium* – "the whole body of students". A university organised on the Paris model was called a *universitas magistrorum* – "the whole body of teachers".[2]

Many universities sprang up in the period 1200-1500. By 1500, there were about 80 universities in Western Europe. Some were celebrated for teaching particular subjects: Paris was famous for theology, Bologna for law, Salerno (southern Italy) for medicine, Oxford (southern England) for science and mathematics. A fully developed university would have four departments or "faculties", teaching theology, law, medicine, and arts. The ideal was to make the university into a centre for preserving and communicating the sum total of all human knowledge.

---

2. *Universitas* is Latin for "whole body"; a centre for preserving and communicating the sum total of all human knowledge.

The normal age for entering a university was 14 or 15. All a man[3] needed was an education in the Latin language and the ability to pay his fees. Latin was the only language spoken in universities; the Western world considered it the proper language of culture and civilisation. A Latin-speaking student from any country could therefore study in any university in any part of Europe: there were no national language-barriers.[4] However, the student bodies of universities were divided up according to nationality. Each national body of students had its own rules and regulations. It was presided over by a university officer called a *proctor*. The proctors elected a *rector* who was head of the university. Each faculty was governed by a *dean*. Almost all lecturers in all subjects were clergymen, and the few laymen had to be celibate; all students, too, had to be unmarried during their time at university. It was a long academic year: 11 months, with just a few weeks off for Christmas and Easter.

The method of education used in universities was twofold: (i) the lecture; (ii) the disputation.

(i) In the lecture, the teacher would read out a set text to the students (*e.g.* Peter Lombard's *Sentences* – see section 3), and make his own comments on the text. The students were expected to take very full notes of what the teacher said. Books were scarce in the days before printing was invented, so we must not imagine that every student had his own copy of the textbook. Probably the university had only one copy which was kept chained up in the library.

(ii) The disputation was a public event in which a teacher and a student would set out to solve a problem. The problem would be two statements which appeared to contradict each other, but which were both found in authoritative texts. To take a theological

---

3. Women were not eligible for university education in the Middle Ages.

4. The first university to teach in the national language of its country, rather than in Latin, was the University of Halle in north-east Germany in 1694.

example, an early Church father might be quoted as saying, "God cannot die." But then another Church father might be quoted as saying, "God died on the cross." The student would have to give all the arguments for and against each statement, by quoting passages from the Bible and great theologians, and offering his own comments on these passages. The teacher would then make remarks on what the student had said, and would offer a solution to the problem. In the example we used, the teacher would probably have said: "Both statements are true, if interpreted properly. In His divine nature, God cannot die. But when He became a man, He took upon Himself a human nature which can die. Therefore on the cross, God suffered death in His human nature. But He remains incapable of dying in His divine nature."

The disputation was a powerful method for training the minds of students in the art of logical thinking and arguing, and enabled them to master the selected areas of knowledge on which they performed their disputations. Lecturers also engaged in disputations over debated subjects; they would draw up a set of statements or "theses", announce that they were going to defend them in debate, and challenge anyone to argue with them and disprove the theses.

When a student had finished his university course, he was awarded the degree of "bachelor". It normally took five or six years to become a bachelor. To obtain the higher degree of "master" or "doctor", which entitled its owner to give his own lectures in a university, took much longer – 14 years of study were necessary to become a doctor of theology.

The growth of the universities produced a theological revolution in Western Christendom. Previously, the great monasteries had been the centres of learning; the leading theologians had been monks who studied theology within the setting of monastic life and worship. The universities challenged this. Theology now became an intellectual subject in its own right, and people studied it in the academic context of university life, outside the constraints of monastic discipline. The great theologians were now university professors who earned their living by teaching doctrine. In one way, this had a liberating effect on Western theology, releasing torrents of intellectual energy, debate, and writing, in the stimulating atmosphere of free academic discourse. In another way, though, it introduced a certain element of division between spiritual life on the one hand, and intellectual and theological pursuits on the other. Many have judged this division to be a deeply harmful feature of Western Christianity since the 1100s.

2. The rise of scholasticism

"Scholasticism" and "scholastic theology" are the names that historians give to the theological teaching which dominated the Western universities of the Middle Ages. The term "scholastic" comes from the word for "school" and simply means "school theology" – the theology taught in the schools (in other words, in the universities). The scholastic theologians are often called "the schoolmen". The schoolmen developed a distinctive approach to theology. We can summarise their style and outlook as follows.

(i) Faith and reason. The scholastic theologians were deeply concerned about the relationship between faith and reason. They wanted to see how far "pure reason" could discover or prove the doctrines of the Christian faith. What could the human mind find out about God by investigating the created world, without referring to God's special revelation in the Bible? For example, what could unaided reason discover of the existence of God the Creator, the Trinity, or providence? If reason alone could not discover or prove a particular doctrine, could it still be shown to be in harmony with reason? For instance, even if we cannot discover the Trinity by pure reason, can we still demonstrate that the Trinity does not contradict reason? Can something be false from the viewpoint of reason, but true according to divine revelation? Different schoolmen gave different answers to these questions, but they were united in asking the same questions.

(ii) Systematic theology. The scholastic theologians wanted to offer a complete, systematic account of Christian truth. This meant examining a particular doctrine logically from every point of view. But it meant more. A typical schoolman would try to bring all Christian doctrines together into a system of theology which set forth and explained the entire body of revealed truth. They called such a system a *summa* (summary). In their pursuit of a universal system of doctrine, the schoolmen often spent a great deal of time and effort inquiring into questions which most Christians in later ages would find pointless. For example, could God have become incarnate as an animal, or as a woman? Can one angel be in two places at the same time? Can two angels be in the same place at the same time? Who sinned most, Adam or Eve?

(iii) Philosophy and the writings of Aristotle. As well as being theologians, the schoolmen were also the philosophers of the Middle Ages. They wanted to give a comprehensive account, not just of Church teaching, but of all truth. So they did not limit themselves to theological questions. They would try to answer deep philosophical questions too. What is matter? What is mind? What is time? What is space? What is being? What is the nature of cause-and-effect?

One of the great debates which the schoolmen carried on was the conflict between "Realism" and "Nominalism". This concerned the relationship between (a) an *individual thing* – e.g. a particular fish, or a particular human being, and (b) what made that individual thing the *same* as other things of the same kind – what makes different fish all to be "fish" (the general idea of "fish"), or what different human beings have in common (the general idea of "humanity"). The general idea was called a "universal". Realists, influenced by the ancient Greek philosopher Plato, held that the universal was more real than the individual thing.[5] So, for instance, the idea of "humanity" was more real than any individual human being, and it existed independently of the various people in whom "humanity" had an individual existence.

---

5. For Plato, see Volume One, Chapter 1, section 1. See also Volume One, Chapter 7, section 2 for Neoplatonism – the new interpretation of Plato that Plotinus put forward.

Nominalists, often influenced by the philosopher Aristotle (see below), held the opposite: individual things were more real than the universal; the general idea of "humanity" was just a name (Latin *nomen* – hence "Nominalism") and had no reality of its own, apart from individual human beings. There were various views which took a middle course between pure Realism and pure Nominalism.

This debate sometimes had serious implications for theology. For example, an extreme Nominalist view would deny any reality to the general idea of "deity", "divinity", or "divine essence", seeing the three persons of the Trinity as each existing in their own right as separate individuals. In that case, how can we avoid saying that Father, Son, and Spirit are three Gods? Among famous scholastic theologians, John Wyclif was an ardent Realist, William of Ockham was a zealous Nominalist, and Thomas Aquinas pursued a middle course.[6]

In the 13th century, scholastic theology came to rely increasingly on the philosophy of *Aristotle* (384-22 BC). Aristotle was one of the greatest of the ancient Pagan philosophers of Greece. A few of Aristotle's works had been known to the early schoolmen, because Boethius in the 6th century had translated them into Latin.[7] However, all of Aristotle's writings became available in Latin in the 1100s, largely through two great Muslim philosophers, the Persian Avicenna (980-1037) and the Spanish Averroes (1126-98). They translated Aristotle from Greek into Arabic for the benefit of the Islamic world; Christian scholars, such as Michael Scotus of Toulouse (1180-1235), then translated the Arabic (along with Islamic commentaries on Aristotle) into Latin for the benefit of the Western Catholic world. Arabic translations of Aristotle found their way into Catholic Europe chiefly through Muslim Spain, especially after 1085 when the Spanish Christians conquered the Muslim city of Toledo, which had been the capital city of the Spanish Muslim kingdom of

---

6. This Chapter deals with Aquinas and Ockham in section 3. For Wyclif, see Chapter 10, section 4.

7. For Boethius, see Volume One, Chapter 11, section 1.

Cordova.[8] Later scholars translated Aristotle into Latin directly from the original Greek.

This rediscovery of Aristotle by Western Europe had a huge impact on Western thought. In the writings of Aristotle, Christian thinkers found an interpretation of God, humanity and the world which seemed logical, convincing, comprehensive – and had been worked out without any reference to the Bible. The problem was that some of Aristotle's teachings were opposed to the Bible. For instance, Aristotle taught that the world had always existed. Some Western thinkers were so enthusiastic for Aristotle, especially as he had been interpreted by the Muslim philosopher Averroes, that they accepted and taught even the anti-Christian elements in his thought. These men were called "Averroists", and their greatest champion was **Siger of Brabant** (1235-1282). Siger taught that the universe had existed from all eternity, and that individual human souls were not immortal but were absorbed into a "world-soul" after death. Siger at first lectured in Paris, but when the Church condemned his teachings as heretical in 1276 he fled to Italy. This did not prove to be much of a safe haven, since Siger was murdered there by a priest whose enthusiasm for orthodoxy proved stronger than his respect for the sixth commandment. To defend themselves against charges of heresy, some Averroists put forward a theory of "double truth". This theory held that human reason, by itself, would compel philosophers to accept certain things as truth; but then divine revelation showed that those things were false, and something else was really the truth. This "double truth" theory set reason and faith in sharp conflict with each other. It meant that if a person followed reason, he was bound to end up believing some things that contradicted revelation.

At first, many Catholic theologians reacted against Aristotle and saw his philosophy as a dangerous alternative to Christianity, especially in view of what the Averroists were saying. Up until then, the Western Church had found the philosophy of Plato

---

8. For Cordova and Spanish Christian-Muslim relations, see Chapter 1, section 5.

to be the most suitable ally of Christian theology, especially since Augustine of Hippo, the greatest Western theologian, had been a Platonist.[9] But Aristotle disagreed with some of Plato's basic teachings. For example, Plato held that the human soul had a direct inner knowledge of a higher spiritual world, and that this knowledge did not depend on our experience of life in the outward physical world. We derive our fundamental ideas (such as beauty and justice) from this inner knowledge. Aristotle, however, taught that all human knowledge arose from experience mediated to the soul through the senses – through what we can see, hear and touch. We can know that a spiritual being like God exists, then, only by reasoning from our experience of the external world; the soul cannot have any direct or immediate spiritual knowledge of God.

Many traditional Catholic theologians preferred Plato to Aristotle, and they led a campaign to ban the study of Aristotle's writings. For a time they enjoyed a measure of success. However, by the 13th century, the tide had turned in Aristotle's favour, and scholastic theologians were hailing him as the great Pagan forerunner of Christian truth, whose philosophy was almost perfectly suited to undergird, express, and explain the theology of the Church. The schoolmen now sought to bring together Aristotle's philosophy and Christian theology into a harmonious unity (much as today's theologians often try to marry theology to the latest scientific theory about the origin of the universe or humankind).

The theological upheavals Aristotle caused in the Western Catholic world had no parallel in the Orthodox East, where the knowledge of Aristotle had never been lost. The Greek in which Aristotle wrote did not need to be translated for Byzantine theologians, as it was their own native language. Eastern theology had absorbed, and adapted to itself, the philosophy of both Plato and Aristotle in roughly equal doses. In fact, in some ways Orthodoxy had something of a bias in favour of Aristotle, because Platonism always formed the philosophical basis on which anti-Christian

---

9. For Augustine, see Volume One, Chapter 9, section 3.

Pagan thought tried (now and then) to make a reappearance in the East – in contrast to the Western Aristotelian Paganism of Siger of Brabant. There was therefore no "revival" of Aristotelian philosophy in the East, no sudden Aristotelian challenge to throw Orthodox theology off balance, and no real Eastern equivalent of Western scholasticism.

3. Great scholastic theologians

Some of the schoolmen were among the greatest Christian thinkers in the history of the Church. We can only pick out a few and try to show their place in the development of Christian theology.

Anselm of Canterbury (1033-1109)

History has awarded Anselm the title of "first of the schoolmen", even though he lived before the rise of the universities. He was born in Aosta, northern Italy, became a monk in the French Benedictine abbey of Le Bec in Normandy, and was elected its abbot in 1078. In 1093 he became archbishop of Canterbury, and spent much of his time in conflict with two kings of England, William Rufus (1087-1100) and Henry I (1100-1135), during the great investiture controversy (Anselm was a supporter of the Hildebrandine reform movement).[10] He was one of the greatest saints of the Western medieval Church: a man of spotless life, unflinching devotion to truth and righteousness, and a profound reverence and burning love for Christ. People today still turn to Anselm's prayers and meditations for spiritual food; they combine thoughtful reflection, deep emotion, and an awe-inspiring sense of intimacy with a great and holy God. In most doctrinal matters, Anselm was content to sit at the feet of Augustine of Hippo.

Anselm's most important writings for the development of scholastic theology were his *Monologion* and *Proslogion*, which tried to prove the existence of God by pure reason, and his *Cur deus homo*, which offered the first systematic theology of the atonement.

---

10. For the Hildebrandine reform movement and the investiture controversy, see Chapter 4, sections 4, 5 and 6.

Anselm of Canterbury (1033-1109)

The Latin words around Anselm's head quote his motto,
"I believe so that I may understand."

We can sum up Anselm's argument for God's existence in the *Monologion* and *Proslogion* as follows. By definition, God is the most perfect of all possible beings. But if God does not exist, He would *not* be the most perfect of all possible beings; for a God who *does* exist would be more perfect than a God who does not exist. Therefore, if God is by definition the most perfect of all possible beings, He *must* exist. Theologians and philosophers have argued for a thousand years about whether Anselm's proof is valid.

Anselm's book on the atonement, *Cur deus homo* ("Why God became man"), had a greater long-term influence on Western theology than the *Monologion* and *Proslogion*. Anselm rejected the view, widespread among many early Church fathers, that Christ's death was a ransom paid to Satan to free sinners from captivity to him. Satan has no "rights" over the human race, Anselm argued; he is a robber and an outlaw who has taken us captive unjustly. Christ's death was paid as a ransom, not to Satan, but to God. Human sin, Anselm reasoned, has outraged God's honour and majesty. The human race must either suffer punishment, or offer compensation ("satisfaction") to God for the outrage. But we cannot offer any satisfaction for so great an outrage. Sin is infinitely serious; so a just satisfaction to God would have to be infinite in value. Only God could offer Himself such an infinite satisfaction.

However, because the Trinity is merciful as well as just, and willed to save sinners, God the Son became human in Jesus Christ; and Christ the God-Man, on humanity's behalf, offered to God the Father an infinite satisfaction for the outrage of sin. That satisfaction was the God-Man's own infinitely valuable life. Because He was without sin, Christ did not have to die, but He freely surrendered His life to the Father on the cross. God then rewarded Christ for His voluntary self-sacrifice by applying the infinite worth or merit of His death to the elect, those sinners predestined to salvation by divine grace (Anselm was an Augustinian in his views of salvation).

Anselm's doctrine of the atonement contained many fruitful ideas which later theologians built into the classic Western understanding of Christ's death. Most, however, would reject Anselm's view that while Christ offered His perfect life as a satisfaction to God, He did not suffer the punishment of sin. The classic substitutionary concept of the atonement sees Christ's "payment" of His life to the Father as being one and the same thing with His suffering sin's punishment on humanity's behalf. However, what Anselm's argument in *Cur deus homo* shows us, clearly and attractively, is the mind of a scholastic theologian at work. He is not content simply to believe that Christ died for sinners. He wants to know *why* Christ had to die for sinners. Why did salvation happen this way, rather than some other way? This search for a rational understanding of Christian truths was the driving force behind scholastic theology. As Anselm put it, his theology was "faith seeking understanding"; or as he also said, "I believe in order that I may understand."

Other great writings of Anselm included his *The Incarnation of the Word*, *The Virgin Conception and Original Sin*, *The Procession of the Holy Spirit* (which defended the Western against the Eastern view – see Chapter 3, section 4), and *The Compatibility of God's Foreknowledge, Predestination and Grace with Human Freedom* (which expounds the Augustinian view).

Peter Abelard (1079-1142)

Abelard was the most brilliant Catholic thinker of the 12th century. He was also its most tragic figure because of the spectacular moral failings of his life and their painful consequences. He was born in Britanny, northern France, and studied at the famous cathedral school of Notre Dame in Paris which was developing into Paris University. Abelard felt dissatisfied with the teaching of the school's head, William of Champeaux (1070-1121), and set up his own rival lectures. The students deserted William to listen to Abelard. This established Abelard's reputation as a genius. He soon became head of the Paris school himself, and students flocked from all over Western Europe to sit at his feet.

However, at the same time that Abelard was rising to these dizzy heights of intellectual fame, his moral downfall was looming. One of the canons[11] of Notre Dame Cathedral, Fulbert, had a 17-year-old niece, the highly intelligent and extremely beautiful Heloise. Abelard fell wildly in love with her. He persuaded Fulbert to take him into his household and appoint him as Heloise's private tutor. She and Abelard, who was more than twice her age, did not confine themselves within the limits of a pupil-teacher relationship; their passion for each other is the most famous love-affair of the Middle Ages. When the affair was discovered (Heloise became pregnant with Abelard's child), Heloise's uncle Fulbert exploded with rage. Presumably acting on the principle that the punishment should fit the crime, good canon Fulbert hired some ruffians who burst into Abelard's bedroom one night and castrated him. A deeply chastened Abelard retired from the Paris school into the Benedictine monastery of Saint Denis, just north of Paris, and Heloise became a nun.[12]

Abelard's most important writing came soon after these tragic events. In 1122 he wrote a book called *Sic et non* ("Yes and no"). In this book Abelard considered 158 theological questions. He set alongside each other statements from the Bible, the early Church fathers, and other authoritative statements of Church teaching, which appeared to contradict each other. Abelard's aim was to provoke people to think for themselves and use reason as a tool for reconciling these apparently conflicting statements. Lawyers were already using this method in legal studies to settle conflicting views on Church law; the greatest of them, **Gratian** (died 1179), an Italian Camaldolese monk who taught in Bologna law school, published his *Decretum* in about 1140, in which he set out all apparent contradictions in the Church's canon law and used rational argument to reconcile them. Gratian's *Decretum* became the fundamental text on which canon lawyers based all

---

11. A "canon" is the title for a clergyman who lives with other clergy in the grounds of a cathedral church. This use of the word should not be confused with two other uses: (i) the canon of Scripture, which means the authoritative list of inspired books; (ii) canon law, which means official Church law.

12. One cannot help thinking that all this would make a good Hollywood film. It has the perfect blend of sex, religion and violence.

future studies. Abelard was the first person to apply to theology this method of using logic to create a harmonious system from the swarm of seemingly conflicting data.

Abelard had a stormy life. He was often in trouble with Church authorities, especially through the lifelong hostility of Bernard of Clairvaux, who regarded Abelard as a dangerously unsound thinker.[13] Nevertheless, Abelard's lectures and writing had a great impact on the 12th century West. They shook the minds of students awake, inspiring them to ask questions and to use reason as a way of investigating and determining the meaning of theological statements.

Peter Lombard (1100-1160)

Peter Lombard has been called "the father of systematic theology". He wrote the most widely used theological textbook of the Middle Ages. Born in Lombardy, northern Italy, he studied at Bologna and Paris (his teacher at Paris was probably Abelard). From about 1140, he taught theology in Paris, and became bishop of Paris in 1159 but died the following year.

Lombard's great work was his *Four Books of Sentences*, produced between 1147 and 1151. *Sentences* means "opinions". This was a collection of quotations from the Bible, the early Church fathers, the ecumenical Councils, and other authorities, dealing with the whole range of theological topics. It was divided into four books: (i) the Trinity and providence; (ii) creation, sin and grace; (iii) the incarnation, salvation and moral virtues; (iv) the sacraments and eschatology. In some ways it was similar to Abelard's *Sic et non*. The difference was that Lombard offered solutions to all difficulties and apparent contradictions, using reason to judge between different authorities. His method was to state the teaching of the Church, prove it from the Bible, give the opinions of the early Church fathers, and then to resolve any seeming contradictions by the careful use of logic.

---

13. For the conflict between Abelard and Bernard of Clairvaux, see Chapter 5, section 3, under *Bernard of Clairvaux* and the *Second Crusade*.

Lombard was the first Catholic theologian to define the number of the "sacraments" as seven: baptism, holy communion, confirmation, penance, marriage, ordination, and extreme unction.[14] However, Lombard's teaching about each sacrament did not always correspond with later Roman Catholic doctrine. For example, in his treatment of penance, Lombard held that the priest did not himself cleanse the sins of the penitent believer by the act of "absolution"; what the priest did was *declare* the cleansing of sin which took place in penance, but the cleansing itself was *brought about* by the Holy Spirit directly. There was no cooperation between God and the priest in the remission of sin. All the priest could *directly* remit by priestly power was the penalties imposed by the Church, *e.g.* excommunication. This was also the view defended by Thomas Aquinas in his *Summa Theologiae*, although Aquinas later changed his mind. (See below for Aquinas.)[15]

---

14.   Confirmation is the ceremony in which a baptised person becomes a full member of the Church by the laying on of a bishop's hands. Penance involves confessing one's sin to a priest, receiving his "absolution" or forgiveness, and submitting to whatever act of discipline the priest imposes (*e.g.* fasting, abstaining from communion). Extreme unction is a ceremony in which the priest anoints a dying person with oil (the oil signifying the Holy Spirit) to prepare him for his journey to the next life; it is often called "the last rites".

15.   Lombard's doctrine of penance, as expounded by Aquinas, was quite complex, and shows that the powers claimed by the medieval priesthood were not necessarily as dreadful as later Protestants imagined. According to Lombard and Aquinas, some priestly acts directly conferred grace by virtue of the power which God had lodged in the priesthood. For example, when a bishop ordained a man by the laying on of hands, that action itself directly caused the grace of apostolic succession to flow upon the man, thus making him into a priest. But absolution was not like this. When a priest absolved someone from his sins, the act of absolution did not itself cause the grace of cleansing to flow into the penitent soul; it merely "disposed" the soul to receive that cleansing through the soul's own act of contrition. God alone cleansed the guilt of the contrite soul. Indeed, as far as Aquinas was concerned, God cleansed the contrite soul at the very moment of its contrition, before priestly absolution. The great value of absolution lay in its power to remit the "temporal penalties" of sin – the penances which had to be carried out either here on earth, or hereafter in purgatory. But the inward and spiritual stain of guilt could be

Lombard's definition of the number of the sacraments as seven became the official Catholic theology through a decision of the Council of Florence in 1439. The Catholic Church saw these seven rituals as both symbolising and actually imparting a special sanctifying grace. Lombard was one of the earliest Catholic theologians to teach clearly that the sacraments were not just *signs* which declared and applied God's grace, but were effective *causes* of grace in believers whenever they received them. By the early 13th century, scholastic theologians had coined the famous phrase *ex opere operato* ("by virtue of the act performed") to express this view of the sacraments. It meant that as long as the sacraments were correctly performed, sanctifying grace flowed through them as an objective force, without regard to the moral or spiritual fitness of the priest performing them, or the person receiving them (although he or she must not set up any positive spiritual barrier to this grace, *e.g.* hatred of God or neighbour).[16]

---

remitted immediately by God the instant a soul was contrite. Aquinas's words are: "Through contrition, a person receives the pardon of his sins as to their guilt, and consequently as to the debt of eternal punishment which is remitted together with the guilt. By virtue of the keys [the priestly power of absolution – a reference to Matt. 16:19] which derive their force from the suffering of Christ, the contrite person's grace is increased, because the temporal penalty is remitted, whose debt continued after the guilt had been forgiven" (*Summa Theologiae*, Supplement, Question 18, article 2). As I said in the main text, Aquinas later changed his mind on this, but in his actual treatment of penance in the *Summa Theologiae* this is the view he expounds at length.

16. The difference between this medieval *ex opere operato* view of the sacraments, and the view upheld by the Protestant Reformers, was (in one sense) only a difference of emphasis. Both Reformers and schoolmen maintained that Christ's presence and power in the sacrament depend neither on the worthiness of the clergyman, nor on the faith of the believer. Christ is objectively present to convey His blessing. The Reformers held that a person must exercise positive faith in Christ if the blessing is to be received; the schoolmen held that a person must not *prevent* the blessing from being received by erecting sinful barriers against Christ in his or her soul. The really serious difference between Reformers and schoolmen lay in their understanding of the *nature* of the blessing Christ conveys in the sacrament.

Lombard's *Sentences* became the standard theological text-book in Western universities until the Protestant Reformation of the 16th century. Writing a commentary on the *Sentences* was a normal part of the process for obtaining a doctorate in theology.

Robert Grosseteste (1168-1253)

Grosseteste was an Englishman, usually remembered today as a pioneer scientist. We do not know much about his early life, but in 1235 he became bishop of Lincoln (eastern England), the English bishopric with the largest territory. Here he devoted himself with white-hot energy to reforming life and conduct among clergy and people alike; he especially insisted on the clergy's duty to preach the Scriptures and the people's duty to come and listen to the Word of God. Grosseteste himself was a great preacher, and he preached in English, not Latin, so determined was he to bring the Gospel to ordinary uneducated people. "The work of a priest," he proclaimed, "is not giving people the mass, but preaching the living truth."

As is the fate of many reformers, Grosseteste spent much of his time waging an unedifying war with those who did not want to be reformed, notably the monasteries, the Lincolnshire nobility, and the clergy of his own cathedral. He quarrelled with the English king, Henry III, denouncing the royal custom of treating bishops as civil servants – a bishop must be a spiritual pastor, Grosseteste declared, free from political entanglements. His zeal for reforming the Church catapulted him into a long and bitter conflict with the papacy too; he protested passion-ately against Pope Innocent IV's grinding taxation of the English clergy, and Innocent's appointment of spiritually unfit Italian friends and relatives (even little boys) to money-making posi-tions in the English Church (Innocent IV was pope from 1243 to 1254). Grosseteste's disgust at the corruptions of the papal court provoked him into explosions of prophet-like condemna-tion, accusing Innocent of being an Antichrist and predicting his eternal damnation in the hereafter. Grosseteste enjoyed such a universal reputation for holiness and intellectual brilliance that Innocent dared not discipline him for these outbursts; but when

Grosseteste died, Innocent exclaimed, "I rejoice, and let every true son of the Roman Church rejoice with me, that my great enemy is removed!"

Grosseteste was one of the most learned Europeans of his day, skilled in Latin, Greek, and Hebrew, and well-read not only in Christian but also in Jewish and Muslim works, as well as the writings of Aristotle. He was one of the first great Western thinkers to absorb Aristotle's teachings on logic and physics, although his own theological and philosophical outlook remained basically Augustinian. Grosseteste's scientific treatises on the nature of light and motion are highly regarded by historians of science; he was an important influence on **Roger Bacon** (1214-92) of Oxford, often hailed as the greatest medieval forerunner of modern science. As far as English Christians were concerned, Grosseteste came to be seen as a precursor of John Wyclif and ultimately of English Protestantism, owing to his zeal for Biblical preaching and his outspoken opposition to a corrupt papacy (although Grosseteste's theology was typically medieval).

Alexander of Hales (1170-1245)

Alexander was another Englishman, born in Hales, near Gloucester (south-western England). After working his way up to the rank of archdeacon in the English Church (and becoming quite wealthy as he climbed), from 1220 he lectured on theology in Paris University. He was soon recognised as its most distinguished teacher; his students called him the "king of theologians". His greatest student was Bonaventura (see below). Alexander's life and theology left three landmarks in Church history:

(a) He was the first schoolman to join (in 1236) the new religious order of preaching monks or "friars" known as the Franciscans (see Chapter 8, section 4). Like a mighty magnet, Alexander's brilliant and far-famed mind helped to attract the Franciscan movement into the scholastic world – an event which would not have pleased Francis of Assisi, the movement's founder.

(b) He was the first schoolman to use Peter Lombard's *Sentences*, rather than the Bible, as his textbook for theology lectures. This helped to elevate the *Sentences* to their central place in Western theology for the next 300 years.

(c) Alexander contributed a number of important developments to Western theology. In particular, he defined the crucial doctrine of the "treasury of merits" of the saints (see under Thomas Aquinas), and argued (against Peter Lombard) that in the sacrament of penance the priest's absolution itself cleansed inward spiritual guilt.

Landmarks (b) and (c) meant that Alexander became a notable theological villain in the eyes of the Protestant Reformers of the 16th century.

Bonaventura (1221-74)

Bonaventura's real name was Giovanni di Fidanza. Born in Tuscany, north-western Italy, he joined the Franciscans in 1243 – which was when he took the name Bonaventura (Latin for "good fortune"). He then studied at Paris University under the great English schoolman Alexander of Hales, and himself taught theology in Paris from 1248 to 1255, writing an outstanding commentary on Peter Lombard's *Sentences*. In 1257 Bonaventura became the head ("minister general") of the Franciscans. In this capacity he produced in 1263 the *Legenda Maior*, a new official life of Francis of Assisi, the founder of the Franciscans. Bonaventura also wrote what became the authoritative exposition of the Franciscan rule. In 1273 he was made (against his will) a cardinal and bishop of Albano by Pope Gregory X (1271-76), but died the following year.

In Bonaventura's day, the West had rediscovered Aristotle, who was becoming highly influential on scholastic theology. Like Grosseteste, Bonaventura knew and made use of Aristotle's philosophy, but again like Grosseteste he built it into a basically Platonist view of reality, because Augustine of Hippo was always Bonaventura's supreme theological guide. Drawing his inspiration from Augustine and Pseudo-Dionysius the Areopagite,[17] Bonaventura's theology was above all a theology of spiritual experience. It is best summed up in his book *Itinerarium Mentis in Deum* ("The Journey of the Mind to God"). Bonaventura taught that it was impossible truly to know God through reason, but only through experiencing Him in the soul. The seeker after God must detach himself from material things; he must gaze upon the physical world, not for its own sake, but to discover in it traces or shadows of God. Then the seeker must look within himself, discovering God's presence in the depths of his own spirit. Finally, illuminated by God's grace, he must rise up beyond all created things and behold the ultimate truth of the Trinity, becoming united with God not through the light of reason but through the fire of love.

People usually describe Bonaventura as a "mystical" theologian – the "prince of mystics", according to Pope Leo XIII (1878-1903).[18] The great flowering of Catholic mysticism in the 14th and 15th centuries probably owed something to Bonaventura's teaching.[19] Some think that his profound Augustinianism, and stress on personal experience and devotion to God, may have helped to pave the way for the Protestant Reformation.

Thomas Aquinas (1225-74)

Aquinas was the greatest of all the schoolmen. He was born in the castle of Roccasecca, near Aquino, in the territory of Naples (southern Italy), the younger son of a Lombard noble. Against the wishes of his family, in 1244 he joined the new religious order of "preaching monks" called Dominicans (see Chapter 8, section 4), just as Bonventura had joined the Franciscans. However, Aquinas's family were so opposed to his decision that they kidnapped him and imprisoned him in Roccasecca castle for over

---

17. For Pseudo-Dionysius, see Volume One, Chapter 12, section 3.

18. "Mysticism" is hard to define, but it revolves around the idea of union with God in feeling and experience. See the heading *Neoplatonism* in Volume One, Chapter 6, section 2, and *Pseudo-Dionysius* in Chapter 12, section 3.

19. See Chapter 10, section 6.

a year, to try to force him to change his mind. They even hired a young woman of beautiful appearance but dubious morals to enter his prison cell and tempt him sexually! Aquinas resisted all the pressure and his family finally gave up and allowed their heroically obstinate son to join the Dominican order. He studied at the universities of Naples, Paris, and Cologne (north-western Germany).

Thomas Aquinas (1225-74)

At Cologne, Aquinas's teacher was the illustrious German Dominican schoolman, **Albertus Magnus** ("Albert the Great", 1193-1280). Albertus was one of the most important Western champions of Aristotle's philosophy, writing commentaries on all Aristotle's works. Albertus and his pupil Aquinas became lifelong friends. When other students mocked Aquinas for his slowness of speech and called him "the dumb ox", Albertus responded, "This dumb ox will make such a roaring in theology that he will be heard through all the earth!" Albertus outlived his brilliant pupil by six years, and spent the last years of his own life constantly declaring that Aquinas had been the flower and glory of the Church.

From 1252, Aquinas taught theology in Paris, and from 1261 he was part of a travelling papal college teaching in various Italian cities. He became a famous lecturer during his lifetime, but it was only after his death that the Church recognised Aquinas's greatness as a theologian. As well as being the deepest of Catholic thinkers, he was also a man of humble and blameless life. He never finished his masterpiece of systematic theology, the *Summa Theologiae*, because towards the end of his life (in December 1273) he abandoned writing entirely. When asked why, he replied that everything he had written seemed like "a piece of straw". Some have traced this to a sort of nervous breakdown, others to a glorious spiritual experience Aquinas is alleged to have had during holy communion which (he said) made his writings appear worthless in comparison with the experience.

Aquinas's theology was based on his attempt to reconcile Catholic teaching with Aristotle's philosophy. Unlike Bonaventura, who used Aristotle only in a very limited and selective way, Aquinas brought about an intimate blend between Aristotle and the Catholic faith, like water mixed with wine. Human reason, Aquinas taught, could discover much that was true about the world and even about God. Aristotle's philosophy was the supreme achievement of human reason, the best account of the universe that humanity's unaided intelligence could give. Divine revelation did not overthrow this philosophy, but brought it to perfection by revealing truths like the Trinity which human reason alone could never have discovered. So for Aquinas, Aristotle's philosophy laid the foundation for a rational knowledge of the universe; divine revelation then built the temple of Christian truth on that foundation.

Aquinas's distinction between humanity's rational understanding of the world, and God's revelation which perfected that understanding, corresponded to what Aquinas called the two realms of "nature" and "grace". "Nature" was human nature as God created it in Adam – complete in itself, but subject to potential tension and conflict between the impulses of the body and the soul, and between emotion and reason within the soul. To enable Adam to keep his body in perfect obedience to his soul, and emotion in obedience to reason, Aquinas held that God added to Adam's nature an extra gift of "supernatural grace" (or "original righteousness"). It was this gift of grace which Adam forfeited by sin. The fall left him a "natural man"; Adam still possessed all the natural powers and faculties of human nature, but the loss of the gift of original righteousness left him without the ability to keep body in proper subjection to soul, or emotion in subjection to reason.

All humanity was involved in this fall of Adam – Aquinas taught the imputation of Adam's guilt to all his offspring, because Adam was the head and source of the human race. Fallen in Adam, human beings have kept all their natural powers, but they have entirely lost the gift of original righteousness, which has resulted in an absence of harmony between body, soul, emotion, and reason. This, Aquinas said, has gravely weakened our capacity for virtue (which for Aquinas was basically the same as being rational). In this way Aquinas rather watered down Augustine's doctrine of original sin, which did not make the same sort of distinction between "nature" and "grace". For Augustine, Adam did not merely lose some extra gift distinct from his nature when he fell; he fundamentally perverted his actual nature, making it radically corrupt in all its moral inclinations and actions.

It was Aquinas's understanding of the fall which enabled him to ascribe such a high ability to the natural human mind, even in a Pagan like Aristotle, to discover so much truth about the universe and God. Still, we must not think that Aquinas blindly accepted everything that Aristotle taught. Where he believed that Aristotle contradicted Christian teaching, *e.g.* Aristotle's view that the world is eternal, Aquinas corrected the philosopher in the light of the Bible.

Aquinas wrote a large number of books. His two masterpieces were: (i) the *Summa contra Gentiles*[20] ("Handbook against the Pagans"); (ii) the *Summa Theologiae* ("Summary of Theology").

(i) The *Summa contra Gentiles* was intended to enable Christians to present Christianity to non-Christians, such as Jews and Muslims, and to refute their errors. It was divided into four parts. In parts one to three, Aquinas argued on the basis of reason and philosophy to establish the existence of God, and the doctrines of creation and providence. In part four, he explained those truths which only divine revelation could make known – the Trinity, the incarnation, the resurrection.

(ii) The *Summa Theologiae* was a systematic theology – one of the greatest ever written. Aquinas intended it to replace Peter Lombard's *Sentences* as the standard theological textbook, although it took several hundred years for this to happen. He arranged the *Summa* in the form of a disputation. It was divided into three parts: (a) God and creation; (b) human nature, sin and virtue; (c) Christ, salvation, and the sacraments. Aquinas looked at 512 disputed questions, and divided each question into a number of "articles" or points of inquiry (sometimes as many as 17). Matters of theology, philosophy, morality, and politics came under Aquinas's scrutiny.

He began each point of inquiry by presenting evidence which seemed to oppose his own view – philosophical arguments, quotations from the Bible and the early Church fathers. Then he offered a reason or quotation for the view he favoured. Next he presented detailed arguments for this view. Finally he responded to the arguments against his own view and disproved them. By

---

20. Pronounced "Gen-teel-ez".

this method Aquinas tried to give a complete account of the question he was dealing with (see the end of the Chapter for some examples). Aristotle was the philosopher he quoted most often – Aquinas referred to him simply as "the philosopher". Among theologians, Augustine of Hippo was his favourite. Although Augustine had been a Platonist, and Aquinas was an Aristotelian, Aquinas still had a high regard for Augustine (he broadly agreed, for instance, with Augustine's views of predestination, despite Aquinas's diluted version of Augustine's doctrine of the fall), and tried to combine many aspects of Augustine's theology with Aristotle's philosophy.

Aquinas's theology became particularly famous for three things:

(i) Aquinas claimed that the existence of God could be proved by reason. Anselm of Canterbury, of course, had made the same claim, but Aquinas rejected Anselm's proof. Because Aquinas had embraced Aristotle's philosophy, he believed that all human knowledge arose from our experience of life in the outward physical world. Therefore God's existence had to be proved from the world, rather than (as Anselm had tried to do) from the inner ideas of the mind. Aquinas offered five such proofs for God's existence, usually referred to as the "five ways" of arguing from the world to God. These five ways were all based on the fundamental idea that the world is an "effect" which needs a "cause", and the cause is God. For example, Aquinas argued that everything in this physical universe was "contingent"; its existence was not *necessary* – it did not *have to* exist. Therefore it existed only because it depended on a being whose existence *was* necessary – and this being was God. Aquinas thought that anyone trained in philosophy could reason in this sort of way from creation to the existence of the Creator. He accepted, however, that most people lacked such training, and that in any case, the Christian would believe in God on the authority of divine revelation, without any need for philosophical reasoning.

(ii) Aquinas taught that all our knowledge of God is through *analogy*. This meant that whatever we say about God, our language refers in the first place to created things. This, of course, followed from Aquinas's belief that all human knowledge was mediated to the soul through the senses. So, for example, if we call God "strong", our idea of strength has come from seeing a strong man or a strong animal. But God is not strong in exactly the same way that a man or an animal is. Therefore, when we say "God is strong," we are really speaking by way of "analogy": making a comparison between human or animal strength and God's strength, but also acknowledging that there is a difference. So we must realise that all our knowledge and language about God are necessarily imperfect. In Aquinas's own words, "God surpasses human understanding and speech. The person who knows God best is he who recognises that whatever he thinks and says falls short of what God really is."

Aquinas's theory that we can know God only by analogy has remained controversial down to our own day. Critics would say, "Suppose we do make an analogy between (for instance) a human mind and God's mind. Once we have stated what the differences between them are, and removed from our definition of God's mind all those aspects of a human mind which are not true of God's, we are left no longer with an analogy but with a direct definition of God's mind (as far as our finite minds can define it at all)." Aquinas would reply that such views failed to take seriously the finite nature of human existence and the infinite nature of God. For Aquinas, we can indeed ascribe to God such properties as intelligence and love, which we understand from our own experience; but we must then strip them of everything that makes them finite (all the limitations that apply to human intelligence and love). The result, Aquinas maintained, was that we can have no *positive* idea of what intelligence and love are in the infinite God – only a negative idea of what they are *not* (they are not limited by time, space, change, contingency, fallibility, *etc.*).

(iii) Aquinas was the first Catholic theologian to offer a full account of the doctrine of *transubstantiation*. As we saw in Chapter 4, section 7, by the 11th century the view had prevailed in Catholic Europe that the bread and wine of the mass were entirely transformed into the flesh and blood of Christ. In the 12th century, Hildebert of Tours (died 1134) invented the word "transubstantiation" ("change of substance") to describe this view, and the Fourth Lateran Council in 1215 officially sanctioned both the word and the view it signified.[21]

Aquinas used the philosophy of Aristotle to give a theological explanation of what happened when the bread and wine were transubstantiated. Aristotle had distinguished between the "substance" and "accidents" of an object. What Aristotle meant by substance was the *inner reality* that gives any object its particular form and identity. This inner reality of substance is not physical, and the bodily senses of sight, hearing, touch, taste, and smell cannot grasp it; only the *mind* can perceive a substance by the intellectual power of reason. For example, if you are walking in a field and see a tree, there is obviously "something there" that looks like a tree. The substance is the inner reality of the "something there", giving that thing its distinct form and identity as a tree – making it a tree, rather than a stone, a frog, a human being, or an angel. Your mind, by its power of reason, perceives and grasps the substance (the inner reality) of the tree, and understands that what you are looking at is a tree.

Substance, then, is this non-physical inner reality of an object which controls its outward form. The *accidents*, by contrast, are the various physical properties, dimensions, and qualities which make an object *appear* the way it does to our bodily senses. In the case of the tree, the accidents would be the particular kind of wood, leaves, and fruit, with their particular colours, odours, and textures. Because accidents are physical, they are grasped by the senses; they are those aspects of a thing which we see, hear, touch, taste, and smell. So in the case of any object, we have (a) a basic "inner something" (the substance) which the mind alone perceives, and (b) an outward form presented to us through physical qualities (the accidents), which are grasped by the bodily senses.

Aquinas applied this reasoning to the bread and wine of the eucharist. When the priest pronounced the words, "This is My

---

21. For the 4th Lateran Council, see Chapter 8, section 2.

body, this is My blood," the substance (the non-physical inner reality) of the bread and wine was miraculously changed into the substance of Christ's flesh and blood. However, the accidents of the bread and wine (the physical form, taste, and smell) remained the same; as far as human bodily senses were concerned, they were still bread and wine.

Aquinas's doctrine of transubstantiation, if rightly understood, actually avoided many of the problems which Protestants were later to discover in it. According to Aquinas, the bread and wine of the eucharist do *not* become the flesh and blood of Christ *physically*. This is because physical qualities, which can be seen, touched, and tasted, are what Aquinas called accidents, not substance. The bread and wine remain physically bread and wine in all their visible and touchable qualities (accidents). But accidents are only the outward form of an object; its substance – its innermost truth and essence – is non-physical, and is therefore not something which the bodily senses of sight, touch, or taste could ever grasp. For Aquinas, substance is a mysterious invisible reality, lying beyond the realm of the merely outward and physical. It is this invisible, untouchable, inward *essence* of the bread and wine which (Aquinas argued) is changed into the equally invisible, untouchable, inward essence of Christ's body and blood. The substance of the Saviour's flesh and blood in the eucharist is seen and grasped by the mind, not by the senses – in this case, seen and grasped only by the believing mind, by an act of faith. Because substance is not physical, it is also not *local* – not contained in a space. Aquinas therefore, by defining the change in the eucharist as a change of substance, ruled out any belief in a local presence of Christ in the space occupied by the bread and wine.

According to Aquinas, then, those who take part in the eucharist are not eating the *physical* body and blood of the Lord, but the *substance* (the non-physical essence, the inner reality) of His body and blood. This inner essence of a thing, which our senses can never perceive, was – in Aquinas's thinking – more *real* than mere physical qualities and dimensions. When people today react against Aquinas's theology of the eucharist, it is often because they see an object's physical qualities as the most real thing about it. But for Aquinas, reality lay ultimately beyond the outward physical form, in the inward and hidden realm of "substance".[22]

Aquinas also developed the view that the entire flesh and blood of Christ were present *both* in the bread *and* in the wine. So it did not matter if laypeople ate only the bread, and did not drink the wine; they still received the whole of Christ in the bread. This taking of the bread alone by the laity, while only the priest drank the wine, was quite a late development in the Western Church. It became widespread only in the 13th century, and seems to have grown out of a fear (by both the laity themselves and the theologians) that the blood of the Saviour would be dishonoured if any of the wine were spilt. Similar fears led to the use of a special wafer instead of ordinary bread: the wafer did not crumble, so no transubstantiated bits of Christ's body could fall on the floor and be trodden on. Giving only the bread to the laity was a purely Western Catholic practice. The Eastern Orthodox Church continued to serve both the bread and the wine to the laity, and also used real bread.

Aquinas's mighty intellect offered the fullest explanation of various other doctrines and practices (particularly in regard to the sacraments) that had come to prevail in the Western Church, and this is as good a place as any for us to consider them. For example, Aquinas brought out very clearly the distinction between the mass as a *sacrament* and as a *sacrifice*:

---

22. Here is a crude illustration of transubstantiation. Imagine a football filled with air. You cannot see or touch the air inside the football; yet the air is what gives the football its shape and bounce. Now imagine that someone lets the air out of the football and fills it instead with some other gas, *e.g.* helium. The football's outward form, shape and texture have not changed; it looks and feels the same as before. In fact, outwardly, it *is* the same as before. But its "inner reality" has changed from air to helium; it is now helium, not air, which is giving the ball its shape and bounce. In a similar way in the eucharist, Aquinas held that the outward physical qualities of the bread and wine do not change; but "inside", beyond sight and touch, the inner reality has become the body and blood of Christ. Of course, however intellectually brilliant Aquinas's doctrine may be, his critics still reject it as lacking in Biblical foundation.

> This sacrament is at the same time both a sacrifice and a sacra-
> ment. It has the nature of a sacrifice to the extent that it is *offered*,
> but it has the nature of a sacrament to the extent that it is *eaten*.
> Therefore, it has the effect of a sacrament in the one who eats it,
> but the effect of a sacrifice in the one who offers it, or in those
> for whom it is offered (*Summa Theologiae*, Part 3, question 79,
> article 5).

In other words, the mass had a twofold aspect. When people ate
the wafer, it was a sacrament, feeding the believer by means of
Christ's very flesh and blood. But in fact, as we saw in Chapter 2,
section 3, a Western medieval congregation hardly ever ate the
wafer at a celebration of mass; normally, they just watched the
priest celebrating it. Indeed, by Aquinas's time, the Catholic mass
had become a sort of spiritual "spectator sport". People fought to
get the best seat in church, so that they could see the wafer being
held up by the priest for their adoration; the wafer was placed
in a special device called a "monstrance". At Church festivals like
Corpus Christi ("body of Christ") in June, there was a great religious procession in which the priest carried the wafer through the
streets in a golden monstrance.[23] So for ordinary Catholics, their
normal act of worship at mass was looking at the wafer, rather
than eating it. So much was this the case that the 4th Lateran
Council in 1215 had to insist that Catholics must actually eat the
wafer at least once a year.

So when Aquinas distinguished between the mass as
a *sacrament* and as a *sacrifice*, his point was that even when the
congregation did not eat the wafer, the mass still had value, because the priest was offering a sacrifice. The mass (so to speak)
"tapped into" and took hold of Christ's once-for-all sacrifice on
the cross, making that past sacrifice present in all its power. The
result was that the mass washed away the sins of those for whom
it was offered. This enabled Aquinas to explain theologically how
a priest could offer mass as a sacrifice both for the living and the

---

23.   Pope Urban IV (1261-64) established the festival of *Corpus Christi* in
1264, in honour of a communion wafer which (it was alleged) miraculously
shed blood in Bolsena, near Rome.

dead – for those still on earth, and for souls in purgatory. In the case of souls in purgatory, offering masses for them would apply Christ's sacrifice to them, thus helping to pay off their debt of sin and hastening their progress to heaven. Indeed, rich people often left legacies in their wills to pay for priests to say masses for their departed souls, in order to secure for them a swifter release from purgatory. Masses for the dead were called "requiem" masses, from the Latin prayer *requiem in pace*, "rest in peace".

Aquinas also worked out in detail the difference between "mortal sins" and "venial sins". The Church had long held that there *was* a distinction between more serious and less serious sins, relying on texts such as 1 John 5:16-17. The Church's age-old system of penance applied to the more serious sins, and the patristic era had experienced several controversies over whether serious sin (adultery, murder, idolatry) after baptism could be forgiven, and if so, on what terms. For the Western medieval Church, Aquinas now gave a fresh, clear, and decisive shape to this approach to sin and penance. To serious sin he gave the name "mortal sin". This was a sin that "killed" the soul – turned it away from God as its true goal, thus destroying the soul's inner principle of spiritual life. As examples of mortal sins, Aquinas suggested blasphemy, oath-breaking, murder, and adultery. By contrast, a less serious sin was a "venial sin". ("Venial" means "pardonable".) This was a sin that only "wounded" the soul; such a sin did not actually turn the soul away from God, but it did bring spiritual disorder into the soul's life. Aquinas suggested "speaking a careless word" and "laughing too much" as examples of venial sins.

Because mortal sins killed the soul, there was nothing the soul could do by its own resources to restore itself; only divine grace could bring it back to life. God bestowed this grace through the sacrament of penance, unless circumstances unavoidably prevented the repentant sinner from confessing his mortal sins to a priest. Normally, then, penance was necessary to salvation for all who had mortally sinned.[24] Venial sins, by contrast, were

---

24. In Western Catholicism, there came to be a general perception of "grace" as a supernatural power, a sort of spiritual medicine, poured or "infused" into

forgiven through various means – private prayer, personal acts of contrition, participation in mass, *etc.*

Next, Aquinas gave classic expression to the Western Catholic doctrine of the "merits" of the saints and the power of indulgences. According to Aquinas, the sins of human beings incurred a twofold punishment: (i) mortal sins deserved eternal punishment, which could be removed only by Christ's atoning death; (ii) but all sins, both mortal and venial, brought "temporal punishment" on the sinner. ("Temporal" simply means "not eternal".) Temporal punishment was necessary to purify the soul of the spiritual effects of sin. And if the sinner willingly accepted his temporal punishment, it became a way of proving the sincerity of his repentance, and of making compensation to God for the dishonour done to Him by sin. This temporal punishment of sin, Aquinas explained, could be paid off during a person's earthly life either by the sacrament of penance, or by an indulgence. But if a believer died without paying all his temporal punishment by penance or indulgences, he had to pay it off by sufferings in the fire of purgatory. The pope, however, had the power to release souls from purgatory, because God had given the papacy control over the "treasury of merits" of the saints.

This "treasury of merits" was a central concept of Catholicism in the later Middle Ages; it described acts of obedience, above and beyond what God strictly required, performed in their earthly lives by the saints now in heaven. Catholic theologians referred to this "extra" obedience of the saints as their "merits". The pope, Aquinas argued, could transfer this surplus of saintly merit to souls in purgatory by means of an indulgence, thus paying off their temporal punishment for them and releasing them.[25]

---

the soul by God through the sacraments. When this grace existed in the soul as an enduring quality or "habit", it was called "created grace". However, since mortal sin could kill the soul, that obviously meant depriving it of all grace. A soul could therefore move many times into, and out of, a state of grace – out of grace by mortal sin, back into grace by the sacrament of penance.

25. For indulgences, see also Chapter 5, section 5. This view of merits, purgatory, and indulgences was purely Western Catholic, and was rejected by Eastern Orthodoxy.

Thomas Aquinas, along with Augustine of Hippo and John Calvin, is one of the three master theologians of the Western Church, in terms of the intellectual depth and breadth of his thought and its long-lasting historic impact. Many even of the great Protestant theologians of the 16th and 17th centuries drew considerable inspiration from the *Summa Theologiae*, despite their serious disagreements with some of its teachings (see Part Three for Calvin and the Protestant Reformation). Aquinas's theology is known as *Thomism* (pronounced "Toemizzum" – it comes from Aquinas's first name, Thomas). Thomism is still highly influential today, especially among conservative Roman Catholics, but also among some Anglo-Catholics and Calvinists.[26]

Duns Scotus (1265-1308)

John Duns Scotus was born in Scotland, probably near Roxburgh. In his youth he joined the Franciscan order, and studied at Oxford and Paris Universities. He lectured on Peter Lombard's *Sentences* at Cambridge, Oxford, and Paris in the period 1297-1307, before moving to Cologne where he died the following year. His chief writings were two commentaries on Lombard's *Sentences*. Scotus formed much of his theology in opposition to the teachings of Thomas Aquinas. He began a revolutionary new trend in scholasticism by separating theology from philosophy. Scotus insisted, for example, that reason could not establish the existence of the Christian God; all it could do was prove the existence of a Being who was infinite. However, the human mind could know the attributes and character of this Being only through special divine revelation. Scotus also denied that other important truths, such as the immortality of the soul, could be proved by reason; they could be discovered only from revelation. So where Aquinas had "married" theology with philosophy, Scotus started proceedings for their divorce. This would soon alter the whole character of the scholastic enterprise.

---

26. Modern conservative Protestant admirers of Aquinas include Norman Geisler, John Gerstner, R.C. Sproul, and Arvin Vos.

Scotus had another way of emphasising that reason could not penetrate the mystery of God. He taught that God's *will*, not God's *understanding*, was His supreme attribute. The world was what it was, not because reason demanded it, but because God's will had freely and sovereignly chosen to make things this way. Scotus applied this outlook to the atonement: Christ's death had saving power, not because of any inherent worth or value possessed by Christ or His sacrifice, but simply because God sovereignly willed to accept it as a sufficient payment for sin. It was therefore impossible for human reason to show that Christian doctrines were "reasonable", because what God had done was not required of Him by reason, but freely chosen. We cannot reason about what God must have done or must do; we can only accept, by faith in His revelation, what He has chosen to do. This new stress in Scotus's writings on the supremacy of God's revelation laid the basis for a theology which was more Biblical and less philosophical in character.

The conflict between Scotus and Aquinas centred most famously on the doctrine of the "immaculate conception" of the Virgin Mary. This is the belief that Mary was conceived without original sin ("immaculate" means "without blemish"). Radbertus in the 9th century seems to have been the first to suggest this idea.[27] However, it was rejected by Anselm, Bernard of Clairvaux, and Bonaventura. Thomas Aquinas was the theologian who made the most detailed criticisms of the doctrine of the immaculate conception. He felt it would mean that Mary did not need salvation. Mary was conceived with original sin like all human beings, Aquinas taught, and was purified from sin at some point between her conception and her birth. Thus Mary too had to be cleansed from the stain of sin, and therefore saved by God's grace, even though in her case it happened while she was still in the womb.

Scotus, however, argued that it was a more perfect exercise of God's grace to preserve an individual from ever having original sin, than to purify an individual from its stain. Since Christ, the

---

27. For Radbertus, see Chapter 2, section 4, under the heading *Radbertus, Ratramnus, and the communion controversy.*

Second Adam, was free from original sin, it seemed fitting that Mary, the Second Eve, should also be free from it. Therefore, Scotus concluded, since Scripture and Church tradition did not deny it, it seemed probable that Mary was conceived without original sin. (Scotus – at least in the surviving texts he wrote – never went further than saying that the immaculate conception was "probable": it appeared to follow from other known doctrines. His followers were less hesitant, and proclaimed the immaculate conception as a definite truth.)

The two religious orders to which Scotus and Aquinas belonged, the Franciscans and the Dominicans, followed their leading thinkers on this issue. Franciscans upheld the immaculate conception, Dominicans denied it. Nuns joined in the controversy. **Bridget of Sweden** (1303-73), founder of the Brigittine order of nuns, had a wonderful vision which revealed to her that the immaculate conception was true. On the other hand, the great Italian mystic, Catherine of Siena (1347-80), had a wonderful vision which revealed to her that the immaculate conception was false.[28] It was not until 1854 that the immaculate conception became an official Roman Catholic doctrine. Eastern Orthodoxy and Protestantism both reject it.

Duns Scotus's theology is called *Scotism*. Because of the complex and intricate nature of his thought, Catholics nicknamed him "the subtle teacher". The Christian humanists of the Renaissance were less kind; if they reckoned any theologian's writings were over-complicated and obscure, they would insultingly refer to him as a "duns" (from which comes our word "dunce").[29] Despite Scotus's ultimate victory over Aquinas on the immaculate conception, his general theology has few followers today.

William of Ockham (1285-1349)

William of Ockham was born at Ockham in Surrey, southern England. He studied theology at Oxford University where he

---

28. Such are the perils of relying on visions for one's theology. For Catherine of Siena, see Chapter 10, section 6.

29. For the Renaissance and Christian humanism, see Volume Three.

joined the Franciscan order. While giving lectures at Oxford on Peter Lombard's *Sentences,* Pope John XXII (1316-34) summoned him in 1324 to Avignon in Provence, southern France (where the papacy was then residing),[30] to answer charges of heresy. At Avignon, Ockham became involved in a controversy within the Franciscan order. A party called the "spiritual Franciscans" wanted all members of the order to practise absolute poverty, as their founder Francis of Assisi had intended.[31] Ockham supported this view, but it was condemned by Pope John XXII in 1328. Ockham and the head of the Franciscans, Michael of Cesena, fled to Germany. There, Ockham was protected by the Holy Roman Emperor, Louis the Bavarian (1314-47), a violent enemy of the papacy. John XXII excommunicated Ockham, who spent the rest of his life in Louis' service. He wrote against the papacy for Louis, teaching that an ecumenical council of the whole Church was superior to the papacy, that popes could err but an ecumenical council and the Bible were infallible, that the pope had no power to depose kings and Emperors, but an Emperor had the power to depose an erring pope.

Ockham was a highly influential thinker. He took further the divorce between theology and philosophy that Scotus had started. Ockham held that reason could not positively prove the existence of God; all it could do was suggest arguments to show that, at best, God probably existed. Ockham also maintained that all our human knowledge was strictly limited to our experience of individual things. And (agreeing in this with Aristotle) Ockham held that all our experience of realities other than the mind comes through our bodily senses. So the only things the mind can know directly are the individual things that it experiences through the senses of sight, hearing, touch, *etc.* This view obviously meant that unaided reason could have no knowledge of God, since He is not an individual thing in the physical world.

---

30. See Chapter 10, section 1. Provence was an independent county bordering on south-eastern France.

31. For the spiritual Franciscans, see Chapter 8, section 4, under *The Franciscans.*

For Ockham, then, there was no pathway from reason or experience to spiritual realities or to God. Reason shows us a spiritually dark and Godless world; only the light of divine revelation in Scripture manifests God to us. The proper religious task of reason, Ockham said, was not to "prove" Christian doctrines or show how "reasonable" they were, but simply to examine the various statements of Scripture. By teaching this, Ockham had in some ways abandoned the whole scholastic attempt to build a theology with rational foundations.

Ockham was also influential in reviving Semi-Pelagianism.[32] The great schoolmen before Ockham had – on the whole, and with various modifications – been followers of Augustine of Hippo and his theology of grace and predestination. Ockham, however, taught that an unbeliever could merit God's grace by "doing his best". God would bestow sanctifying grace on those who did their best by their own natural wills, and this grace then enabled them to achieve eternal salvation. Ockham denied that it was strictly a reward for goodness when God gave grace to sinners who did their best; it was, he said, simply because God in His freedom had sovereignly *decided* to give His grace to such people. In this way Ockham tried to preserve the free character of grace. However, by placing salvation effectively in the power of the natural human will and its moral striving, Ockham had certainly turned away from the teachings of Augustine. Ockham denied that humanity's fallen will was in bondage to sin, and made God's predestination depend on His foreknowledge of those unbelievers who would "do their best" by their own natural capacity.

Ockham's type of Semi-Pelagianism placed a far stronger emphasis on the power of the human will than the older Semi-Pelagians had done – they had not held that a sinner could merit grace by doing his natural best, but that unbelievers could freely accept the *unmerited* grace which alone converts and saves.[33] Ockham's teaching was in fact much closer to pure Pelagianism;

---

32. For Pelagianism and Semi-Pelagianism, see Volume One, Chapter 9, section 3.

33. See Volume One, Chapter 7, section 3.

we could more accurately describe it as "neo-Pelagianism" (the "new Pelagianism"). This neo-Pelagian trend in scholasticism, begun by William of Ockham, came to its highest point in the great German theologian **Gabriel Biel** (1420-95), sometimes called "the last of the schoolmen", who taught theology in Tubingen university (south-western Germany) in the 1480s.

Other schoolmen, who were faithful Augustinians in their theology, strongly opposed Ockham's neo-Pelagianism – men like **Thomas Bradwardine** (1290-1349), **Gregory of Rimini** (1300-1358), and John Wyclif (1325-84).[34] The Englishman Bradwardine was professor of theology at Oxford University, chaplain to King Edward III, and briefly archbishop of Canterbury for 40 days in 1349 (before dying of plague). He published an important book in 1344 entitled *Concerning the Cause of God against Pelagius*, attacking Ockham's views of salvation as a betrayal of Scripture and the Augustinian tradition. The book earned Bradwardine the nickname "the profound teacher". The Italian schoolman, Gregory of Rimini (north-eastern Italy), joined in the attack on Ockham. Gregory was probably the most brilliant and profound student of Augustine's writings in the entire Middle Ages; he lectured on theology in Paris University from 1341 to 1351, and in 1357 he became head of the Augustinian order of friars to which he belonged. Gregory's theological masterpiece was a commentary on the first two books of Peter Lombard's *Sentences*.

The theology of Ockham and Gabriel Biel became known as the *via moderna*, the "modern way", in contrast to the *via antiqua*, the "old way" of the previous schoolmen. The *via moderna* dominated scholastic theology until the dawn of the Protestant Reformation. This helps us to understand the forceful way in which the Protestant Reformers denounced scholasticism: they were, in part, condemning the neo-Pelagian theology of Ockham, Biel and the *via moderna*, which made salvation into the fruit of natural human free-will and merit, rather than (as the Reformers believed) the fruit of God's sovereign grace.

---

34. For John Wyclif, see Chapter 10, section 4.

Important people:

The Church

Anselm of Canterbury (1033-1109)
Peter Abelard (1079-1142)
Peter Lombard (1100-1160)
Gratian (died 1179)
Alexander of Hales (1170-1245)
Robert Grosseteste (1168-1253)
Bonaventura (1221-74)
Thomas Aquinas (1225-74)
Albertus Magnus (1193-1280)
Siger of Brabant (1235-1282)
Roger Bacon (1214-92)
Duns Scotus (1265-1308)
William of Ockham (1285-1349).
Thomas Bradwardine (1290-1349)
Gregory of Rimini (1300-1358)
Bridget of Sweden (1303-73)
Gabriel Biel (1420-95)

Others

Aristotle (384-22 BC)

A schoolman's heart: Anselm on "faith seeking understanding"

Come along now, little man,
Leave your daily work for a while,
Get away for a while from the swirling storm of your thoughts.
Put those heavy anxieties to one side,
Free yourself for God for a little while,
And rest for a little while in Him.
Retreat into the innermost room in your soul,
Lock out everything else except God
And whatever can aid you in seeking Him;

And when you have closed the door,
Then seek Him.
Now, my whole heart, say to God,
"I seek Your face;
Lord, it is Your face I am seeking" ...
I confess, O Lord, with thanksgiving,
That you have made me in Your image,
So that I can remember You,
Think of You,
And love You.
But Your image in me is so worn away,
So blotted out by faults,
So darkened by the smoke of sin,
That it cannot do the thing it was made for,
Unless You renew it and remake it.
Lord, I am not trying to climb up to Your height;
My understanding is simply not equal to that.
But I do want to understand a little of Your truth
Which my heart already believes and loves.
I do not seek to understand so that I may believe;
I believe so that I may understand.
More than that,
I believe that unless I do believe
I will not understand.

Anselm of Canterbury
Proslogion, **chapter 1**

Anselm on sin and satisfaction

Anselm: We must ask, then, on what basis God forgives human sin. So that we may do this more clearly, let us first see what "sin" means, and what "satisfaction for sin" means.

Boso: It is for you to explain, and for me to listen.

Anselm: If angels or human beings always gave God what they owed Him, they would never sin.

Boso: I cannot contradict you.

Anselm: To sin, then, is the same thing as not to give God
               what is owed to Him.

Boso: What is the debt which we owe to God?

Anselm: Every desire and every attitude of a created being
               who possesses reason ought to be subject to the
               will of God.

Boso: Nothing could be more true.

Anselm: This is the debt which angels and human beings
owe to God. No-one sins if he pays this debt; everyone who
does not pay it sins. This is the justice or uprightness of the
will, which makes human beings just or upright in heart, that
is, in will. This is the only and entire honour which we owe
to God, and which God requires from us. Only an upright
will does works which are pleasing to God, when it is able to
act; and when it cannot act, an upright will pleases God by
itself alone, since no work is pleasing apart from it. Anyone
who does not give this honour to God takes away from God
what belongs to Him and dishonours Him; and this is sin.
On top of this, as long as the sinner does not repay what he
has stolen, he remains at fault. And it is not enough to return
what was taken away. Because of the insult committed against
God, he must give back more than he took away. If you injure
someone's health, it is not enough to restore his health, without also making some compensation for the pain and injury
suffered. Likewise, if you violate someone's honour, it is not
enough to restore the honour, unless you also make some sort
of restitution which will please the person you dishonoured,
according to the extent of the injury and dishonour. We must
also observe that, when someone pays back what he unjustly
took away, he also ought to give something which could *not* be
required of him if he had *not* stolen the other's property. So
then, everyone who sins must repay to God the honour that
he has taken away; and this is the satisfaction that every sinner
ought to make to God.

Boso: Although you make me rather afraid, I have nothing to say against any of these statements, since we promised to follow reason.

Anselm: Now let us go back and see whether it is fitting for God to forgive sins by simple mercy alone, if the sinner offers Him no payment for the honour he has taken away from Him.

Boso: I do not see why that should not be fitting.

Anselm: To forgive sin in this way is the same as not to punish it. But to deal rightly with sin, when no satisfaction is offered, is the same thing as to punish it. Therefore, if God does not punish sin when no satisfaction is offered, He forgives in a disorderly way.

Boso: What you say makes sense.

Anselm: But it is not fitting for God to permit anything disorderly in His kingdom ... Therefore either the honour that was taken away from Him must be paid back, or else punishment must follow ... Every sin is necessarily followed either by satisfaction, or by punishment.

[Anselm proceeds to argue that Christ offered satisfaction to God on behalf of believers, and therefore we are not punished.]

Anselm of Canterbury
Cur deus homo, **chapters 11-13, 15**

The medieval heart's love for the Virgin Mary

[The most profound theologians of the Middle Ages loved and cherished the Virgin Mary in the depths of their hearts, with a sweetness of affection which today's Protestants may find it hard to understand. Anselm's grasp of the sovereignty of God's grace in salvation surpassed that of many modern Evangelicals;

yet here is Anselm pouring out his heart's devotion, not to his
Lord, but to his Lady, the Saviour's blessed Mother:]

O Mary, great Mary,
The most blessed of all Marys,
The greatest of all women,
O great Lady, great beyond reckoning:
With all my heart I long to love you,
With my lips I desire to praise you,
In my mind I wish to honour you,
In my inmost being my joy is to pray to you,
Into your protection I entrust myself completely ...
O Woman, full of grace and overflowing,
From you streams the Bounty [Christ] which makes all created
     things
Fresh with life again!
O blessed Virgin, blessed for ever,
Your blessing rests on all nature;
Not only is creation blessed by its Creator,
The Creator is blessed by His creation too.
O highly exalted Mary,
My heart's love tries to follow after you,
But you somehow elude the sharpness of my sight.
O you who are so beautiful to gaze upon,
O you who are so lovely to look at,
O you who are so sweet to love,
Where do you vanish to, where do you escape
From the embrace of my heart?
O Lady, please wait for me, this weak man who follows after you;
See the smallness of the soul that seeks you,
And do not hide yourself!
Be gracious, O Lady,
To this soul that thirsts and longs for you ...

No created thing is equal to Mary,
And the only thing greater than Mary is God Himself.

From God's heart was born God's own Son,
The Only One who is equal to God;
For God loves His Son to the same degree that God loves
    Himself.
God gave this Son to Mary,
And then from Mary a Son was born –
The same Son, not another –
So that, by nature, one person might be
Both Son of God
And Son of Mary.
All nature has been created by God – and God is born of
    Mary!
God created all things – and Mary gave birth to God!
The God who made all things made Himself human through
    Mary,
And in this way He created afresh everything which He had
    made ...
He was born of a Mother to take our nature,
So that He might make us into the sons of His Mother by
    restoring our life;
Now He invites us to acknowledge that we are His brothers
    and sisters.
Yes, our Judge is our Brother,
The Saviour of the world is our Brother,
And finally, our God is our Brother – through Mary.
So then, let us have confident hope,
Let us be comforted and free from all fear!
For our salvation or condemnation depends on the will
Of a Brother who is so good and a Mother who is so devoted.

O how great our affection ought to be for this Brother and this
    Mother;
How intimately we should surrender ourselves to them,
With what security of mind we should run to them!
For our good Brother pardons us when we sin,
He wards off what our errors deserve,

He bestows on us what our repentance asks for.
And the good Mother prays for us and makes supplication for
    us;
She asks and pleads that He may hear us with grace.
She prays to the Son on behalf of the sons,
To the Only-begotten on behalf of the adopted,
To the Lord on behalf of the servants.
And the good Son hears the Mother on behalf of His brothers,
The Only-begotten hears on behalf of those He has adopted,
The Lord hears on behalf of those He has liberated.
O Mary, O Mother and Lady, how much we owe you
Through whom we have such a Brother!

From Anselm's
Third Prayer to Mary

The schoolman as sinner: Peter Abelard's love for Heloise

There lived in the same city of Paris a young girl called Heloise, the niece of canon Fulbert. Her uncle's affection for her was equalled only by his desire to give her the best possible education. She was beautiful, but stood out even more by her great academic knowledge. This virtue is not often found in females; because of its rarity, it made Heloise twice as excellent, the most praiseworthy of her sex in the whole kingdom ... I was totally on fire with passion for this girl. So I tried to discover ways in which I could see her, be close to her, and speak with her every day. To achieve this, I persuaded the girl's uncle, with the help of some of his friends, to take me into his household (he lived next to my school) in return for a little rent ... Fulbert committed Heloise entirely to my care. He begged me to act as her tutor whenever I was free from my lecturing duties, by day or by night, and to punish her sternly if she neglected her education. The man was so naive that I was utterly amazed; I would have been just as struck with astonishment if he had entrusted a tender lamb to the care of a ravenous wolf ...

Why should I say more? Heloise and I were brought together first by the household that concealed our love, and then by our hearts that burned with love's fire. Pretending to be at study, we spent our time in the happiness of love; the pursuit of knowledge supplied the secret opportunities which our desire longed for. We spoke more about love than about the books that lay open before us; our kisses outnumbered our words of reason ... As this passionate rapture consumed me more and more, I devoted less and less time to philosophy and teaching. In fact I began to hate going to my school or lingering there. The work was burdensome; my nights were consecrated to love, my days to study. My lectures became completely careless and dull. I lost all inspiration and just did everything out of mere habit ...

Heloise and I could not really hide the obvious passion we felt for each other, and indeed I think the only person who knew nothing about it was her uncle, Fulbert, the one exposed to the most disgrace by it. Many people often enough hinted to him about what was going on, but he could not believe it, partly because of his boundless affection for Heloise, partly because of the famous reputation for purity of life which I had earned before I fell into sin. It is hard for us to suspect that those whom we most love are guilty of evil; a devoted love will not hear any whisper of suspicion. As Saint Jerome says in his letter to Sabianus, "We are normally the last people to know about the evil things that are going on in our own households, and we are usually ignorant of the sins committed by our own children and our own wives, even though our neighbours are singing about them at the top of their voices!"[35]

From Peter Abelard's
History of my Calamities

How to read the Scriptures and the best theologians
In the midst of so many words, some things the saints have said appear to contain discrepancy or even contradiction. But we must not rashly judge those men who will judge the world, as it is written, "The saints shall judge the world" (1 Cor. 6:2) ... Nor should we arrogantly rebuke those men, or despise them as being in error,

---

35. For Jerome, see Volume One, Chapter 9, section 2.

since the Lord has said to them, "Whoever hears you hears me, and he who despises you despises me" (Luke 10:16). Instead let us reflect on our own weakness, and believe that we are the ones who lack grace in understanding, and not they who lacked it in writing. For the Truth Himself said to them, "It is not you who speak, but the Spirit of your Father who speaks in you" (Matt. 10:20). So why should we be surprised if we ourselves lack understanding of what they wrote, when we lack that Spirit who instilled into those writers the things they wrote and said?

We are particularly hindered in understanding by their manner of speech, which is foreign to us, and often by different meanings for the same word, which brings it about that the same sound will sometimes stand for one meaning, sometimes another. For each writer abounds in his own meaning and his own words. Indeed, Cicero says that in all matters, sameness produces fullness (that is, weariness), so that it is right sometimes to vary the words even in the same matter, and not to communicate everything in ordinary and common words. Saint Augustine says that certain matters are veiled so that we may not despise them; instead, they acquire all the more relish, to the degree that we need greater zeal in studying them, and master them with greater difficulty ...

Therefore, if anything in Scripture seems absurd, we must not say that the writer of that book did not hold the truth. We must rather say that the manuscript is at fault, or that the translator made a mistake, or that you the reader lack understanding ... Jerome speaks of the canonical Scriptures of the Old and New Testaments as tools, and says that it is heretical to assent that anything in the Scriptures dissents from the truth ... For, says Jerome, if even pleasant falsehoods have found their way into holy Scripture, what authority will be left in them? All will be delivered up to the liberty of private interpretation ... Within those books which certainly belong to the canon, there is no distinction; so that for example, what Paul says, Christ says. With the fathers we may indeed be critical; for we must weigh, not the pre-judged opinion of the teacher, but the reason behind his doctrine. As it is written, "Test all things; hold fast to what is good" (1 Thess. 5:21). But this is spoken of the commentators, not of the canonical Scriptures, to which it is right to give an implicit faith.

Therefore I have made this present collection as a basis for discussion in the schools, according to the fashion recommended by Aristotle to all serious students. For through doubt we are prompted to inquire, and through inquiry we grasp the truth. As the Truth Himself said: "Seek and you shall find; knock and it shall be opened to you" (Matt. 7:7).

From the *Preface* to Abelard's

Sic et non

The father of systematic theology: Peter Lombard on Christology and sacraments

Is Christ an adopted son of God in His human nature?

If we ask whether Christ is an adopted son in His humanity, or in some other way, we reply that Christ is not an adopted son in any way, but only a natural Son. He is Son by nature, not by the grace of adoption. However, we do not call Him "Son by nature" in the same way that we call Him "God by nature". The thing that makes Him "Son" is not the thing that makes Him "God". For He is Son by virtue of being begotten, but He is God by virtue of the divine nature. Still, we use the term "nature" or "Son by nature" because Christ is God's Son naturally, having the same nature as the Father who begot Him.

Again, He is not an adopted Son, because He did not first exist and then become adopted as a son. This is what happens to us; we are called adopted sons because when we were born, we were "sons of wrath" (Eph. 2:3), but we have become "sons of God" by grace. But there never was a time when Christ was not a Son, and therefore He is not an adopted son ...

Thus Augustine says in his commentary on John, "The Only-begotten is equal to the Father, not by grace, but by nature. However, it is not by nature, but by grace, that a human being was united with the Only-begotten's person [in the incarnation]." So Christ is not the adopted son either of God or of man; He is Son of God naturally, and He is Son of Man naturally and by grace ...

Why were the sacraments instituted?
The sacraments were instituted for three reasons: as a way of increasing humility, as a method of instruction, and as a stimulus to activity.

As a way of increasing humility: so that human beings submit themselves, out of reverence for God's command, to visible things which by nature are beneath us. By this humility and obedience, we are more pleasing and worthy to the God by whose command we seek salvation in things lower than ourselves – not that salvation comes from them, but from God through them.

The sacraments were also instituted as a method of instruction, so that the mind may perceive the outward visible form [of the sacrament], and be instructed to understand the inward invisible power [which the sacraments signify and impart]. Before sin entered, human beings saw God without any medium; but sin has made us so dull that we no longer know how to grasp divine things unless human things incite us.

Likewise, the sacraments were also instituted as a means of stimulating us into activity. Human beings cannot remain inactive; the sacraments supply us with a useful and healthy stimulus to turn us away from futile and harmful activities. For when habitual practice makes us free to devote ourselves to goodness, the tempter cannot easily capture us. As Jerome warns, "Be seriously engaged in some work at all times, so that the devil may find you occupied."

Peter Lombard
The Four Books of Sentences,
Book 3, distinction 10, chapter 2,
and Book 4, distinction 1, chapter 5

The schoolman as mystic: Bonaventura on union with God

Keep on labouring, my friend, towards the mystic vision. Give up what your senses tell you, and the workings of your logical reason. Leave behind you all things visible and invisible, being and non-being. As far as you can, embrace without sight Him who goes beyond all essences and all knowledge. In this uplifted state of the soul, which is the highest and beyond measuring, forget all created things as one who has been unbound from them. Rise above yourself, beyond all that is made, and you will find yourself within the beam of light that shines forth from the divine mystery of darkness.

But if you would know how to bring about these things, do not ask for education, but for grace. Do not ask for understanding, but for desire. Do not ask for the ability to work hard in study, but for the groanings of prayer. Do not seek the teacher, but the Bridegroom. Do not seek any human being, but God. Do not seek bright clearness, but dark mystery. Do not seek light so much as fire, which inflames the soul totally, filling it with divine anointing and holy desires, raising you out of your very self, right up to God. Indeed this fire *is* God, whose "furnace is in Jerusalem" (Isa. 31:9). The man Jesus kindled this fire on the earth by the fervour of His most ardent sufferings. We share in this fervour when we can say, "My soul chooses strangling and my bones death" (Job 7:15). He who chooses such a death shall see God, for without doubt it is true that "no man shall see Me and live" (Exod. 33:20). Let us die, then, and through death's door let us enter into this darkness. Let us bring silence upon our anxieties, our lustful desires, and the workings of our imaginations. With Christ crucified, let us pass from this world to the Father, so that when He is revealed to us we may say with Philip, "It is enough for us!" (John 14:8). Let us listen with Saint Paul to the words, "My grace is sufficient for you" (2 Cor. 12:9). Let us cry out in triumph with David, "My heart and my flesh fail, but God is the strength of my heart and my portion for ever!" (Ps. 73:26). "Blessed be the Lord for evermore; and let all the people say, Amen and amen!" (Ps. 89:52).

Bonaventura
The Journey of the Mind to God, **chapter 7, sections 5 and 6**

Aquinas on predestination

Article 5. Is God's foreknowledge of good works the cause of predestination?

Objection 1. It seems that foreknowledge of good works is the cause of predestination. For the apostle says, "Whom He foreknew, He also predestined" (Rom. 8:28) ...

Objection 2. Divine predestination involves the divine will, and God's will can never be without a reason for what it does. As Augustine says, predestination is the purpose to show mercy. But there can be no other reason for predestination than God's foreknowledge of our good works. Therefore this must be the cause and reason for predestination.

Objection 3. Again, "There is no unrighteousness with God" (Rom. 9:14). But it would seem to be unjust if unequal things are given to equal persons. All human beings are equal in their nature and in original sin. Any inequality arises from the good or bad character of their works. Therefore God does not prepare unequal things for us by His predestination and reprobation, except on the basis of His foreknowledge of our good and bad works.

On the other hand, the apostle says, "Not by works of right-eousness which we have done, but according to His mercy He saved us" (Titus 3:5). But God saved us because He predestined us to salvation. Therefore His foreknowledge of our good works is not the cause or reason of His predestination.

Response: As we said previously, God's predestination in-volves His will. So we must seek the reason for predestination in the same way that we seek the reason for God's will. Now, as we have already shown, we cannot find any cause for God's will in His act of willing, but we can find a cause in the things which He wills. For God wills one thing on account of another thing. Therefore nobody has been mad enough to say that good works actually cause God to perform the act of predestination. But the question is whether His predestination has any cause in terms of one of its effects depending on another; or, in other words, whether God foreordained to give the final result of predestina-tion to anyone on account of any good works.

Some have thought that God foreordained the results of predestination for some people because of good things they had done in a previous life. This was the view of Origen, who held that human souls were created from all eternity, and that according to their works God awarded them different conditions in the world when these souls were united to bodies.[36] But the apostle disproves this view when he says, "The children not yet being born, and not having done any good or evil ... not of works but of Him who calls, it was said to her, The elder shall serve the younger" (Rom. 9:11-12).

Others said that good works we have already done in this present life are the reason and cause behind the results of predestination. The Pelagians taught that we ourselves take the first step in doing good, and God then brings it to completion. In this view, God gives the results of predestination to one person, and not to another, because the one took the first step by preparing himself, but the other did not. Against this, however, we must set what the apostle says: "Not that we are sufficient of ourselves, to think of anything as coming from ourselves" (2 Cor. 3:5) ...

It is impossible that the whole result of predestination in general should have any cause in ourselves. For whatever is in a human being, disposing him towards salvation, is all included *within* the results of predestination. Even a person's preparing himself to receive grace is the effect of predestination; such preparation is impossible apart from divine assistance, as the prophet Jeremiah says: "Turn us back to You, O Lord, and we will be restored" (Lam. 5:21). In this way, as far as its results are concerned, the reason for predestination lies in the moral excellence of God. All the results of predestination are directed towards God's moral excellence as their end, and predestination proceeds from God's moral excellence as its first cause and principle ...

Response to objection 1. God's foreknowledge of how we will use His grace is not what causes Him to bestow grace on us, except in the sense that God bestows grace in order that we may make a good use of it.

---

36. For Origen, see Volume One, Chapter 5, section 1.

Response to objection 2. The basis of predestination lies in the moral excellence of God, as regards its general results. But if we consider the various things that happen as a result of predestination, one thing is the cause of the next.

Response to objection 3. The reason why some souls are predestined to glory and others reprobated can be found only in the moral excellence of God. He made all things through His moral excellence, so that He might display it in all things. Now, God's moral excellence is one and undivided in itself, but it is revealed in many different ways in His creation, because created things cannot attain to the simple oneness of God. The perfection of the universe requires different grades of being, some holding a higher place in the universe, and others a lower. To preserve these many grades of being, God allows some evil things, without which many good things would never happen. We must therefore consider the whole human race in the same way that we consider the whole universe. God chooses to reveal His moral excellence in human beings. He reveals it through His mercy in those whom He predestines to glory, by pardoning them; in others whom He reprobates, He reveals His moral excellence through His justice, by punishing them. This is the general reason why God elects one part of humankind and rejects the other ... Yet why in particular He chooses *these* people for glory but reprobates *those* – there is no reason for this except His own will. As Augustine says, "Why He draws one but not another, do not seek to know, unless you wish to go astray."

Thomas Aquinas

Summa Theologiae, Part 1, question 23, article 5

Aquinas on baptismal regeneration

Article 2. Can a human being be saved without baptism?

Objection 1. It seems that no human being can be saved without baptism. For our Lord said, "Unless a man is born again of water and the Holy Spirit, he cannot enter the kingdom of God" (John 3:5). But only those who enter God's kingdom are saved. Therefore no-one can be saved without baptism, by which a person is born again of water and the Holy Spirit.

Objection 2. In the book *Concerning Church Doctrines*, chapter 41, it says, "We believe that no catechumen who dies doing good works will have eternal life, unless he suffers martyrdom, which contains all the sacramental power of baptism." But if it were possible for anyone to be saved without baptism, this would especially be the case with catechumens who do good works, for they seem to have the "faith that works by love" (Gal. 5:6). Therefore it seems that no-one can be saved without baptism.

Objection 3. As we have previously stated, the sacrament of baptism is necessary for salvation. Now a thing is necessary if, without it, something else cannot be. Therefore it seems that no-one can obtain salvation without baptism.

On the other hand, Augustine says, "Some have profitably received an inward sanctification without outward sacraments; but though it is possible to have an outward sanctification consisting in an outward sacrament, this will be to no profit without an inward sanctification" (*On Leviticus*, chapter 84). Therefore, since the sacrament of baptism relates to outward sanctification, it seems that a person can – by means of an inward sanctification – obtain salvation without the sacrament of baptism.

Response: The sacrament of baptism may be lacking to a person in two ways. First, it may be lacking both in reality and in desire. This is the case with those who are not baptised and do not wish to be baptised. In those who have the use of free-will [*i.e.* not babies], this clearly shows contempt for the sacrament. As a result, those who lack baptism in this way cannot obtain salvation, because they are not incorporated into Christ either in their minds or sacramentally, and it is only through Christ that salvation can be obtained.

Second, the sacrament of baptism may be lacking to a person in reality but not in desire, as when a person wishes to be baptised but, through ill fortune, death cuts him off before his baptism. Without being actually baptised, such a person can obtain salvation on account of his *desire* for baptism. This desire is the effect of "faith working by love", by which God sanctifies people inwardly – for God is not tied to outward sacraments. Thus Ambrose says of Valentinian, who died as a catechumen,

"I lost the one whom I was to regenerate, but he did not lose the grace for which he prayed."[37]

Response to objection 1. As Scripture says, "Man looks on the outward appearance, but the Lord looks on the heart" (1 Sam. 16:7). If a man desires to be born again of water and the Holy Spirit by baptism, he is regenerated in heart, though not in body. Thus the apostle says, "circumcision is of the heart, in the Spirit, not in the letter, and their praise is not from men but from God" (Rom. 2:29).

Response to objection 2. No human being obtains eternal life unless he is free from all guilt and debt of punishment. This full remission is given when a person receives baptism, or suffers martyrdom. That is why it says that martyrdom "contains all the sacramental power of baptism", that is, for the full deliverance from guilt and punishment. Therefore, if a catechumen has the desire for baptism (for otherwise he could not die doing good works, which can be done only through the faith that works by love), he would not after dying come immediately to eternal life, but would suffer punishment for his past sins [in purgatory]; "but he himself will be saved, yet so as through fire" (1 Cor. 3:15).

Response to objection 3. We say that the sacrament of baptism is necessary for salvation to this extent, that a person cannot be saved without at least the desire for baptism, "which God accepts for the deed itself", as Augustine says (on *Psalm 57*).

Thomas Aquinas
Summa Theologiae, **Part 3, question 68, article 2**

Aquinas on transubstantiation
Article 1. Is the body of Christ in this sacrament in very truth, or only as in a symbol or a sign?

Objection 1. It seems that Christ's body is not in this sacrament in very truth, but only as in a symbol or a sign. For it is written that when our Lord had spoken these words, "Unless you eat the flesh of the Son of Man and drink His blood," many of

---

37. For Ambrose and Valentinian, see Volume One, Chapter 7, section 3, under *Church worship*.

His disciples on hearing it said, "This is a hard saying," and He responded, "It is the Spirit that gives life; the flesh profits nothing" (John 6:60-63). As if He were saying, according to Augustine's exposition of *Psalm 4* [actually *Psalm 98*], "Give a spiritual meaning to My words. You are not to eat this body which you see, nor to drink the blood which those who crucify Me will shed. I am setting a mystery before you; in a spiritual sense it will give you life, but the flesh profits nothing."

Objection 2. Our Lord said, "Behold, I am with you always, even to the end of the age" (Matt. 28:20). Explaining this, Augustine makes this observation: "The Lord is in heaven until the world ends. Still, the Lord's truth is with us here. The body in which He rose again must be in one place, but His truth is spread abroad everywhere" (*Tract 30 on John*). Therefore the body of Christ is not present in the sacrament in very truth, but only as in a sign.

Objection 3. A body cannot be in several places at the same time. Not even an angel can do this. If it could, it could be everywhere. But Christ has a real body which is in heaven. So it seems that His body is not in very truth present in the sacrament of the altar, but only as in a sign.

Objection 4. The Church's sacraments are ordained for the profit of believers. But according to Gregory [the Great][38] in *Homily 28 on the Gospels*, the ruler is rebuked for demanding Christ's bodily presence [John 4:46-54]. Again, the apostles were prevented from receiving the Holy Spirit because they were too attached to Christ's bodily presence, as Augustine says on John 16:7, "Unless I go away, the Paraclete will not come to you" (*Tract 94 on John*). Therefore Christ is not in the sacrament of the altar according to His bodily presence.

On the other hand, Hilary [of Poitiers][39] says, "There is no room for doubt concerning the truth of Christ's body and blood. For by our Lord's own declaration, and by our faith, His flesh is truly food and His blood is truly drink" (*On the Trinity,*

---

38. For Gregory the Great, see Volume One, Chapter 11, section 2.

39. For Hilary of Poitiers, see Volume One, Chapter 8, section 3.

chapter 8). And Ambrose says, "As the Lord Jesus Christ is God's true Son, so it is Christ's true flesh which we take, and His true blood which we drink" (*On the Sacrament*, chapter 6).

Response: Neither the senses nor the understanding can detect Christ's true body and blood in this sacrament. Only faith can detect it, resting on divine authority. Thus commenting on Luke 22:19, "This is My body which is given for you," Cyril[40] says, "Do not doubt that this is true. Rather take the Saviour's words with faith. For He is the Truth and does not lie." This is appropriate, first for the perfection of the New Covenant. For the sacrifices of the Old Covenant contained only in a symbol the true sacrifice of Christ's suffering, as it says in Hebrews 10:1, "For the law, having a shadow of the good things to come, and not the very image of the things". So the sacrifice of the New Covenant which Christ instituted had to have something more – namely, that it should contain Christ crucified, not merely in sign or symbol, but also in very truth. Thus this sacrament, which as Dionysius [Pseudo-Dionysius the Areopagite][41] says contains Christ Himself, is the perfection of all the other sacraments, which participate only in Christ's power [not His bodily presence].

Second, this belongs to Christ's love, which inspired Him to take a true body of our nature for our salvation. It is the special mark of friendship to live together with one's friends, as Aristotle says. Therefore Christ promises us His bodily presence as our ultimate reward, saying, "Where the body is, there the eagles gather together" (Matt. 24:28). Yet even during our pilgrimage He does not deprive us of His bodily presence, but unites us with Himself in this sacrament through the truth of His body and blood. Thus He says, "Whoever eats My flesh and drinks My blood abides in Me and I in him" (John 6:56). Therefore this sacrament is the sign of supreme love, uplifting our hope, because of the intimate union between Christ and us which it brings.

---

40. This is either Cyril of Jerusalem or Cyril of Alexandria. I have not been able to find the reference.

41. For Pseudo-Dionysius the Areopagite, see Volume One, Chapter 12, section 3.

Third, this belongs to the completeness of faith, which relates to Christ's humanity equally with His deity, according to John 14:1, "You believe in God, believe also in Me." Now faith concerns things which are unseen. So just as Christ shows us His deity invisibly, He also in this sacrament shows us His flesh in an invisible way.

Some people, then, not paying heed to these things, have argued that Christ's body and blood are not in this sacrament except as in a sign. We must reject this as a heresy, because it contradicts Christ's words. Thus Berengar, the first inventor of this heresy, was afterwards forced to withdraw his error and confess the truth of the faith.[42]

Response to objection 1. The heretics have taken occasion from Augustine's authority to err by understanding his words falsely. When Augustine says, "You are not to eat this body which you see," he does not intend to exclude the truth of Christ's body [in the eucharist], but that it was not to be eaten in this form in which they then saw it. When he says, "I am setting a mystery before you; in a spiritual sense it will give you life, but the flesh profits nothing," his intention is not that Christ's body is in the sacrament merely by mystical symbolism, but that Christ's body is present spiritually, that is, invisibly and by the Spirit's power. Thus he expounds John 6:64: "The flesh profits nothing. That is, as they understood it; for they thought that His flesh was to be eaten by being divided into pieces from a dead body, or as if sold in the meat-market, rather than as enlivened by the Spirit ... Let the Spirit draw near to the flesh, and the flesh will then profit very much. For if the flesh profits nothing in any sense, the Word would not have become flesh to dwell among us" (*Tract 27 on John*).

Response to objection 2. This saying of Augustine, and all others like it, must be understood as referring to Christ's body as people saw it in its own proper form. As our Lord Himself said, "You do not always have Me with you" (Matt. 26:11). Even

---

42. For Berengar of Tours, see Chapter 4, section 7.

so, He is present invisibly under the form of this sacrament, wherever it is performed.

Response to objection 3. Christ's body is not "in" the sacrament in the same way that a body is "in" space. When a body occupies space, its dimensions measure the same as the place it is in. But Christ's body is in the sacrament in a special way which is peculiar to the sacrament. Thus we say that Christ's body is on many altars, not as if it were in many different places, but in a sacramental way. This does not mean we think that Christ is there only as in a sign, but that Christ's body is there in a special way peculiar to the sacrament, as already stated.

Response to objection 4. This argument is true as regards Christ's bodily presence, when He is present in the way that a body is, by way of visible appearance. But it is not true regarding the presence of His body in a spiritual way, invisibly, according to the way and the power of the Spirit. Thus Augustine says: "If you have understood Christ's words about His flesh spiritually, they are spirit and life to you; but if you have undersood them in a fleshly way, they are still spirit and life, but not to you" (*Tract 27 on John*).

Thomas Aquinas
Summa Theologiae, **Part 3, question 75, article 1**

Duns Scotus on salvation

When humankind had become God's enemy through guilt, God purposed that He would not forgive that guilt, or give any assistance towards forgiveness, or towards the obtaining of heavenly bliss, except by means of something offered to Him – something which He would accept with a delight greater than the displeasure and disgust which humanity's sin had caused Him. However, nothing can be found which would bring to the Trinity a pleasure greater than the displeasure and disgust caused by the total guilt and sin of the human race. Nothing, that is, unless some obedience could be offered by a person more worthy of love than the sinful human race would have been, if it had not sinned. The human race could not produce from itself such a beloved person, since it was entirely God's enemy, one great mass of damnation.

Therefore the Trinity purposed to give this beloved person to the human race, and to incline this person to offer obedience on behalf of the whole race; and this person is Christ alone, to whom God gave without limit the Spirit of love and grace.

Christ's obedience manifested the greatest love, because He offered Himself even to death for the sake of righteousness. Therefore, upon human pilgrims toward heaven, the Trinity bestows saving help only by means of this offering of Christ on the cross, which He made both as a person most beloved and out of the greatest love. Thus Christ's suffering was the cause which merited our salvation, because through His suffering God bestows on human pilgrims the goodness which merits heaven ...

To bestow such remedies on His human enemies is a work of the greatest mercy on God's part. But it is also a work of the greatest justice, on account of the obedience so excellent of a Person so beloved, to bestow such a remedy on those for whom He offered that obedience. It was the greatest mercy on Christ's part to offer Himself for the enemies of the supreme Object of His love, the Trinity. But it was also a work of the greatest justice, with regard both to God and to fallen humanity. For Christ would not seem to love God and His neighbour in the greatest degree, unless He were willing to offer obedience to God for the sake of such a great common blessing, the heavenly bliss of humankind, to which God had foreordained humankind, decreeing that we should obtain it only through Christ's obedience.

Duns Scotus

Opus Oxoniense, Part 3, article 19

William of Ockham on the papacy

According to Pope Nicholas, Christ gave or entrusted to blessed Peter the rights of both heavenly and earthly power.[43] But we must expound his words in a way that goes against what may seem the obvious interpretation, in case they appear to have a heretical savour. The same applies to other things said by this pope in the same chapter – for example, when he says, "Christ

---

43. Pope Nicholas I (858-67). See Chapter 3, section 4.

alone instituted, founded, and set up the Roman Church on the rock of the faith which was then just springing up"; and when he says, "The Roman Church inaugurated all supreme bishoprics, whether the highest dignity of any patriarch, or the supremacy of any bishop's throne, or the chairs of bishoprics, or indeed the dignity of churches of any rank."

Unless we interpret these words carefully, they appear to contradict the divine Scriptures and the writings of the holy fathers. For Christ did not found the Roman Church on the rock of the faith which was then just springing up, since the Roman Church was not set up at the beginning of the faith, nor did Rome establish all the other churches. Many churches were established before the Roman Church, and many were exalted to ecclesiastical dignity even before the origin of the Roman Church; for before the Roman Church existed, blessed Matthew was chosen for the dignity of apostleship. Before the Roman Church began, seven deacons were chosen by the apostles; and before the Roman Church existed, they "had peace throughout all Judaea and Galilee and Samaria" (Acts 9:31). Before the Roman Church existed, blessed Paul and Barnabas were exalted to apostolic dignity by divine command; before the Roman Church enjoyed the power of appointing bishops, Paul and Barnabas appointed elders throughout the various churches (Acts 14:23). Before the Roman Church had any authority, the apostles and elders met in a general council (Acts 15:22).

And before the Roman Church had any power of setting up bishops, blessed Paul said to the elders he had called from Ephesus (as we are told in Acts 20:28), "Take heed to yourselves, and to all the flock, among which the Holy Spirit has made you overseers, to shepherd the Church of God." Before the Roman Church held the primacy, the churches of Antioch had so multiplied that Christ's disciples were first called Christians in that place (Acts 11:26). For the same reason, the blessed Peter had his apostolic throne in Antioch before he went to Rome, and thus he set up churches and ecclesiastical dignities in the Antiochene Church before he ever did this in the Roman Church. So then, we must give a proper interpretation to the words of Pope

Nicholas referred to above, in case they directly contradict the divine Scriptures.

William of Ockham

Eight Questions on the Power of the Pope, **Question 2, chapter 7**

8
The age of Innocent III

The claims and might of the papacy reached their high noon during the reign of Pope *Innocent III* (1198-1216). If Hildebrand was the most heroic pope, Innocent was the most powerful.[1] He did not have so negative an attitude to kings and Emperors as Hildebrand had displayed a hundred years before. However, Innocent made Hildebrand's lofty view of the papacy as the political and spiritual head of Western Europe into a far more effective reality than Hildebrand himself had ever achieved.

Innocent's real name was Lothario Conti. Born in 1160, he belonged to one of Rome's oldest aristocratic families. Having studied theology and law at Rome, Bologna, and Paris, he became a lecturer at Bologna law school, before being made into a cardinal deacon of Rome in 1190. In 1198, at the youthful age of 37, the other cardinals unanimously elected him pope, and he took the name "Innocent III". A short, stout man with wide staring eyes, he was a cool, calculating, far-seeing ruler of the Western Church, patient and determined, a perfect genius at turning even hostile circumstances to his own advantage.

We can look at the problems and achievements of Innocent's reign under the following headings.

1. The papacy in Italy and Europe
Innocent was the first pope who made the title "vicar of Christ" central to the claims of the papacy. ("Vicar" means a person who

---

1. For Hildebrand, see Chapter 4, section 5.

stands in someone else's place.) Previously, popes had claimed that their special position was as the "vicar of the apostle Peter", standing in Peter's place and exercising Peter's supreme apostolic authority. Even Hildebrand had claimed no more than this. Not that "vicar of Christ" was an *entirely* new title; Christians had previously spoken of the bishop (any bishop), or all bishops together, as vicar of Christ on earth. From the 12th century, others (*e.g.* Bernard of Clairvaux) had spoken in these exalted terms of the pope in particular. However, before Innocent III, people normally gave the titles "vicar of Christ" and "vicar of God", not to the pope, but to kings, especially the Holy Roman Emperor; it had been part of the Western "sacred kingship" ideal – the king represented God or Christ on earth.[2]

Innocent was the first pope who positively rejected the old papal title of "vicar of Peter", and the first to refer to himself officially and regularly by the title "vicar of Christ". He declared: "We are the *successor* of Peter the prince of the apostles, but we are not his *vicar*, nor are we the vicar of any man or any apostle; we are the vicar of Jesus Christ Himself." Innocent also took to himself the traditional title of kings and Emperors, "vicar of God". He was claiming that he, as pope, was the visible manifestation of Christ on earth, exercising Christ's supreme authority, not just over the spiritual kingdom of the Church, but over all human beings, all earthly kingdoms, and even the angels and demons. "The Lord Jesus Christ," Innocent proclaimed, "has established one sovereign [the pope] over all as His universal vicar, whom all things in heaven, earth and hell should obey, even as they bow the knee to Christ." This was the doctrine of the pope's "plenitude of power" – that all spiritual and political authority flowed from him. From Innocent's reign onwards, then, "vicar of Christ" became the customary title by which the popes both defined and described themselves and their exalted position. Kings and

---

2. For Bernard of Clairvaux, see Chapter 5, section 3, under *Bernard of Clairvaux and the Second Crusade*. For "vicar of Christ" and "vicar of God" as titles for bishops and kings, see Chapter 2, section 2, under the heading *Emperor and pope*.

ordinary bishops would have to be satisfied with lesser names from now on.

The political circumstances of Western Europe at that time enabled Innocent to translate these elevated claims into a practical reality. The papacy's greatest rival, the Holy Roman Empire, had lost its grip on Italy due to the sudden death of the Emperor Henry VI (1190-97) in 1197; a war between two rival claimants to the imperial throne, Philip of Swabia and Otto of Brunswick, then plunged Germany into utter confusion. Innocent took advantage of the Empire's descent into chaos to enlarge the political power of the papacy and its lands in Italy. He abolished the last remaining signs of imperial authority in Rome, winning over the city prefect (the Emperor's representative) to swear an oath of allegiance to the papacy. By this time, Rome's economy largely depended on the papacy through the business of the papal court (the "curia"); Innocent exploited this fact to secure full control of the city from the Roman aristocracy.

Having made himself political master of Rome, Innocent then began spinning a steel web of influence over the whole of central Italy, forming alliances with Italian cities against their German governors. He also persuaded one of the imperial claimants, Otto of Brunswick, to make concessions to the papacy in Italy in return for papal support in Otto's struggle with Philip of Swabia. Innocent recognised Otto as Holy Roman Emperor; Otto promised never to intervene in northern Italy, to acknowledge the independence of the papal states, and to give up all imperial authority over the German Church. The previous Emperor, Henry VI, had virtually destroyed the papacy's independence by uniting the Empire with Naples and Sicily, thus surrounding Rome with imperial territory and power. Innocent was determined to prevent this happening again. He managed to bring Sicily within his grasp when the widow of Henry VI surrendered it to his protection, in order to guarantee the title of her young son, Frederick, to the Sicilian crown. (She placed Frederick himself, the future Emperor Frederick II, in Innocent's care.) By these actions, Innocent re-established the papal states in Italy as an independent political dominion; they survived in the basic form Innocent gave them until the 19th century.

Having restored the papacy's independence in Italy, Innocent succeeded in making the Hildebrandine concept of papal supremacy effective in the politics of Western Europe. He insisted on the absolute right of the papacy to control the beliefs and moral conduct of the entire Catholic world. This had the gravest implications for secular rulers, since it involved the pope's right to depose a king or Emperor who broke the Church's laws.

Innocent made his power felt in all three of Western Europe's great monarchies – Germany, England, and France. In Germany, as we saw, rival claimants to the throne, Philip of Swabia and Otto of Brunswick, had split the Holy Roman Empire. Innocent had backed Otto in return for pledges of papal independence in Italy. Otto's rival Philip was assassinated in 1208, and Innocent crowned Otto as Emperor in 1209. However, no sooner was the crown on Otto's head than he promptly broke his promises to Innocent, and marched his troops into Naples; he wanted to recreate the union between Germany and Sicily which had destroyed the papacy's independence under the previous Emperor, Henry VI. In a cold fury of indignation, Innocent excommunicated the treacherous Otto and recognised Henry VI's son Frederick as Emperor, after first making him promise to give up the Sicilian throne as soon as he had mastered Germany. Innocent then headed the first great conflict of international military alliances in European history: he supported Frederick and King Philip Augustus of France against Otto of Brunswick and King John of England. In 1214 the papal alliance won a decisive victory at the battle of Bouvines (then in north-eastern France, now in Belgium). Frederick, Innocent's candidate, was settled on the German throne as the Emperor Frederick II (1210-50).[3]

The end result of these conflicts was the permanent weakening of the Holy Roman Emperor's authority. In the 17 years of civil war (1197-1214) since Henry VI's death, the local rulers

---

3. For more about Frederick II, see Chapter 5, section 3, and the account of the Sixth Crusade.

(counts, dukes, princes) of the individual German states had effectively won back their power against the centralising policies of the German monarchy. Innocent III had quite deliberately presided over the political disintegration of Germany in the interests of papal independence.

Innocent had even greater success against **King John of England** (1199-1216). In a disputed election to the archbishopric of Canterbury, Innocent intervened to set aside John's candidate and appoint one of his own cardinals, the Englishman Stephen Langton (died 1228), to the position in 1207. John refused to accept Langton. Innocent threatened to place England under an "interdict" – that is, to forbid all English clergyman to perform any of their sacramental or spiritual functions (except funerals, and baptism if the candidate was in danger of death) until King John submitted. John swore he would expel all the clergy from England if Innocent dared to do this. Innocent dared, and placed England under an interdict in 1208.

For four years England went without any Church services. Still John refused to submit or accept Langton as archbishop. In 1212, Innocent used his ultimate weapon: he excommunicated John, released all English nobles from their oath of loyalty to him, and summoned the other kings of Europe to dethrone John in a crusade. John gave in. His submission was as grovelling as his defiance had been proud: in 1213, he surrendered his entire kingdom to Innocent – England became the property of the pope. John also promised to pay a special annual tax to the papacy. And he accepted Stephen Langton as his archbishop of Canterbury. Innocent removed the interdict which had, by now, put a stop to all religious services in England for six years. The English monarchy, in many ways the most successful in Europe, lay prostrate in the dust at the feet of Innocent III.

Innocent also humiliated the French monarchy. In 1193, the king of France, **Philip Augustus** (1180-1223), had married the 18-year-old Ingeborg, sister of King Canute VI of Denmark. But almost immediately afterwards, Philip lost interest in Ingeborg, forced his French bishops to cancel the marriage, and had the unfortunate girl locked away in a nunnery. Innocent took up

Ingeborg's cause after becoming pope in 1198. When Philip contracted a second marriage with Agnes of Meran, Innocent responded by placing France under an interdict in 1200, in order to force Philip to repudiate Agnes and be reconciled to Ingeborg. At first Philip refused, but when Agnes died he submitted to Innocent, released Ingeborg from her imprisonment and took her back as his wife.

Innocent, then, had compelled the three greatest kingdoms in Catholic Europe – Germany, England, and France – to bow to his will as the vicar of Christ. This was the papacy at the dizzying height of its political power.

2. Internal Church affairs

Innocent carried out an important series of ecclesiastical reforms. Many of these were aimed at creating a more centralised government of the Church, with the pope as absolute monarch. For example, Innocent expanded the system of papal "legates" (ambassadors). These were officials appointed directly by the pope and responsible to him; their function was to oversee Church affairs in different localities, and make sure that bishops were carrying out the pope's policies. Innocent also established the right of the papacy to appoint bishops in disputed cases – a right Innocent exercised in the Langton case in England. In 1199, he imposed the first general income tax on all Catholic clergy, to be paid to the papacy.

Innocent's concern for reforming the Church enjoyed its greatest moment in the Fourth Lateran Council of 1215. It was the best attended of any council, local or ecumenical, to be held in the West up to that time; 412 bishops, 800 abbots and priors, and many other delegates of absent bishops and secular rulers were present. The Council's reform measures were wide-ranging, dealing with the moral lives of the clergy, the importance of preaching, and Church discipline. The Council, for instance, decreed that all Catholics must confess their sins privately to their priest at least once a year, and receive holy communion at least once a year at Easter.

The most significant decree of the Council had to do with the theology of the mass, for the Fourth Lateran Council gave the first official Catholic definition of the doctrine of transubstantiation.[4] The definition reads:

> There is indeed one universal Church of the faithful, outside which no-one at all is saved, and in which the Priest Himself, Jesus Christ, is also the sacrifice. His body and blood are truly contained in the sacrament of the altar, under the appearances of bread and wine, the bread being transubstantiated into His body by divine power, and the wine into His blood, so that we receive from Him what He received from us [flesh and blood]. Thus the mystery of unity [between Christ and us] is accomplished. Indeed no-one can perform this sacrament except the priest, properly ordained according to the power of the keys of the Church, which Jesus Christ Himself granted to the apostles and their successors.

The Council condemned the teachings of the Waldensians and Cathars – whom we will consider in the next section. It also demanded that in Christian societies, Jewish people who did not accept Christianity should wear distinctive Jewish clothing and live in special Jewish areas of towns and cities, separate from the Christian population. This pronouncement of the Council reflected the increasing anti-Judaism (religious hostility to Jews) that marked Western society in the later Middle Ages. This anti-Jewish attitude led to the expulsion of all Jews from England in 1209, and from France in 1306 and then again more effectively in 1394. There was a general massacre of Jews in Spain in 1391, and the Spanish monarchy officially expelled them in 1492; the Portuguese expelled them in 1496. The Jews were not ejected from Germany owing to its lack of centralised government, but popular hatred of Jews was probably stronger in Germany than elsewhere in Western Europe; German Christians often massacred German Jewish communities in outbursts of anti-Jewish feeling. In 1349, for example, a Christian mob in Strasbourg marched the city's entire Jewish community (some 2,000) to Strasbourg's cemetery, and burnt at the stake all who refused to convert to Christianity.

---

4.   For an explanation of transubstantiation, see the account of Thomas Aquinas's theology in the previous Chapter, section 3.

This popular Christian hostility to the Jews was fuelled by stories that Jews kidnapped and murdered Christian babies, and practised religious rituals in which they treated the wafer of holy communion with blasphemous mockery and contempt. There is no reason to think these stories were true; but they do show the shocking social and religious gulf which now existed between the Church and Israel. A more down-to-earth explanation for Christian anti-Judaism was that until the end of the Middle Ages, the Church forbade all Christians to practise usury (lending money for interest). Jews therefore became the great medieval money-lenders, putting many Christians in their debt. It seemed quite intolerable to Christians that the unbelieving Jews should exercise such economic power over them.[5]

3. The Church, its adversaries and the inquisition

Innocent had to deal with a number of dissenting religious movements which operated outside the Catholic Church. There was a great upsurge of religious dissent and heresy in Catholic Europe from about 1150 onwards. This was probably related to serious changes that were taking place in the Western world's social and economic system at this time. In the Netherlands, western Germany, northern Italy, and France, the growth of towns, cities, trade, and industry was undermining the old land-based social system,[6] by creating new wealth and a new economy which was based increasingly on money rather than land, thus laying the foundations of *capitalism* (an economic system based on *capital*, i.e. money). As a result, the rich became visibly richer and more numerous; the poor became visibly and distressingly poorer. Nobles began to be able to buy soldiers, and so profit assumed greater importance than the old relationships of personal loyalty.

---

5. Anti-Judaism is not quite the same as anti-Semitism. Anti-Semitism is racial hostility to all Jews, based on theories of racial purity that developed in the 19th century. Anti-Judaism is religious hostility to non-Christian Jews based on opposition to the religion of Judaism.

6. For the social system that emerged after the collapse of centralised Roman authority in the West, see Chapter 4, section 2.

Middle-class merchants were now even richer than the nobility. At the same time, the population was growing, so that the old land-based way of life was less able to support those who lived in rural areas.

The real losers in this process of deep social change were the peasants, especially if they left the over-populated land to live in towns and cities. In the old manorial village, the lord of the manor personally looked after his peasant workers – he could not afford to let them starve. By contrast, a town-dwelling peasant who was unemployed would indeed starve. He no longer belonged to a lord, and to that extent he had gained personal freedom. However, with this freedom went the destruction of those close bonds of community, which had previously ensured that even the lowest classes had a place in society and were cared for. This loss of the sense of security and belonging, and the growth of great social inequality, created a fertile soil in which new religious movements could flourish. The two most widespread of these movements were the Waldensians and the Cathars.

The Waldensians

The founder of the Waldensians was a wealthy French merchant of Lyons called **Valdes** or Waldes. (In later accounts he is given the first name Peter, and his surname is spelt "Waldo", but there is no solid evidence for the truth of these traditions.) The date of Valdes's birth is uncertain; he died around 1205. Some time between 1173 and 1176, Christ's command to the rich young ruler deeply impressed him: "If you want to be perfect, go, sell what you have and give it to the poor, and you will have treasure in heaven; and come, follow Me" (Matt. 19:21). Valdes obeyed this command literally, gave away all his wealth to the poor, and began a new life as a lay preacher, living only on voluntary contributions of food, clothing and money from others. He soon had a band of followers in Lyons, known as "the poor men of Lyons". However, the archbishop and clergy of Lyons were hostile; Church law restricted preaching to the clergy. Valdes appealed to the 3rd Lateran Council of 1179. Pope Alexander III (1159-81) praised his devotion to poverty, but denied him and his followers the right to preach without the approval of their local bishop. Valdes and his "poor men", however, refused to give up preaching, and the archbishop of Lyons excommunicated them in 1182 and expelled them from the city. Most of them went to the region of Languedoc (the south-eastern coastland of France) and Lombardy. In 1184, Pope Lucius III (1181-85) excommunicated all Waldensians.

Forced out of the Catholic Church against their wishes, the Waldensians began thinking afresh about many matters of Christian belief. Their most crucial decision was that the Bible, especially the New Testament, should be the supreme rule of Christian belief and practice. Thus they rejected the infallible teaching authority of the papacy. They gave up believing in transubstantiation, purgatory, prayers for the dead, and indulgences, but continued to venerate the Virgin Mary. Waldensians also studied the Bible in translations made into their native tongues, and celebrated holy communion among themselves if a Catholic priest would not give it to them. They set up schools to train preachers, sending out both male and female evangelists. Some of their social attitudes were quite radical – they rejected oaths and military service (although some practised armed self-defence if attacked).

The Waldensian movement spread out from its original homelands of Languedoc and Lombardy into Spain, Austria, and eastern Germany, and (next after the Cathars) became the second most widespread and influential non-Catholic group in Western medieval Europe. As well as those who were committed Waldensians, there was a large number of Catholics who sympathised with them; known as "friends" or "believers", they gave financial support to Waldensian preachers and training schools, and attended Waldensian Bible studies, but themselves remained members of the Catholic Church.

In some ways, the Waldensians were "Protestants before the Reformation". Many Waldensians died as martyrs, especially after the inquisition was established (see below). However, they survived in northern Italy, and linked up in the 16th century with the Protestant Reformation (see Volume Three). The Waldensian Church in Italy today is the oldest "Protestant" body in the world.

The Cathars

The other great dissenting movement, and the most widespread, was the Cathars (Greek for "pure ones"). A previous generation of Protestant scholars saw them as essentially akin to the Waldensians – an Evangelical movement of dissent. This then gave way to the view that they were a basically Gnostic movement. Now some modern scholars deny they existed at all. The present volume takes the view that they did exist and were basically Gnostic. One reason for taking this view is that there was a parallel movement in the Eastern Byzantine world, the Bogomils, who were Gnostic – the Eastern Cathars, as it were, whose existence there seems no reason to doubt.

The Cathars were divided up into many sects. Sometimes they were known as *Patarenes* (from the Pataria district of Milan in northern Italy), and sometimes as *Albigensians* (from the town of Albi in southern France, one of their chief centres of influence). They originated in northern Europe in about 1140, but soon moved south and became strongest in northern Italy (Lombardy and Tuscany), and above all in Languedoc. By 1200, they had become a powerful force in southern France, enjoying the support and protection of many French nobles who sided with them out of a shared hostility to the Church – although in the case of the nobility, this was motivated less by serious religious idealism, more by the desire to refuse paying tithes and to seize Church land for themselves. French Cathars were called Albigensians, and it was the Albigensians that aroused the greatest anxiety and hostility from the Catholic Church.

The beliefs and practices of the Cathars were basically identical with those of the Gnostics from the early Church period, and the Paulicians and Bogomils of the Byzantine Empire (Bogomil missionaries were at work in Western Europe in the 12th century, and joined forces with the Cathars).[7] They taught that the physical world of space, time and matter had been created by Satan, who was as eternal and powerful as God. The soul, they

---

7. For the Gnostics, see Volume One, Chapter 4, section 1. For the Paulicians and Bogomils, see Chapter 3, section 6 of the present volume.

said, was an angelic spirit, kidnapped by Satan from heaven and imprisoned in an evil physical body. The ultimate sin was sexual reproduction, because it increased the number of evil bodies for Satan to use as prisons for kidnapped spirits. Christ did not have a physical body, did not really die, and did not experience a bodily resurrection. Salvation did not come through the cross, but through spiritual enlightenment (accepting and following the Cathar teachings). Cathars rejected water baptism and holy communion.

The Cathars were divided into two classes, an outer group of "believers" and an inner group of "the perfect". To join the perfect, a believer had to renounce marriage and property, and abstain from meat, cheese, eggs, and milk, since these were the evil products of sexual reproduction. There was a special ceremony called the *consolamentum* which initiated believers into the ranks of the perfect. This involved the laying on of hands by the perfect, and the placing of a copy of John's Gospel on the believer's head or breast; the believer confessed all his sins, and then received the kiss of peace. (Most believers delayed receiving the *consolamentum* until they were on their deathbeds.) The perfect were organised as clergy, with deacons and bishops; all bishops were equal. Women members of the perfect were not allowed to be deacons or bishops, but they had authority over all mere believers, male and female. Cathars held that they alone were the true Church of Christ; there was no salvation outside their number. The Catholic Church, they claimed, was the great prostitute of Revelation 17, and the papacy was the Antichrist.

The Albigensian Crusade

The missionary efforts of the Catholic Church failed to make any impression on the Cathars. Their grip on southern France in particular (where, as we saw, they were called Albigensians) seemed unbreakable. However, Pope Innocent III had one weapon left to him: the crusade. The event which led him to employ this weapon was the death of Innocent's legate in southern France, Peter of Castelnau. Peter had excommunicated **Raymond of Toulouse** (1156-1222), the greatest noble of southern France and a protector of Albigensians. When one of Raymond's servants murdered Peter in 1208, Innocent sternly resolved on exterminating the Albigensian heretics by the sword. He proclaimed a crusade against them in 1209 – the "Albigensian Crusade" – promising to all who took part the same spiritual rewards as various popes had promised to Crusaders who fought the Turks in the Holy Land.[8]

The nobility of northern France were only too eager to carry out Innocent's will, since it meant conquering fresh land for themselves. The French king, Philip Augustus, also looked with favour on the Crusade as a way of crushing his rebellious southern nobility. The Albigensian Crusade lasted 20 years (1209-29). Led by the northern French noble Simon de Montfort,[9] it brought horrific bloodshed and destruction to the south of France. The Crusaders behaved with great savagery, slaughtering men, women, and children; they wiped out the Albigensians, and shattered the power of the southern nobility. At the start of the Crusade, Languedoc and the surrounding regions had been one of the most prosperous and cultured parts of Europe. When the Crusaders had done their work, it was a desolate wasteland.

The Albigensian Crusade not only put an end to the Albigensians of southern France. It also destroyed the French Waldensians. The Crusaders did not distinguish between one heretic and another. Suppressed in their French homeland, the Waldensians henceforth had their chief place of residence and influence in the Alpine valleys around Turin in northern Italy.

The Petrobrusians

This group was named after its founder **Peter de Bruys**. Little is known of his life, except that he was a Catholic priest in

---

8. See Chapter 5 for the Crusades.

9. Simon de Montfort had also, through marriage, acquired land in England; his English title was the "earl of Leicester". We must not confuse him with his more famous son, also named Simon de Montfort (died 1265), a great English political reformer who pioneered the idea that kings should be held in check by parliamentary influence.

southern France[10] who, in about 1105, started a reform movement which the Church eventually condemned as heretical. The
authorities burnt Peter at the stake in 1126. Henry of Lausanne,
a Benedictine monk and eloquent preacher, took over the leadership of the movement. He was arrested and imprisoned for
heresy; we do not know what became of him.

Peter the Venerable, abbot of Cluny from 1122 to 1157, wrote
a treatise against the Petrobrusians, in which he identified five
chief errors they taught: (i) They denied infant baptism, baptising only those who made a profession of faith; (ii) they denied
the holiness of church buildings and altars; (iii) they refused to
venerate the sign of the cross – Peter de Bruys, indeed, made
a point of showing great disrespect to crosses, breaking and burning them; (iv) they denied the doctrine of transubstantiation and
the sacrifice of the mass; (v) they denied that any prayers or good
works done on earth could help those who had already died. Peter
the Venerable also tells us that the Petrobrusians opposed the
celibacy of the clergy and rejected singing as a true act of worship.

Like the Waldensians, the Petrobrusians seem in many ways
to have been Protestants (even Baptists) before the Reformation.
However, they do not appear to have survived as a distinct group
after the death of Peter de Bruys and the imprisonment of Henry
of Lausanne. Their followers dispersed among the Cathars,
Waldensians, and other dissenting groups.

Joachim of Fiore (1135-1202)

Joachim was a Cistercian monk, abbot of Curazzo in Calabria
(south-western Italy), who in 1192 founded the new monastery
of Saint John in Fiore, near Curazzo.[11] Joachim's monastery at
Fiore became the centre of a new order of Saint John, recognised
by Pope Celestine III (1191-98) in 1196. However, Joachim's
real fame rests on his mystical writings, collectively known as *The*

---

10. Southern France, for some reason, was a very fertile ground for religious
dissent in the 12th and 13th centuries. The Cathars, Waldensians, and
Petrobrusians all flourished there.

11. Fiore is sometimes spelt Flore or Flora.

Everlasting Gospel. He divided the history of the world into three stages, corresponding to the three persons of the Trinity. The Old Testament was the age of God the Father, when humanity lived under the Law; it was characterised by fear. The New Testament was the age of God the Son, when humankind lived under the grace of the Gospel; it was characterised by faith. But a new age was about to dawn, the age of God the Holy Spirit, which Joachim identified with the "thousand years" of Revelation 20:1-6. In this new age of the Spirit, Christ would purify the Church from all corruption, a new monastic order would arise which would evangelise and convert the whole world (including the Jews), and humanity would enter a "golden age" of spiritual freedom and contemplation – the world itself would become one vast and holy monastery. As fear and faith characterised the first two ages, love would characterise the third. Joachim predicted that the age of the Spirit would begin in the year 1260.

Joachim's ideas were very influential on dissenting movements opposed to the papacy in the 13th century and onwards. They took Joachim's teaching about the corruption from which the "new age" would free the Church, and interpreted that corruption as the papacy itself, or at least the papacy in its present form. The most important group Joachim influenced was the spiritual Franciscans, who saw themselves as the new monastic order prophesied by Joachim (see section 4). Joachim's teaching about a spiritual "golden age" on earth before Christ's return also influenced some of the Radical Reformers in the 16th century.[12] It may be one source of the "postmillennial" view of history that was widely held by English-speaking Protestants in the 17th, 18th, and 19th centuries, which taught that the conversion of the Jews and a time of worldwide spiritual blessing would occur before the return of Christ.

The inquisition
During the progress of the Albigensian crusade, Pope Innocent III took another step towards centralising Church organisation

---

12. For the Radical Reformers, see Volume Three.

around the papacy. He set up a system of special legates appointed by himself to seek out any surviving heretics in southern France. Previously, the Western Church had left the investigation of heresy to local bishops, who were often ineffective. Innocent turned the investigation of heresy into a centrally controlled systematic operation, carried out by special papal agents. His actions laid the basis for what in 1227 became the "inquisition" (or "holy office", as it was called). The inquisition was a separate organisation within the Catholic Church, free from episcopal control and subject only to the pope, dedicated exclusively to uncovering and punishing heretics in Catholic Europe. It developed into the most feared organisation of the later Middle Ages. Once the inquisition had accused a person of heresy, it was almost impossible for him to prove his innocence. Those who confessed had financial penalties or acts of penance (*e.g.* going on a pilgrimage) imposed on them. Those who refused to confess received varying degrees of punishment, depending on the seriousness of the heresy; some had all their property confiscated, others were imprisoned perhaps for life, and the worst offenders were handed over to the secular authorities and burnt to death at the stake.[13]

The activities of the inquisition forced dissenting movements (like the Waldensians) to meet in secret. This is the main reason why we know so little about the history of religious dissent in medieval Catholic Europe, compared with what we know of the history of the Catholic Church itself.[14]

---

13. It was never actually the Catholic Church that burnt heretics at the stake; it was the state, the civil government, that did this, once the Church authorities had found someone guilty of deadly heresy. But the Church, of course, *expected* the state to burn a deadly heretic; this was part of the state's duty, according to official Church teaching. Appeal was often made to the "two swords" of Luke 22:38, interpreted allegorically: one was the "spiritual sword" of Church discipline, the other was the "civil sword" of the state which punished physically those whom the Church had judged spiritually.

14. Some notable Catholics of the Middle Ages opposed the use of force in dealing with heretics. The most famous was Bernard of Clairvaux. See Chapter 5, section 3, under *Bernard of Clairvaux and the Second Crusade.*

The Eastern Orthodox Church

Innocent III also tried to end the schism between Western Catholicism and Eastern Orthodoxy which had been brought about by cardinal Humbert in 1054.[15] Innocent's attempt at ending the East–West split came about almost by accident when (as we have already seen) the French army of the Fourth Crusade, organised by Innocent himself, captured Constantinople in 1204 and overthrew the Byzantine Empire.[16] Innocent had forbidden the Crusaders to attack Constantinople, and condemned them furiously for what they had done:

> How are we to bring the Greek Church back into the unity of the Catholic Church and devotion to the apostolic throne [the papacy], when they are afflicted with such trials and persecutions? They have seen in the Latins nothing but an example of damnation and the works of darkness, so that they now despise us as worse than dogs. For you who are meant to serve Christ rather than your own interests, you who should have used your swords only against the Pagans, are dripping with the blood of Christians! You have spared nothing that is sacred, neither age nor sex. You have given yourselves up to prostitution, adultery, and debauchery in the eyes of all the world. You have satisfied your guilty passions, not only on married women, but on women and virgins dedicated to the Saviour.

Despite his condemnation of the Crusaders, Innocent decided to exploit the capture of Constantinople in the interests of the Western Church. So he set up a Western Catholic patriarch of Constantinople. The new French rulers of the old Byzantine territories forced the Eastern Orthodox inhabitants to submit to the authority and worship of the Western Church. However, Western control of Constantinople came to an end in 1261 when a Byzantine army recaptured it. Innocent's establishment of a Western patriarch in Constantinople on the ruins of the city's

---

15. See Chapter 3, section 8.

16. See Chapter 3, section 1, and the account of *The Fourth Crusade* in Chapter 5, section 3.

conquest by the Crusaders ultimately widened the gulf between the Eastern Orthodox and Western Catholic Churches.

4. New religious movements within the Church: the Franciscans, Dominicans, Carmelites and Augustinians, and the Beguines and Beghards

Two of the most important religious developments in the Catholic Church during Innocent III's reign were not Innocent's doing. They were the founding of two new religious orders: the Franciscans and the Dominicans.

The Franciscans

The Franciscans were founded by the most well-known and popular of medieval Catholic saints, *Francis of Assisi* (1182-1226). Francis was the son of a wealthy cloth merchant, Peter Bernadone of Assisi in Umbria (northern Italy). After an early life as a soldier, Francis had a number of religious experiences in his twenties (including seeing visions and hearing heavenly voices) which led him to embrace a life of poverty. He renounced his father, who thought Francis was mad, and determined that from now on God alone would be his Father. Then one day in 1209 he heard Matthew 10:7-10 (the sending out of the Twelve) read in a church, and took it as a call to himself from God to be a preacher.

Francis was a highly attractive figure, and within months he had a small band of devoted followers. In contrast to the complicated theological systems of the schoolmen, Francis emphasised the childlike simplicity of faith; a poet and singer, he found God in nature,[17] and among the poor and the outcasts of society. His whole life became a symbolic acting-out of his main message: Jesus is the loving Lord of the humble and the poor. As soon as he had a group of disciples, Francis wrote a rule for them in 1209 to govern their life together. The rule exalted poverty, not as a means to a spiritual end, but as an end in itself. Franciscans absolutely renounced the ownership of all property; they were

---

17. See his *Canticle of the Sun* at the end of the Chapter.

spiritually married to "Lady Poverty", and begged for their food.
Because Franciscans begged, they were called *mendicants* (from
the Latin word for "beg"). In 1210, Francis went to Rome to ask
Innocent III to give the new movement his backing. After some
hesitation, Innocent agreed – a dream deeply influenced him, in
which he saw Francis holding up the great church building of
Saint John Lateran in Rome as it was about to collapse. This was
a historic decision by Innocent. It meant that the Franciscans
would remain within the Catholic Church, and not be forced out
as the Waldensians had been.

Under the supervision of the papacy, the Franciscans became
a monastic organisation which spread all over Catholic Europe.
They were called the "Little Brothers" or "Friars Minor" ("friar"
comes from the Latin word *frater*, "brother"). They were known
popularly as the "Grey Friars" because they dressed in dark grey.
There was also a Franciscan organisation for women called the
"Poor Clares", named after **Clare of Assisi** (1193-1253), Francis's
friend and fellow worker. Even during Francis's lifetime, the
Franciscans lost some of their original freshness, due to the conflict between Francis's simplicity and idealism, and the desire
of the papacy to turn the Franciscans into a proper monastic
order. In 1216 Pope **Honorius III** (1216-27) appointed **Cardinal
Ugolino** (who became Pope Gregory IX in 1227) to oversee the
Franciscans, and Ugolino's influence became increasingly more
important than that of Francis himself. Francis did not really
want his followers to have any sort of fixed or disciplined organisation, but by 1217 there were so many Franciscans, even
outside Italy, that Francis had no choice but to appoint local
leaders ("ministers") for different areas.

Cardinal Ugolino was the inspiration behind a new rule for
the Franciscans in 1221, revised in 1223. The new rule set aside
Francis's ideal of absolute poverty, introduced traditional monastic discipline, and added the new duty of complete submission to
the papacy. Francis himself resigned as leader ("minister general")
of the Franciscans in 1220, having lost faith in the direction his
movement was taking. He retired from public affairs, lived something of a hermit's life, and died, sick and blind, in 1226.

However, on one point Francis had stood firm and made sure it remained part of the Franciscan order. At his insistence, the Franciscan rules of 1221 and 1223 included something which had never before appeared in any monastic rule: "I firmly order the brothers to obey their ministers in all those things which they promised the Lord they would observe, *as long as they are not contrary to their conscience or to our rule*." This provision for the rights and freedom of the individual conscience was entirely new in monastic rules; it reflected Francis's belief in the importance of individual human beings and their personal relationship with God.

Francis was one of the first medieval Catholics to take any positive interest in missionary work among Muslims. He toured Syria and Egypt in 1219, preaching to the Sultan al-Kamil and his soldiers. Francis impressed the Sultan deeply but did not win any converts. He was also the first known person to experience the *stigmata* (Latin for "marks") – a mysterious bleeding from the hands, feet, and side, the places where Christ's body was pierced. Francis received the stigmata in 1224. Since then, some 300 others are known to have undergone the experience, many of whom were later "canonised" (officially declared to be saints by the papacy). The stigmata are a Roman Catholic phenomenon, unknown within Eastern Orthodoxy or Protestantism (although some Anglicans have more recently experienced them).

After Francis's death, the Franciscans drifted still further from Francis's original ideals. Even the moderate renunciation of property required by the rule of 1223 did not seem practical to many in the order, so they compromised by having wealthy monasteries and churches that were (in theory) not owned by them, but by a "spiritual friend". Franciscans also abandoned their opposition to scholastic theology; some of the greatest school-men of the later 13th and 14th centuries were Franciscan friars, *e.g.* Alexander of Hales, Bonaventura, Duns Scotus, and William of Ockham.[18]

---

18. For Alexander of Hales, Bonaventura, Duns Scotus, and William of Ockham, see Chapter 7, section 3.

Another outstanding Franciscan intellectual was **Nicholas of Lyra** (1270-1349). Born in Lire (France), he taught theology at Paris University from 1308 and was minister of the French Franciscans from 1319. Lyra was the most brilliant Bible scholar the Western medieval Church ever produced. He insisted that the literal, grammatico-historical meaning of Scripture must reign supreme over any allegorical interpretation. To apply this principle to the Old Testament, Lyra mastered the Hebrew language, immersing himself in studies of the Old Testament by Jewish rabbis; he drank especially deeply from the French rabbi "Rashi" (Solomon ben Isaac of Troyes, died 1105), who had himself pioneered a fresh emphasis on the grammatico-historical method of Scripture interpretation within Judaism. Lyra wrote two complete commentaries on the Bible, the *Postillae Litterales* or "Literal Postils" (1322-33) and the *Postillae Morales* or "Moral Postils" (1339) (a "postil" was an explanation or homily on Scripture). When the printing press was invented in around 1450, Lyra's was the first Bible commentary ever printed; in fact, between 1471 and 1600, over a hundred editions of Lyra rolled from the press. Lyra's massive scholarship, harnessed in the service of Scripture's literal sense, helped pave the way for the Protestant Reformation. The great Reformer Martin Luther was a disciple of Lyra; the enemies of Protestantism in the 16th century used to say, "If Lyra had not played his lyre, Luther would never have danced."[19]

However, many Franciscans did not approve of the way their order was developing, notably in its acceptance of wealth and property; they wanted to go back to the original values of Francis, especially his practice of absolute poverty. This party was known as the "spiritual Franciscans". Those who opposed them were called the "conventual Franciscans". The writings of Joachim of Fiore profoundly influenced some of the spiritual Franciscans; they saw themselves as the new monastic order which Joachim had predicted would convert the world, ushering in the new age of the Holy Spirit. The greatest spokesman of the spiritual

---

19. For Luther and the Protestant Reformation, see Volume Three.

Franciscans was William of Ockham. When Pope John XXII (1316-34) settled the dispute between spiritual and conventual Franciscans in favour of the conventuals in 1317-18, many of the spiritual Franciscans refused to submit to the papal decision, condemned John XXII as the Antichrist, and became a dissenting movement. These dissenting Franciscans were known as the *Fraticelli* (which, like Friars Minor, also means "Little Brothers"). Sympathetic Franciscan monasteries sheltered some of the Fraticelli; others established their own groups, and even their own priests, outside the Catholic Church. The Fraticelli were especially active in Italy and southern France, but the inquisition fiercely persecuted them, burning many of them at the stake.

Despite Pope John XXII's attempt to crush the spiritual Franciscans, they remained active within the order, and became known as "observant" Franciscans – those who wanted to observe Francis's original ideals. In 1517, on the eve of the Protestant Reformation, Pope Leo X (1513-21) divided the Franciscans into two separate orders, the observant Franciscans and the conventual Franciscans, each having their own officers and governing bodies.

The Dominicans

The Dominicans, the other great new preaching order of the 13th century, were founded by **Dominic Guzman** (1171-1221), a native of Calaroga in Castile, northern Spain. Destined for a clerical career since his childhood, Dominic was ordained when he was 25 and became a canon in the Spanish cathedral at Osma. His outstanding abilities prompted Dominic's superiors to send him in 1206 as a missionary to Languedoc, at a time when Waldensian and Albigensian influence were at their height. Dominic believed that the dissenting movements had to be fought with their own weapons – with Catholic missionaries who were as simple and pure in lifestyle, and as good at preaching, as the Waldensian and Albigensian evangelists. Dominic dedicated himself to this task, and went preaching in market places and on roadsides, living in poverty and begging for his food. At first he had little success, and had to abandon his mission when Innocent III launched the

Albigensian Crusade in 1209. However, Dominic stayed faithful
to his original convictions, and in 1214 he gathered a group of
followers, training them to become missionary preachers who
would live by begging (so the Dominicans, like the Franciscans,
were a "mendicant" order, begging for their food).

In 1215 Dominic travelled to Rome and sought the backing of the 4th Lateran Council to organise his disciples into
a new religious order of preaching monks. The Council praised
Dominic's efforts but told him to adopt one of the already existing monastic rules. He chose the rule of Augustine. However,
the following year Pope Honorius III gave his personal support
to the Dominicans, and in 1217 they took the name "the order
of Friars Preachers". They were known popularly as the "Black
Friars", because Dominicans wore black in distinction from the
grey dress of the Franciscans.

The initial mission of the Dominicans was to preach chiefly to
the religious dissenters of southern France, but under Dominic's
leadership they soon became an international organisation devoted to evangelising and teaching theology across the whole of
Catholic Europe. They were not as well-liked as the Franciscans;
Francis of Assisi was above all a lover of people and indeed of
all living creatures, whereas Dominic was first and foremost a
servant of the Catholic Church. However, the Dominicans enjoyed strong papal support; the Franciscan pope, Gregory IX
(1227-41), granted them the unique right to preach anywhere
and everywhere. Unlike the Franciscans, the Dominicans were
from the very outset committed to scholastic theology. Theirs
was to be an order which cultivated the study of theology above
all else; to concentrate on this, they abolished the requirement
for monks to do manual labour, which until then had been an
essential feature of the monastic life. Dominican influence was
concentrated in academic centres like Bologna, Paris, and Rome,
and they did indeed produce outstanding theologians, most
famously Thomas Aquinas, greatest of the schoolmen.[20] Their
preaching and teaching did much to keep the people of Western

---

20. For Aquinas, see Chapter 7, section 3.

Europe loyal to the Catholic faith, especially in the cities. There was also an order of Dominican nuns which later became well-known for providing education for girls.

Intense rivalry existed between the Dominican and Franciscan orders, for example over the doctrine of the immaculate conception of the Virgin Mary, which Dominicans opposed and Franciscans upheld.[21] One reason why the Dominicans were especially unpopular with Franciscans (and other religious orders) was because it was Dominicans who staffed the "holy office" of the inquisition. This gave the Dominicans a fearsome power over other orders, which they exercised in (for instance) persecuting and martyring the spiritual Franciscans.

The Carmelites and Augustinians

Not long after Innocent III's reign, two more important mendicant orders of friars came into being: the Carmelites in 1247, and the Augustinians in 1256. The Carmelites had first been established in the Crusader kingdom of Jerusalem in 1154, on Mount Carmel. The fall of the various Crusader states to the Turks brought many Carmelites into Western Europe, where they reorganised themselves as a mendicant order in 1247. From their white dress they were known popularly as the "White Friars". The Augustinians were originally a society of hermits, but soon abandoned their eremitic lifestyle to become an active mendicant order, basing their organisation on the Dominicans. Their monastic rule was that of Augustine of Hippo. The most famous Augustinian friar was to be Martin Luther, the great Protestant Reformer.

The Franciscans, Dominicans, Carmelites, and Augustinians presented a new kind of monasticism to the world. Rather than withdrawing from society to create communities of the spiritually minded, the whole purpose of the mendicant orders was to go out into society, preaching and winning disciples, both in Catholic Europe and in the unevangelised world of Muslims and

---

21. See the account of this under the heading *John Duns Scotus* in previous Chapter, section 3.

Pagans (see section 5). Other differences between the mendicant friars and traditional monks included (a) the mendicant practice of begging for food rather than cultivating it themselves in their monastery, (b) not being bound to a specific monastery by an oath of "stability", and (c) exemption from the authority of the local bishop (which often resulted in serious hostility between mendicants and bishops). Most of the great Catholic preachers and theologians of the later Middle Ages came from the mendicant orders. Ultimately, through Martin Luther, the Protestant Reformation itself came from this source.

The Beguines and Beghards

The Beguines (pronounced "bay-geens") and Beghards (pronounced "beg-ards") were laypeople who lived together in communities devoted to cultivating the spiritual life, but without taking vows of lifelong celibacy or obedience to a superior, and without following a monastic rule. Beguine communities were "sisterhoods" with an exclusively female membership. They may have got their name from a priest of the Netherlands, Lambert le Begue (died 1177), who gave away all his property, and founded a hospital and a house for women in Liege; people mockingly called the house a "beguinage" after its founder (or so one account says). Other Beguine communities sprang up in the Netherlands, Germany, and France in the late 12th and early 13th centuries. Like the Franciscans and Dominicans, Beguines begged for their food, but also supported themselves by weaving, looking after the sick, and other activities. Beghards (Dutch for "beggars") were the male counterpart of Beguines, all-male communities organised along the same lines.

Beguines and Beghards were not a dissenting movement, but dissent and heresy often tainted many of their communities, especially through connections they had with the spiritual Franciscans. Some embraced Waldensian or Cathar beliefs. They also aroused suspicion because of their independence – they were lay organisations, directed neither by a priest nor by a monastic order. Various Church councils criticised them, until in 1311 Pope Clement V (1305-14) condemned the entire movement at the Western ecumenical Council of Vienne. However, his successor John XXII (1316-34)[22] reversed this decision and extended papal protection to Beguine and Beghard communities, as long as they adhered strictly to Catholic teaching. By about 1400, most Beguine and Beghards had joined one or other of the monastic orders, to guard themselves against accusations of heresy.

The Beguines nurtured one of the greatest mystical poets of the Middle Ages, *Mechthild of Magdeburg* (1212-80). Mechthild lived most of her life as a Beguine in the north German city of Magdeburg, where she experienced a variety of visions which inspired her poems. She collected her spiritual poetry into an important seven-part work called *The Flowing Light of the Godhead*. This influenced the Italian poet Dante (1265-1321), generally considered the greatest Christian poet of all time.[23] Mechthild's poetry blended intense religious emotion, vivid visual imagination, and keen analysis of the soul's spiritual life. "O Lord," she said in one place, "You have taken from me everything that I had of You. Yet by Your grace, leave me at least the gift that even a dog has by nature: the gift of being true to You in my distress, when I am deprived of all spiritual comfort. I desire this more fervently than Your heavenly kingdom."

5. Missionary expansion

Franciscans and Dominicans were at the forefront of a new wave of Catholic missionary enterprise to Muslims and Mongols. After the pioneering work of Francis of Assisi and Raymond Lull[24] among Muslims, other missionaries followed in their footsteps. One of the most important was *Raymond of Penafort* (1175-1275), a Spanish Dominican, chaplain of Pope Gregory IX, and

---

22. There was a two-year gap between the end of Clement V's reign and the start of John XXII's, because for two years the cardinals could not agree on a successor to Clement V.

23. Dante's masterpiece was *The Divine Comedy*, an allegory of the soul's salvation. One of the figures in the *Comedy*, Matilda, may be Mechthild of Magdeburg. See Chapter 10, section 7 for Dante.

24. For Raymond Lull, see Chapter 1, section 6.

famous for putting the Western Church's canon law into a more organised shape. Raymond evangelised Muslims in Spain and North-West Africa from 1240 to 1275. It was Raymond who persuaded Thomas Aquinas to write his *Summa contra Gentiles* as a handbook for teaching Christianity to Muslims. Another Dominican, **William of Tripoli**, tried to convince Pope Gregory X (1271-76) that he must abandon the "Crusade" attitude to Muslims and work for their peaceful conversion. William put his own theories into practice, working as a missionary in Palestine and baptising a thousand Muslims. A Franciscan, **Conrad of Ascoli**, evangelised Muslims in Libya, and is said to have baptised 6,000. The Dominicans and the Franciscans each set up separate organisations called the "Society of Pilgrim Brothers", which sent out missionaries on a regular basis to different parts of the Muslim world.

Meanwhile, Lawrence of Portugal, **John of Plano Carpini** (1180-1252), and **William of Ruysbroeck** (1215-95) spearheaded Catholic evangelism among the Pagan Mongols. After emerging from Mongolia under Genghis Khan in 1205, the Mongols had created a vast empire which covered China, central Asia, Persia, and southern Russia.[25] These four regions were each governed by a *khan* (ruler); the rulers of Mongolia and China were called the "great khans". The Mongols were merciless in war, but tolerant in religious matters once they had conquered. There was clearly a great mission field here, both for Christianity and Islam. The papacy and the Latin kingdoms of the Middle East also had great hopes of creating a military and political Catholic-Mongol alliance against the Muslim Turks. In 1246, Pope Innocent IV (1243-54) sent John of Plano Carpini, a Franciscan friar, to the Mongol Great Khan Guyuk (1246-51) at Karakoram, in present-day Mongolia. Guyuk treated John and his companions with great respect, but had no intention of becoming a Christian. Instead, he sent a message back to Innocent IV exhorting him and all other Western Catholic rulers to submit to God's divinely appointed world-leader, Guyuk!

---

25. For more about the Mongols and Genghis Khan, see Chapter 6.

In 1253 the mission of another Franciscan, William of Ruysbroeck, to Guyuk's successor Mongka (1251-59), met with a similar response. Mongka treated him well, and William stayed as a guest in the great khan's court for eight months, discussing religion with him and his courtiers many times, but without converting Mongka to Christianity. Mongka expressed the typical Mongol attitude to religion when he told William:

> We Mongols believe that there is only one God, in whom we live and die. But as God has given different fingers to the hand, so He has given to humankind different ways to Himself. To you Christians, He has given the holy Scriptures; to us Mongols, He has given wizards and diviners.

The missions of John of Plano Carpini and William of Ruysbroeck launched a hundred years of religious and cultural contact between the Mongols and the Catholic West. Trade and commerce also played a part in opening up the Mongols to Catholic influence. The great Mongol ruler **Kublai Khan** (1260-94) came in touch with Western Christianity through the travels of the Polo family, merchants of Venice, who were in China from 1260 to 1269, and again from 1275 to 1291. Their most famous family member was **Marco Polo** (1254-1324), who was in the service of Kublai Khan throughout 1275-91. After his return to Italy in 1292, Polo wrote an account of his travels in China, entitled *Il Milione*, "The Million", published in 1299 – the English title is *The Travels of Marco Polo* – which revolutionised Western awareness of the East.[26]

As a result of this contact with the Polos, Kublai Khan in 1269 invited the West to send 100 Christian scholars to prove to Mongol scholars "by just and fair argument that the faith professed by Christians is superior to any other and based on more evident truth". The Catholic Church did not immediately take up the invitation. In 1289, Pope Nicholas IV (1288-92)

---

26. Modern historical scholarship has questioned whether Marco Polo ever got further than Constantinople on his Eastern travels. This does not alter the effect his *Il Milione* had on Western ideas of the East.

sent an Italian Franciscan missionary, *John of Monte Corvino* (died 1328), to Kublai, but when John arrived in Peking in 1294 Kublai had just died. However, his successor Timur received John warmly. By 1305 John had baptised some 6,000 people; in 1307, Pope Clement V appointed him the first Catholic archbishop of Peking. John translated the New Testament and Psalms into the Mongolian language. Despite this initial success, however, the mission went into decline after John's death, and was brought to an end in 1369 when the ethnic Chinese captured Peking from the Mongols. The Chinese, under their new ruling Ming dynasty, were anti-Christian, and expelled all Westerners. This terminated all Christian missions in China for the next 200 years. The work of the Franciscan missionaries left no visible fruit behind; the majority of Mongols in the far East drifted from their ancestral Paganism into Buddhism, which has remained their ethnic religion to the present day.[27]

Meanwhile, the Nestorians of Persia were enjoying a season of prosperity under the new Mongol regime.[28] The Mongols had conquered Islamic Persia in the 13th century, capturing Baghdad in 1258 and Damascus in 1260, thus becoming the political masters of the Nestorian Church. In the Mongol spirit of religious tolerance, Kublai Khan allowed the Nestorians to establish bishoprics throughout central Asia, and even an archbishopric in Kublai's capital city of Peking in China. But it was not to last. Islam enjoyed far greater success than Christianity (Nestorian or Catholic) among the Mongol kingdoms of central Asia and Persia, largely because Islam was the established faith of the native peoples; as so often in history, the conquerors adopted the culture and religion of the conquered.

The triumph of Islam was sealed by the rise to power of the great Mongol warrior-leader *Tamerlane* (1360-1405) in

---

27. Most of today's far Eastern Mongols live in China. The country of Mongolia is racially Mongol; but animistic spirit-worship is the prevailing religion, with Buddhism the next most popular.

28. For the origin of the Persian Nestorians, see Volume One, Chapter 10, section 5.

Samarkand. Tamerlane, one of the most highly educated and most cruel rulers of the Middle Ages, was a fiercely intolerant Muslim, who embarked on a long and devastating campaign of Islamic conquest throughout central Asia and Persia. He unleashed a storm of bloody persecution on the Nestorians which virtually destroyed the Persian Church. Only a few Nestorians escaped by fleeing into the mountains. His repressive rule also put an end to Catholic mission among his Mongol subjects. Asia, which had been open for a century to Christian influence, closed up again with what seemed like a violent finality.

The Franciscan and Dominican missionaries faced an equally destructive problem at home: the "Black Death". This was a plague that swept through Europe from 1347 until about 1400. A third of Europe's population perished – in some countries, half the population. The great Italian poet, Francesco Petrarch,[29] has left us the following description:

> When will our descendants be able to believe that there was a time when, without fire falling from heaven or kindling on earth, without war or any other visible calamity, not just this or that country but almost the whole earth became uninhabited – empty houses, deserted cities, fields growing wild, the ground covered in dead bodies, and everywhere a vast and dreadful silence?

Under the devastating impact of the Black Death, the Franciscans and Dominicans found they simply could not keep up their supply of missionaries to the East. As a result, the whole Catholic missionary programme shrank to a tiny size. The Church did not effectively revive it for another 200 years.

Important people:

The Church

Peter de Bruys (active 1105-26)
Valdes (died around 1205)

---

29. For Petrarch, see Volume Three and its discussion of the Renaissance.

Joachim of Fiore (1135-1202)
Pope Innocent III (born 1160; pope 1198-1216)
Dominic Guzman (1171-1221)
Francis of Assisi (1182-1226)
Pope Honorius III (1216-27)
Pope Gregory IX (1227-41) (cardinal
  Ugolino, prior to becoming pope)
Clare of Assisi (1193-1253)
Raymond of Penafort (1175-1275)
Mechthild of Magdeburg (1212-80)
William of Tripoli
Conrad of Ascoli
John of Plano Carpini (1180-1252)
William of Ruysbroeck (1215-95)
John of Monte Corvino (died 1328)
Nicholas of Lyra (1270-1349)

Political and military

King John of England (1199-1216)
King Philip Augustus of France (1180-1223)
Raymond of Toulouse (1156-1222)
Kublai Khan (1260-94)
Tamerlane (1360-1405)

Others

Marco Polo (1254-1324)

Innocent III on Church and state

The Creator of the universe set up two great lights in the firmament of heaven, the greater light to rule the day, the lesser light to rule the night. Likewise, for the firmament of the universal Church, which is spoken of as heaven, He appointed two great powers: the greater to exercise rule over souls (corresponding to the days), and the lesser to exercise rule over bodies (corresponding to nights). These powers are the papal authority and the office of king. Further, the moon derives its light from the sun, and is inferior to the sun in its size, quality, and position, as well as in its effect. Likewise, the kingly office derives its splendour from the papal authority: and the more closely the kingly office adheres to the shining sphere of papal authority, the less brightly does kingship itself shine out; but the further away it removes itself from the papacy, kingship increases its own glory.

Innocent III

Letter 1 (**1198**)

Innocent III receives England as his property from King John

Innocent, bishop, servant of the servants of God, to his well-beloved son in Christ, John, illustrious king of the English, and to his free-born heirs for ever. The King of kings and Lord of lords, Jesus Christ, a priest for ever according to the order of Melchizedek, has set up His kingdom and His priesthood in the Church so that the one is a kingdom of priests and the other a royal priesthood, as testified by Moses in the Law and by Peter in his epistle. Over all He has set one person whom He has appointed as His vicar on earth, so that all men should obey His vicar and strive to live as one fold with one shepherd, even as every knee bows to Jesus in heaven, on earth and under the earth. All secular kings venerate this vicar for God's sake, so that they doubt if they are reigning properly unless they serve him faithfully.

To this, my dearly beloved son, you have paid wise attention; and by the gracious inspiration of Him in whose hand lie the hearts of kings which He turns wherever He pleases, you have chosen to submit yourself and your kingdom in a secular sense to him who already ruled them spiritually [*i.e.* Pope Innocent III], so that kingdom and priesthood might be united like body and soul in the single person of Christ's vicar. He has condescended to work this miracle, who is alpha and omega, causing the end to follow the beginning, and the beginning to anticipate the end, so that the provinces which have been under the spiritual teaching authority of the Holy Roman Church from oldest times should now also accept her as their secular sovereign. God has chosen you as a suitable servant to bring this about by a devout and free act of will; and on the general advice of your barons, you have offered and surrendered yourself and your kingdoms of England and Ireland, with all their rights and all that pertains to them, to God and to His apostles, Saint Peter and Saint Paul, and to the Holy Roman Church, and to us and our successors, to be our right and our property, giving us an annual payment of a thousand marks ...

Innocent III
Letter to King John of England (1214)

Joachim of Fiore: The end of this present age and the dawn of the new

The evening has almost fallen. We have arrived at the sunset of this life. We must endure weeping for an hour, so that in the morning we may find joy. It is time now for the elect to weep over the coming destruction of the newest Babylon, that we may not share in her sins, and be forced to share her punishments, as those not having the letter Thau written on our foreheads (Rev. 7:3, 14:1) and thus unable to escape her looming destruction. "Behold, the day of the Lord comes, cruel, with both wrath and fierce anger, to lay the land desolate; and He will destroy its sinners from it" (Isa. 13:9) ...

If only those who were born of the flesh would stop persecuting those who desire to walk in the Spirit! Yet have I not told my brothers, day and night, how Joseph was sold into bondage and taken into Egypt by his owners? Yes, those who despise prophecy and try to quench the Spirit must exist, even now. There is no comfort here! Perhaps it is not God's will that we can soon bring this mystery to its fulfilment. So many things distract me and hinder me in so many different ways, so that he who is holy is still made holy by his faith, but he who is filthy is still made unclean (Rev. 22:11), until that hour of testing suddenly comes to try all who dwell on the earth ...

Where faith is, and the desire for understanding, let the entire Church know that dangerous times are coming, in which her children will become barren. After the present time of testing, they will then cry out. Christians will be seen coming to the

Lord, not too late, and He will set them free from the hand of the persecutor. When He has liberated them, they will once more profit from the peace God has given them. The Lord will hand them over to their enemies to teach them not to blaspheme. But after the time of anger and hour of testing have ended, the Lord will look upon His people; His heart will rejoice in them, and no-one will take His joy from them. There will be a short time when the humble will not see their King, because the wicked will rule over the earth. Then there will be another short time. And then they will begin to see a time of peace, like nothing that has ever existed since the human race was first born on the earth!

From Joachim of Fiore
The Everlasting Gospel

Glory to God for nature

O most high, almighty, good Lord God, to You belong praise, glory, honour and all blessing!

Praised be my Lord God with all His creatures, and especially our brother the sun, who brings us the day and the light; he is fair and shines with a very great splendour. O Lord, he represents You to us!

Praised be my Lord for our sister the moon, and for the stars, so clear and lovely, which He has set in the heavens.

Praised be my Lord for our brother the wind, and for air and clouds, for calm and for all weather by which You uphold life in all creatures.

Praised be my Lord for our sister water, who is very useful to us, and humble and precious and clean.

Praised be my Lord for our brother fire, through whom You give us light in the darkness; he is bright and pleasant and very mighty and strong.

Praised be my Lord for our mother the earth, which sustains us and keeps us, and brings forth various fruits and flowers of many colours, and grass.

Praised be my Lord for all those who forgive one another for His love's sake, and who endure weakness and tribulation;

blessed are they who peacefully endure, for You shall give them a crown, O Most High.

Praised be my Lord for our sister the death of the body, from which no-one escapes. Woe to him who dies in mortal sin! Blessed are they who are found walking by Your most holy will, for the second death shall have no power to do them harm.

Praise and bless the Lord, and give thanks to Him, and serve Him with great humility.

Francis of Assisi
Canticle of the Sun

Francis of Assisi: The Franciscan Rule

I advise, admonish, and exhort my brothers in the Lord Jesus Christ, that when they go about in the world, they do not quarrel or contend with words, or judge others. Let them be humble, peaceful, and modest, gentle and lowly, speaking with courtesy to all, as is fitting. They should not ride on horses, unless clear necessity or bodily weakness forces them. Whenever they enter any house, they should say, "Peace to this house." They are free to eat whatever food is set before them, as the holy Gospel says (Luke 10:5). I firmly command that none of the brothers receive coins or money in any way, either personally or through a second party ...

Those brothers to whom the Lord has granted the grace of working should carry out their work faithfully and with commitment, so that they avoid idleness, the enemy of the soul, and do not quench the Spirit of holy prayer and devotion, which everything else in our earthly life must serve. As payment for their work, they may take whatever is necessary for their bodily needs and the needs of their brothers, but not money in any form. They should take their payment humbly, as is fitting for servants of God and disciples of most holy Poverty.

The brothers must not obtain any property of their own, neither a house nor a place nor anything at all. Rather, with total trust in God, let them beg for gifts of charity, as pilgrims and strangers in this world, serving the Lord in poverty and humility.

Let them not be ashamed, for the Lord made Himself poor in this world for our sakes. My dearly beloved brothers, this is the summit of that highest poverty which has established you as heirs and kings in the kingdom of heaven. It has made you poor in earthly things, but has exalted you in virtue. Let this be your portion which leads you into the land of the living. My dearly beloved brothers, devote yourselves totally to this, and for our Lord Jesus Christ's sake, do not ever desire to have anything else under heaven ...

Those brothers who are the ministers and servants of the other brothers should visit and admonish their brothers, correcting them humbly and lovingly, and not command them to do anything which violates their conscience or our Rule. Likewise, the brothers who are subject to them should remember that they have surrendered their own wills for God's will. Therefore I firmly order the brothers to obey their ministers in all those things which they promised the Lord they would observe, as long as they are not contrary to their conscience or to our Rule.

From Francis's
***Later Rule* of 1223**

Francis in the words of his contemporaries
How he always loved spiritual joy in himself and in others
It was always the supreme and highest desire of blessed Francis to possess an abiding spiritual joy outside of times of prayer and divine worship. This was the virtue that he specially loved to see in his brothers, and he often blamed them when they showed signs of gloom and sadness. He used to say, "If the servant of God strives to obtain and preserve, both outwardly and inwardly, the joyful spirit which springs from purity of heart and is acquired through devout prayer, the demons have no power to hurt him – they say, 'We can find no way to get at him, or hurt him, because this servant of God preserves his joy both in trouble and in triumph.' But the demons are delighted when they discover ways to quench or disturb the devotion and joy which springs from true prayer and other holy practices. For if Satan can gain a hold

over one of God's servants, he will soon transform a single hair into a log to throw at him, unless he is a wise man and takes care to remove and destroy it as quickly as possible by the power of holy prayer, contrition, confession and penance. Therefore, my brothers, since this spiritual joy springs from purity of heart and the purity of constant prayer, it must be your first concern to obtain and preserve these two virtues, so that you may possess both inwardly and outwardly this joy which I so greatly desire and love to see both in you and in myself, which edifies our neighbour and reproaches the enemy. It is the fate of Satan and his servants to be sorrowful, but ours is always to rejoice and be glad in the Lord."

Concerning the serious temptation he endured for more than two years

While he was living in the friary [a monastery of friars] of Saint Mary, a very serious temptation was inflicted on him for the good of his soul. He was so tormented in mind and body that he often withdrew from the company of the friars because he could not show them his normal cheerfulness. Nevertheless, he continued to discipline himself by abstaining from food, drink, and speaking; he prayed more constantly and shed more abundant tears, so that the Lord might be pleased to grant some remedy powerful enough for such a great trial. When he had been troubled in this way for more than two years, he happened to be praying in the Church of Saint Mary one day, when in his spirit he heard the words of the Gospel, "If you have faith, even though it is as small as a mustard seed, you will say to this mountain, Move from here to there, and it will move" (Matt. 17:20). At once, blessed Francis asked, "Lord, what is this mountain?" The reply came, "This mountain is your temptation." "In that case," said blessed Francis, "may it be to me as You have said." And from that moment, he was completely set free, so that it seemed to him as if he had never had any temptation. Likewise, in the holy mountain of Alverna, when he received the stigmata of the Lord in his body, he suffered such trials and temptations from the demons that he could not appear to his brothers with his normal joy, and he used to say to his friends, "If the friars knew the many and terrible afflictions the

demons bring upon me, they would all be moved to compassion
and pity for me."

Leo of Assisi
The Mirror of Perfection, **chapters 95 and 99**

Clare of Assisi: We must, like the Virgin Mary, be Christ-bearers

Therefore, dearly beloved, may you too rejoice in the Lord always.
May no bitterness, no cloud of sorrow overwhelm you, O dearly
beloved lady in Christ, you who are the joy of the angels and the
crown of your sisters. Set before your mind the Mirror of eternity
(Wisdom 7:26). Set your soul in the Radiance of God's glory
(Heb. 1:3). Set your heart in the Image of God's essence (Heb.
1:3 again). Transform your whole being into the likeness of Deity
itself through contemplation (2 Cor. 3:17). Then you too will feel
what His friends feel, as they taste the hidden sweetness which
God has reserved from the beginning for those who love Him.
You have cast aside all things which enslave their blind lovers in
this deceitful and restless world. Now love Him utterly, who gave
Himself utterly to win your love! The sun and moon stand in
awe of His beauty; there is no limit to the abundance, price and
greatness of His gifts. I speak of Him who is the Son of the Most
High Father, the One whom the Virgin brought forth, remaining
a Virgin after His birth. Cling to His most sweet Mother who
carried a Son whom the heavens could not contain – and yet she
carried Him in the little enclosure of her holy womb, and held
Him on her virgin lap.

Who does not fear the treacheries of humanity's enemy?
Through the arrogance of deceptive glories which do not last, he
tries to reduce to nothing what is greater than heaven itself. For
the soul of the believer is greater than heaven, because the grace
of God has made it the most worthy of all created things. The
heavens and the rest of creation cannot contain their Creator;
the believing soul alone is His dwelling place. This is possible
only through the love which wicked souls do not possess. For
the Truth said: "Whoever loves Me will be loved by My Father,
and I will love him too, and We will come to him and make our

home in him" (John 14:21). Therefore, just as the glorious Virgin of virgins carried Christ *physically* in her body, surely you too in your chaste virgin body can always carry Him *spiritually*, by following in His footsteps, especially His poverty and humility. You will then hold Him by whom you and all things are held together (Col. 1:17). Thus you will possess Him who is the most secure of possessions, compared with the fleeting possessions of this world.

Clare of Assisi
Third Letter to Agnes of Prague

Christian behaviour

When you pray, make yourself small with the greatness of humility.

When you confess sins, be honest.

When you perform penances, be committed.

When you eat, be restrained.

When you sleep, be disciplined.

When you are alone, be faithful.

When you are with others, be wise.

When someone teaches you to practise virtues, be attentive.

When someone rebukes you, be patient.

When you do a good work, reckon yourself poor.

When you do something wrong, seek God's grace immediately.

When you are behaving in a conceited way, be afraid.

When you are disturbed, trust God with great faith.

When you work with your hands, be swift, so that you may banish evil thoughts.

Mechthild of Magdeburg

9

The Byzantine Empire: from the Crusades to the fall of Constantinople

1. Political and military history

After the Byzantine Empire's golden age under Emperor Basil II (976-1025),[1] there followed an era of decline and defeat. A new power was rising in the East: the *Seljuk Turks*. Originally Pagans, this great warrior people swept in from central Asia, conquered most of Muslim Persia, converted to Islam, and in 1055 entered Baghdad, capital of the Islamic Empire. The caliph of Baghdad, Cayem, recognised the mighty Seljuk leader, ***Tughril Bey*** (1038-63), as *Sultan* (ruler), governing the Empire's secular affairs on Cayem's behalf. The caliphs continued to reign in theory as Muhammad's successors, but the real political power in the Muslim world had now passed from the Arabs to the Seljuk Turks. In 1065 the Seljuks invaded Armenia, subduing it by 1067. Their troops then marched into Anatolia, which was the heart of the Byzantine Empire in Asia Minor. The Byzantine Emperor Romanus IV (1067-71) took a huge army to fight off the Seljuks and reconquer Armenia in 1071; the two sides met in battle at Manzikert. It was one of the truly decisive conflicts of world history, and a turning point in Christian-Muslim relationships. The Turks completely wiped out the Byzantines, then invaded and took control of all Asia Minor. The Byzantine Empire never really

---

1. See Chapter 3, section 1.

recovered from this crushing defeat. In the same fateful year, the Byzantines lost the city of Bari, their last stronghold in southern Italy, to the Catholic Normans.

The continued existence of the Byzantine Empire now became bound up with military intervention by the Catholic West. The Emperor Alexius I Comnenus (1081-1118) recovered the western half of Asia Minor from the Turks with the help of Western Catholic troops in the First Crusade (1096-99), which temporarily broke Turkish power in the Middle East.[2] But instead of handing Syrian and Palestinian territory back to the Byzantines, the Western leaders set up their own "Crusader states". The Byzantine Empire now fell under Western economic control, through the commercial sea-power of Venice (northern Italy); Alexius gave the Venetians special trading privileges in return for their help against the Turks. The effects of Catholic intervention in the Middle East did not last long. In the 1140s Islam went back on the offensive, reconquered most of the Crusader states and, in 1176, destroyed the Byzantine army at the battle of Myriocephalum (southern Asia Minor). Once again, the whole of Asia Minor fell under Muslim control. Exploiting Byzantium's weakness, Hungary, Serbia, and Bulgaria all threw off their allegiance to the devastated Empire.

Further Catholic involvement in the East proved ultimately disastrous for the Byzantines. As we have seen in the Chapters on the Crusades and Innocent III, a French army of Crusaders arrived at Constantinople in 1203. They had at first intended to conquer Egypt from the Muslims, but they were being ferried there in Venetian ships; and Venice insisted, as part of the payment, that the French first of all conquer for them the city of Zara in Dalmatia (modern Croatia). While the French were in Dalmatia, Alexius Angelus – son of the deposed Byzantine Emperor, Isaac II (1185-95) – persuaded them to help him regain the Byzantine throne. In return, Alexius promised the French Crusaders large payment, and the submission of the Orthodox Church to the papacy. So the French army went to

---

2. See Chapter 5 for a detailed account of the Crusades.

Constantinople, deposed the Byzantine Emperor, and placed Alexius on the throne. But when Alexius could not keep his promises of payment, the French and Venetians did what the Muslims had never been able to do – they besieged and captured Constantinople in 1204. Amid scenes of great brutality, the French soldiers destroyed property, murdered men, and raped women. The treasures of the Byzantine capital were looted and taken West. A French noble, Baldwin of Flanders, was made Emperor of a new Catholic kingdom of Constantinople; large parts of the Byzantine Empire were shared out among other French nobles. A Western Catholic patriarch of Constantinople was appointed, and the Orthodox Church was made subject to the pope. However, except where Western force compelled them, the Orthodox people of Byzantium remained loyal to their own Church and their own patriarch. The French and Venetian conquest of Byzantium had a deadly effect on the relationship between Eastern and Western Christianity; the Orthodox world never forgot, and never forgave, what the Catholic West did to Constantinople in 1204.

The defeated Byzantines formed themselves into three separate states to carry on the resistance against their Catholic conquerors. These three states were the Empire of Nicaea (northern Asia Minor), the Empire of Trebizond (a coastal strip along the southern shore of the Black Sea), and the Despotate of Epirus (southern and western Balkans). They fought fiercely with each other, the Catholics, and the Bulgars. The Empire of Nicaea, where the Orthodox patriarchs of Constantinople now resided, came out the winner. In 1261, Nicaea's ruler, Michael VIII Palaeologus (1259-82), reconquered Constantinople from the Catholics and recreated the Orthodox Byzantine Empire.

Michael was an able ruler in military and political matters, but he brought fierce religious division into Orthodoxy by engineering the "Union of Lyons" in 1274 (see section 4 for a more detailed account). This was a union between Constantinople and Rome, in which Byzantium submitted to the papacy. However, the Union of Lyons was fatally wounded through its utter rejection by most Orthodox believers, and it did not survive Michael's death. The Emperors who followed him restored the spiritual independence of Constantinople, but they were not very gifted in the arts of war and government. The Empire was disturbed by civil strife; serious economic problems were caused by Venice and Genoa, the two great Italian trading powers that now dominated the Byzantine economy. By 1354 the Ottoman Turks, the new Muslim rulers of the East, had deprived the Byzantine Empire of Asia Minor again. By 1400, the Turks had invaded and conquered the Balkans too. There was nothing left of the once glorious Byzantine Empire except parts of Greece and the holy city of Constantinople itself.

Byzantine Emperors made desperate attempts to persuade the Catholic West to come to their aid. But the price of Catholic support was always the same: the Orthodox Churches of the East must submit to the papacy, as they had done in the short-lived Union of Lyons in 1274. At the Council of Florence in Italy in 1439, Byzantine *Emperor John VIII* (1425-48) and Patriarch Joseph II of Constantinople (1416-39) yet again accepted this humiliating condition, in an agreement known as the "Union of Florence" (see section 4). But once more, most Orthodox believers scornfully rejected this official Union, and no real Catholic military aid was forthcoming. In 1453, Turkish forces under the Ottoman Emperor Muhammad II besieged and captured Constantinople; the last Byzantine Emperor, Constantine XI (1448-53), died heroically defending his city. The Byzantine Empire, founded in 330 by the first Christian Emperor of Rome, Constantine the Great, was no more; and therefore the last vestige of the Roman Empire, which had existed for 1,500 years, died too.

2. Theology and philosophy in Byzantium: Michael Psellus and John Italus
One of Byzantium's brightest intellects of this era was *Michael Psellus* (1018-78). A native of Nicomedia in Bithynia, Psellus was an ardent disciple of the Pagan philosophers of ancient Greece, especially Plato and Aristotle. He was a true marvel of learning. Philosophy, theology, music, rhetoric, mathematics, astronomy,

medicine, military strategy: nothing seemed to escape Psellus's masterful mind – with the possible exception of humility, as he never lost any opportunity of telling everyone how great his knowledge and achievements were. Emperor Constantine IX (1042-55) appointed this conceited genius as head of the philosophy department in Constantinople University. In fact, Psellus was Constantine's chief agent in completely reorganising the University, which he accomplished so successfully that it outshone all other academic establishments in the Christian and Muslim world of its day, attracting students from as far away as Babylon in the East and Ireland in the West. Psellus's teaching and writings inspired a whole new generation of students. In some ways he was Byzantium's equivalent of the West's Peter Abelard (1079-1142),[3] supporting the systematic use of reason as a tool for resolving problems in theology. His foes accused him of being more a Platonist than a Christian – he referred adoringly to "My Plato!" Psellus, however, managed to avoid being disciplined by the Byzantine Church authorities; whenever seriously challenged, he simply made professions of absolute theological orthodoxy, accompanied by strangely dismissive language about "My Plato".

As well as being a brilliant thinker and teacher, Psellus was constantly involved in Byzantine politics as a counsellor to various Emperors; he lived through 13 changes of government, and wrote a vivid and colourful court history covering all the Emperors from Basil II (976-1025) to Michael VII (1071-78).

Psellus may have escaped Church discipline; his pupil **John Italus**, who succeeded him as head of Constantinople University's philosophy department, was less fortunate. Italus, a bold free-thinking spirit, went much further than Psellus in positively reinterpreting orthodox doctrines to make them fit in with Platonic philosophy; he believed, for example, that human souls had existed from all eternity, and denied the physical nature of the resurrection body. Italus's Platonised Christianity reminds us of the great 3rd century theologian Origen, placed on the official list of heretics by the fifth ecumenical Council of Constantinople

---

3. For Abelard, see Chapter 7, section 3.

in 553.[4] Italus suffered a similar fate. Two patriarchal tribunals in 1076-77 and 1082 condemned him and issued 11 anathemas against his theology, the seventh of which rejected the idea that the Pagan writings of ancient Greece and Rome (which meant in particular Plato, Aristotle, and the Neoplatonists) could be treated as an independent source of truth, rather than simply a tool for Christian educational purposes.

Italus's condemnation marked another turning point in the divergence between East and West. It showed that Byzantine Orthodoxy would refuse to accept any fusion between philosophy and theology – in contrast to the marital union the West was soon to celebrate between Catholicism and Aristotle. In Byzantium, theologians carried out the enterprise of systematic theology within the traditional context of studying the early Church fathers, rather than the framework of Aristotelian logic and philosophy adopted by Western scholasticism. The reverence which Catholic thinkers like Thomas Aquinas gave to Aristotle, quoting him as an almost infallible authority in their doctrinal writings, was unthinkable for the majority of Eastern Churchmen, and just seemed to them to prove how ungodly the Catholics were. The monastery, not the university, remained the wellspring of theological study and creativity in the Orthodox world.[5]

3. Gregory Palamas and the hesychastic controversy

The triumph of the iconodules in the iconoclastic controversy[6] led to an era of outstanding prosperity for the monasteries of the Byzantine world. Monks had supplied the iconodules with their foremost champions and martyrs; with the victory of their cause came honour, expansion (especially in the cities), and lavish

---

4. For Origen, see Volume One, Chapter 5, section 1. For his condemnation by the second Council of Constantinople, see Volume One, Chapter 12, section 2.

5. Certainly Orthodoxy made use of philosophical concepts in its theology, but never granted Pagan philosophy the almost independent status it acquired in large sections of Western scholasticism. See Chapter 7 for scholasticism.

6. For the iconoclastic controversy, see Chapter 3, section 3.

support from Emperors and the ruling classes. Many monastic communities developed into great landowners, possessing slaves and peasant workers in abundance. Church life in the East became dominated by the monasteries to a degree that was unknown in the West.

The monasteries provided the Byzantine Empire with one of its most distinctive expressions of spirituality – *hesychasm* (from the Greek *hesychia*, "quietness, peace").[7] As we saw back in Chapter 3, section 5, the life and teachings of Simeon the New Theologian (949-1022) had given a great impetus within Orthodoxy (especially the monasteries) to the growth and development of hesychasm as a disciplined pattern of praying. A person who practised this prayer-discipline was called a *hesychast* ;[8] his purpose was to conquer his passions, attain inner peace and silence, and through constant prayer to aspire to the vision of God as eternal light. Hesychasts employed two special prayer-techniques:

(i) They recited a special prayer, known as the "Jesus prayer": "Lord Jesus Christ, Son of God, have mercy on me" (or "have mercy on me, a sinner"). The hesychast would speak this prayer, first by his lips, then silently in his mind, over and over again. The idea was to make the prayer so much a part of a person's life and being, that he would be ceaselessly praying it in his heart, whatever else he was doing.

(ii) Hesychasts emphasised the importance of the body in prayer. To assist contemplation, they recommended that a person should rest his chin on his chest and gaze at his heart. The hesychast would breathe *in* as he prayed the words "Lord Jesus Christ, Son of God", and breathe *out* as he said "have mercy on me". These special practices of posture and breathing, however, were secondary to the Jesus

---

7. *Hesychasm* is pronounced "hezzy-kazzum".

8. Pronounced "hezzy-kast"

prayer itself; teachers of hesychasm regarded the physical techniques simply as useful aids to concentration. Pure inner mental prayer was their goal.

Non-Orthodox readers may wonder what it actually felt like to *be* a hesychast and practise the Jesus prayer. The best description occurs in the great 19th century classic of Russian Orthodox spirituality, *The Way of a Pilgrim* (author unknown). The pilgrim gives this account of his own experience of the Jesus prayer:

> I became so accustomed to the prayer that I prayed it all the time. In the end, I felt it going on by itself, within my mind and in the depths of my heart, without any prompting of my own. Not only when I was awake, but even when I slept, the prayer went on. Nothing broke into it; whatever I was doing, the prayer never stopped for a single moment. My soul was always giving thanks to God, and my heart melted away with ceaseless joy ... The self-acting prayer in my heart was a comfort and consolation as I travelled. Whatever happened to me, the prayer never ceased to make me glad, although it did so to different degrees at different times. Wherever I was, whatever I did or gave myself to, the prayer never hindered my activities, nor did they hinder the prayer. If I am working at anything, the prayer goes on by itself in my heart, and I work all the faster. The prayer never stops, even if I am listening carefully to something or reading. I am aware both of what I am doing and of the prayer, at one and the same time, just as though I were two persons, or as though my body contained two souls. O Lord, what a mysterious thing man is! How manifold are Your works, O Lord; in wisdom You have made them all!

One of the greatest leaders of the hesychast movement was *Gregory of Sinai* (died 1346). Gregory was a native of Asia Minor who was taken captive and enslaved by Turkish Muslims in his youth. After being ransomed by fellow Christians, he became a monk in the Saint Catherine monastery on Mount Sinai (hence his name). Gregory then spent time on the island of Crete where a hermit called Arsenius taught him hesychasm. This was the turning point in Gregory's life; from now on, he was to be a devout disciple of John Climacus[9] and Simeon the New Theologian, refining and popularising their philosophy of inner prayer. He journeyed to Mount Athos, took up residence there, and attracted multitudes of followers, to whom he imparted the wisdom of holy living in general and hesychastic praying in particular. One of his pupils said:

> When Gregory taught us about purifying the heart and deifica-
> tion through grace, his words awakened in our souls a kind of
> irresistible divine desire for virtue, and a love for God which
> knew no limits.

Gregory went on to found a monastery in the wilderness of Paroria in Thrace (on the south-eastern borders of Bulgaria). Gregory's Paroria monastery became the second greatest centre of hesychastic spirituality in the Orthodox world, eclipsed only by Mount Athos itself; from Paroria, Gregory scattered the seeds of hesychasm throughout Bulgaria and Serbia. Gregory summed up the teaching and practice of hesychasm in his major work, a treatise on inner prayer divided into 150 chapters.

Another mighty champion of hesychasm was **Theodosius of Trnovo** (died 1363). A disciple of Gregory of Sinai at Paroria, Theodosius was a Bulgarian who returned to his homeland after Gregory's death and founded the monastery of Kilifarevo, financed by the Bulgarian tsar John Alexander. From Kilifarevo, Theodosius continued Gregory's work of spreading hesychastic spirituality in Bulgaria.

Paroria and Kilifarevo were vitally important in propagating hesychasm in Eastern Europe, beyond the political boundaries of Byzantium. However, the true stronghold of hesychasm remained the great Orthodox "monastic republic" of Mount Athos. It was the hesychasm of the Athonite monks that set the scene for the great hesychastic controversy – the most far-reaching theological dispute in the East since the iconoclastic controversy of the 8th

---

9. For Climacus, see Volume One, Chapter 12, section 6.

and 9th centuries. The controversy broke out as a result of a frontal attack on the hesychastic spirituality of Mount Athos; and it was a monk of Athos who stepped forth as the supreme advocate of hesychasm, and the most famous and influential Orthodox spiritual thinker since Simeon the New Theologian – **Gregory Palamas** (1296-1359).

Palamas was born in Constantinople, the son of a Byzantine noble; brought up in the court of the pious Emperor Andronicus II (1282-1328), he trained for a career in the civil service. However, the young Palamas was concerned for his eternal destiny as well as his career, and entrusted his soul to the oversight of metropolitan **Theoleptus of Philadelphia**. Theoleptus was a slightly eccentric character whose life reads like a script for an epic film. His spiritual odyssey began as a married deacon in his native Nicaea. However, when Emperor Michael VIII engineered the submission of the Byzantine Church to the papacy in 1274 (see section 4, below), Theoleptus – an ardent foe of all things papal – abandoned his wife and fled from Michael's persecuting fury to the monastic Mountain of Saint Auxentius in Bithynia. Here he embraced the life of a monk, and never returned to his beautiful and devoted wife, despite her tears and pleas.[10] Still, Michael's agents arrested the new monk, and the Emperor had him tortured and imprisoned for several years.

After spending time on Mount Athos, Theoleptus found himself catapulted into fame by the death of Michael VIII in 1282. The new Emperor, Andronicus II, dissolved the Byzantine Church's union with Rome and showered honours on all who had suffered for opposing it. Among the honoured were Theoleptus; Andronicus appointed him metropolitan of Philadelphia in 1283, where his career continued to be highly colourful. Theoleptus was also a devout hesychast who wrote a celebrated little discourse on inner prayer called *A Word which Expounds the Secret Doing in Christ*.

---

10. Theoleptus's desertion of his wife – praised in his own day as an act of spiritual heroism – shows the lengths to which people in the Middle Ages could go in valuing celibacy over marriage.

Gregory Palamas (1296-1359)

This, then, was the man whose spiritual influence inspired a young Gregory Palamas, in 1316 at the age of 20, to abandon secular life and settle on Athos as a monk. There Palamas lived for the next 20 years, apart from a three-year period in Thessalonica where he was ordained to the priesthood. On Athos, Palamas tried as far as possible to live in solitude as a hermit – from 1331, in the Saint Sabbas hermitage above the Great Lavra monastery.[11] However, despite his love of the hermit's way of life, Palamas's growing reputation for personal holiness and spiritual wisdom eventually won him an army of disciples. Although he lived and taught on Athos at the same time as the other great hesychast leader, Gregory of Sinai, we possess no certain knowledge of any relationship they may have had with each other.

The spark which ignited the flame of the hesychast controversy was a full-scale assault on hesychasm made by an Orthodox monk from southern Italy, **Barlaam of Calabria** (died 1350). Barlaam was a learned theologian, well respected within Byzantine Orthodoxy. Famous for his writings on logic and astronomy, he came to Constantinople in 1338, lectured at its University (notably on Pseudo-Dionysius the Areopagite), and then in 1339 become a Byzantine ambassador to the papacy, which was at that time resident in the French city of Avignon.[12]

Strangely, it was Barlaam's writings against Western Catholic theology in defence of Eastern Orthodoxy which first made Palamas aware that Barlaam was on a collision course with the teachings of Mount Athos. Barlaam argued that Western reliance on Aristotle and his logical methods had given birth to an arrogant over-confidence among Catholic scholastic theologians, especially Thomas Aquinas and his followers, as if with their intellects they had actually mastered God's being and His ways. Barlaam held strong Eastern "apophatic" views on the incomprehensible nature of God, nurtured by his studies of Pseudo-Dionysius.[13] These views led Barlaam to affirm that human beings could know God only in an indirect, second-hand sort of way, glimpsing His shadow from created things; but no actual knowledge of the all-transcendent God Himself was possible to the human soul, however carefully and brilliantly it

---

11. For the Great Lavra and Mount Athos in general, see Chapter 3, section 5.

12. For the "Avignonese captivity" of the papacy, see Chapter 10, section 1.

13. For Aquinas, see Chapter 7, section 3. For the "apophatic way" and Pseudo-Dionysius, see Volume One, Chapter 12, section 3.

reasoned. Barlaam intended this to be the East's response to the mighty claims and complex systems of Catholic scholasticism. It was equally an attack on Eastern monastic piety, which held that human beings could enjoy a genuine personal knowledge of God through prayer and spiritual experience.

Barlaam and Palamas were soon waging a fierce literary war with each other. Having returned to the Byzantine Empire, Barlaam tried to find out more about his new critic's outlook by joining a hesychastic hermitage, first in Thessalonica, then in Constantinople. Here Barlaam tasted hesychastic disciplines of prayer at their wellsprings. Instead of refreshing his mind with sympathy, they filled Barlaam with bitter shock and hostility.

> "The hesychasts have initiated me," he wrote, "into monstrosities and absurd doctrines that a man with any intelligence, or even a little common sense, can hardly debase himself by describing. They are the offspring of false belief and reckless imagination."

That was enough for Barlaam; he launched a sweeping and influential campaign against the entire theory and practice of hesychasm, focusing on two chief points:

(i) He attacked and ridiculed the hesychasts for their *physical* prayer-techniques of posture and breath-control: staring at the heart, breathing in for the first part of the Jesus prayer and out for the second. These practices, he argued, were mere superstition. They had no place in a true Christian understanding of prayer.

(ii) Hesychasts claimed that the soul could enter into a direct personal experience of God – indeed, union with God – and they laboured to attain the fullness of this blessed experience in prayer. Barlaam, by contrast, held that God could be known only in an indirect way, by means of created things. The light that shone from Christ on the mount of transfiguration, and which Simeon the New Theologian and other hesychasts had experienced in prayer, was (according to Barlaam) a merely created light, not a light that actually shone forth from God's very essence. How could God be a pure Spirit, Barlaam asked, if He shone with a light that a human being's physical eyes could see?

To Barlaam's damaging criticisms, Palamas responded – especially in his *Triads in Defence of the Holy Hesychasts* – as follows:

(i)   The posture and breath-control techniques of hesychasm were not ridiculous, Palamas argued, but part of a truly Biblical doctrine of human nature. Humanity was both body and soul; and the body was not the soul's enemy, but its friend and partner in the spiritual life. When the Son of God became man, He took human flesh as well as a human soul, and thus sanctified body and soul alike. Therefore, said Palamas, when Christians prayed, it involved their whole being, body as well as soul; the physical techniques of hesychasm were simply a way of bringing body and soul into harmony in the supreme act of prayer.

(ii)   Palamas agreed with Barlaam that God was incomprehensible and unknowable in His divine nature or essence: this was crucial to the whole "apophatic" tradition of the East. However, Palamas said, although God remained for ever beyond us in His *essence*, human beings could know Him and be united with Him in His *energies*. Earlier Eastern theologians, *e.g.* the Cappadocian fathers, Maximus the Confessor, and Simeon the New Theologian, had accepted this distinction between God's essence and His energies.[14] Even so, Palamas explored it more deeply than any previous Eastern thinker, and made it central to his entire understanding of union with God. What did he mean?

---

14.   For the Cappadocian fathers, see Volume One, Chapter 8, section 3. For Maximus the Confessor, see Volume One, Chapter 12, section 4.

Palamas reasoned thus: clearly the Bible taught that Christians became united with God through Jesus Christ. But this could not be a union of *natures* – our human nature cannot be united with the divine nature. If that were the case, we would be the same as Christ the God-man; we too would be God and man, divine and human, in one person. And that was impossible, for Christ is unique. Our humanity must therefore be united with the divine *energies*, rather than with the divine nature or essence. We have met this doctrine of "energy" before, in the great Monothelete controversy of the 7th century, where the Church decided that there were "two energies in Christ", a human and a divine energy, corresponding to Christ's two natures (see Volume One, Chapter 12, section 4). We remember that energy means the distinctive actions, activities, works, and operations which a particular nature performs, revealing its identity.

By the "divine energies", then, Palamas was not referring to something different from God, but God Himself present in divine activity, operation, grace and power. For Palamas, God's existence could be approached and expressed in two ways: (a) His innermost nature and essence, which He did not share with any created person, and (b) the activities and energies that streamed forth from His nature, like light and heat radiating from the sun. Through the saving work of Christ and the Holy Spirit, Palamas maintained, Christians were truly united with God – but in His outflowing energies, not in His hidden essence. So the Church enjoyed a real union with God, and thus a real experience and knowledge of God Himself, without in any way trespassing on His mysterious inner essence which remains for ever beyond our grasp.[15]

---

15. The following illustration may help readers who find it hard to understand Palamas's distinction between God's essence and God's energies. Imagine yourself speaking to someone. The words you speak are not your human *nature*. But they flow out of your nature, out of your soul through your lips, and reveal what you are thinking. So in a sense, the words you speak are *you*; they are *your* words, embodying, expressing, and communicating your thoughts and feelings. Your spoken words are *you active in speech*. But they are not your human nature. This is similar to what Palamas meant when he distinguished between God's

Palamas further argued that God's energies manifested them-selves in the world as *light* – the divine light that transfigured Christ on Mount Tabor (Matt. 17:1-8, Mark 9:2-8, Luke 9:28-36). This light, Palamas maintained, was not like the created light of the sun, stars, or fire; it was the uncreated eternal light of God's own energies, shining forth from His invisible essence, revealing the deity of Christ. Human beings could indeed see this light with their physical eyes, as Peter, James, and John did on Mount Tabor, but not by natural eyesight – only by the supernatural op-eration of the Holy Spirit. By defining this light in terms of God's energies, not His essence, and by contending that people could see it only by the sanctifying grace of the Spirit, Palamas tried to set aside Barlaam's criticism that the hesychasts had made God into a physical being who could be physically seen.

Barlaam was a learned and hard-hitting opponent, but two councils in Hagia Sophia (Constantinople's chief church) upheld Palamas's teaching in 1341, in June and August, condemning Barlaam. Destiny, however, then dealt Palamas a very wild card. The Emperor Andronicus III (1328-41) had died just after the June council; his son was still a child, so power passed into the fumbling hands of Andronicus's Italian wife Anne. By August, political instability had flung the Empire into civil war. It was a grim struggle between, on the one hand, John Cantacuzenus, who had been Emperor Andronicus's best friend, prime minister, and the real power behind his throne; and on the other hand, the mighty noble Alexis Apocaucus, "bloody and venomous", and his ally, Patriarch John XIV of Constantinople, "a proud and feeble old man".[16] The spoils of victory fell at first to the venomous Apocaucus and the proud patriarch. This resulted in the solemn farce of Palamas being excommunicated by Patriarch John in 1344 for having backed Cantacuzenus. For a time, Barlaam and his theology were back in fashion for political reasons.

---

nature (or essence) and His energies. God's energies are God Himself active in work, power, and operation, expressing His essence but not identical with it.

16. The barbed descriptions of Edward Gibbon, *Decline and Fall of the Roman Empire*, chapter 63.

But it was not to last. Cantacuzenus regained power in 1347 – in fact, he fought his way to the throne, becoming Emperor John VI (1347-54) – and Palamas was restored to favour and elevated to the rank of archbishop of Thessalonica. A series of councils, the last of them in 1351, triumphantly vindicated his theology. Palamas's defence of hesychasm thereby passed into the mainstream of Orthodox thought. The distinction he had forcefully expounded between God's essence and His energies, however, was foreign to Western Catholic theology. Barlaam was so opposed to Palamas's doctrine that he abandoned Orthodoxy and joined the Catholic Church.

Palamas's teaching gave a powerful undergirding to the central Eastern concept of salvation as *deification* (the idea was known in the West, but not particularly emphasised or developed). Through Christ, humanity becomes divine: not in the sense of sharing God's essence, which is impossible, but in the sense of participating in God's energies. The union between the divine and human natures in Christ meant that Christ's humanity was flooded with the divine energies, thus deifying it; the human nature of the Saviour has, therefore, become the source of the divine life which alone can cleanse, heal, and sanctify our sinful humanity. Through the Holy Spirit, Palamas held, believers enter into saving union with Christ, so that His deified human life comes streaming into our souls (and ultimately, in the resurrection, even into our bodies). The believer therefore becomes holy and immortal with God's own holiness and immortality – but only through Christ's glorified humanity, by grace, always in utter dependence on God, and never to the same infinite degree as God Himself. This is what Orthodoxy means when it speaks about "becoming a god" through Christ. It does not mean that believers stop being human, but that through union with Christ their human nature is glorified and perfected by sharing in God's own sanctifying energies.

Palamas himself, whatever one thinks of his theology, remains one of the most attractive figures of the later Byzantine world. As archbishop of Thessalonica from 1347, he preached sermons setting forth a Christ-centred theology and spirituality with lucid simplicity, and condemned social injustice with scathing audacity. He also displayed a remarkable tolerance towards Islam. When he spent a year as a prisoner of the Turks, Palamas held friendly religious discussions with the son of Turkish emir Orkhan, expressing the hope that "a day will soon come when we [Christians and Muslims] will be able to understand each other." The citizens of modern Thessalonica venerate Palamas today as one of their most beloved saints.

4. East and West: Attempts at healing the schism of 1054

Through the East–West schism of 1054, the one holy, Catholic, apostolic and Chalcedonian Church of Europe, Russia and the Middle East had been rent asunder into two separate and hostile Churches. Perhaps not surprisingly, several attempts at reconciliation were made. Only 44 years after the schism, discussions between Orthodox East and Catholic West were held at Bari (southern Italy) in 1098, although they came to nothing.

A more serious effort at reunion dominated the reign of Byzantine Emperor **Michael VIII Palaeologus** (1259-82). Michael, chief general of the empire of Nicaea, had recaptured Constantinople from its French Crusader conquerors in 1261, thus recreating the Greek Byzantine Empire. Yet no sooner had Michael performed this political miracle than he unleashed storms of religious discord on his kingdom. First, on Christmas day 1262, he blinded the boy-Emperor John IV, Michael's rightful lord, of whom Michael was legally the guardian and regent. He hoped by this cruel act to destroy John's ability to become Emperor in his own right, thus securing the crown of the reborn Empire for Michael alone, without having stained himself with the guilt of actually murdering John. The plan failed. Patriarch **Arsenius** (1255-67), outraged by Michael's treacherous violence, excommunicated him. None of Michael's attempts at professing repentance impressed the pious and high-minded Arsenius, who on one occasion slammed the door of his prayer-room in Michael's face, leaving the Emperor kneeling and weeping outside. Michael finally lost all patience; deposing and exiling

Arsenius, he installed a new and more pliable patriarch, Joseph I (1268-75). This created the bitter schism of the "Arsenites", those loyal to Arsenius; the movement proved particularly fertile among the monks of Asia Minor, who remained stubbornly out of communion with apostate Constantinople for 40 years, until 1310.

Having split Byzantine Orthodoxy over Arsenius, Michael then plunged it into even darker waters through his negotiations for spiritual reunion with Rome. His motives were political and military: Byzantium was under threat from the Ottoman Turks in the East, and from Charles of Anjou, Catholic king of Sicily, in the West. Since 1261 the popes – Urban IV (1261-64), Clement IV (1265-68), and Gregory X (1271-76)[17] – had been poised to launch the Western powers on a crusade against Michael, in order to restore the French Catholic kingdom of Constantinople. Surrounded by a host of foes, Michael decided that his only safety lay in winning the papacy over to his side; and the stiff but unvarying price of papal favour was the submission of Orthodoxy to Rome. After delaying for as long as he could, Michael finally sent ambassadors who arrived in the French city of Lyons in 1274, bearing a letter in which the Byzantine Emperor declared his belief in the *filioque* clause, purgatory, and the supremacy of the pope. On July 6th, the decree of union was signed – the "Union of Lyons".

It provoked outrage among ordinary Easterners, who had not been consulted at any stage. Constantinople seethed with riots; Michael's patriarch, Joseph, no longer pliable, resigned in protest at what his Emperor had done. Michael simply appointed another patriarch (his third), John XI (1275-82). Then he put to work all the repressive machinery of the Byzantine state to crush dissent. His most famous victim was **Meletius the Confessor**, a hermit of the Mountain of Saint Auxentius in Bithynia, home to many monasteries. Meletius was an accomplished

---

17. The reason for the three-year gap between Clement IV and Gregory X is simply that the cardinals quarrelled for three years over whom to elect as the new pope.

theologian, well versed in the early Church fathers, author of exquisite religious poetry, and (above all) a holy man with a high reputation for sanctity and miracles. His best-loved writing was *The Alphabetalphabetos*, otherwise known as *The Garden*; covering a vast variety of doctrinal and spiritual subjects, it was a poem arranged according to the 24 letters of the Greek alphabet, with each "letter" containing 24 verses, each verse 24 lines, and the first word of each verse beginning with the letter of the alphabet under which it was classified. Appalled by the Union of Lyons, Meletius journeyed to Constantinople together with his friend Galaction, a hieromonk of Mount Auxentius, to protest personally to Emperor Michael. Michael's savage response was to inflict on Meletius and Galaction a long ordeal of exile, imprisonment, starvation, and trial for heresy; he finally had Meletius's tongue torn out and Galaction blinded. Other opponents of the Union received similar treatment.

However, Michael's brutal efforts bore no fruit. The great mass of Easterners – clergy, monks, and laity – rejected the Union with scorn. Members of Michael's own family conspired to topple him from the throne. Things also turned sour in the West. The papacy had assumed that if the Emperor of Byzantium converted to Catholicism, his people would submissively follow. Now, seeing the Union so widely spurned in the East, Rome blamed Michael: obviously his conversion was not sincere. Pope Martin IV (1281-85) decided he could tolerate the situation no longer, and excommunicated Michael as a heretic and schismatic in November 1281.

In December 1282 Michael died, universally despised in both East and West. The people of Byzantium hated him so deeply that his son, the new Emperor, Andronicus II (1282-1328), dared not give him a public funeral; he buried his detested father secretly, in a remote monastery at night. Andronicus then deposed the pro-Union patriarch, John XI, reinstated the anti-Union Joseph I, and officially dissolved the Union. Those who had been imprisoned or exiled for their loyalty to Orthodoxy came home in triumph, including Meletius and Galaction; despite his blindness, Galaction was given the honour of freshly consecrating

Hagia Sophia for Orthodox worship, by sprinkling the cathedral with holy water. So ended the first East–West reunion in dismal failure. It had proved that whatever Emperors and patriarchs did, ordinary Orthodox people would deny the right of their rulers to humiliate their Church at the feet of the papacy, or change its theology in a Romeward direction.

It seems, however, that this potent lesson was wasted on popes and Byzantine Emperors alike. A second and far more concerted attempt at Church reunion on Rome's terms was made 150 years later, at the Council of Florence in Italy. The Council (a Western Catholic Council) first met in Basel, Switzerland, in 1431, to try to resolve the internal crisis in the Catholic Church which had been triggered off by Catholicism's "Great Schism" of 1378-1417 (when there were first two, then three rival popes), and the revolutionary "conciliar movement" which tried to make the papacy subject to the authority of ecumenical Councils.[18]

In 1437 pope Eugenius IV (1431-47) transferred the Council from Basel to Ferrara in Italy, and then in 1439 to Florence. At Ferrara and Florence, the Council welcomed a glittering and impressive delegation from the Orthodox world, headed by no less a figure than the Byzantine Emperor himself, John VIII (1425-48), and the patriarch of Constantinople, Joseph II (1416-39). Other important Orthodox delegates included Metropolitan *John Bessarion* of Nicaea (1403-72), Metropolitan *Mark Eugenicus of Ephesus* (died 1444), and Metropolitan Isidore of Kiev (head of the Russian Orthodox Church).[19] They and the papacy opened negotiations for healing the breach between East and West. What gave this more weight than the Lyons affair was the presence of so many Orthodox bishops: this was to be no mere government-decreed union, but a reconciliation of East and West based on theological discussion and the approval of Orthodoxy's leading clergy. In reality, though,

---

18. See Chapter 10, sections 2 and 3, for a detailed account of the Great Schism and the conciliar movement.

19. For more about Isidore and the consequences of his involvement with the Council of Florence, see Chapter 6, section 3.

Emperor John VIII's motives were purely political and military, as Michael VIII's had been; John wanted Western help to defend the Empire against the Ottoman Turks, who had by now almost overwhelmed Byzantium. To secure Western help, John was willing to submit to Western religion.

Mark of Ephesus (died 1444)

Submission, however, did not come easily; there were nine months of exhausting negotiations, mostly on the *filioque* clause. The most active spokesmen on the Orthodox side were John

Bessarion and Mark of Ephesus. Bessarion was one of the most learned men of his day in East or West; passionately concerned for both the Christian and Pagan wisdom of the ancient Greek and Roman world, he was an expert on the early Church fathers and the writings of Platonist and Neoplatonist philosophers. The intellectual brilliance of Western scholastic theology captivated Bessarion, making him ashamed of the comparative ignorance of his Eastern colleagues; he swiftly became the moving spirit in the pro-union party among the Orthodox delegates. With Byzantium about to crumble under the Muslim onslaught, Bessarion felt that the Western Church – so theologically talented, so devoted to academic learning – was alone capable of preserving the noble cultural and spiritual inheritance of Greece and Rome.

Mark of Ephesus was Bessarion's intellectual equal, but otherwise stood at the opposite end of the ecclesiastical spectrum. A disciple of Gregory Palamas, Mark regarded all learning as subservient to spiritual life. His passion was for truth; and if reunion with Rome meant sacrificing the truth, Mark would fight it with his last breath. He therefore spent all his mighty theological energies at the Council of Florence arguing against Western Catholic doctrines not recognised in the East, especially the *filioque* clause and purgatory. But the metropolitan of Ephesus was almost a lone voice; the other Orthodox delegates became increasingly irritated with his awkward insistence on truth rather than political expediency.

A plan of reunion – the Union of Florence – was finally signed on July 6th 1439.[20] By the terms of the Union, the Orthodox agreed to accept three points of Western Catholic doctrine: (a) the theology of the *filioque* clause, that the Holy Spirit proceeds from the Son as well as from the Father, although Easterners were not required actually to utter the clause when they recited the Nicene Creed in worship; (b) the doctrine of purgatory; (c) the supremacy of the pope. The Catholics agreed to allow the Orthodox to use leavened bread in communion. Of the 33

---

20. The Union of Lyons and the Union of Florence were both signed on July 6th: evidently an unlucky day for Orthodoxy.

Orthodox delegates, only Mark of Ephesus refused to submit to the agreement. "The testimonies of the Western teachers I neither acknowledge nor accept," he famously declared. "I conclude that they are corrupted. There can be no compromise in matters of the Orthodox faith." When it was reported to pope Eugenius that the Orthodox delegates had signed the decree of Union, he instantly asked: "Did Mark of Ephesus sign?" When he was told that Mark had refused, Eugenius exclaimed in despair, "Then we have achieved nothing!"[21]

Eugenius's words were prophetic. Mark wrote a circular letter to all Orthodox Christians, exhorting them to shun the Union of Florence. Byzantine Emperor John VIII, enraged by Mark's intrepid one-man opposition to the Union, had him arrested and imprisoned, despite the fact that the metropolitan of Ephesus was a sick man; but Mark continued his anti-Union campaign from his prison cell by personal witness and by letter. And indeed, the Union of Florence proved empty and barren. Almost all the Orthodox bishops and people of the East rejected it with contempt as a sell-out to the papacy. Ordinary Orthodox laypeople refused to worship in churches whose clergy had submitted to the Union; Hagia Sophia, the patriarch of Constantinople's church, was virtually deserted. Isidore of Kiev, head of the Russian Orthodox Church, was treated with such violent hostility on arriving back in Russia that he fled the country, returning to Italy. There, both he and John Bessarion pursued new careers as cardinals in the Catholic Church. Bessarion went on to make a rich contribution to the Italian Renaissance.[22]

Meanwhile the other Eastern patriarchs, of Antioch, Jerusalem and Alexandria, who had not been present at Florence, denounced the Union officially in a public letter sent forth from Jerusalem in 1443. The only Orthodox delegate at Florence to emerge with any honour was Mark of Ephesus; for his

---

21. Two other delegates, Isaiah of Stavropolis and the bishop of Tver, walked out of the Council before the day of Union. Mark remained so that his refusal to sign would be a positive and public act.

22. See Volume Three, Chapter 1, section 2.

uncompromising resistance to the Union, and consequent sufferings, he was recognised throughout the East as "the conscience of Orthodoxy" and (after his death in 1444) a hero and a saint.

Despite the Union, no effective Western military assistance came to the Byzantines, and Constantinople fell to the Turks in 1453, thus bringing an end to a thousand years of Byzantine history. The Muslim conqueror of Byzantium, the Turkish sultan Muhammad II, appointed a new patriarch of Constantinople, Gennadius Scholarius (1405-72), a disciple of Mark of Ephesus. Gennadius was totally opposed to the Union of Florence. Under his leadership the Union became a dead letter; in 1472, it was authoritatively rejected by a synod of bishops meeting in Constantinople.[23]

5. Other great Orthodox figures in this period

The period between the East–West schism and the fall of Constantinople produced an abundant crop of illustrious Byzantine believers. We have met many of them in the previous four sections. Here we will consider some others who did not figure so prominently in the main controversies of the day.

One of Byzantium's great writers of popular Christian literature was **Theophylact of Ochrid** (1050-1109), metropolitan of Bulgaria. A native of the Greek island of Euboia, Theophylact was educated by Michael Psellus in Constantinople (see section 2), and became a deacon and distinguished preacher in Hagia Sophia. In 1090 Emperor Alexius I Comnenus (1081-1118) appointed him metropolitan of the capital city of Bulgaria, Ochrid (Bulgaria had been part of the Byzantine Empire since 1018). Here Theophylact earned a reputation for religious tolerance, by recommending a policy of combating Paulicians and Bogomils by persuasion not persecution.[24] He also championed the Eastern side of the great schism of 1054 in his *On the Errors of the Latins*, in which he argued – with a calmness and moderation

---

23. For more about Scholarius and Byzantine Orthodoxy after 1453, see Volume Three, Chapter 9.

24. For the Paulicians and Bogomils, see Chapter 3, section 6.

surprising for those days – that the only important point in the dispute was the *filioque* clause. However, his greatest achievement was his commentary on the entire New Testament (apart from the book of Revelation); from that day to this, Theophylact's has been the most widely read Bible commentary among Orthodox people in Greece, Russia, Bulgaria, and Serbia – the Orthodox equivalent of Protestantism's Matthew Henry. The commentary is a skilful weaving together of previous Biblical writings by the early Church fathers, especially John Chrysostom,[25] with illuminating remarks by Theophylact himself. He also wrote commentaries on Hosea, Jonah, Nahum, and Habakkuk.

Another great Byzantine Bible commentator who lived at the same time as Theophylact was **Euthymius Zigabenus** (active 1081-1118). A monk in the Monastery of the Virgin Mary near Constantinople, he was treated with the highest honour by Emperor Alexius I Comnenus and his remarkable daughter **Anna Comnena** (1083-1153). Anna wrote a colourful account of her father's reign, *The Alexiad*, which is both a treasury of knowledge about that era, and an enduring monument to Anna's own fascinating, complex personality.[26] In *The Alexiad* Anna praised Zigabenus as having "an unrivalled knowledge of doctrine". Emperor Alexius asked him to write a refutation of all the heresies which then disturbed Byzantium, especially Bogomilism; Zigabenus obediently produced his *Dogmatic Panoply*, which exposed the errors not only of the Bogomils, but the Paulicians, Jews, Muslims and Western Catholics too. The *Panoply* is our chief source of information about the Bogomils. Zigabenus also wrote an important series of commentaries on the Psalms, Gospels and letters of Paul. They were unusual in the way that Zigabenus emphasised the literal historical meaning of the text, in contrast to the allegorical method which was more fashionable at that time.

---

25. For John Chrysostom, see Volume One, Chapter 9, section 1.

26. Anna's *Alexiad* makes it clear that she virtually worshipped her father and violently hated her brother, Emperor John II (1118-43), whom – in true sisterly fashion – she tried to assassinate. John exiled her.

Eustathius of Thessalonica (died 1194) was the most learned Byzantine of his day. A native of Constantinople, he became a monk early in life at the Monastery of Saint Florus. Impressed by his mighty intellect, the Emperor Manuel I (1143-80) appointed Eustathius tutor to his son John; he then made him a deacon of Hagia Sophia, and finally metropolitan of Thessalonica, the most important Byzantine city after Constantinople. Eustathius won a golden renown as metropolitan, famed for his wisdom, integrity, courage, and spiritual-mindedness, his commitment to social justice for the ordinary people of his city, and his sermons on practical religion, in which he ceaselessly rebuked mere nominal Christianity (especially among monks) and summoned his hearers to the spirit and practice of holy love. Not everyone appreciated Eustathius's outspoken criticisms of tyranny, immorality, and superstition; his enemies managed to get him exiled from Thessalonica for several years, but he returned in triumph by popular demand.

Eustathius also championed the rights of the Orthodox to their own faith and worship against the oppressions of Catholicism. When the Catholic Normans of Sicily captured Thessalonica in August 1185, it was a dark day for East–West relations; the Normans massacred some 7,000 civilians, raped countless women and girls, and destroyed Orthodox churches and icons – all described in chilling detail by Eustathius in his *History of the Latin Conquest of Thessalonica*, the only eyewitness account of the event. Not surprisingly after this, Eustathius regarded Western Catholics as no better than savage barbarians. (Thessalonica was liberated from the Normans three months later.)

Eustathius's writings range over a wide area: monumental and brilliant commentaries on the Pagan Greek poets Homer and Pindar, a famous work *On the Reformation of Monastic Life*, treatises on various ecclesiastical topics, and a multitude of sermons and letters.

Michael Acominatus of Athens (died 1222) was Eustathius's greatest pupil. Born in Chonae, Phrygia (Asia Minor), he rose to the heights of becoming metropolitan of Athens, the ancient capital of Greece. Acominatus was dazzled by the city's glorious past as the birthplace of European philosophy, where Socrates, Plato and Aristotle had once lived and taught. However, his heart was broken by the actual Athens of his own day – the superstitious, uncultured people he had to baptise, preach to, marry, and bury. In his sermons, he was for ever exhorting his flock to live up to the noble heritage of their forefathers, and for ever weeping and complaining about their miserable failure to heed his words. "O city of Athens, mother of wisdom, to what ignorance you have sunk!" Acominatus's life is a study in the triumph of harsh reality over starry-eyed idealism. When the French Catholic Crusaders conquered Constantinople in 1204 (see section 1), they expelled Acominatus from Athens, replacing him with a Catholic bishop. He fled to the tiny Greek island of Ceos, where he died in 1222. His legacy was a collection of sermons, speeches, letters, and poems which offer many valuable insights into the spiritual, social, and cultural life of his day.

Michael Acominatus's brother **Nicetas Acominatus** (died 1216) has also secured a place in history. He wrote an important theological treatise, *Treasury of Orthodoxy*, a bursting storehouse of Eastern doctrine and a refutation of all religious errors. The *Treasury* has a special fascination because Nicetas was not a monk or clergyman, but a career politician who achieved great eminence in the Byzantine court, until the fall of Constantinople forced him to flee to Nicaea. He produced the *Treasury* to inspire his fellow Orthodox to remain true to their faith amid the persecutions heaped on them by their Catholic conquerors. It reminds us that the figure of the learned lay theologian, although unknown in the Catholic West, was not uncommon in the Eastern Orthodox world. Nicetas also wrote a useful *History* of Byzantium from 1118 to 1206, highly esteemed by scholars for its accuracy and wealth of political information. It contains Nicetas's own eyewitness account of the capture of Constantinople by the Crusaders and the brutalities they inflicted on the fallen city, its churches and people.

Nicholas Cabasilas (born 1322 or 1323, died some time after 1387) was a native of Thessalonica. He spent the first half of his life as a high-flying civil servant, a close friend of Emperor

John VI Cantacuzenus. But Cantacuzenus was deposed in 1354, retiring into a monastery. Cabasilas followed his example, abandoned politics, and joined the monastery of Manganon, near Constantinople, where he dedicated himself to theology and philosophy. He was probably ordained to the priesthood, but if so, we are not sure when. Nothing certain is known of the date of his death.

The fame of Cabasilas rests on his two great treatises, *Commentary on the Divine Liturgy* and *The Life in Christ*. The second of these is perhaps the most readable spiritual masterpiece in the history of Byzantine Orthodoxy. At the heart of Cabasilas's understanding of the Christian life we find a powerful concept of union with Christ which probably reflects the influence of Gregory Palamas. Cabasilas's basic approach to Christ was by way of the incarnation: the second person of the Trinity, God the Son, has sanctified and deified human nature by taking it into union with His divine nature. Now exalted in heaven, He draws believers into the most intimate life-giving union with His own humanity through the Church's mysteries (or sacraments, as Westerners would say), although Cabasilas mentioned only three – baptism, eucharist, and chrism – at a time when the West had generally accepted that there were seven.

This outlook enabled Cabasilas to combine a high doctrine of Church and sacraments with a spiritually rich emphasis on the individual believer's participation in Christ's sanctifying life through the Church. Cabasilas placed particular stress on the eucharist as spiritual food for the weary, struggling, tempted soul: here Christ gives His entire glorified body and soul to the body and soul of the Christian. From this closest of unions with the God-man flows the true believer's own life of love towards God and his neighbour.

Important people:

The Church

Theophylact of Ochrid (1050-1109)
Euthymius Zigabenus (active 1081-1118)

Eustathius of Thessalonica (died 1194)
Michael Acominatus of Athens (died 1222)
Patriarch Arsenius of Constantinople (1255-67)
Meletius the Confessor (active 1270s and 80s)
Theoleptus of Philadelphia (1250-1322)
Gregory of Sinai (died 1346)
Barlaam of Calabria (died 1350)
Gregory Palamas (1296-1359)
Theodosius of Trnovo (died 1363)
Nicholas Cabasilas (born 1322 or 1323, died some time after 1387)
Mark Eugenicus of Ephesus (died 1444)
John Bessarion (1403-72)

Political and military

Tughril Bey, leader of Seljuk Turks (died 1063)
Emperor Michael VIII Palaeologus (1259-82)
Emperor John VIII (1425-48)

Others

Michael Psellus (1018-78)
John Italus (active 1070s and 80s)
Anna Comnena (1083-1153)
Nicetas Acominatus (died 1216)

Sexual morality

"You have heard that it was said to those of old, 'You shall not commit adultery.' But I say to you that whoever looks at a woman to lust for her has already committed adultery with her in his heart" (Matt. 5:27-28). In other words, if a man stands there looking at a woman and examining her, setting alight the flame of his desire by gazing at her, and then gazing at her again in order to desire her even more, he has already prepared the sinful thing in his heart. If he did not actually commit the deed itself because he did not have the opportunity, what does that matter? If he could have done it, he would instantly have committed the sin. Still, understand this: if we have lusted, and then something stopped us from committing the deed, obviously God's grace protected us. Furthermore, if a woman makes herself look beautiful with the aim of being sexually attractive to men, but does not actually succeed in inflaming their desire, she stands guilty of mixing the poison into the cup, even though nobody drank it ...

"But I say to you that whoever divorces his wife for any reason except sexual immorality causes her to commit adultery, and whoever marries a woman who is divorced commits adultery" (Matt. 5:32). Christ does not abolish the laws of Moses, but reforms them by making the husband afraid of hating his wife without reason. If he divorces her for a good reason, because she has committed adultery, Christ does not condemn him. But if she has not been guilty of sexual immorality, Christ does condemn him, because by divorcing his wife he forces her to commit adultery [by remarriage]. And the man who marries her also commits adultery, for if he had not married her, she could have returned to her true husband and submitted to him.

Theophylact of Ochrid
Commentary on Matthew's Gospel, **Chapter 5:27-28, 32**

The hardship and the glory of becoming a monk

You have sold all your goods, you have forsaken your parents, brothers, relatives, friends, acquaintances, money, houses, lands, even your own body. In exchange for all these, you laid hold upon the pearl of great price, Christ, who is every blessing, yes, beyond every blessing. Having Christ, you have every blessing. What do you miss? Why are you complaining? What do you lack? Why are you upset? You have tasted Christ, the bread from heaven, the true manna. You have drunk the water of life. You know that the Lord is good. You have learned that there is no lack to those who fear Him. In the treasury of your love, you have stored Christ, the treasure of life. You have rejected the pleasures of this world, by renouncing the things which belong to this world. At the gate of your soul, you have planted the fear of God, to guard you and persuade you to undergo all suffering in this world – for His sake, who suffered wounds on your behalf, and gave you a share in His glory, as you accept the various sorrows that come upon you and imitate His endurance.

Those who are rich in this world's goods become poor and go hungry, because the desire for perishable things deceives them, and they believe they can possess things which cannot be possessed. Therefore they will go hungry and suffer in the world to come, because – forsaking true riches – they cling to the fading objects and false joys of this passing world, which are like spiders' webs, spun out and disappearing. These people become poor and are eaten up by famine, not only in the world to come, but even here on earth, many times, because the things of this present world are so unstable. However, there are others who have rejected everything, not even sparing their bodily life, because they prefer Christ, the true life; and they seek the Lord day and night, for they have turned away from the world, denied themselves, and are following after Christ. They will not lack any good thing, for they are truly seeking the Lord. He who possesses that Good which is perfect and incomparable lacks nothing; he always enjoys every blessing, and rejoices eternally, because the Lord is his joy, as the apostle decrees, "Rejoice in the Lord always!" We cannot live without Him; likewise without Him, we cannot rejoice always or rejoice truly.

Theoleptus of Philadelphia
Letter 3

Calling on Christ in prayer

My beloved friend, as we have already said,
We must at all the times mingle prayer
With deep attentiveness,
And especially blend it with that source of salvation
Which everyone desires –
The prayer of calling on the Logos, the God-man,
The prayer that gives special delight to all who pray.
When this prayer becomes a habit
By constant practice,
It makes a person keep a sharp look-out in God's presence
Concerning what his senses and his perception tell him,

Just as a person always looks after the apple of his own eye.
Yes, prayer banishes far away from us
All earth-begotten menaces
That aim themselves at the body or the soul.
Delight yourself in prayer, then,
For she loves to be loved –
She, the radiant one, the illuminator,
The bringer of light and warmth,
The sweetest one,
Giver of fairest pleasure to all.
Like heavenly lightning,
Turn prayer about in your heart,
Crying out with a secret voice
To Him who knows all secrets:
O Son of God, help me;
O my Christ, protect me!
Say this always, keep it ever in your mind,
And you will be enlightened,
You will attain to wisdom,
You will acquire divine grace –
In a word, you will be called an angel in the flesh.
For the Lord is not looking so much
For words from the lips
Or cries from the mouth,
But for speechless groans from the heart
And inner cries.
This is the voice, well-tuned and clear,
That swiftly flies up to the Master's ear,
And instantly moves Him to mercy.

Meletius the Confessor
The Alphabetalphabetos, **Letter Eta, section 10**

Gregory Palamas: Knowing God

In His love for humanity which is beyond all other love, the Son of God joined His divine person to our human *nature*, thus taking upon Himself as a garment a living body and a thinking soul, so that He might show Himself on earth and live with human beings. But O the wonder beyond wonders, and full of glory, He also joins Himself to human *persons*, by joining Himself to each believer through our fellowship in His holy body [in the eucharist]. For Christ becomes one body with us, making us a temple of the whole Deity; for in Christ's own body "all the fullness of the Godhead dwells bodily" (Col. 2:9). How then would He fail to give light to those who, in a worthy manner, share in the divine splendour of His body within us, shining on their souls as He once shone forth on the bodies of the apostles on Mount Tabor? Christ's body, the wellspring of shining grace, was at that time not yet joined with our bodies; it shone outwardly on those who drew near it worthily, sending its light through their senses to their souls. But today, since His body is now joined to us and dwells within us, it sheds light on our souls inwardly ...

God makes Himself known "face to face, not in dark sayings" (Num. 12:8). As the soul is joined to the body, so God makes Himself one with those who are worthy, thereby making them members of Himself. He joins Himself to us by coming in His fullness to dwell in the whole of our being, so that we also may dwell in Him. Through the Son, the Spirit is richly poured out upon us; yet the Spirit is not on that account a created spirit [that is, our knowledge of God is not – as Barlaam held – through created things alone, for we know God through the Holy Spirit who is not created] ...

This knowledge of God, which goes beyond human reason, is shared by all who have trusted in Christ. Christ will come again in the glory of the Father, and the righteous will shine like the sun in that glory; they will be light, and they will see light, a blessed and holy vision, the reward bestowed only upon purified hope (1 John 3:2-3). This light shines out in part today, a token bestowed on those who, by overcoming their passions, have left behind them all that is forbidden, and by pure mental prayer have journeyed even beyond what is merely pure. But on the last day, the brightness of this light will deify the sons and daughters of the resurrection; they will rejoice for everlasting and cry out joyously in fellowship with the One who has given divine glory and brightness to our nature ...

Each and every believer has known the Son by the Father's voice speaking to us from heaven; and the Holy Spirit Himself, who is light beyond words, has shown us that Jesus is truly the Beloved One of the Father. The Son Himself has made the Father's name known to us, and as He was going up into heaven He promised to send us the Holy Spirit to stay with us for ever. This same Spirit has now come down to us, and dwells with us, teaching us all truth. So how can it be true that we know God only through created things? Think about those who have not had personal experience of marriage. Can they have no understanding of the near union between God and His Church, because they have nothing like this in their own human experience? If so, you would have to tell everyone to flee from virginity, in order to reach the true knowledge of God about which you speak. But the apostle Paul overthrows your arguments. Paul was not married, yet he was the first to cry out, "This is a great mystery, but I speak concerning Christ and the Church" (Eph. 5:32) ...

No-one can share in God in His innermost being; His essence-above-all-essence is utterly beyond being shared. But we find something *between* the divine essence which cannot be shared, and those who do indeed share in God; and this "something between" is what enables us to share in God [this "something between" is the divine energies, which mediate between the divine essence and creation]. If you take away what stands between those who share, and That Which cannot be shared, you are cutting us off from God – O the emptiness! You wreck the link, thus opening up a huge gulf which cannot be bridged, between God on the one side, and on the other side the creation and government of those who are created. Then we would have to go looking for another God, One who not only has in Himself His own purpose, energy, and deification, but One who would also be a loving God, who would not merely want to gaze at Himself ... Thus God makes Himself present to everything by the ways in which He shows Himself forth, and by His creative and providential energies. To put it all in a few words, we must look for a God in whom we can share in some way, so that by sharing in Him, each one of us – in a way fitting to each, and in keeping with the nature of sharing – may have being, life, and deification bestowed upon him.

Gregory Palamas
Triads in Defence of the Holy Hesychasts,
1:3:38, 1:11:29, 2:3:66-67, 3:2:24

Christ's atoning death

The One who died was God; the One whose blood was shed on the cross was God. What could be more costly or awe-inspiring than this death? What a great sin human nature had committed, if it needed such a great penalty to atone for it! What a great wound it must have been, if it needed the power of this remedy! Some penalty was necessary to abolish sin, so that we – by paying a righteous penalty – might be cleared of accusation for the sins we have committed against God. For he who has been punished for his deeds will never again be called to account for them. But among human beings, there was no-one without guilt who could have suffered on behalf of the rest. Indeed, no-one was able to suffer even on his own behalf. Therefore the entire human race could not pay the penalty it deserved, even if it had died ten thousand times. What suitable penalty could a miserable slave suffer, who had totally destroyed the image of his King and acted with such contempt towards so great a majesty?

Therefore the sinless Master Himself suffered many terrible things, and died, and endured the stroke. Thus He sets the human race free from accusation, and grants liberty to the prisoners, because He, our God and Master, was in no need of being liberated Himself. These, then, are the reasons why true life flows to us through the Saviour's death. And the way in which we receive this life into our souls is by being initiated into the mysteries [sacraments], being washed [baptism] and anointed [chrism] and partaking of the holy table [the Lord's supper]. When we do these things, Christ comes to us and lives in us; He is united with us, and grows into oneness with us. He treads down sin in us, pouring into us His own life and worthiness, to make us share in His triumph. O the greatness of His goodness! He crowns those who have been washed, and declares to be victors those who partake of His banquet!

Nicholas Cabasilas
The Life in Christ, Book 1, chapters 10 and 11

Do not be afraid to return to God

Of the many things that are an obstacle to our salvation, the greatest of all is when, having sinned, we do not immediately turn back to God and ask Him to forgive us. Because we feel shame and fear, we think that the way back to God will be hard, that He is angry and foul-tempered towards us, and that we need to prepare ourselves with great effort before we can approach Him. But God's lovingkindness completely banishes this thought from the soul. Scripture says, "While you are still speaking, He will say, Here I am" (Isa. 58:9, Septuagint). If anyone really knows how kind God is, what can stop him from going to God immediately for pardon for the sins he has committed? Here is the scheme and device which our common enemy uses against us: he incites us to sin with rashness and daring, but then – after we have ventured on the most dreadful deeds – he fills us with shame and with a groundless fear. First he prepares our downfall, and then he does not allow us to rise up from it. He both leads us away from God, and then also prevents us from returning to God. So by opposite paths Satan carries us to ruin.

Nicholas Cabasilas
The Life in Christ, Book 6, chapter 6

The Council of Florence: Catholics and Orthodox dispute about purgatory

[The Catholic side triumphantly presented proof of the doctrine of purgatory from the writings of the great Eastern theologian, Gregory of Nyssa (330-95), one of the Cappadocian fathers. The Orthodox response ran as follows:]

Gregory, the blessed priest of Nyssa, seems to speak more to your advantage [about purgatory] than any of the other fathers. We preserve all the respect which is due to this father; but we must point out that he was only a mortal man. And however great the degree of holiness a man may attain, he is still very liable to error, especially on subjects like this, which have not been examined before, or settled by an ecumenical Council of the fathers ... We must not pay heed to what each theologian has written in his own private capacity, but look at the universal teaching of the Church, and take holy Scripture as our rule.

Reported in Dorotheus of Mytilene's

History of the Council of Florence

10
The Catholic Church in Crisis: from the Avignonese Captivity to the Hussites

1. *The Avignonese captivity of the papacy (1309-77)*

The papacy had reached the height of its political power in Western Europe under Innocent III. His death in 1216 was followed by a period of eclipse and finally disaster. The popes continued to struggle against the Holy Roman Emperors; their conflict with Frederick II (1210-50), whom Innocent III himself had settled on the German throne, was especially bitter.[1] However, the long warfare between papacy and Empire had permanently weakened the power of the German monarchy, by undermining Germany's national unity. Real power lay in the hands of the local German princes, not the Emperor. The threat to the independence of the papacy no longer came from Germany, but from France.

In contrast to the situation in Germany, the French monarchy was growing in strength. It reached dangerous levels, as far as the papacy was concerned, under King *Philip the Fair* (1285-1314). Philip was a ruthless tyrant who had the highest views of his own absolute authority over all French affairs. Conflict broke out between Philip and Pope *Boniface VIII* (1294-1303) over taxation. In 1295 Philip levied a tax on the French clergy to finance a war with England. The French clergy complained to

---

1. For more about Frederick II, see the account of the Sixth Crusade in Chapter 5, section 3; see also Chapter 8, section 1.

Boniface, who decreed the excommunication of all who imposed or paid such taxes without papal permission. Philip responded by forbidding the export of gold and silver from France; this crippled the economy of Rome. Boniface had to compromise and allow the French clergy to make "voluntary" contributions to Philip's war.

Then in 1301 Boniface sent a special papal legate, Bernard of Saisset, to Philip's court to complain about various high-handed acts of Philip, *e.g.* his seizure of Church property. Philip had Bernard arrested and charged with high treason. The conflict escalated. Boniface ordered the release of Bernard and summoned Philip to Rome. Philip called a national assembly of French nobles, clergy and commoners, which supported him in his defiance of the papacy. Boniface reacted by issuing his famous papal edict (or "bull") in 1302, entitled *Unam sanctam*, which made the most awe-inspiring political and spiritual claims for the papacy.[2] The bull asserted that all political authority is subject to the pope, and that submission to the pope is necessary for salvation:

> We are forced by the faith to believe and hold, and we do indeed firmly believe and sincerely confess, that there is one holy Catholic and apostolic Church, and that outside this Church there is no salvation or forgiveness of sins ... There is one body and one head of this one and only Church – not two heads, like a monster – and that is Christ, and Christ's vicar is Peter and the successor of Peter ... Both the spiritual and the civil sword are in the power of the Church. The civil sword is to be used *for* the Church, the spiritual sword *by* the Church: the spiritual sword is to be used by the priest, the civil sword by kings and captains, but only at the will of the priest and by priestly permission ... We declare, state, define and pronounce that it is absolutely necessary to salvation for every human being to be subject to the Roman pope.

---

2. Bull comes from the Latin *bulla*, "seal", referring to the wax seal by which a pope impressed the sign of his authority on a papal edict. Bulls were known by their opening words in Latin. The name of the *Unam sanctam* bull comes from its opening declaration, "We are forced to believe in one holy Catholic Church" (*Unam sanctam* is Latin for "one holy").

Philip's response was to declare that Boniface was unfit to occupy the papal throne, and he summoned the pope to appear before an ecumenical Council of the whole Church. The French parliament, clergy and Paris University all joined in this declaration. Boniface prepared to excommunicate Philip, but before he could do so, the French king resorted to violence and had Boniface kidnapped and imprisoned. Philip's agents demanded that he resign from the papacy; Boniface refused. Allies rescued him from imprisonment, but Boniface died a month later, an old and broken man, while the struggle was still raging.

The papacy was now in serious trouble. Philip had appealed to French national opinion against the claims of Rome, and had succeeded. Nationalism as a political and anti-papal force had arrived on the European scene.

Worse was still to come. When Boniface's successor, Pope Benedict XI (1303-4), died after a reign of only eight months, the French faction of cardinals succeeding in electing a French pope, Clement V (1305-14). Clement was a weak man who simply became the tool of King Philip. He never set foot in Rome, and after four years of wandering around southern France, in 1309 Clement established the papal court in Avignon (pronounced "Avvin-yon"), a city on the river Rhône. Today Avignon is in the south-east of France, but in 1309 it was in Provence, an independent county; Pope Clement VI (1342-52) purchased it in 1348, making it into a papal city.[3] Still, Avignon was surrounded by French territory and under French political influence. The papacy remained in Avignon for nearly 70 years (1309-77), a captive of the French monarchy and its policies. Those hostile to France referred to this period as the "Babylonian captivity" of the papacy; modern historians call it the "Avignonese captivity". There were seven popes in this period, all Frenchmen, and they made sure that most of the cardinals were French too. It had a devastating effect on the prestige and influence of the papacy. According to Catholic theory, the apostle Peter had been the bishop of Rome and (therefore) the first pope; that is why the

---

3. Avignon remained a papal city until the French Revolution.

church and bishop of Rome were paramount. With the popes now in Avignon, torn loose from their ancient historic seat in Rome, it seemed to many that the papacy had lost its true identity and become nothing more than a mere political pawn in the hands of the French kings.

The Avignonese captivity led to several remarkable attacks on the papacy by Christian thinkers. Most of them came from the Holy Roman Empire, which was even more hostile to the papacy now that it was in Avignon under French domination. The most radical critiques of papal claims were made by the English schoolman William of Ockham,[4] and the Italian **Marsilius of Padua** (1280-1343). Marsilius was rector of Paris University from 1313. His attacks on the papacy forced him to flee for his safety to Germany in 1326, placing himself under the protection of the Holy Roman Emperor **Louis the Bavarian** (1314-47), as William of Ockham did in 1328. Louis was a determined foe of the papacy, who was excommunicated by Pope John XXII in 1324. Louis supported the spiritual Franciscans against John XXII's condemnation of them,[5] invaded Italy, and even managed to capture Rome and set up a short-lived rival pope, Nicholas V, in 1328. Marsilius of Padua's great anti-papal treatise was his *Defensor Pacis* ("Defender of Peace"), written in 1324 when he was still in Paris.

In *Defensor Pacis*, Marsilius argued that authority lay with "the people" – the whole body of citizens in the state, and the whole body of believers in the Church. (Marsilius had learned this theory from the political writings of Aristotle, of whom he was a devoted student.[6]) Political and spiritual leaders, therefore, were appointed by the people and accountable to the people. The supreme legislative power in the Church was not the papacy, but an ecumenical Council representing the entire body of believers. Scripture alone was the source of Christian teaching; if there was any dispute over what Scripture meant, an ecumenical Council

---

4. For William of Ockham, see Chapter 7, section 3.

5. See Chapter 8, section 4.

6. For the influence of Aristotle, see Chapter 7, section 2.

must settle it. Pursuing this line of thought, Marsilius distinguished between the *Catholic* Church and the *Apostolic* Church (William of Ockham also made this distinction). The Catholic Church included the Western Church, the Eastern Orthodox, and all who believed in Christ; all members of the Catholic Church were within God's grace. The Apostolic Church was the Church of Rome, which was an embodiment and manifestation of the Catholic Church, but was not infallible – Rome could err.

The Roman pope, Marsilius taught, was not the leader of the Church by divine right; his leadership flowed simply from the political fact that he was bishop of the Roman Empire's capital city. Furthermore, the pope had no right to depose kings and Emperors. The clergy, Marsilius insisted, were in all secular matters subject to the state, like all other people. The only power priests had was the power to teach, warn, persuade and rebuke. Since Marsilius accepted that Church and state were the spiritual and political aspects of a single Christian society, he also taught that a Christian state had the right to call Church councils, appoint clergy, and control Church property.

The Protestant Reformers of the 16th century took up many of Marsilius's ideas (see Volume Three). Roman Catholic historians have called Marsilius a forerunner of Martin Luther and John Calvin.

2. The Great Schism (1378-1417)

The papacy finally returned to Rome in 1377 under Pope Gregory XI (1370-78); the great Italian mystic, Catherine of Siena (see section 6), inspired him to make the move. Gregory died the following year. The French cardinals would gladly have gone back to Avignon, but the Roman population was determined to keep the papacy in Rome and demanded an Italian pope. Pressurised by a mob, the cardinals elected Urban VI (1378-89), an Italian who wanted to liberate the papacy from French control. However, a few months after Urban's election, 12 of the 16 cardinals declared that the election was null and void, because it had been carried out under threat of popular violence. They chose another Frenchman as pope – Clement VII (1378-94). Clement and his cardinals returned to Avignon and set up court there. Urban VI stayed in Rome.

There were now two rival popes. This had happened before, when an Emperor had set up a rival pope for political reasons, or when aristocratic factions in Rome had put up opposing candidates (until the Hildebrandine reformers had placed the right of electing a pope in the hands of the cardinals). However, this time the two popes had both been elected by the Church itself – by the same body of cardinals. The two rival popes, Urban VI and Clement VII, excommunicated each other. Since there was no higher authority in the Church above a pope who had been elected by the cardinals, there was no power that could choose between them. This rending asunder of the Catholic Church is known as the "Great Schism" (not to be confused with the great East–West schism of 1054). Catholic Europe was split down the middle. The Roman pope, Urban VI, won the support of northern and central Italy, England, the Scandinavian countries, and most of Germany. The Avignonese pope, Clement VII, had the backing of France, Spain, southern Italy, Scotland, and some parts of Germany. Urban VI died in 1389, and the Roman line of popes carried on with Boniface XI (1389-1404), Innocent VII (1404-1406) and Gregory XII (1406-15). In Avignon, Clement VII was succeeded by Benedict XIII (1394-1417).

If the Avignonese captivity had damaged the reputation of the papacy, the Great Schism caused it to sink even lower. The visible unity of the Catholic Church was broken. And the situation dragged on for nearly 40 years. In France, during the reign of the mad King Charles VI (1380-1422), the Schism provoked his nobles to issue in Charles's name in 1398 a royal document called the *Subtraction of Obedience*, in which the French monarchy took over all papal powers within the French kingdom: the king of France would now appoint all French bishops and receive the taxes they had previously paid to the pope. France withdrew the *Subtraction* in 1403, but it had created quite a sensation while it lasted.

Nor did the anti-papal agitation die away. In 1407 the French struck again, setting forth a document entitled *The Liberties of the Gallican Church* ("Gallican" is the Latin word for "French"), which rejected the pope's authority over all secular and political affairs, restricting it to purely spiritual things. Here were the foundations of "Gallicanism" – the belief that the French Church was independent of the papacy in matters of internal organisation, although accepting the pope's right to define doctrinal and moral matters. Gallicanism would cause serious problems for the papacy in France in the 17th century. Meanwhile, in the 15th century, it was painfully obvious that the Great Schism was stirring up feelings of autonomy in the Churches of the Catholic nations, thus threatening the universal authority of the papacy.

In these circumstances, the minds of many loyal and sincere Churchmen began to feel that the answer to the scandal of the Great Schism must be found in an ecumenical Council of the whole Catholic Church – and in making the papacy subject to the Council.

3. The conciliar movement

Those who wanted to end the Great Schism and reform the Church by placing the papacy under the authority of an ecumenical Council were called "conciliarists" (from the Latin *concilium*, "council"), and their efforts at reform are known as "the conciliar movement". The movement began in Paris University, and its two outstanding leaders were the French theologians **Peter d'Ailly** (1350-1420) and *John Gerson* (1363-1429). D'Ailly, a celebrated preacher, was rector of the college of Navarre on the borderlands between France and Spain. In 1389 he became chancellor of Paris University. Gerson, who studied under d'Ailly in Navarre, succeeded him as chancellor of Paris University in 1395, and was famous both as a preacher and a writer on the Christian life. Gerson also founded the branch of Catholic doctrine known as "Josephology" – the systematic study of the life of Joseph, the Virgin Mary's husband, and of his role in the history of salvation. Both men were zealous disciples of William of Ockham and his neo-Pelagianism in their theology. Another great conciliarist writer was the profound German thinker, **Nicholas of Cusa** (1401-64), who differed from the neo-Pelagian d'Ailly and Gerson in being a faithful disciple of Augustine, as well as an admiring student of Pseudo-Dionysius, Bonaventura and Eckhart.[7] Cusa, lecturer in canon law at Cologne University and (from 1450) bishop of Brixen (northern Italy), was one of the most learned men of the 15th century – a genius at mathematics, astronomy, geography (he produced the first geographical map of Europe), history, and philosophy.

D'Ailly, Gerson, and Cusa taught that the Catholic Church was superior to the Roman Church, and that infallibility did not belong to the papacy, but to the Church as a whole, represented by an ecumenical Council (by "ecumenical Council" they were referring only to a council of the whole Western Catholic Church – for most of the conciliarists, the East no longer counted after the schism of 1054). Church authority, they argued, rested ultimately in the entire body of believers, to whom even the pope was accountable. The Catholic Church bestowed authority on the papacy, to be exercised for the Church's good; if a pope abused his authority, an ecumenical Council could depose him. Even within the Roman Church, authority did not belong to the pope alone, but to the pope and the cardinals together; the cardinals had the power to restrain an erring pope, and in a crisis they could summon an ecumenical Council on their own authority. These conciliar views were not entirely new; William of Ockham and Marsilius of Padua had already said most if not all the things that d'Ailly, Gerson, and Cusa were now saying. However, Ockham and Marsilius had put their anti-papal ideas forward on behalf of the Holy Roman Empire in its political conflict with the papacy. D'Ailly, Gerson, and Cusa gave conciliarism a fresh cutting edge by propagating it in the name of the Church, at a time when (due to the Schism) there was no effective papacy.

The first attempt to end the Great Schism by an ecumenical Council took place in 1409 at the Council of Pisa (north-western Italy). The Council was summoned by the cardinals acting on their own authority. It deposed both rival popes, Gregory XII

---

7. For Pseudo-Dionysius, see Volume One, Chapter 12, section 3. For Bonaventura, see Chapter 7, section 3. For Eckhart, see below, section 6.

(Rome) and Benedict XIII (Avignon), and asserted that ecumenical councils were superior to the papacy. The Council then elected a new pope, Alexander V (1409-10). Unfortunately, this meant that there were now *three* rival popes! England and France acknowledged the new Pisan pope, Alexander V, but Italy and much of Germany continued to support Gregory XII of Rome, while Spain and Scotland stayed loyal to Benedict XIII of Avignon.

In 1414-18 the Council of Constance (in north-eastern Switzerland) made another attempt to end the Schism. This time it was the Holy Roman Emperor **Sigismund** (1410-37) who summoned the Council. Sigismund acted in alliance with Pope John XXIII (1410-15), the successor to Alexander V who had been elected by the Council of Pisa. However, once the Council of Constance met, it deposed John XXIII for scandalous misconduct, and persuaded Pope Gregory XII of Rome to resign. The Avignonese Pope Benedict XIII proved stubborn, and refused to step down; but Sigismund persuaded Benedict's backers, Spain and Scotland, to disown him. The Council then officially deposed Benedict in 1417. Then the cardinals, together with representatives of the nations present, elected the Italian cardinal, Colonna, as the new pope; he assumed the name Martin V (1417-31). Finally the Council decreed that a new Council should meet in five years' time, then another in seven years, and then once every 10 years.

The Council of Constance was revolutionary. It had ended the Great Schism, but only by subjecting the papacy to the authority of an ecumenical Council. It seemed that the conciliarists had demolished the absolute papal monarchy of Hildebrand and Innocent III, and replaced it by a more limited, constitutional, democratic form of Church government. However, the new pope, Martin V, after ascending the papal throne, abandoned whatever conciliarist convictions he may have had, and there was much friction between him and the next two ecumenical Councils at Pavia-Siena (1423-24) and Basel (1431-49). Martin V died only months after the Council of Basel (north-western Switzerland) opened; *Eugenius IV* (1431-47) succeeded him.

Eugenius tried to adjourn the Council, but it refused to disband and declared its own superiority over him as pope. The Council then began a great programme of administrative and moral reforms. It appeared that Pope Eugenius was captive to the Council.

However, Eugenius turned the tables completely in 1437 by removing the Council to the north-eastern Italian city of Ferrara, where he received the Byzantine Emperor John VIII (1425-48), the patriarch of Constantinople, Joseph II (1416-39), and other delegates of Eastern Orthodoxy. The Byzantines wanted to negotiate a union with the Catholic Church in return for Western military support against the Ottoman Turks. The Council at Basel was split; a minority followed the pope to Ferrara. In 1439 Eugenius moved the Council again, to Florence (south of Ferrara). He successfully concluded a union with the Orthodox, the "Union of Florence", which sent his personal prestige soaring.[8] The Council at Basel reacted rather foolishly by deposing Eugenius and electing a new pope, Felix V (1439-49). This act dealt a mortal blow to the influence of the conciliarists; they were seen as plunging the Church into schism again. Nicholas of Cusa, the distinguished conciliar thinker, was so disgusted by the Council's antics that he went over to Pope Eugenius and spent the rest of his life as a committed servant of the papacy. Indeed, more and more members of the Council defected to Eugenius. Eventually, what was left of the Council dissolved itself in 1449.

This marked the end of the conciliar movement. The papacy had triumphed. In fact, the Orthodox Churches of the East scorned the agreement its delegates had made with Pope Eugenius, but it had served Eugenius's purposes well. He had re-established the papacy as the true leader of Western Catholicism. The conciliar theory lived on in the Church, but the incredible incompetence of the conciliarists at Basel had ruined any hope of making the Catholic Church into a more democratic institution.

---

8. For an account of the Union of Florence, see Chapter 9.

4. Heresy: John Wyclif and the Lollards

During the Avignonese captivity and the Great Schism, a new and potentially deadly challenge to the papacy arose in England. It came from a theologian at Oxford University by the name of *John Wyclif* (1330-84), a native of Yorkshire in northern England. His contemporaries tell us that Wyclif was a thin man who never enjoyed good health. He had an open, honest, forthright character which made him precious to his fellow countrymen, and was gifted with a fearlessly independent and questing mind, one of the finest of its age. When dealing with abuses in the Church, he also possessed a painfully harsh way of speaking and writing, which (even so) never sank into rudeness or crudeness. Wyclif's only obvious defects were his "pluralism" and "absenteeism" – that is, accepting appointment as parish priest in several churches at the same time, and receiving payment for spiritual services which he mostly failed to perform. This was a common enough practice at the time; and "curates" (assistants to a priest) would have carried out the priest's duties.

After studying theology at Oxford, where he achieved fame as a lecturer in theology and philosophy in the 1360s, Wyclif became a religious advisor to the court of the English king, Edward III (1327-77). Wyclif had developed theological views which the English monarchy and nobility found useful in their conflict with the papacy; this conflict revolved around the papacy's claim to own England, based on the fact that King John had surrendered England to Pope Innocent III in 1213.[9] Wyclif put forward a doctrine of "dominion" or "lordship", according to which God was the only source of true authority. God had delegated a portion of His authority over secular things to the state, said Wyclif, and over spiritual things to the Church. However, human rulers could exercise this delegated authority only on condition that they served God faithfully. If they did not, they lost their right to lordship. Therefore, Wyclif taught, if bishops failed to live pure and blameless lives, the state (which had dominion over secular things) was entitled to strip them of their property

---

9. See Chapter 8, section 1.

and possessions. This idea appealed to the English nobility, who were only too eager to seize the vast wealth and property of the English Church.

John Wyclif (1330-84)

Bishop Courtney of London summoned Wyclif to appear before his tribunal in London in February 1377 to answer for his views, but the protection of King Edward III's younger son, John of Gaunt, prevented Courtney from harming Wyclif. In May 1377, Pope Gregory XI (1370-78) summoned Wyclif to appear in Rome within 30 days, charged with no fewer than 19 deadly errors; Wyclif refused to go. (King Edward III died in June 1377; his young grandson Richard II, the son of Edward III's deceased eldest son, succeeded to the throne.) When archbishop Sudbury of Canterbury tried to put Wyclif on trial in January 1378, a mob of London citizens who supported Wyclif broke up the meeting. At this point Wyclif was in favour with the court and nobility, and a popular hero. There seems during this period to have been a widespread hostility among Englishmen to the higher clergy. Ordinary priests, friars and laypeople alike denounced them as corrupt, greedy and immoral. English writers of that time – such as **William Langland** (born 1332, died around 1400), who took "minor orders" in the Church[10] and wrote the poem *Piers the Ploughman,* and the court poet Geoffrey Chaucer (1344-1400), who wrote the more famous *Canterbury Tales* – certainly paint a rather unedifying picture of English Church life in general. Wyclif rode on the back of this popular anticlerical mood.[11]

When the Great Schism broke out on the death of Pope Gregory XI in March 1378, Wyclif's theology began to become more radical. He published a book called *The Truth of Holy Scripture,* in which he argued that the Bible was the only source of Christian doctrine, by which believers must test all the teachings of the Church, including the early Church fathers, the papacy and ecumenical Councils. All Christians should read the Bible, so it must be translated from the Latin of the Vulgate into the native languages of the various nations.

Wyclif's views here were quite revolutionary. In the Middle Ages in Western Europe, people had come to regard the Bible as the clergy's book; priests and theologians alone could interpret it correctly and teach laypeople what it meant. The Catholic Church looked with great suspicion, even outright hostility, on the idea that a layperson should study the Bible for himself. The French council of Toulouse in 1229 had actually forbidden the laity to read the Bible, either in the Latin of the Vulgate (all

---

10. There were four minor orders in the Western Church – doorkeepers, lectors, exorcists, and acolytes. Doorkeepers were church caretakers; lectors read out the Scriptures in services; exorcists laid hands on and prayed for catechumens and those thought to be either demon-possessed or mentally disturbed; acolytes assisted priests and deacons at the altar.

11. "Anticlerical" means "opposed to the clergy".

educated people could understand Latin), or in a translation into their native tongue. What chiefly prompted the Church to oppose Bible-study by the laity was the anti-Catholic interpretations of Scripture made by the various dissenting movements (Cathars, Waldensians, *etc.*).[12]

Despite this official hostility to lay Bible reading, however, some scholars had made a number of translations of the whole Bible or parts of it into the native languages of Western Europe. One of Wyclif's arguments for translating the Bible into English was that it had already been translated into French.[13] Not that translating it into English solved all the problems: most ordinary people in England (and other Western European countries) were illiterate – they could not read at all! However, if the Bible was translated into their native tongue, they could at least listen to the Bible being read out to them, even if they could not read themselves.

Later in 1378, Wyclif wrote another important book entitled *On the Church*. This revealed him as a student and interpreter of Augustine of Hippo (Wyclif had studied under Thomas Bradwardine, the great English Augustinian).[14] Wyclif defined the Church, not in terms of an outward organisation controlled by papacy and priesthood, but as the whole body of the elect, those eternally predestined to salvation by the pure grace of God. And if from the viewpoint of eternity the Church was the elect, on earth at any given point in time it was the entire company of true believers in every land. The Church was thus a spiritual and invisible body, rooted in God's eternal predestination, infallibly known to God alone, and its head was not the pope but Christ

---

12. For the Cathars and Waldensians, see Chapter 8, section 3.

13. It was only in the 1360s that English started to become the national language of England's ruling and educated classes. From 1066 onwards it had been French, owing to the influence of the Norman Conquest, when William the Conqueror and his French-speaking nobles had invaded and conquered England.

14. For Bradwardine, see Chapter 7, section 3, under the heading *William of Ockham*.

Himself. The pope, Wyclif said, could be the head only of the outward and visible church that existed in the city of Rome, which was made up of both the elect and the non-elect.

In 1379, Wyclif wrote *The Power of the Pope*. Here he argued that the papacy was of human not divine origin, and denied that the pope had any authority over any secular government. If a particular pope imitated the apostle Peter by living a holy and humble life, he could then claim to exercise Peter's authority; but a pope who did not follow Christ was Antichrist. Later Wyclif declared that all popes, not just the bad ones, were Antichrist. Then in 1380 came his boldest stroke: he attacked the Catholic doctrine of holy communion in his *On the Eucharist*. Wyclif rejected transubstantiation and went back to the earlier views of Augustine and Ratramnus.[15] The bread and wine of communion, Wyclif argued, remained bread and wine in their own inner nature – their "substance" was not miraculously changed. However, Christ's flesh and blood were truly present in the bread and wine in a spiritual manner. Wyclif used the following illustration: the soul of a human being is truly present in his body; yet if an animal ate a man's body, the animal's mouth would not thereby consume the man's soul. Likewise in holy communion, Wyclif taught, the believer (and only the believer) truly feeds on Jesus Christ's body and blood as he eats the bread and drinks the wine; however, he does not receive Christ's life-giving flesh in a crude physical way into his mouth, but spiritually into his soul by faith. The true view of the eucharist, Wyclif argued, had vanished from the Western Church since the 11th century, but was still preserved in the Eastern Orthodox Church.[16]

---

15. For Ratramnus, see Chapter 2, section 4, under the heading *Radbertus, Ratramnus, and the communion controversy.*

16. The Eastern Orthodox believed in the real presence of Christ in the bread and wine (more strongly than Wyclif did), but not in the Western theory of transubstantiation. It was this theory that Wyclif was basically attacking, with its philosophical distinction (derived from Aristotle) between "substance" and "accidents", and its idea that the accidents of bread and wine could remain when their substance no longer existed. See Chapter 7, section 3, under *Thomas Aquinas*, for the theory of transubstantiation.

This was not the only appeal Wyclif made to the Eastern Church; he also held it up as an example in other matters, *e.g.* allowing the clergy to marry. Thus John Wyclif began the great tradition of Western reformers using the Eastern Church as a weapon with which to attack the corruptions of Rome. It was a clever strategy. For in many disputed matters, if Rome claimed that it had the ancient practice of the Church on its side, a reformer could simply point to the Eastern Orthodox and say, "But they are as ancient as you, and they don't do this or believe this!"

By Catholic standards, Wyclif's denial of transubstantiation had made him into a dangerous heretic, and the English court and nobility (including John of Gaunt) broke off their support for him. Oxford University also turned against him, expelling his followers. Wyclif retired to Lutterworth in the English midlands, where he was the parish priest. He spent the last three years of his life writing popular pamphlets, in which he set out his views vigorously and effectively in the English language, and several academic works in Latin in which he explained his views in a more scholarly way. He organised a team of his disciples to translate the Latin Vulgate Bible into English, a task not finished until after Wyclif's death.

The first of these translations (the first complete English Bible) appeared in 1384; it was a very stiff and literal translation of the Vulgate. Wyclif's secretary **John Purvey** (1353-1428) produced a second version in 1396, with a preface by Purvey in which he defended the right of lay Christians to have God's Word in their native tongue. Purvey's translation was much more popular than the 1384 version (its use of the English language was more natural); it had a wide circulation in the period between its appearance and the Protestant Reformation in the 16th century.[17] Wyclif also sent out preachers to proclaim the Gospel, and provided sermons for them. For Wyclif, the essence

---

17. Over 235 copies of the Purvey Bible have survived. This is remarkable, considering that they are all hand-written; the printing press was not invented until about 1450, and even then no printer dared to print Purvey's English Bible, for fear of being branded a heretic.

of the ordained ministry was preaching the Word, rather than celebrating the sacraments; it was preaching that made unbelievers into true Christians, and it was preaching above all that built Christians up in the faith by helping them to understand what it meant.

Wyclif died in 1384, and was buried in the Lutterworth church graveyard. 34 years later the Church authorities dug up his body, burnt it for heresy, and threw its ashes into the river Swift. Protestants have hailed Wyclif as "the morning star of the Reformation".

Wyclif's followers were called Wycliffites, or "Lollards" (a term of abuse which probably means "mumblers" – Catholics had already applied it to Beguines and Beghards in the Netherlands).[18] The Lollards became the English equivalent of the Waldensians. They grew throughout the closing years of the 14th century during the reign of King Richard II (1377-99). In 1395, a group of Lollard members of parliament published a manifesto called *The Twelve Conclusions*, which denounced the English Church's bondage to the papacy, advocated the marriage of the clergy, and condemned transubstantiation, prayers for the dead, pilgrimages, and the holding of political office by bishops.

However, in 1399, a political revolution brought a new dynasty to the English throne, the family of Lancaster; and in an attempt to win the Church's favour, the first Lancastrian king, Henry IV (1399-1413), passed a new law which, for the first time, made the burning of heretics legal in England. This savage law was aimed against the Lollards.[19] Persecution became fierce under King Henry V (1413-22), owing to Henry's conflict with a leading Lollard, Sir John Oldcastle (1378-1417), a soldier, member of parliament, and important landowner, otherwise known by his title of "Lord Cobham". The Church courts convicted Oldcastle of Wycliffite heresy in 1413 and sentenced him to death, but he escaped from prison and organised a Lollard

---

18. For the Beguines and Beghards, see Chapter 8, section 4.

19. Ironically, Henry IV was the son of John of Gaunt who had been Wyclif's greatest protector.

conspiracy to kidnap Henry in 1414. The king discovered and crushed the plot. Oldcastle escaped again, but Henry finally caught and executed him in 1417.

Oldcastle's rebellion destroyed whatever support for Lollardy may have been left among the English ruling classes. Henceforth it would be a movement among ordinary people, completely outside the political establishment. Like the Waldensians, the Lollards became a secret underground sect. They were found mainly in London and the surrounding areas in southern England; it was a family-based heresy, passed on from father to son. Despite persecution, the Lollards survived until the Protestant Reformation, and in many ways helped to prepare the way for it by circulating Lollard tracts and the Bible in English. When the Reformation came to England, the Lollards were its earliest supporters, and they soon merged into the mainstream of English Protestantism.

5. Revolution: John Huss and the Hussites
Wyclif's ideas had a far greater success in the Holy Roman Empire than they did in England. King Richard II of England had married Anne of Luxembourg, the sister of the king of Bohemia in the east of the Empire (today Bohemia is known as the Czech Republic). This brought about close relations between England and Bohemia, at the very time when Wyclif and the early Lollards were active and flourishing. A number of Bohemian students studied theology at Oxford University and took Wyclif's views and writings with them back to Bohemia, especially to the University of Prague, Bohemia's capital city. There was already a religious reform movement in Bohemia, aimed at purifying the Church from worldliness and returning to the Bible. Wyclif's ideas spread rapidly in such a setting. There was no effective opposition from a discredited papacy: this was the period of the Great Schism.

The most outstanding of the Bohemian reformers was *John Huss* (1372-1415), preacher at the Bethlehem chapel in Prague from 1402, and rector of Prague University from 1409. Huss studied and greatly admired Wyclif's writings – some of Huss's own works reproduce Wyclif's almost word-for-word. However, he was more moderate than Wyclif in his criticisms of prevailing conditions in the Catholic Church; Huss, for instance, continued to accept the doctrine of transubstantiation. The campaign for reform which Huss championed took on the features of a Bohemian nationalist movement, with the support of the Bohemian King Wenceslas (1373-1419), the Bohemian nobility, Prague University, and ordinary Bohemians. This nationalism sprang from the fact that Bohemians belonged to the Slavic race, and wanted to assert their Slavic identity against the overwhelmingly German character of the Holy Roman Empire.

John Huss (1372-1415)

Dark clouds began gathering around Huss in 1411 when he launched an attack on indulgences, declaring them useless since God Himself bestowed His forgiveness freely on all who truly repented. Pope John XXIII (1410-15), the claimant to the papal throne supported by Bohemia during the Great Schism, was stung into taking action; he was himself selling indulgences on a massive scale to finance a war against his rival, Pope Gregory XII (1406-15). John excommunicated Huss and threatened to place Prague under an interdict. To save the city, Huss retired from Prague into southern Bohemia, protected by friendly Bohemian nobles. He continued to propagate his views, notably in two important books, *Concerning the Church*, and *Exposition of the Faith, the Ten Commandments, and the Lord's Prayer*.

Huss's assault on the theology of indulgences made enemies for him in Bohemia, especially in Prague University. Many who had supported his demands for moral and spiritual reform drew back when he started attacking basic doctrines of the Catholic Church. Two religious parties now came into being in Bohemia, a traditionalist Catholic group and the Hussites (although for a long time Huss and his followers were called "Wycliffites"). The quarrel between the two parties centred on their doctrine of the Church. Huss argued that the Church was the entire body of the elect in all ages, known to God alone, who had predestined them to belong to Himself by His free grace; and of this Church, Christ alone was the head, not the pope. Popes were not infallible, said Huss; they had erred many times. One of Huss's arguments for denying the pope's supremacy over the Church was that the Eastern Orthodox were true Christians who managed to exist perfectly well without the papacy – another example of a Western reformer appealing over the pope's head to the East (as Wyclif had done). Huss further taught that Christians should not follow or obey immoral and unworthy clergy. The Christian secular rulers of the state should step in and reform the Church, if the Church was not willing to reform itself. Finally, Huss also accepted Wyclif's view that preaching, not celebrating the sacraments, was the true heart of the ordained ministry. To traditional Catholics, of course, these Hussite views were diabolical heresy.

When the reforming Council of Constance met in 1414, the religious turmoil in Bohemia was one of the issues it had to settle. The Council summoned Huss to appear before it. Huss knew he was in danger of being condemned and burnt as a heretic; his theology was unacceptable even to the conciliarist reformers like John Gerson who controlled the Council. However, Huss was given a promise of safe-conduct by the Holy Roman Emperor Sigismund (1410-37), brother of Bohemian King Wenceslas. Huss therefore went to Constance. But the Council ignored the safe-conduct and threw Huss in prison almost immediately on his arrival. He was kept captive for six months in the most horrific conditions which destroyed his health – he became subject to headaches, fever, bleeding, and vomiting. While Huss languished in prison, his disciples in Prague started giving the wine as well as the bread to the laity in holy communion: an act of open defiance of Catholic practice (Huss was in full agreement with what his followers did).

Finally, in June 1415, the Church authorities brought the sick Bohemian reformer before the Council, which refused to allow him to defend himself, bullied him mercilessly for three days in an attempt to force him to renounce his "heresies", and finally condemned him and deposed him from the priesthood. In a humiliating ceremony, six bishops stripped off Huss's priestly vestments, put on his head a cap covered in pictures of red demons, and solemnly committed Huss's soul to the devil. "And I," said Huss, "commit myself to my most gracious Lord Jesus." The Council then handed Huss over to Emperor Sigismund, the man who had promised him safe-conduct; Sigismund's soldiers burnt Huss at the stake on July 6th 1415. Huss died with serene courage, refusing a last minute offer of pardon if he would abandon his beliefs: "I shall die with joy today in the faith of the Gospel which I have preached."

Huss's martyrdom created an uproar in Bohemia. He became a popular national hero. The Bohemians were further enraged when, at Emperor Sigismund's insistence, the Council also burnt Huss's foremost disciple, the noble and learned layman ***Jerome of Prague*** (1371-1416), in 1416. Jerome's martyrdom made an even greater impression than Huss's. An eyewitness, Poggio Bracciolini, who was not a Hussite, wrote:

> It was wonderful to see with what words, how persuasively, with what arguments, what a spirit, and what calmness Jerome answered his enemies, and how fairly he put his case. He stood there utterly fearless, not just scorning death but seeking it. He went to his fate with a joyful and willing spirit. When the executioners wanted to start the fire behind his back so that Jerome would not see it, he told them, "Come here and light the fire in front of me. Had it frightened me, I would not have come to this place."

Many onlookers wept, overcome by the spectacle of the martyr's peaceful boldness.

Bohemia was now smouldering with rage, ready to blaze up against any further provocation. The spark which ignited the blaze came in 1419, when King Wenceslas died. Wenceslas's brother, the Holy Roman Emperor Sigismund, should by rights have succeeded to the Bohemian throne, but he was the most hated man in Bohemia, stained with the holy blood of Huss and Jerome. Passions boiled over, and civil war erupted between the nation and its monarch. Pope Martin V came to Sigismund's aid, declaring a crusade against the heretical Bohemians, but to the astonishment and fury of their foes, the Bohemians defeated the crusading armies again and again. Two of the greatest generals of the Middle Ages, the one-eyed *John Ziska* (1360-1424) and the priest *Procopius the Great* (1380-1434), led the Bohemian armies to one stunning victory after another, carrying the war from Bohemia into Germany. It seemed that not all the armed might of Catholic Europe could crush the Hussite troops.

Meanwhile, the Hussites themselves divided into two parties:

(i)   The *Utraquists* (from the Latin *utraque*, "both"), or as they were also called, the *Calixtines* (from the Latin *calix*, "cup"). They demanded that the laity receive both the bread and the wine in communion, and insisted that they be allowed to use a Bohemian translation of the Bible in Hussite worship, and that their priests be allowed to preach the Hussite gospel freely in Bohemia. However, they wanted to remain within the Catholic Church. The Utraquist centre of influence was Prague.

(ii) The *Taborites* (after the Biblical mount Tabor, a name the Taborites gave to a hill in southern Bohemia where they gathered in great numbers in 1419). They were much more radical in their rejection of Catholic doctrines and practices than the Utraquists were (*e.g.* Taborites denied transubstantiation, the invocation of saints, and prayers for the dead), and wanted to break away entirely from the Catholic Church. They were also politically more radical than the Utraquists; Taborites rejected private property and held everything in common, on the pattern of Acts 2:44-45. The Bohemian military chiefs, Ziska and Procopius, were both Taborites.

Despite their differences, Utraquists and Taborites united against the Catholic crusading armies. By 1433, after 14 years of fierce warfare, it had become clear that the Catholics could not defeat the Hussites on the field of battle. So for the first time in its history, the Catholic Church was forced to sit down and negotiate with a dissenting group. The Council of Basel managed to reach a compromise agreement with the Hussites, called the Four Articles of Prague. These Articles stated that the Hussites would remain within the Catholic Church, on condition that four principles were recognised: (i) Hussites must be allowed to receive both bread and wine in communion; (ii) Hussite priests could preach the Word of God freely without interference; (iii) all clergy were under obligation to live simple, humble lives, devoted to the Gospel, and not be rich political figures; (iv) mortal sins should be punished by the secular courts. This compromise caused open warfare between the Utraquists, who accepted the Articles, and the Taborites, who rejected them. A combined

Utraquist and Catholic army decisively crushed the Taborites at the battle of Lipany in 1434; the Taborite leader, Procopius the Great, was killed.

There were further struggles, but the end result of the Hussite wars was that most Bohemians (the Utraquists) remained within the Catholic Church, although as a distinct body with their own Hussite traditions and practices. Some, led by Constantine Anglicus, who described himself as "a humble priest of Christ", entered into negotiations with Constantinople to be admitted into the Orthodox Church, but the fall of Constantinople to the Turks in 1453 brought this intriguing episode to an end. A significant minority of Hussites stayed loyal to the defeated Taborite cause, linked up with some of the Waldensians, and remained outside the national Bohemian Church; from about 1458, they formed a separate body called the "United Bohemian Brotherhood". By 1500, the Brotherhood had three or four hundred congregations in Bohemia and Moravia, with their own confession of faith and their own Hussite hymns.

Relations were always uneasy between Hussite Bohemia and the papacy. With the advent of the Protestant Reformation in the 16th century, most Bohemians welcomed it, and the Hussite movement flowed into the mightier ocean of Protestantism.

6. The 14th century Catholic mystics and the "devotio moderna"

The 14th century saw a great flowering of mysticism in the Catholic Church. A new thirst for direct personal experience of God burned in many souls. In Germany, three great Dominican preachers, **Eckhart von Hochheim** (1260-1327), usually called "Meister (Master) Eckhart", and his two disciples *Johann Tauler* (1300-1361) and **Heinrich Suso** (1295-1360), promoted this mysticism. Eckhart, Tauler, and Suso, three of the best-loved mystics in Christian history, pastored Dominican nuns and Beguines in western Germany; the influence of their preaching and writings gave rise to a wider group of German and Swiss mystics, who called themselves "the Friends of God". It was someone from the "Friends of God" movement who wrote the anonymous *Theologica Germanica* ("German Theology"), one of the most profound and beautiful of Christian mystical writings. In the Netherlands, the leading mystic was **Jan van Ruysbroeck** (1293-1381), head of an Augustinian monastery in Groenendael. His most influential writings were his *The Spiritual Espousals* and *The Sparkling Stone*. Italy's contribution to the mystical flowering came through **Catherine of Siena** (1347-80), a Dominican "tertiary"[20] from Siena in north-western Italy, who acted as spiritual guide to an admiring circle of followers. She wrote a mystical treatise called *Divine Dialogue* and some 400 letters of spiritual counsel. Catherine also involved herself in the highest levels of Church politics during the Avignonese captivity, corresponding with popes and many other concerned Catholics, and journeying across Italy and France, trying to bring the captivity to an end (see section 2).

In England, mysticism found expression in the life and writings of a number of hermits – **Richard Rolle** (1300-49) of Hampole in Yorkshire (northern England), author of *The Fire of Love*; **Walter Hilton** (died 1396) of Thurgarton in Nottinghamshire (central England), author of *The Scale of Perfection*; and most famous of all, the lady **Julian of Norwich** (1342-1416), an anchoress from Norwich in Norfolk (on the English east coast), author of the highly imaginative and enchanting *Revelations of Divine Love* (see the end of the Chapter for a quotation). The English mysticism of this period also appeared in an anonymous treatise called *The Cloud of Unknowing*, which put the theology and spirituality of Pseudo-Dionysius the Areopagite into popular 14th century English. Finally we have **Margery Kempe** (1373-1440), a lay person from Bishop's Lynn in Norfolk and friend of Julian of Norwich. Her *Book of Margery Kempe* recounted Margery's remarkable visions and her international pilgrimages to Rome, Jerusalem, Compostela (in Spain), Wilsnack (in Germany), and Canterbury.

---

20. A tertiary is a lay person who places himself or herself under the spiritual discipline of a monastic order but takes no monastic vows.

These Catholic mystics of the 14th century shared a number of distinctive qualities. They used the native language of their country (rather than Latin), and aimed their ministries at ordinary lay people as well as scholars and clergy. They emphasised the centrality of preaching and teaching in the Church, the high value of studying and knowing the New Testament Scriptures, and the importance of practical holiness in daily living. Their whole approach to Christianity was eminently Christ-centred; Christ, they stressed, was always immediately available to the believing soul – He was not "locked up" inside the priesthood and sacraments.

The teaching of the mystics often brought them under great suspicion from Church authorities, who feared that mysticism would lead people to despise the official doctrines and structures of the Catholic Church. Pope John XXII, for instance, condemned Eckhart in 1329 (two years after his death). Eckhart, along with some other mystics, sometimes taught (or appeared to teach) that there was an uncreated and eternal "divine spark" in the human soul; orthodox theologians rejected this idea because it destroyed the distinction between Creator and creature. However, Eckhart did not mean to offer a deliberate alternative to Catholic doctrine. He admitted that he had used unhelpful language, and tried to give orthodox explanations of those parts of his teaching which had offended the theologians.[21] He and the vast majority of Catholic mystics were loyal members of the Catholic Church, and had no intention of undermining its authority. Even so, it is interesting that the German mystics deeply influenced the great Protestant Reformer, Martin Luther; he praised Johann Tauler's sermons as a source of "pure theology", and himself had the *German Theology* reprinted twice, in 1516 and 1518, with introductions from his own pen. Luther said of the *German Theology*, "I have discovered no book, except the Bible and the writings of Saint Augustine, which has taught me more about God, Christ, human nature, and all things."[22]

---

21. Whether he succeeded is a matter of opinion.

22. For Luther, see Volume Three.

Possessing some similarities with mysticism was the movement known as the *devotio moderna* ("the modern way of serving God"). It began in the Netherlands with **Gerard Groote** (1340-84) of Deventer, a friend and admirer of Jan van Ruysbroeck. Groote's ideal of the religious life was to set up communities of Christian men and Christian women ("brotherhoods" and "sisterhoods") who would live, pray, and follow Christ together, but without becoming monks or nuns; they would work for a living "in the world" and take no monastic vows. These communities proved very popular, and spread throughout the Netherlands and western Germany. In time, the majority of the female communities adopted some form of monastic discipline, but most of the male communities – the "Brothers of the Common Life" – stayed true to Groote's ideals. They devoted much of their energy to copying and distributing religious literature. When the printing press was invented in the mid-15th century, the Brothers turned their attention to teaching boys in publicly funded city schools and also in schools they themselves established.

The "modern way of serving God" was marked by a sense of God's closeness to the individual believer and a focusing of the mind on Christ's life and sufferings as recorded in the Gospels. The most influential and well-known writing to emerge from this spiritual movement was *The Imitation of Christ*, written by **Thomas a Kempis** (1380-1471). Thomas was born in Kempen (north-western Germany); in 1399 he joined the Mount Saint Agnes community, near Zwolle in the Netherlands, where his elder brother John was prior (Mount Saint Agnes was one of the monasteries founded for Brothers of the Common Life who wanted to practise a full monastic life). There, Thomas studied the Bible and the early Church fathers, preached impressive sermons, and wrote a biography of Gerard Groote and many works on the spiritual life, such as *Prayers and Meditations on the Life of Christ*.

Thomas's most famous and enduring work, however, was *The Imitation of Christ*; it has had more readers, and been translated into more languages, than any other Christian book except the Bible itself. Rooted in a deep knowledge of the Scriptures, and bathed in the spirituality of Augustine of Hippo and Bernard of Clairvaux,[23] the *Imitation* is a handbook on how to live a true Christian life. It is simple, direct (it is addressed to "you", the reader), and governed by the twin thoughts of (a) setting the heart on eternal realities and (b) walking with Jesus in every aspect of daily life. Thomas's masterpiece has always found wide acceptance among all Western Christians, including Protestants, despite the strong medieval Catholic emphasis which the *Imitation* places on the mass.

7. The Christian poet: Dante

The period covered by this Chapter embraces the life and work of a man usually ranked as the greatest Christian poet of all time – **Dante Alighieri** (1265-1321). Dante was born in the Italian city of Florence. The first part of his life saw him actively committed to Florentine politics, which proved complex and catastrophic. Although Florence was a Guelf (papalist) city in the conflict between pope and Holy Roman Emperor, the Florentine Guelfs were themselves divided into White and Black Guelfs.[24] Dante was a White Guelf – a papalist, but opposing Pope Boniface VIII's ambitions for secular dominion. In 1302 the Black Guelfs seized power in Florence and exiled the leading White Guelfs, including Dante, who never set foot inside his native city again. He spent the rest of his life wandering across northern Italy, dying of malaria in Ravenna in 1321. Dante's bitter experience of banishment hardened his political views into a more anti-papal form; his treatise *De Monarchia* ("Concerning Monarchy") argued that papacy and Empire were equal in authority, each having its own sphere, and that in civil, secular affairs the Emperors were not subject to papal decrees. An enraged papacy had Dante's book publicly burnt.

Dante's emotional and spiritual life was dominated by a woman – Beatrice Portinari. Just a few months older than

---

23. For Bernard, see Chapter 5, section 3, under *Bernard of Clairvaux and the Second Crusade*.

24. For the term "Guelf", see Chapter 2, section 2, footnote 17.

Beatrice, Dante first met her when they were nine, and then again when they were 18. He was utterly and for ever enchanted by Beatrice's grace and beauty; her image in his mind had a sweetening influence which expelled all impure thoughts. Unfortunately for lovers of romance, Beatrice married another man in 1289, and then died a year later at the age of 25, without enjoying even a single kiss from Dante. Even so, she lived on in Dante's heart and imagination for the rest of his life as the ideal of perfect womanhood. Dante himself married three years after Beatrice's death, but his own wife Gemma had no chance of winning his affections away from his adored Beatrice; in fact, when the Black Guelfs banished him from Florence in 1302, Dante left Gemma behind and never saw her again.

Dante's poetic masterpiece was his *Divine Comedy*, divided into three books – *Inferno*, *Purgatory*, and *Paradise*. It begins with Dante lost in a gloomy forest (symbolising sin), where he meets the great Pagan Roman poet Virgil (70-19 BC), who symbolises human philosophy. Virgil guides Dante through hell and purgatory, where among other suffering souls he sees numerous popes. Leaving purgatory, now cleansed from his own sins, Dante meets his beloved Beatrice, who symbolises the light of divinely revealed truth; she now guides him to the exalted heights which Virgil (philosophy) cannot reach – heaven. For the vision of God, even Beatrice must give place to Bernard of Clairvaux, Dante's most admired saint, who presents him to the Virgin Mary; and through Mary's intercession, Dante receives a glimpse of the Trinity in all its glory.

Students of poetry have generally regarded the *Divine Comedy* as the most glorious Christian poem ever written, the Christian equivalent of Homer's *Iliad*. Its outlook is that of a devout medieval Catholic; Dante was a disciple of Thomas Aquinas in doctrinal matters.[25] However, his imaginative and moving depiction of the central Christian theme – the salvation of the soul from sin by the mercy of God in Christ – has won admiration among believers of every shade of theology; and his hostility

---

25. For Aquinas, see Chapter 7, section 3.

to a corrupt papacy and its pretensions to world dominion has endeared Dante to Protestants.

Important people:

The Church

Pope Boniface VIII (1294-1303)

Dante Alighieri (1265-1321)

Marsilius of Padua (1280-1343)

John Wyclif (1330-84)

William Langland (born 1332, died around 1400)

Gerard Groote (1340-84)

John Huss (1372-1415)

Jerome of Prague (1371-1416)

Pierre d'Ailly (1350-1420)

John Purvey (1353-1428)

John Gerson (1363-1429)

Pope Eugenius IV (1431-47)

Nicholas of Cusa (1401-64)

Thomas a Kempis (1380-1471)[26]

Mystics:

Eckhart von Hochheim (1260-1327)

Richard Rolle (1300-49)

Heinrich Suso (1295-1360)

Johann Tauler (1300-61)

Catherine of Siena (1347-80)

Jan van Ruysbroeck (1293-1381)

Walter Hilton (died 1396)

Julian of Norwich (1342-1416)

Margery Kempe (1373-1440)

---

26. Some would classify Thomas as a mystic. As I have said before, the term is slippery.

Political and military

King Philip the Fair of France (1285-1314)
Holy Roman Emperor Louis the Bavarian (1314-47)
John Ziska (1360-1424)
Procopius the Great (1380-1434)
Holy Roman Emperor Sigismund (1410-37)

Conciliarism: The claims of the Council of Constance

This holy Council of Constance, being an ecumenical Council, lawfully assembled in the Holy Spirit for God's praise and for ending the present schism, for the union and reformation of God's Church in head and members, in order to bring about this reformation more easily, securely and perfectly, ordains and declares and decrees as follows: First, this Council, lawfully assembled, is an ecumenical Council, representing the Catholic Church militant, and has its authority directly from Christ. Everybody, of whatever rank or position, including the pope, is bound to obey this Council in things relating to the faith, the ending of the schism, and a general reformation of the Church in its head and members. Likewise the Council declares that if anyone, of whatever rank, condition or position, including the pope, refuses to obey the commands, statutes, decrees or orders of this holy Council, or of any other holy Council properly assembled, with respect to ending the schism and reforming the Church, he shall be subject to the proper penalty; and if he does not repent, he shall be duly punished; and other tools of justice shall be used, if necessary.

The decree *Sacrosancta*
Council of Constance, 1415

Marsilius of Padua: The papacy and the state

The Roman bishops have taken a title which they declare is theirs – the title "plenitude of power" – by means of which they seek to accomplish their wicked designs. They claim that Christ gave them this title in the person of Saint Peter, since they are the particular successors of that apostle. Through this accursed title, and through the double-talk of cunning arguments which all believers everywhere must always reject as false in every way, the Roman bishops have up till now reasoned falsely, and are still reasoning falsely, and are striving to continue their false reasoning, so that they can put in bondage to themselves all the rulers, peoples, groups and individuals in the world. For they took this title "plenitude of power" under the cloak of piety, charity and mercy, firstly in the sense (apparently) of the universal care of souls, a universal pastorate, and then in the sense of the power to absolve all people from guilt and punishment.

But then they gradually and secretly brought about a great change, and ended up claiming the title "plenitude of power" in the sense of a universal authority and supreme jurisdiction or coercive lordship over all rulers, nations, and secular matters. This change and the arrogant claim resulting from it are based wrongly on their allegorical interpretation of texts.

So that the deceptions of these bishops may now be revealed, I – a herald of truth – urgently declare and say to you kings, princes, nations, tribes, and people of all tongues, that this statement of theirs is most clearly false in every sense, and by it the Roman bishops with their gang of clergymen and cardinals do the greatest injury to you all. They are striving to bring you into bondage to themselves, and they will succeed if you allow this statement to go unchallenged, especially if you let it have the force and validity of law ...

This "plenitude of power" has in the past been used by the Roman bishops always for the worse, and is still being used thus, especially against the [Holy] Roman Emperor and government. On him the Roman bishops can carry out this vicious outrage of enslaving governments to themselves, because discord and strife among [Holy] Roman citizens themselves and against their Emperors have been stirred up in the past, and are still being stirred up and strengthened, by these so-called "bishops" and "most holy fathers" ...

The Roman bishop is not Saint Peter's particular successor by God's direct appointment, nor the successor of any other apostle in a way that gives him superiority over other bishops ...

This treatise will be called *Defensor Pacis*, because it discusses and explains the chief causes by which political peace and tranquillity exist and are preserved, and by which strife arises and is checked and crushed. My treatise reveals the authority, cause, and agreement of divine and human laws and of all coercive governments, which are the standards of human actions, in whose proper free process we enjoy political peace and tranquillity ...

The ruler will also learn that he must do nothing apart from the laws, especially on important matters, without the agreement of the multitude of his citizens, or the law-making assembly. He must not provoke the multitude of citizens and the law-making assembly, for the virtue and authority of government lie in their expressed will ... The multitude of citizens will also learn what it may do to make sure that its ruler, or any other part of the community, does not assume an arbitrary power to enact policies or perform any other political acts which are apart from the laws or against the laws.

Marsilius of Padua

Defensor Pacis, **prologue**

English Church life in the 14th century

A heap of hermits with their hooked staves went to Walsingham [on pilgrimage to a shrine of the Virgin Mary], with their wenches following after. These great long loafers, who loathed work, were clothed in clergy's capes to distinguish them from laymen, and behaved as hermits for the sake of an easy life.

I found the friars there too – all the four orders [Franciscans, Dominicans, Augustinians, and Carmelites] – preaching to the people for what they could get for their bellies. In their greed for fine clothes, they glossed the Gospel to suit themselves. Many of these master friars can dress up as they please, for their money and their merchandise [preaching] march together. For ever since charity has been a business matter, and become confessor-in-chief to absolve wealthy lords, many miracles have happened in a few years; unless the friars and the holy Church hold better together, the worst mischief on the earth is mounting up fast.

There also preached a pardoner [a Church officer who sold indulgences], as if he were a priest. He brought forth a document with bishops' seals on it, and said that he had power to absolve all the people from all broken fasts and broken vows. The laymen believed him and liked his words. They came up kneeling to kiss his documents. He blinded their eyes with his letters of indulgence thrust into their faces, and with his parchment he raked in their rings and broaches. Thus you give your gold to help gluttons, and lend it to louts who live in lechery. If the bishop were a blessed man and worth both his ears, his seal would not be sent to deceive the people. But it is not against the bishop that this boy preaches; for the parish priest and the pardoner part the silver between them – which the poor of the parish would have if it were not for these men.

William Langland
Piers the Plowman, **prologue**

Wyclif's New Testament
[Spelling modernised]

And Jesus, seeing the people, went up into an hill; and when He was set, His disciples came to Him.

And He opened His mouth, and taught them, and said,

Blessed be poor men in spirit, for the kingdom of heavens is theirs.

Blessed be mild men, for they shall wield the earth.

Blessed be they that mourn, for they shall be comforted.

Blessed be they that hunger and thirst [for] righteousness, for they shall be fulfilled.

Blessed be merciful men, for they shall get mercy.

Blessed be they that be of clean heart, for they shall see God.

Blessed be peaceable men, for they shall be called God's children.

Blessed be they that suffer persecution for rightfulness, for the kingdom of heavens is theirs.

Ye shall be blessed, when men shall curse you, and shall pursue you, and shall say all evil against you lying, for me.

Joy ye, and be ye glad, for your meed [reward] is plenteous in
  heavens; for so they have pursued also prophets that were
  before you.

Ye be salt of the earth; that if the salt vanish away, wherein shall
  it be salted? To nothing it is worth over, no but that it be cast
  out, and be defiled of men.

Ye be light of the world; a city set on an hill may not be hid;

Nor men tendeth not a lantern, and putteth it under a bushel,
  but on a candlestick, that it give light to all that be in the
  house.

So shine your light before men, that they see your good works,
  and glorify your Father that is in heavens.

John Huss on the Council of Constance and the papacy: a letter from prison to his faithful followers in Bohemia

I ought to warn you, my well-beloved, not to let yourselves be
alarmed by the sentence of those who have condemned my books
to be burned. Remember that the Israelites burned the writings
of the prophet Jeremiah, without, nevertheless, being able to avoid
the fate which he predicted for them... Two councils of priests
condemned Saint Chrysostom as a heretic; but God made their
lie manifest after the death of him who was surnamed Saint John
of the Golden Mouth.

   Knowing, therefore, these things, let not fear prevent you
from reading my books, and do not deliver them up to my enemies to be burned. Give a response to these preachers who teach
that the Pope is God on earth; that he can sell the sacraments,
as the canon lawyers declare; that he is the head of the Church
in administering it purely; that he is the heart of the Church in
vivifying it spiritually; that he is the source from which springs all
virtue and all good; that he is the sun of the holy Church, the sure
asylum, where it is important that all Christians should find refuge. Behold! already this head is, as it were, severed by the sword;
already this terrestrial god is enchained; already his sins are laid
bare; this never-failing source is dried up – this divine sun is

dimmed – this heart has been torn and branded with reprobation, that no-one should seek an asylum in it. The Council has
condemned its chief, its own head, for having sold indulgences,
bishoprics, and other things... [The Council of Constance deposed Pope John XXIII for scandalous misconduct.]

Truly, already have the malice, abomination, and depravity of
Antichrist been revealed in the Pope and other members of this
Council. The faithful servants of God may now understand these
words of the Saviour, who has said, "When you shall behold the
abomination of desolation foretold by the prophet Daniel," etc.
Truly, the supreme abomination is pride, avarice, and simony
in deserted places, that is, in high ranks in the Church, where
neither goodness nor humility, nor any virtue, are now to be
found, as we now witness in those who are high in honour and
places. Oh! how much I desire to unveil all the iniquities that
I am acquainted with, in order that the faithful servants of God
may keep on their guard against them! But I hope that God
will send after me more vigorous champions; and there are now
already those who will better expose all the cunning tricks of
Antichrist, and who will expose themselves to death for the truth
of our Lord Jesus Christ, who will give unto you and me eternal
blessedness!

I write this letter on the day of Saint John the Baptist, in
prison and in chains, and I bear in mind that Saint John was
beheaded in prison for the word of God.

The reality of God

We should not let ourselves rest content with a god we have
set up in our own thoughts, because when our thought slips
out of our mind, our "god" will slip out too. It is the reality of
God Himself that we desire, and that reality rises far beyond
any human thought or any created thing. When we accept God
as He truly is in His divine being, God in all His inner reality,
then He illuminates all things. Everything then will have the taste
of God; everything will reflect Him. The more a person looks
on everything as being divine in this way – more truly divine
than it is in its own nature – the more God will take pleasure in

that person. This needs hard work and devoted love on our part, a thorough nurturing of our inner life, and a vigilant, sincere, energetic supervision of all a person's attitudes towards things and other people. We cannot gain this by retiring from the world, or fleeing from outward affairs. Instead, a person needs to acquire an internal solitude of spirit. He needs to acquire the art of seeing right into things and finding God there. To obtain this, you will have to exercise yourself spiritually. And lastly, a person should be clothed with the bright presence of God without having to put it on by conscious effort.

Eckhart von Hochheim
Talks of Instruction 6

Divine election

O Lord, most fair and most tender,
    My heart is adrift and alone;
My heart is so weary, so thirsty,
    It thirsts for a joy unknown.
From a child I've followed it, chased it,
    Through wilderness, wood and hill;
I never have seen it or found it –
    Yet I must follow it still.

In the bygone years I sought it
    In the sweet fair things around;
But the more I sought and thirsted,
    The less, O my Lord, I found.
When closest it seemed to my grasping,
    It fled like a vanishing thought.
I never have known what it is, Lord;
    Too well I know what it is not.
"It is I! It is I, the Eternal,
    Who chose you My own to be –
Who chose you before the ages –
    Who chose you eternally!
I stood in the way before you,
    In the ways that you would have gone;

For this is the mark of My chosen –
    They shall be Mine alone."

A poem by Heinrich Suso
[**from Frances Bevan,** *Hymns of Ter Steegen, Suso and Others,*
First Series]

The weary day

"For me to live is Christ." And yet the days
    Are days of toiling men;
We rise at morn, and tread the beaten ways,
    And lay us down again.

Our common need, and weariness, and strife,
    While common days wear on –
How is it that this base, unsightly life
    Can yet be Christ alone?

Then I saw how, before a Master wise,
    A shapeless stone was set.
He said: "In this a form of beauty lies,
    Though none can see it yet.

"When all beside it shall be hewn away,
    That glorious shape shall stand
In beauty of the everlasting Day,
    In the pure virgin Land."

So it is with the homely life around.
    There, hidden, Christ abides:
Still by the single eye for ever found,
    That seeks for none besides.

When hewn and shaped till self no more is found –
    Self, ended at Your cross –
The precious freed from all the vile around
    (No gain, but blessed loss) –

Then Christ alone remains: the former things
> For ever passed away;
And so to Him the heart in gladness sings
> All through the weary day.

A poem by Heinrich Suso

[**from Frances Bevan, *Hymns of Ter Steegen, Suso and Others,***

First Series]

True and false seeking of God

Even though our desires have been focused on God, we can
sometimes be overcome with worry and sadness; we begin to fear
we were not really seeking God at all, and that now all is lost.
That fear may at times be the product of a naturally melancholic
temperament, or it could be the effect of the air or the weather,
or it could even be caused by the devil. We must conquer all these
things with a gentle persistence.

Some people try to conquer these afflictions in a violent way,
by a single blow. But all they do is hurt themselves by causing
such turmoil. Others will go running to get the advice of experts
or those who truly know God. However, no-one can really offer
much help to such folk, and their bewilderment only gets worse.
When a storm like this bursts on the soul, the best thing to do
is act like those who have been caught in a shower; they shelter
themselves under a covering and wait for the storm to end. This
is what we ought to do when we are sure it is God alone we are
truly seeking. When the problem arises, we should disregard it
until we have found peace, waiting for God with a submissive
heart and an uncomplaining self-surrender in our agony. Who
can tell where and when and how God will choose to visit us
with His gifts?

It is a hundred times more blessed to stand uncomplainingly
beneath the shelter of God's will than to seek a heroic state of
virtue and its bloated emotional gratification which we prize
so highly. For when we wait humbly for God, there can be no
keeping hold on our own selfhood, which befalls us very easily
when we experience spiritual passion and comfort. In the grip of
great feelings, our nature claims as its own the gifts of God, and

takes delight in them. But this brings a stain on the soul, because God's gifts are not God. Our delight should be in God Himself, not His gifts.

Johann Tauler
Sermon for the Sunday after Ascension

God's love is greater than our sins

Our Lord, because of His gentle respect for us, does not want His servants to despair, even if they fall into sin frequently and terribly. Our falling does not stop Him loving us. *His* peace and love are always working in us, even though *we* are not always in peace and love. But God wants us to understand that He is the foundation of our whole life in love, and that He is our everlasting protector and our strong safe-keeper against our foes, who are so fierce and so wicked. Alas, our need is all the greater, because by our failures we give our foes so many opportunities! It reveals the royal friendship of our gentle and respectful Lord that He holds on to us with such tenderness when we fall into sin, and that His touch is so sensitive when He shows our sin to us by the soft light of His mercy and grace. When we see ourselves to be so vile, we know that God is angry with us because of our sin. The Holy Spirit then moves us to pray with repentance and a desire to change our lives as best we can, so that we may avert God's displeasure, and find rest for our souls and a peaceful conscience. Then we hope that God has forgiven us our sins.

And indeed He has! And then our Lord in His gentle respect reveals Himself to the soul, joyfully and with a glad countenance, giving the soul a warm welcome as though it had been suffering in a prison. "My beloved," He says, "I am glad that you have come to Me. In all your afflictions I have been with you. Now you can see how much I love you. We are made one in blessedness." So our sins are forgiven through God's merciful grace, and whenever we experience the gracious work of the Holy Spirit and the power of Christ's suffering, God receives our souls with honour and joy, just as they will be received on arriving in heaven ...

From the time these things were first revealed to me, I had often wondered what our Lord meant by it all. More than 15 years later, the answer came to me in my spirit's understanding. "Do you wish to know our Lord's meaning in this? Know it well. Love was His meaning. Who showed it to you? Love. What did He show you? Love. What was His reason for showing it to you? Love. Keep hold of this, and you will more and more understand love. But you will never learn or understand anything else from what He has shown you – only love." Thus I learned that love was our Lord's meaning. I saw very clearly that before God made the world, He loved us, and that His love has never grown cold and never will. In this love, He has performed all His works; in this love, He has made all things to be beneficial to us; in this love, our life is everlasting. We began to exist when God made us; but the love in which He made us never had any beginning, and this eternal love is what gave us our beginning. All this we shall see in God throughout eternity. May Jesus grant this. Amen.

Julian of Norwich

Revelations of Divine Love, **chapters 39, 40 and 86**

Close friendship with Jesus

When Jesus is with us, all is well, and nothing seems hard. But when Jesus is not with us, everything is hard. When Jesus does not speak to our hearts, nothing comforts us. But if Jesus speaks one word, we have great comfort. Did not Mary rise instantly from the place where she wept, when Martha said to her, "The Master has come, and He is asking for you"? Happy the hour when Jesus calls us from tears to spiritual joy! How dry and hard your heart is, without Jesus. How foolish and empty you are, if you desire anything except Jesus. Does this not hurt you more than if you lost the whole world? What can the world give you, without Jesus? To be without Jesus is a dreadful hell. To be with Jesus is a sweet paradise. If Jesus is with you, no enemy can harm you. He who finds Jesus finds a rich treasure, a blessing above every blessing. He who loses Jesus loses so much – more than the whole world. Poorest of all people is the person who lives without Jesus. Richest of all is the person who has the favour of Jesus.

It is a great art to converse with Jesus, and to know Jesus and keep Him is true wisdom. Be a humble and peaceful person, and

Jesus will dwell with you. But if you turn aside to worldly things, you will soon lose the grace of Jesus and cause Him to leave you. And if you make Jesus leave, and lose Him, with whom will you then take refuge? Whom will you then seek as your friend? You cannot live happily without a friend. And if Jesus is not your greatest friend, you will be a very sad and lonely person. How foolish you are, then, to trust or delight in any other. It is better to have the whole world against you, than to give offence to Jesus. Therefore, of all that is precious to you, love Jesus first and foremost.

Thomas a Kempis
The Imitation of Christ, **Book 2, chapter 8**

Glossary

ABBESS

The head of a community of nuns. The word is the feminine form of "abbot".

ABBEY

The dwelling place of a community of monks led by an abbot, or a community of nuns led by an abbess.

ABBOT

The head of a community of monks. From the Aramaic abba, "father".

ADOPTIANISM

The view, current in the West in the 8th and 9th centuries, that Christ was an adopted son of God in His human nature, just as He is the eternal Son of God in His divine nature. This was condemned as a revival of the Nestorian heresy, because it meant logically that there were two sonships, two sons, and therefore two persons, in Christ. See Chapter 2, section 2, under *Religious policy*.

ALBIGENSIANS

Gnostic Cathar heretics who were widespread in southern France. From the town Albi, one of their chief centres of influence. See Chapter 8, section 3.

ANCHORESS

A female hermit. The feminine form of "anchorite".

ANCHORITE

Another word for a hermit. From the Greek *chorizo*, "to separate".

ARISTOTELIANISM

The system of philosophy derived from the Pagan Greek philosopher Aristotle (384-22 BC). Its view of knowledge was influential – that the mind's knowledge of everything (apart from the laws of reason) is mediated to the mind from the external world through the senses. See Chapter 7, section 2.

ATHOS, ATHONITE

Mount Athos in northern Greece is the chief centre of monastic life in Eastern Orthodoxy. Situated on one arm of the Halkidiki peninsula, no women are allowed to set foot there. In its heyday it was home to some 40,000 monks. Athos was particularly influential in the development of hesychasm. See Chapter 3, section 5, and Chapter 9, section 3.

AUGUSTINIAN

(i) Relating to the theology of the early Church father Augustine of Hippo (354-430), especially his understanding of sin and salvation. We can sum it up like this: (a) the whole human race fell in Adam; (b) the fallen human will is in helpless bondage to sin and Satan; (c) God's sovereign grace alone can liberate the fallen will and cause it to repent and believe in Christ; (d) those whom Christ liberates are eternally chosen for this destiny in the mystery of unconditional election. Most of the great Western medieval theologians and reformers – Anselm of Canterbury, Bernard of Clairvaux, Peter Lombard, Thomas Aquinas, Gregory of Rimini, John Wyclif, John Huss – moved within an Augustinian spectrum of thought. For Augustine, see Volume One, Chapter 9, section 3.

(ii) The Augustinians were an order of friars which emerged in the 13th century, living according to the monastic rule of Augustine of Hippo. See Chapter 8, section 4.

AUTOCEPHALOUS

A term describing a national Church of the Eastern Orthodox faith which has its own independent Church government under a metropolitan or patriarch.

AVERROISM

After the Muslim philosopher Averroes (1126-98). A Pagan form of Aristotelianism which taught that the material universe is eternal and that individual souls are absorbed in a world-soul after death. See Chapter 7, section 2.

AVIGNONESE CAPTIVITY

The period 1309-77, when the papacy resided not in Rome but in the French city of Avignon, and was dominated by the French monarchy and its political interests. This led to much disenchantment with the papacy among non-French Catholics, and several remarkable attacks on the papacy by Western thinkers like Marsilius of Padua (1280-1343) and William of Ockham (1285-1349). See Chapter 10, section 1.

BEGHARDS

Laymen who lived together in communities devoted to cultivating the spiritual life, but without taking vows of lifelong celibacy or obedience to a superior, and without following a monastic rule. They flourished in the Netherlands, Germany and France in the period 1200-1400. See Chapter 8, section 4.

BEGUINES

Pronounced "bay-geens". The female equivalent of Beghards.

BENEDICTINE

Relating to Benedict of Nursia (480-547) and the "rule" he wrote for monastic life, widely used in the West. For Benedict, see Volume One, Chapter 11, section 1.

BLACK FRIARS

Popular name for Dominicans, from their black garb.

BOGOMILS

A Gnostic movement, originating in Bulgaria in the 10th century, named after its founder Bogomil ("dear to God"). Bogomil taught that the Supreme God had two angel-sons, Satanael the elder, and Christ the younger. Satanael rebelled against the Supreme God and seduced many lesser angels to follow him. He then persuaded these fallen angels to inhabit bodies of flesh which he had created as part of an evil world of matter – so that human souls are really angels who have fallen away from heaven. To set mankind free from the tyranny of Satanael and his monstrous world of matter, Bogomil taught that the Supreme God sent his younger son, Christ, to the earth as Jesus of Nazareth. Satanael killed Jesus, but he was resurrected in a spirit-body and returned to heaven. Likewise, after death, God would give eternal spirit-bodies to all the Bogomil followers of Jesus. Bogomils flourished in Bulgaria in the 10th century; by 1150, there were Bogomil missionaries working in Western Europe, where they enjoyed close relationships with the Cathars and Albigensians. However, they died out in their native Bulgaria after 1393, when the Muslim Turks conquered the land. See Chapter 3, section 6.

BULL

A papal edict. It comes from the Latin *bulla*, "seal", referring to the wax seal by which a pope impressed the sign of his authority on the edict. Bulls were known by their opening words in Latin.

BYZANTINE EMPIRE

The Eastern Roman Empire with its capital in Constantinople. "Byzantine" comes from Byzantium, the site on which Constantinople was built. Historians call them Byzantines, but the Byzantines called themselves "Romans", and we should remember that the Byzantine Empire was a direct continuation of the Roman Empire which did not "fall" in the East until 1453.

CALIPH

The title for the leader of the Islamic Empire. Caliph literally means "successor" – standing in succession to Muhammad.

CALIXTINES

The moderate wing of the Hussite movement. From the Latin *calix*, "cup" – referring to their insistence that the cup must be given to the laity in holy communion, as against the Catholic practice of withholding it. They are also known as the Utraquists. See Chapter 10, section 5.

CAMALDOLESE
A monastic order founded in 1012 under the influence of the Cluniac revival.

CARDINAL
Originally a title for the deacons and priests of Rome, and the bishops of Rome's suburban churches. Later, bishops who were geographically remote from Rome began to be nominated as cardinals to act as the pope's representatives. The Hildebrandine reform movement placed the election of new popes in the hands of the cardinals.

CARMELITES
An order of mendicant friars, first established in the Crusader kingdom of Jerusalem in 1154 on Mount Carmel (although at that point they were not mendicants). The loss of much Crusader territory to the Turks brought many Carmelites into Western Europe, where they reorganised themselves as a mendicant order in 1247.

CAROLINGIAN
The important Frankish royal dynasty which came to power in 751. The word comes from the Latin *Carolus*, "Charles", after the dynasty's greatest king, Charlemagne.

CAROLINGIAN RENAISSANCE
The flowering of culture which took place under Charlemagne and the Holy Roman Empire in the late 8th century and 9th century. See Chapter 2, section 2.

CATHARS
Greek for "pure ones". The most widespread dissenting movement in Western medieval Christendom. They were divided

up into many sects, but all shared a Gnostic religious outlook. They became especially numerous in southern France where they were called Albigensians. Cathars taught that the physical world of space, time and matter had been created by Satan, who was as eternal and powerful as God. The soul was an angelic spirit kidnapped by Satan from heaven and imprisoned in an evil physical body. The ultimate sin was sexual reproduction, because it increased the number of evil bodies for Satan to use as prisons for kidnapped spirits. Christ did not have a physical body, did not really die, and did not experience a bodily resurrection. Salvation did not come through the cross, but through spiritual enlightenment (accepting and following the Cathar teachings). Cathars rejected water baptism and holy communion. See Chapter 8, section 3.

CENOBITIC
The community form of monastic life.

CHALCEDONIAN
Pertaining to the Creed of Chalcedon, drawn up by the fourth ecumenical Council of Chalcedon in 451. Chalcedon taught that Christ is one person in two distinct natures, human and divine. Large sections of the Eastern Church rejected Chalcedon in favour of the Monophysite view that Christ is one person with a single divine-human nature. See Volume One, Chapters 10 and 12.

CHIVALRY
From the French *chevalerie*, "cavalry". A code of moral and spiritual ideals by which the Western Church sought to Christianise the knights of Western Europe. See Chapter 5, section 2.

CHRISTENDOM
"The Christian domain". The nations and territories of Eastern and Western Europe and parts of the Middle East, which – despite political and cultural differences – were united by the fact that Christianity was the public faith in each of them. People often use the word today to refer to the idea of a society publicly committed to the Christian religion. From the reign of Roman

emperor Theodosius the Great in the 4th century up to the French Revolution in the 18th, it also meant the political union of Church and state, whichever of the two was the dominant partner.

CISTERCIANS

A monastic order, a reformed branch of the Benedictines. They originated from the French monastery of Citeaux (in Latin, *Cistercium*), founded in 1098. See Chapter 5, section 3, under *Bernard of Clairvaux and the Second Crusade*.

CLUNIAC

Pertaining to the French monastery of Cluny, founded in 909. It initiated a revival of strict Benedictine monasticism in Western Christendom, and introduced the idea of a special organisation of monasteries, bound together by particular ideals, with a single leader (in this case, the abbot of Cluny) at the top. The Cluniac revival was also influential in helping to rebuild the Christian culture of Western Europe in the 10th and 11th centuries. See Chapter 4, section 3.

CONCILIARISM

From the Latin *concilium*, "council". A movement in the Western Church in response to the Great Schism of 1378, when there were two (later three) rival popes. The conciliarists wanted to restore the unity of the Church by making the papacy subject to the higher authority of a general or ecumenical Council of the Church. Leading conciliarist thinkers were John Gerson, Peter d'Ailly and Nicholas of Cusa. See Chapter 10, section 3.

CONVENTUAL FRANCISCANS

The progressive wing of the Franciscan movement which wanted to modify and adapt the order's original commitment to absolute poverty (in contrast to the more conservative "spiritual" Franciscans). In 1517 pope Leo X established the conventual Franciscans as a distinct order with its own governing body. See Chapter 8, section 4.

CRUSADES

A series of military expeditions to the Middle East by Western Catholics, inspired and blessed by the Catholic Church, with the aim of recapturing the Holy Land (especially Jerusalem) from the Muslims. There were four main Crusades: (i) 1096-99, (ii) 1147-49, (iii) 1189-92, and (iv) 1202-4. Later crusades were used within Western Christendom against dissenters, *e.g.* the Albigensian Crusade of 1209-29 and the crusade against the Hussites in the 15th century. See Chapter 5.

DEIFICATION

"Becoming divine". This was the accepted understanding of salvation in the Eastern Church. It does not mean that human beings are gods by nature or become God by nature. It means that through union with Christ, believers share by grace in the glory and immortality of God, and in that sense become divine – "partakers of the divine nature" (2 Pet. 1:4). In many ways, "deification" in Eastern theology is the equivalent of "sanctification" in Western theology.

DEVOTIO MODERNA

"The modern way of serving God". A spiritual movement beginning in the mid-14th century in the Netherlands. It was marked by a sense of God's closeness to the individual believer, and a focusing of the mind on Christ's life and sufferings as recorded in the Gospels. It inspired the creation of communities of Christian men and Christian women ("brotherhoods" and "sisterhoods") who would live, pray and follow Christ together, but without becoming monks or nuns; they would work for a living "in the world" and take no monastic vows. The most influential and well-known writing to emerge from the *devotio moderna* was *The Imitation of Christ*, written by Thomas a Kempis (1380-1471).

DISPUTATION

A public educational event in a university, in which a teacher and a student would set out to solve a problem. The problem would be two statements which appeared to contradict each other, but which were both found in authoritative texts. The student would have to give all the arguments for and against each statement, by quoting passages from the Bible and great theologians, and offering his own comments on these passages. The teacher would then make remarks on what the student had said, and would offer a solution to the problem. Lecturers also engaged in disputations over debated subjects; they would draw up a set of statements or "theses", announce that they were going to defend them in debate, and challenge anyone to argue with them and disprove the theses.

DOMINICAN

An order of mendicant friars founded in 1214 by Dominic (1171-1221). The order devoted itself especially to the study of theology, producing great theologians like Albertus Magnus and Thomas Aquinas. Dominicans ran the inquisition, which made them unpopular with the other monastic orders. They had the unique right to preach anywhere and everywhere; the 13th and 14th centuries saw many Dominican missionaries working in the far East among the Mongols. See Chapter 8, sections 4 and 5.

DONATION OF CONSTANTINE

A document which began to circulate in the mid-8th century. It claimed to be a letter from the first Christian emperor, Constantine the Great (312-37), in which he acknowledged that the pope was superior to the emperor, and granted the papacy the right to govern the city of Rome and all imperial territory in Italy and the West. The document was a forgery, exposed by the great Italian scholar Lorenzo Valla in 1440; but for 700 years the popes used the Donation of Constantine to support their claims.

EASTERN ORTHODOXY

A title often given to the Eastern Greek-speaking Chalcedonian Church of the Byzantine Empire, and its daughter Churches in Russia, the Balkans and elsewhere. Strictly speaking, we should only refer to it in this way after the great East–West schism of 1054; it was only at that point that Eastern and Western Chalcedonians separated into two mutually hostile bodies.

ECUMENICAL COUNCIL

A conference of bishops from all parts of the Christian world to decide questions of doctrine and discipline. There were seven ecumenical Councils recognised by both East and West – Nicaea (325), Constantinople (381), Ephesus (431), Chalcedon (451), Second Constantinople (553), Third Constantinople (680-81), and Second Nicaea (787). The Western Church had other Councils it regarded as ecumenical after 787, but these were not recognised by the East. Most Protestants have not accepted the 2nd Council of Nicaea for theological reasons (rejecting its doctrine of the veneration of icons). "Ecumenical" comes from the Greek for "the inhabited world"; when used in the phrase "ecumenical Council", it has nothing to do with the modern "ecumenical movement".

EREMITIC

The hermit's way of life. From the Greek *eremia*, desert.

EUCHARIST

The Lord's supper or holy communion. From the Greek *eucharisteo*, "to give thanks".

FILIOQUE CLAUSE

Filioque is Latin for "and from the Son". This phrase was added to the Nicene Creed by the Western Church, first by Spanish Christians at the council of Toledo in 589, and at length by the papacy in the early 11th century. The addition altered the Creed's teaching about the Holy Spirit; it originally said that the Spirit "proceeds from the Father", but after the insertion of the *filioque* clause, Western versions of the Creed now said that the Spirit "proceeds from the Father and from the Son". This generated fierce controversy between East and West. The East protested that (a) the West had no right to alter an ecumenical Creed by unilateral action, and (b) this particular alteration was theologically incorrect – in the eternal relationships of the Trinity, the Spirit proceeds from the Father alone. The *filioque* clause was the chief theological difference between East and West which led to the great schism of 1054. See Chapter 2, section 2, under *Religious policy*, and Chapter 3, section 8.

FRANCISCANS

An order of mendicant friars founded in 1209 by Francis of Assisi. They were originally committed to absolute poverty – no ownership of any property – but this was modified in various ways as the order developed. Many great medieval thinkers were Franciscans – Alexander of Hales, Bonaventura, Duns Scotus, William of Ockham, Nicholas of Lyra. The Franciscan order produced many missionaries to the far East in the 13th and 14th centuries. See Chapter 8, section 4.

FRATICELLI

The "little brothers". A dissenting movement among the "spiritual" wing of the Franciscans. When in 1317-18 pope John XXII settled the controversy between "spiritual" and "conventual" Franciscans in favour of the conventuals, many spiritual Franciscans refused to submit. Sometimes the Fraticelli established their own groups and priests outside the Catholic Church. Despite being persecuted fiercely by the inquisition, they were numerous in Italy and southern France. See Chapter 8, section 4, under *The Franciscans*.

FRIARS

From the Lain *fratres*, "brothers". A new form of monastic order which arose in the 13th century with the Franciscans and Dominicans. Rather than withdrawing from society to create communities of the spiritually minded, the purpose of the friar-monks was to go out into society, preaching and winning disciples, both in Catholic Europe and in the unevangelised world of Muslims and Pagans. Other differences between the friars and traditional monks included (a) the friars' "mendicant" practice of begging for food rather than cultivating it themselves in their monastery, (b) not being bound to a specific monastery by an oath of "stability", and (c) exemption from the authority of the local bishop. Most of the great Western Catholic preachers and theologians of the later Middle Ages were friars.

GHIBILLINES
Supporters of the Holy Roman emperors in their conflict with the papacy. The word comes from Waiblingen, a German town noted for its allegiance to Germany's anti-papal Hohenstauffen dynasty.

GREAT EAST–WEST SCHISM
The separation of Eastern and Western Chalcedonians in 1054 into two mutually hostile Churches, the East centred in Constantinople and the Byzantine Empire, the West centred in Rome, the papacy and the Holy Roman Empire. The most important issues leading to the schism were the authority claims of the papacy and the *filioque* clause. See Chapter 3, section 8.

GREAT SCHISM
The period 1378-1417 when there were two, then three rival popes, each commanding the loyalty of different parts of Western Christendom. See Chapter 10, section 2.

GREY FRIARS
Popular name for the Franciscans, from their grey garb.

GUELFS
Supporters of the papacy in its conflict with the Holy Roman emperors. The word comes from duke Welf of Bavaria, who opposed the anti-papal Hohenstauffen dynasty's claim to the German throne, and sided with the papacy as a natural ally against the common foe.

HAGIA SOPHIA
The "Holy Wisdom", Constantinople's chief church.

HESYCHASM
From the Greek *hesychia*, "quietness", "peace". A spiritual discipline of prayer popular in the Eastern Church. It involves the unceasing mental recitation of the "Jesus prayer" – "Lord Jesus Christ, Son of God, have mercy on me, a sinner" – as a means of conquering the passions and attaining to the vision of God as light. Hesychasm

was especially associated with the monks of Mount Athos. It provoked much controversy in the 14th century, but a series of councils vindicated the practice and the undergirding theology developed by Gregory Palamas. See Chapter 9, section 3.

HILDEBRANDINE REFORM MOVEMENT

The great 11th century movement for the reformation of the Western Church. Its main concerns were to promote the independence of the Church from state control, the supreme authority of the papacy over Church and state, and moral fitness and celibacy of the clergy. Named after its leading figure, Hildebrand, later pope Gregory VII (1073-85). See Chapter 4, sections 4-6.

HOLY ROMAN EMPIRE

The political and religious entity created by pope Leo III on Christmas day 800, when he crowned the Frankish king Charlemagne as "emperor of the Romans". The Holy Roman Empire claimed that it, not Byzantium, was the true successor to Constantine and the Christian Roman Empire in the West. Its territories constantly shrank and grew under different emperors; at its greatest, the Empire embraced Germany, the Netherlands, Bohemia, Austria, Switzerland, much of Italy, and parts of eastern France. It was marked by prolonged conflict between popes and emperors over which of them held the supreme authority in the Empire. See Chapter 2.

HOSPITALLERS

Another name for the Knights of Saint John, one of the great Crusading monastic orders. They were founded in 1048, and given papal recognition in 1113. The name "Hospitallers" came from a hospital for sick pilgrims in Jerusalem which the Knights of Saint John ran. See Chapter 5, section 4.

HUSSITES

The most successful dissenting movement in the Western medieval world. Hussites were followers of the 15th century Bohemian reformer John Huss. Eventually they separated into two parties, the Utraquists who remained within the Catholic Church but with their own Hussite practices (preaching from the Bible in Bohemian, the wine as well as the bread served to the laity in communion), and the United Bohemian Brotherhood which broke away from the Catholic Church and was doctrinally more radical (rejecting transubstantiation, prayers for the dead, the invocation of saints). See Chapter 10, section 5.

ICON
A pictorial representation of Christ, saints or angels. The word is Greek for "image" and usually restricted to the Eastern Church's use of such images. They are two-dimensional (not statues), and regarded not as works of human art but God-given points of contact with the spiritual world.

ICONOCLASM, ICONOCLAST
Literally "image-smashing". Iconoclasts were those who, in the "iconoclastic controversy" of the 8th and 9th centuries, were opposed to the presence of icons in the Eastern Church. See Chapter 3, section 3.

ICONODULE
One who honours icons. The party that supported icons against the iconoclasts in the Eastern Church during the iconoclastic controversy. See Chapter 3, section 3.

ICONOGRAPHY
The artistic theory and technique of painting icons.

ICONOPHILE
Another name for an iconodule.

IMMACULATE CONCEPTION
The opinion that the Virgin Mary was conceived free from original sin. Its great champions were Duns Scotus and the Franciscans; its great opponents were Thomas Aquinas and the Dominicans. It was not until 1854 that the immaculate conception was elevated

to the status of official Roman Catholic dogma. See Chapter 7, section 3, under *Duns Scotus*.

IMPERIALISM, IMPERIALIST

The view that the emperor, not the pope, was the supreme authority in the Holy Roman Empire.

INDULGENCE

A pardon which released a sinner from the obligation to pay the "temporal penalties" of sin. Temporal penalties included penitential acts of Church discipline and sufferings in purgatory. Only the pope could issue an indulgence. His right to do so stemmed from his power over the "treasury of merits" – the merits of the saints by which they had performed acts of obedience above and beyond the call of duty. Such merits the pope could transfer to sinful souls on earth and even in purgatory. The sale of indulgences produced several indignant protests in the late Middle Ages, and were the spark which finally ignited the Reformation. See Chapter 7, section 3, under *Thomas Aquinas*.

INQUISITION

The "holy office", a separate organisation within the Western Catholic Church, free from episcopal control, subject only to the pope, dedicated to the forcible suppression of heresy and dissent. Pope Innocent III (1198-1216) laid the basis for the inquisition during the Albigensian Crusade. In 1227 Innocent's system was consolidated as the "holy office". Staffed by Dominicans, the inquisition became the most feared organisation in the Middle Ages. See Chapter 8, section 3.

INTERDICT

A papal edict which put a stop to all religious services (except funerals and baptism if the candidate was in danger of death) within a particular locality, as a disciplinary measure. It was used most famously by pope Innocent III against England between 1207 and 1213 in an attempt to force the English king John to submit to Innocent's will.

INVESTITURE CONTROVERSY
The controversy over whether a clergyman's spiritual office flowed from the king as Christ's representative, or from the bishop who ordains. See Chapter 4, sections 2, 5 and 6.

JESUS PRAYER
The prayer at the centre of hesychasm – "Lord Jesus Christ, Son of God, have mercy on me, a sinner."

LAITY, LAYPEOPLE
From the Greek *laos*, "the people". All Church members who are not clergy. This includes most monks, the majority of whom are not priests.

LEGATE
An ambassador or representative of the pope.

LOLLARDS, LOLLARDY
The followers of the English reformer John Wyclif (1330-84). It is uncertain what "Lollard" means – possibly "one who mumbles or mutters". Wyclif anticipated many of the views of the Protestant Reformers, *e.g.* his rejection of the papacy and transubstantiation, his conviction that preaching not the sacraments lay at the heart of the ministry, and his championing of the Bible as supreme authority in the Church, with the right and duty of all believers to study it in their native language. See Chapter 10, section 4.

MEDIEVAL
Pertaining to the Middle Ages.

MENDICANT
Begging for one's food. The friars were mendicants.

MERIT
(i) Often used in Latin theology to mean "virtue", "goodness", not necessarily implying any idea of earning salvation.

(ii) More specifically, the obedience of the saints above and beyond what God strictly required of them, sometimes called their "works of supererogation". According to the later Western medieval theory, the pope could transfer these merits to sinners on earth and in purgatory by means of an indulgence.

MIDDLE AGES

The period of history "in the middle" between the patristic age and the Renaissance and Reformation. I have taken this period as beginning around about the late 7th century (after the sixth ecumenical Council of Constantinople in 681) and ending with the Hussites in the mid-15th century.

MONOPHYSITES

Those who rejected the Creed of Chalcedon (451) because it taught that Christ has two distinct natures, human and divine. Monophysites held that Christ has a single divine-human nature. There were Monophysite majorities in Egypt, Ethiopia, Syria and Armenia.

MORTAL SIN

According to later medieval Western theology, a serious sin which kills the spiritual life of the soul. This life must be restored by the sacrament of penance.

MYSTICISM

This has always been a hard term to define. Mysticism is rooted in the belief that a person can enter into a state of spiritual "union" with God, and that this union – the ultimate experience – can be pursued by certain disciplines or techniques. But there are seemingly endless varieties of mysticism: Christian, Muslim, Pagan, and others.

NEO-PELAGIAN, NEO-PELAGIANISM

A term sometimes applied to the teaching of William of Ockham (1285-1349) and his disciples, that God grants saving grace to those who "do their best" by their own natural powers. Ockham's opponents condemned this as a revival of the Pelagian heresy. See Chapter 7, section 3, under *William of Ockham*.

NEOPLATONISTS, NEOPLATONISM

Neoplatonism means "the new Platonism", and is the name given to the philosophy of the great 3rd century Pagan thinker Plotinus (205-70). It had a huge impact on the Church. See Volume One, Chapter 6, section 2.

NESTORIANS, NESTORIANISM

After Nestorius (381-451), patriarch of Constantinople from 428 to 431. Nestorians believed that in the incarnation, Christ not only had two distinct natures, but was two distinct persons – a divine Son of God indwelling a human Son of Mary. The Council of Ephesus in 431 condemned Nestorianism as a heresy. The national Church of Persia became strongly Nestorian in its Christology. See Chapter 1, section 5, and Chapter 8, section 5.

NICENE CREED

Confusingly, this is the Creed drawn up by the Council of *Constantinople* in 381. The Creed which the Council of Nicaea formulated in 325 is not called the Nicene Creed, but "the Creed of Nicaea". The Nicene Creed was recited during the eucharist. The Western addition of the *filioque* clause to the Creed was the major cause of the great East–West schism of 1054.

NOMINALISM

The view that individual things are more real than the general category to which they belong. For example, an individual tree has more reality than the general category "tree". The general category is only a name (Latin *nomen*), not an existing reality. Nominalism is the opposite of Realism. See Chapter 7, section 2.

NUN

A female monk. The word comes from the Latin *nonna*, the feminine form of *nonnus*, "monk".

NUNNERY
The place where a community of nuns live.

ORTHODOXY
Literally "right glory", the correct way of praising God. Term applied to the Eastern Chalcedonian Churches after the great East–West schism of 1054.

PAPACY
From the Latin *papa*, "father". The office of Roman bishop, understood as being founded by the apostle Peter and enjoying first place of honour and dignity above all other bishops. The claims of the Roman bishops became ever more exalted, but the papacy as we know it today, claiming to be the "vicar of Christ" on earth, came to its maturity only in the Middle Ages, in the reign of pope Innocent III (1198-1216). See Chapter 8.

PAPALISM, PAPALIST
The view that the pope, not the emperor, was the supreme authority in the Holy Roman Empire.

PATRIARCH, PATRIARCHATE
From the Greek for "fatherly ruler". The title of patriarch was given from the end of the 4th century to the bishops of Rome, Constantinople, Alexandria and Antioch, and then in the 5th century to the bishop of Jerusalem too. All other bishops were subject to the authority of the patriarch in whose territory their church was situated. A "patriarchate" is the office and jurisdiction of a patriarch.

PATRISTIC
Relating to the early Church fathers. From the Greek and Latin *pater*, "father". There are various ways of defining the patristic period; I take it as covering the first six centuries of Church history (roughly the period of the first six ecumenical Councils). For the end of the patristic period and the beginning of the Middle Ages, see Chapter 1, section 1.

PAULICIANS
A Gnostic group that originated in Armenia in the 7th century, founded by a certain Constantine. Paulicians accepted only the Gospels and Paul's letters as divinely inspired; their reverence for the apostle Paul is the probable reason for their name. They were typical Gnostics in their beliefs, *e.g.* rejecting physical matter as evil. See Chapter 3, section 6.

PELAGIANISM
Named after Pelagius (active 383-417). Pelagius held that all human beings were born into the world as sinless as Adam was before he fell; the apostasy of Adam had not corrupted humanity's nature, but had merely set a fatally bad example, which most of Adam's sons and daughters had freely followed. Pelagius defined God's grace, not in terms of the inner renewing power of the Holy Spirit, but as the moral law, the example of Christ, and the persuasive power of rewards and punishments. Human free-will therefore became the chief source of salvation in the Pelagian scheme. Pelagianism was fought vigorously by Augustine of Hippo (354-430) and condemned by the Council of Ephesus in 431. See Volume One, Chapter 9, section 3.

PETROBRUSIANS
A dissenting movement in southern France. Its founder was a priest, Peter de Bruys, who started a reform movement in 1105 which was eventually condemned as heretical. Petrobrusians rejected infant baptism, transubstantiation, prayers for the dead, and the celibacy of the clergy. See Chapter 8, section 3.

PHOTIAN SCHISM
The breach between East and West which lasted from 863 until 867, when pope Nicholas I and patriarch Photius of Constantinople excommunicated each other. See Chapter 3, section 4.

PLATONISM
The philosophy of the Greek thinker Plato (427-347 BC) – in terms of influence, the world's greatest philosopher. See Volume One, Chapter 1, section 1, under *Philosophy*.

PLENITUDE OF POWER

The doctrine that all spiritual and secular power is lodged in the pope, so that all other authorities derive their legitimacy from him.

PRIOR

Second highest rank in a monastery, after abbot.

PURGATORY

A place between heaven and hell where Christians are purified from sins which they failed to wash away on earth through holy communion and works of love. Some of the early Church fathers teach a form of this doctrine, but not in any developed way; it was Gregory the Great (540-604) who brought the idea to its maturity in the Western Church. The East rejected it.

REALISM

The view that the general category to which things belong is more real than the individual things. For example, the general category "tree" has more reality than an individual tree. The general category was often seen as an idea in the eternal mind of God; the individual thing reflected that idea on earth. Realism is the opposite of Nominalism. See Chapter 7, section 2.

SACRAMENT

A Western Latin word meaning "an oath of allegiance". It was applied to baptism and holy communion. In the East, these were called "the mysteries".

SACRED KINGSHIP

The view that the king is a spiritual figure who receives his authority directly from Christ, that bishops derive their position from the king, and that kings have the right and duty to regulate Church affairs in their realm. This view was widespread in Western Christendom prior to the triumph of the Hildebrandine reformers in the investiture controversy. See Chapter 2, section 2, under *Emperor and pope*.

SCHISM
The act of breaking fellowship with the "one, holy, Catholic and apostolic Church".

SCHOLASTICISM
The type of theology that developed in Western universities during the later Middle Ages. It was marked by a commitment to explore and state rationally the full content of individual Christian doctrines, and a desire to fit them together in a comprehensive system of truth. Scholasticism also tended to include the questions of philosophy within its quest for a system of truth – questions about the nature of space, time, matter, causality, *etc.* Later scholasticism was also marked by its increasing reliance on the philosophical concepts and methods of Aristotle. See Chapter 7.

SCHOOLMEN
The scholastic theologians.

SEMI-PELAGIANS, SEMI-PELAGIANISM
A theological position midway between Pelagianism and the teachings of Augustine of Hippo regarding the origins of the experience of salvation. Pelagianism placed salvation in the power of human free-will; Augustine ascribed salvation (regeneration, the new birth) wholly to God's grace; the Semi-Pelagians held that salvation was initially prompted by God's grace, but depended for its effect on human cooperation. See Volume One, Chapter 9, section 3.

SKETE
A small group of up to 12 monks who lived under the spiritual direction of a more experienced monk and met with other sketes for worship on holy days. Named after the Skete region of Egypt.

SPIRITUAL FRANCISCANS
The conservative wing of the Franciscans who wanted to preserve Francis's original ideal of absolute poverty, in contrast to

the modernising "conventual" Franciscans. In 1517 pope Leo X established the spiritual Franciscans as a distinct order with its own governing body. See Chapter 8, section 4.

STIGMATA

Latin for "marks", which mysteriously appear on the body resembling the wounds of the crucified Christ, often accompanied by bleeding. The first known person to experience the stigmata was Francis of Assisi in 1224.

TABORITES

The radical wing of the Hussite movement which later developed into the United Bohemian Brotherhood. They are named after the Biblical mount Tabor, a name they gave to a hill in southern Bohemia where they gathered in great numbers in 1419. See Chapter 10, section 5.

TEMPLARS

Another name for the great Crusading monastic order of the Knights of the Temple, founded in 1118. Bernard of Clairvaux wrote a new constitution for them in 1128. See Chapter 5, section 4.

TEUTONIC KNIGHTS

A Crusading monastic order founded in 1190. They were almost wholly German, and most of their activities were in Germany and Eastern Europe rather than Palestine. See Chapter 5, section 4.

THEOTOKOS

Greek title for the Virgin Mary. Literally "birth-giver of God", often translated "mother of God" by Roman Catholics and Eastern Orthodox, and "God-bearer" by Protestants. See Volume One, Chapter 10, section 3.

THOMISM

The theology of Thomas Aquinas. See Chapter 7, section 3, under *Thomas Aquinas*.

TREASURY OF MERIT

The merits of the saints which the pope has power to transfer to souls on earth and in purgatory.

UNIVERSALISM

The belief that all human beings, and perhaps the demons too, will finally be saved.

UTRAQUISTS

The moderate wing of the Hussite movement. From the Latin *utraque*, "both" – referring to their insistence that both the bread and the wine must be given to the laity in holy communion, as against the Catholic practice of withholding the wine. They are also known as the Calixtines. See Chapter 10, section 5.

VENIAL SIN

"Venial" means "pardonable". According to later Western medieval theology, a sin that only "wounded" the soul; such a sin did not actually turn the soul away from God, but it did bring spiritual disorder into the soul's life. This disorder could be rectified by individual religious acts – prayer, participation in mass, *etc.* – without priestly absolution.

VULGATE

Jerome's Latin translation of the Bible. "Vulgate" comes from the Latin word for "common" – the common Bible, *i.e.* the one in common use. See Volume One, Chapter 9, section 2.

WALDENSIANS

One of the great dissenting movements of Western Christendom. Originated by a certain Valdes or Waldes in Lyons sometime between 1173 and 1176, they were scattered across much of Western Europe, although their stronghold came to be in the Alpine valleys of northern Italy. In many ways they anticipated the views of the Protestant Reformers, e.g. in rejecting the papacy, transubstantiation, purgatory, prayers for the dead and indulgences, and in upholding the supreme authority of Scripture and the right and duty of all believers to study it in their native language. See Chapter 8, section 3.

WESTERN CATHOLIC
I use this term to describe (especially after the great East–West schism of 1054) the Church of Western Europe, which used Latin as its theological and liturgical language, and looked to the Roman papacy for spiritual leadership, although Western Churchmen did not necessarily accept all the increasingly lofty claims which the popes made for themselves. The term *Roman Catholic* is, arguably, best applied to that branch of the Western Catholic Church which rejected the Protestant Reformation of the 16th century.

WHITE FRIARS
Popular name for Augustinian friars, from their white garb.

Bibliography

Once again I offer here a selection of some of the books which the enthusiastic non-specialist should be able to enjoy and profit from – although, to vary a comment I made in Volume One, it's just as well to have a dictionary and a stiff black coffee at your side with some of these. I have highlighted a few of the books in bold print; these, I think, are especially helpful for those coming to the study of medieval Church history for the first time.

Tamim Ansary, *Destiny Disrupted: A History of the World Through Islamic Eyes* (PublicAffairs, New York 2009)

Thomas Aquinas, *Light of Faith: The Compendium of Theology* (Sophia Institute Press, Manchester, New Hampshire 1998) (very accessible way of getting into Aquinas: his own condensation of his theology into a single volume, and well translated into English)

Reza Aslan, *No God But God: The Origins, Evolution and Future of Islam* (Arrow Books, London 2006)

Geoffrey Barraclough, *The Medieval Papacy* (Thames and Hudson, London 1968)

Fiona Bowie and Oliver Davies, *Hildegard of Bingen* (SPCK, London 1990)

James Bryce, *The Holy Roman Empire* (MacMillan, London 1906)

William R. Cannon, *History of Christianity in the Middle Ages* (Baker, Grand Rapids 1983)

Norman F. Cantor, *The Civilization of the Middle Ages* (HarperCollins, New York 1993)

—*The Medieval Reader* (HarperCollins, New York 1994)

G.K. Chesterton, *Saint Thomas Aquinas* (Hodder & Stoughton, London 1943)

G.G. Coulton, *Studies in Medieval Thought* (Thomas Nelson, London 1940)

S.J. Curtis, *A Short History of Western Philosophy in the Middle Ages* (MacDonald, London 1950)

R.H.C. Davis, *A History of Medieval Europe* (Longman, London 1970)

Margaret Deanesly, *History of the Medieval Church* (Methuen, London 1925)

Gillian Elias, *Bernard of Clairvaux: A Cistercian Saint* (Saint Bernard Press, Coalville n.d.)

G.R. Evans (editor), *The Medieval Theologians* (Blackwell, Oxford 2001)

R.S. Franks, *The Work of Christ: A Historical Study of Christian Doctrine* (Thomas Nelson and Sons, London 1962) (see Part II, *The Mediaeval Theology*)

Christopher Frayling, *Strange Landscape: A Journey through the Middle Ages* (BBC Books, London 1995)

Asterios Gerostergios, *St Photios the Great* (Institute for Byzantine and Modern Greek Studies, Belmont 1980)

Edward Gibbon, *Decline and Fall of the Roman Empire* (the later volumes are a history of the Byzantine Empire in the Middle Ages until the fall of Constantinople in 1453) (John Murray, London 1838. With notes by H.H. Milman)

Elizabeth Hallam (editor), *Chronicles of the Crusades: Eyewitness Accounts* (Guild Publishing, London 1989)

Friedrich Heer, *The Holy Roman Empire* (Phoenix, London 1995)

Maurice Keen, *The Penguin History of Medieval Europe* (Penguin, London 1991)

Gordon Leff, *Medieval Thought: St Augustine to Ockham* (Penguin, London 1958)

Angus MacKay and David Ditchburn (editors), *Atlas of Medieval Europe* (Routledge, London 1997)

John Meyendorff, *Byzantine Theology* (St. Vladimir's Seminary Press, New York 1974)

—*Saint Gregory Palamas and Orthodox Spirituality* (St. Vladimir's Seminary Press, New York 1974)

John Julius Norwich, *Byzantium: The Apogee* (Penguin, London 1991)

—*Byzantium: The Decline and Fall* (Penguin, London 1996)

Ivan Ostroumoff, *The History of the Council of Florence* (Holy Transfiguration Monastery, Boston 1971)

Aristeides Papadakis and John Meyendorff, *The Christian East and the Rise of the Papacy* (St. Vladimir's Seminary Press, New York 1994)

Henri Pirenne, *A History of Europe* (Allen & Unwin, London 1939)

Michael Psellus, *Fourteen Byzantine Rulers* (Penguin, London 1966)

Tamara Talbot Rice, *Everyday Life in Byzantium* (Batsford, London 1967)

Jonathan Riley-Smith, *The Oxford History of the Crusades* (Oxford University Press, Oxford 1994)

Daniel Rogich, *Serbian Patericon: Saints of the Serbian Orthodox Church* (St. Paisius Abbey Press, Platina 1994)

Ghulam Sarwar, *Islam: Beliefs and Teachings* (Muslim Educational Trust, London 2006)

Philip Schaff, *History of the Christian Church* (Eerdmans, Grand Rapids, Michigan 1994) vols.4-6

Philip Sherrard, *Church, Papacy and Schism: A Theological Inquiry* (SPCK, London 1978)

—*The Greek East and the Latin West* (Denise Harvey, Limni, 1992)

Georges Tate, *The Crusades and the Holy Land* (Thames & Hudson, London 1996)

Hugh Trevor-Roper, *The Rise of Christian Europe* (Thames & Hudson, London 1965)

Arvin Vos, *Aquinas, Calvin, and Contemporary Protestant Thought* (Christian University Press, Washington DC 1985)

G.S.M. Walker, *The Growing Storm: Sketches of Church History from AD 600 to AD 1350* (Paternoster, London 1961)

Robert Wallace, *Rise of Russia* (Time/Life, Netherlands 1967)

D.S. White, *Patriarch Photios of Constantinople* (contains 52 of Photios's letters) (Holy Cross Orthodox Press, Brookline 1981)

Herbert Workman, *The Church of the West in the Middle Ages* (2 volumes, Kelly, London 1896)

Esmond Wright (editor), *The Medieval and Renaissance World* (Hamlyn, London 1979)

Serge A. Zenkovsky, *Medieval Russia's Epics, Chronicles and Tales* (Dutton, New York 1974)

Index of Names

446

Index of Subjects

Aachen, 59, 61, 66, 71

Abbey, **445**

Abbots/Abbesses, **445**

Acre, 216, 218

Adoptianist controversy, 59, 62-63, 77, **445**

Afghanistan, 25

Africa, spread of Islam, 23, 25

Aix-la-Chapelle *see* Aachen

Albigensians, 127, 221, 335-37, 346, **445**

Alexandria, 24, 104, 132

Algeria, 34

allegory, and Biblical interpretation, 76

altars, Eastern Orthodox, 98

Amorian dynasty (Byzantine), 96-97

analogy, and knowledge of God, 286-87

Anchorites/Anchoresses, **445**

angels, icons of, 101, 109, 247

Aniane (France), monastery of Benedict, 70

anti-Semitism, 205, 331-32

see also Jews

antidoron bread, 99

Antioch, 24, 97, 104, 132

siege of (1098), 206

Antioch, Principality, 206

apologetic literature, 35-44

Arabia, rise of Islam, 17-18, 22-23, 29

Arabic language

translations of the Bible and Christian liturgy, 33

translations of Greek philosophers, 28, 30-31

architecture, to the praise of God, 12

Aristotelianism, 268-70, 279, 283, 283-84, 368, 376, **446**

applied to the mass, 288

Islam and, 28

Armenia, 97, 125, 365

art

in service of the Church, 12

see also icons

asceticism, 169

Asia Minor

Chalcedonians, 23

Islamic conquest of, 25, 96, 200, 365

restored to Byzantine rule, 206

Athos *see* Mount Athos

atonement

Anselm on the, 270, 272-73

limited, 72

Nicholas Cabasilas on, 400-401

Augsburg, battle of (955), 158

Augustinian friars, 299, 348, **446**

Augustinianism, 12, 71-72, 181, 210, 279, 281, 299, 314, **446**

Autocephalous, **446**

Avars, 57

Averroists/Averroism, 268, **447**

Avignon

captivity of the pope, 297, 376, 405-07, **447**

in the Great Schism, 407-12

Baghdad

caliphate, 28, 29-31

captured by Mongols, 353

university, 30-31

Balkans

Bulgar wars, 96

Chalcedonians, 23

Ottoman conquest of, 368

baptism, 276, 393

baptismal regeneration, 314-16

differing practices, 132&n

Petrobrusians and, 338

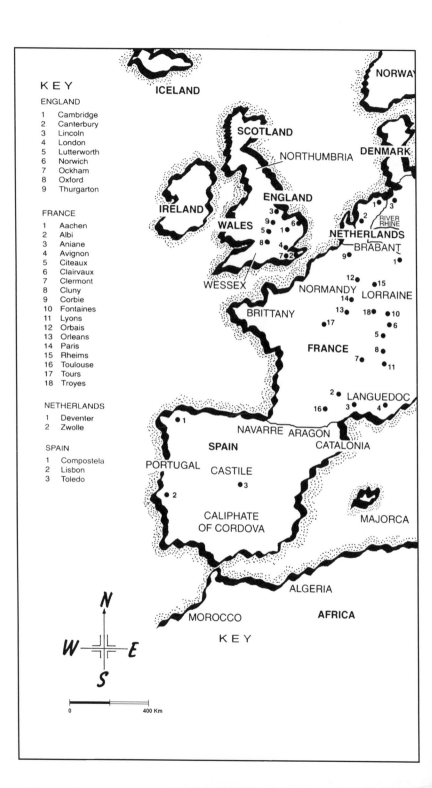

KEY

ENGLAND

1 Cambridge
2 Canterbury
3 Lincoln
4 London
5 Lutterworth
6 Norwich
7 Ockham
8 Oxford
9 Thurgarton

FRANCE

1 Aachen
2 Albi
3 Aniane
4 Avignon
5 Citeaux
6 Clairvaux
7 Clermont
8 Cluny
9 Corbie
10 Fontaines
11 Lyons
12 Orbais
13 Orleans
14 Paris
15 Rheims
16 Toulouse
17 Tours
18 Troyes

NETHERLANDS

1 Deventer
2 Zwolle

SPAIN

1 Compostela
2 Lisbon
3 Toledo

FINLAND

SWEDEN

ESTONIA

3

LATVIA

5

LITHUANIA

PRUSSIA

SAXONY

POLAND

MORAVIA

RUSSIA

7

1

4

6

2

7

GERMANY

THURINGIA

BOHEMIA

FRANCONIA

BAVARIA

RIVER DANUBE

SWABIA

HUNGARY

SWITZERLAND

CROATIA

BULGARIA

ITALY

SERBIA

BALKANS

CALABRIA

SICILY

TUNISIA

LIBYA

For this area
see other map

KEY

RUSSIA

1 Kiev
2 Moscow
3 Novgorod
4 Perm
5 Pskov
6 Radonezh
7 Turov

GERMANY

1 Augsburg
2 Bingen
3 Bremen
4 Brunswick
5 Cologne
6 Fulda
7 Lubeck
8 Magdeburg
9 Mainz
10 Prague
11 Strasbourg
12 Worms

KEY

ITALY

1 Aosta
2 Aquileia
3 Assisi
4 Bologna
5 Canossa
6 Fiore
7 Florence
8 Milan
9 Monte Cassino
10 Naples
11 Padua
12 Ravenna
13 Rimini
14 Rome
15 Salerno
16 Siena
17 Sutri
18 Turin
19 Venice

SWITZERLAND

1 Basel
2 Constance
3 Lausanne

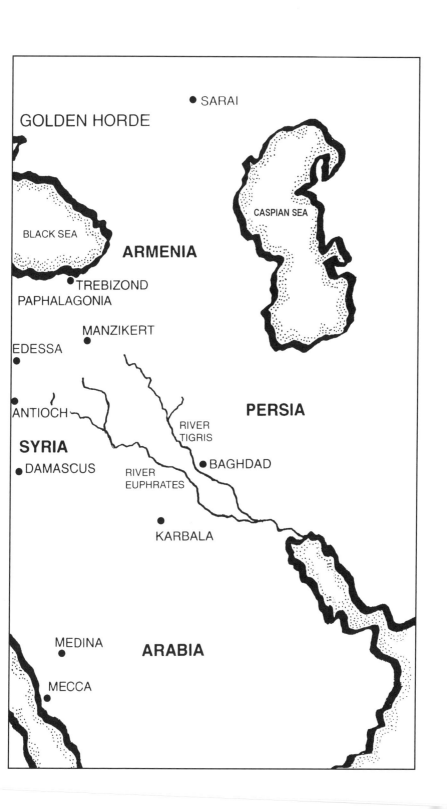